# OCR Gateway
# GCSE Biology
# Teacher Handbook

**Author:**
Simon Broadley • Mark Matthews

**Series Editor:**
Philippa Gardom Hulme

# Contents

| | | |
|---|---|---|
| Introduction | | iv |
| Assessment and progress | | vi |
| Differentiation and skills | | viii |
| Kerboodle | | x |

## Working Scientifically — 2

| WS1 | The power of science | 2 |
|---|---|---|
| WS2 | Methods, models, and communication | 4 |
| WS3 | Asking scientific questions | 6 |
| WS4 | Planning an investigation | 8 |
| WS5 | Obtaining high-quality data | 10 |
| WS6 | Presenting data | 12 |
| WS7 | Interpreting data | 14 |
| WS8 | Errors and uncertainties | 16 |

## B1 Cell-level systems — 18

### B1.1 Cell structures
| B1.1.1 | Plant and animal cells | 18 |
|---|---|---|
| B1.1.2 | Bacterial cells | 20 |
| B1.1.3 | Light microscopy | 22 |
| B1.1.4 | Electron microscopy | 24 |
| B1.1 | Checkpoint | 26 |

### B1.2 What happens in cells?
| B1.2.1 | DNA | 28 |
|---|---|---|
| B1.2.2 | Transcription and translation | 30 |
| B1.2.3 | Enzymes | 32 |
| B1.2.4 | Enzyme reactions | 34 |
| B1.2 | Checkpoint | 36 |

### B1.3 Respiration
| B1.3.1 | Carbohydrates, proteins, and lipids | 38 |
|---|---|---|
| B1.3.2 | Aerobic respiration | 40 |
| B1.3.3 | Anaerobic respiration | 42 |
| B1.3 | Checkpoint | 44 |

### B1.4 Photosynthesis
| B1.4.1 | Photosynthesis | 46 |
|---|---|---|
| B1.4.2 | Photosynthesis experiments | 48 |
| B1.4.3 | Factors affecting photosynthesis | 50 |
| B1.4.4 | Interaction of limiting factors | 52 |
| B1.4 | Checkpoint | 54 |
| B1 | Topic summary | 56 |

## B2 Scaling up — 58

### B2.1 Supplying the cell
| B2.1.1 | Diffusion | 58 |
|---|---|---|
| B2.1.2 | Osmosis | 60 |
| B2.1.3 | Active transport | 62 |
| B2.1.4 | Mitosis | 64 |
| B2.1.5 | Cell differentiation | 66 |
| B2.1.6 | Stem cells | 68 |
| B2.1 | Checkpoint | 70 |

### B2.2 The challenges of size
| B2.2.1 | Exchange and transport | 72 |
|---|---|---|
| B2.2.2 | Circulatory system | 74 |
| B2.2.3 | Heart and blood | 76 |
| B2.2.4 | Plant transport systems | 78 |
| B2.2.5 | Transpiration stream | 80 |
| B2.2.6 | Factors affecting transpiration | 82 |
| B2.2 | Checkpoint | 84 |
| B2 | Topic summary | 86 |

## B3 Organism-level systems — 88

### B3.1 The nervous system
| B3.1.1 | Nervous system | 88 |
|---|---|---|
| B3.1.2 | Reflexes | 90 |
| B3.1.3 | The eye | 92 |
| B3.1.4 | The brain | 94 |
| B3.1.5 | Nervous system damage | 96 |
| B3.1 | Checkpoint | 98 |

### B3.2 The endocrine system
| B3.2.1 | Hormones | 100 |
|---|---|---|
| B3.2.2 | Negative feedback | 102 |
| B3.2.3 | The menstrual cycle | 104 |
| B3.2.4 | Controlling reproduction | 106 |
| B3.2.5 | Using hormones to treat infertility | 108 |
| B3.2.6 | Plant hormones | 110 |
| B3.2.7 | Uses of plant hormones | 112 |
| B3.2 | Checkpoint | 114 |

### B3.3 Maintaining internal environments
| B3.3.1 | Controlling body temperature | 116 |
|---|---|---|
| B3.3.2 | Controlling blood sugar | 118 |
| B3.3.3 | Maintaining water balance | 120 |
| B3.3.4 | Inside the kidney | 122 |
| B3.3.5 | Responding to osmotic challenges | 124 |
| B3.3 | Checkpoint | 126 |
| B3 | Topic summary | 128 |

## B4 Community-level systems — 130

### B4.1 Ecosystems
| B4.1.1 | Ecosystems | 130 |
|---|---|---|

| | | | | | | |
|---|---|---|---|---|---|---|
| B4.1.2 | Abiotic and biotic factors | 132 | | B6.2.3 | Selective breeding | 198 |
| B4.1.3 | Competition and interdependence | 134 | | B6.2.4 | Genetic engineering | 200 |
| B4.1.4 | Pyramids of biomass | 136 | | B6.2.5 | Producing a genetically engineered organism | 202 |
| B4.1.5 | Efficiency of biomass transfer | 138 | | B6.2.6 | Use of biotechnology in farming | 204 |
| B4.1.6 | Nutrient cycling | 140 | | B6.2 | Checkpoint | 206 |
| B4.1.7 | The carbon cycle | 142 | | | | |
| B4.1.8 | Decomposers | 144 | | | | |
| B4.1 | Checkpoint | 146 | | | | |
| B4 | Topic summary | 148 | | | | |

## B5 Genes, inheritance, and selection — 150

### B5.1 Inheritance
| | | |
|---|---|---|
| B5.1.1 | Variation | 150 |
| B5.1.2 | Sexual and asexual reproduction | 152 |
| B5.1.3 | Meiosis | 154 |
| B5.1.4 | Dominant and recessive alleles | 156 |
| B5.1.5 | Genetic crosses (1) | 158 |
| B5.1.6 | Genetic crosses (2) | 160 |
| B5.1.7 | Mutations | 162 |
| B5.1.8 | History of genetics | 164 |
| B5.1 | Checkpoint | 166 |

### B5.2 Natural selection and evolution
| | | |
|---|---|---|
| B5.2.1 | Natural selection | 168 |
| B5.2.2 | Evidence for evolution | 170 |
| B5.2.3 | The theory of evolution | 172 |
| B5.2.4 | Classification systems | 174 |
| B5.2 | Checkpoint | 176 |
| B5 | Topic summary | 178 |

## B6 Global challenges — 180

### B6.1 Monitoring and maintaining the environment
| | | |
|---|---|---|
| B6.1.1 | Sampling techniques (1) | 180 |
| B6.1.2 | Sampling techniques (2) | 182 |
| B6.1.3 | Loss of biodiversity | 184 |
| B6.1.4 | Increasing biodiversity | 186 |
| B6.1.5 | Maintaining biodiversity | 188 |
| B6.1.6 | Monitoring biodiversity | 190 |
| B6.1 | Checkpoint | 192 |

### B6.2 Feeding the human race
| | | |
|---|---|---|
| B6.2.1 | Food security | 194 |
| B6.2.2 | Feeding the world | 196 |

### B6.3–Part 1 Monitoring and maintaining health
| | | |
|---|---|---|
| B6.3.1 | Health and disease | 208 |
| B6.3.2 | Spread of communicable diseases | 210 |
| B6.3.3 | Preventing the spread of communicable diseases | 212 |
| B6.3.4 | Human infections | 214 |
| B6.3.5 | Plant diseases | 216 |
| B6.3.6 | Plant defences | 218 |
| B6.3.7 | Identification of plant disease | 220 |
| B6.3.8 | Blood and body defence mechanisms | 222 |
| B6.3.9 | Monoclonal antibodies | 224 |
| B6.3.10 | Vaccinations | 226 |
| B6.3.11 | Prevention and treatment of disease | 228 |
| B6.3.12 | Aseptic technique | 230 |
| B6.3.13 | New medicines | 232 |
| B6.3–Part 1 | Checkpoint | 234 |

### B6.3–Part 2 Non-communicable diseases
| | | |
|---|---|---|
| B6.3.14 | Non-communicable diseases (1) | 236 |
| B6.3.15 | Non-communicable diseases (2) | 238 |
| B6.3.16 | Treating cardiovascular disease | 240 |
| B6.3.17 | Modern advances in medicine (1) | 242 |
| B6.3.18 | Modern advances in medicine (2) | 244 |
| B6.3–Part 2 | Checkpoint | 246 |
| B6 | Topic summary | 248 |

## B7 Practical skills — 250

| | | |
|---|---|---|
| B1 | Microscopy | 250 |
| B2 | Testing for biological molecules | 252 |
| B3 | Sampling | 254 |
| B4 | Enzymes | 256 |
| B5 | Photosynthesis | 258 |
| B6 | Physiology | 260 |
| B7 | Microbiology | 262 |
| B8 | Osmosis | 264 |

**Answers for all questions** — 266

# Introduction

## About the series

This series has been specifically designed to support the new OCR Gateway GCSE Science suite of resources. The Student Books have been endorsed by OCR, and our author teams and experts have been working closely with OCR to develop a blended suite of resources to support the new specifications.

All resources in this series have been carefully designed to support students of all abilities on their journey through GCSE Science. The demands of the new specifications are fully supported, with maths, practicals, and synoptic skills developed throughout, and all new subject content fully covered.

The series is designed to be flexible, enabling you to co-teach Foundation and Higher tiers, and Combined and Separate Sciences. Content is clearly flagged throughout the resources, helping you to identify the relevant content for your students.

Assessment is an important feature of the series, and is supported by our unique assessment framework, helping students to track and make progress. Users of *Activate* will recognise features of this assessment framework, and this series has been developed to segue perfectly from *Activate* into GCSE.

The series is edited by Philippa Gardom Hulme. Philippa brings a wealth of teaching and authoring experience to her role as Series Editor of OUP's *OCR Gateway GCSE Science* series. She builds on her authoring success with GCSE revision guides, the *Activate Chemistry* Student Book, and numerous Kerboodle resources. A former teacher in a variety of comprehensive schools and more recently an Oxford University PGCE tutor, she understands the demands of modern education and draws on her experience to deliver this new and innovative course that builds upon *Activate* and the legacy of previous *OCR Gateway GCSE Science* editions.

## Your Teacher Handbook

This Teacher Handbook aims to save you time and effort by offering lesson plans, differentiation suggestions, and assessment guidance on a page-by-page basis that is a direct match to the Student Book.

With learning outcomes differentiated you can tailor the lessons and activities to suit your students and provide progression opportunities students of all abilities.

Lesson plans are written for 55-minute lessons but are flexible and fully adaptable so you can choose the activities that suit your class best.

Separate Science-only content is contained within whole topics and clearly flagged from the Combined Sciences content, enabling you to co-teach using one Teacher Handbook.

## Lesson

### Specification links

This indicates the area of the OCR Gateway GCSE (9–1) Biology specification this lesson covers. Relevant Working Scientifically and Mathematical requirements links are also provided.

### Differentiated outcomes

This table summarises the possible lesson outcomes. They are ramped and divided into three ability bands. The three ability bands are explained in the Assessment and progress section. Each ability band has two to three outcomes defined, designed to cover the specification content for different ability levels.

An index of questions and activities is given for each learning outcome, helping you to assess your students informally as you progress through each lesson.

### Suggested lesson plan

A suggested route through the lesson is provided, including ideas for support, extension, and homework. The right-hand column indicated where Kerboodle resources are available.

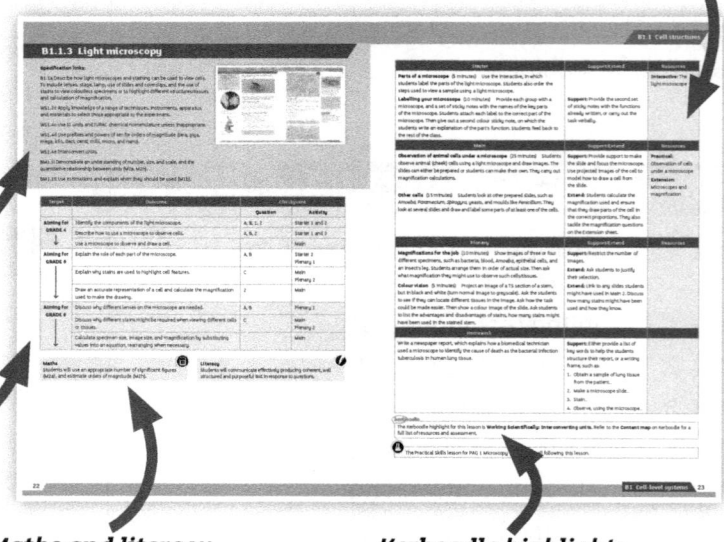

### Maths and literacy

These boxes provide suggestions of how Maths and Literacy skills can be developed in the lesson. Where relevant, the Maths skills are linked to the Mathematical requirements of the specification.

### Kerboodle highlights

A resource from the Kerboodle course for the lesson is suggested here. The Content Map on Kerboodle provides a full list of resources and assessment.

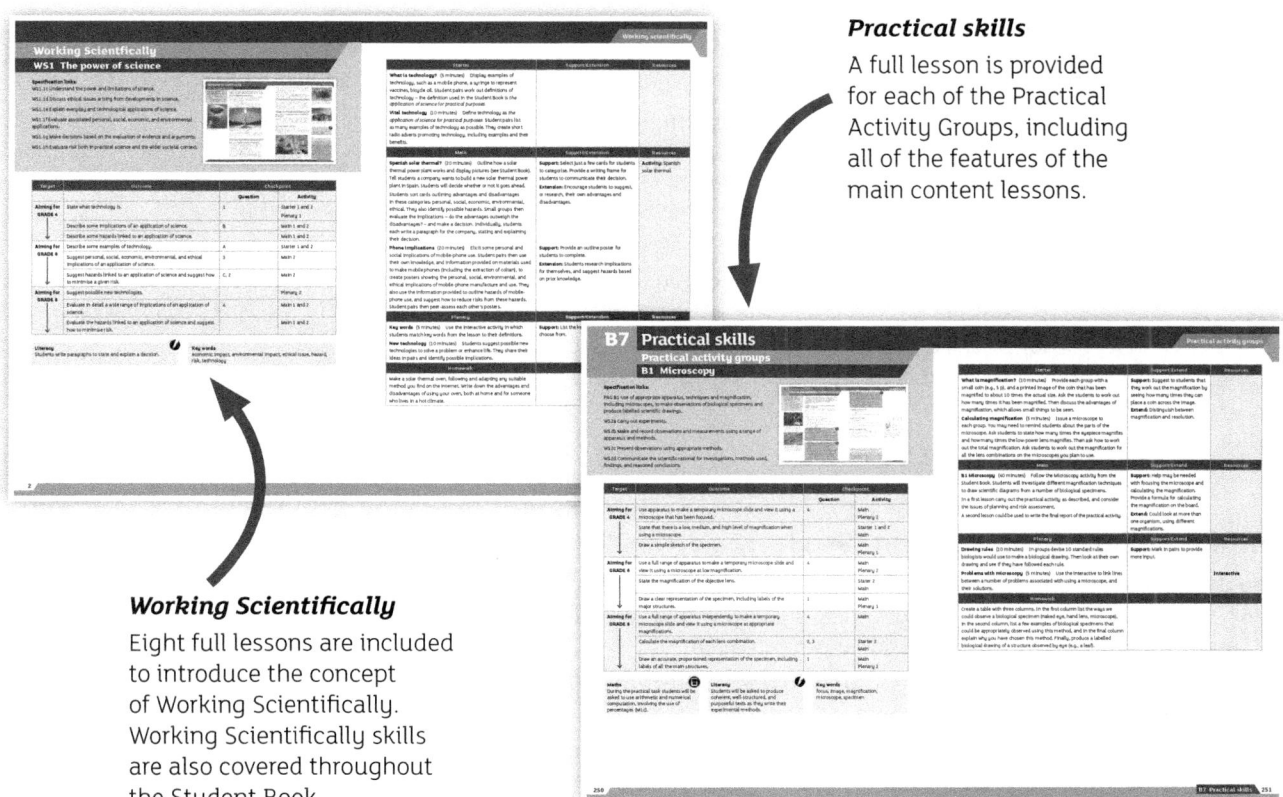

### Practical skills
A full lesson is provided for each of the Practical Activity Groups, including all of the features of the main content lessons.

### Working Scientifically
Eight full lessons are included to introduce the concept of Working Scientifically. Working Scientifically skills are also covered throughout the Student Book.

## Checkpoint lesson

### Overview
The Checkpoint Lesson is a suggested follow-up lesson after students have completed the automarked Checkpoint Assessment on Kerboodle. There are three routes through the lesson, with the route for each student being determined by their mark in the assessment. Each route aims to support students with progressing up an assessment band.

### Chapter overview
This text provides a brief overview of the chapter, including the key concepts students should be confident with.

### Checkpoint lesson plan
This table provides a differentiated lesson plan for the checkpoint follow-up lesson. This includes learning outcomes, starters and plenaries, supporting information for the follow-up worksheets (including any descriptions of relevant practicals), and progression suggestions to support students with progressing up a band.

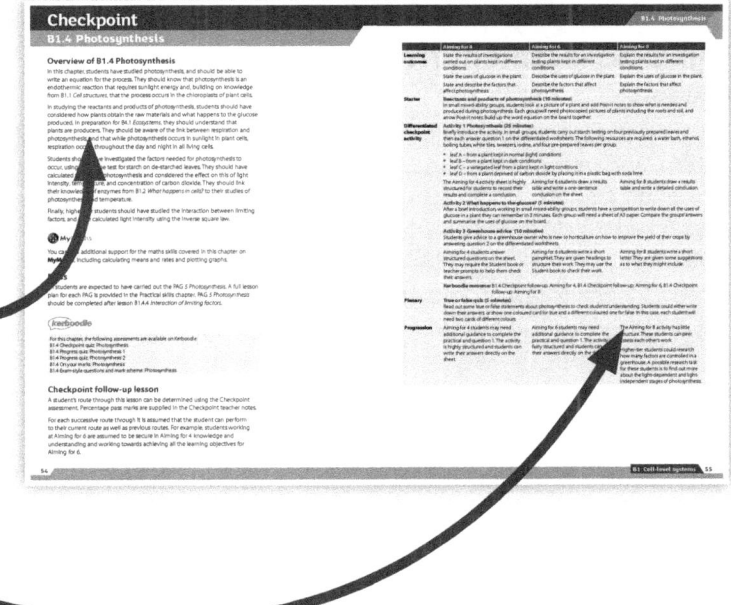

# Assessment and progress

### Dr Andrew Chandler-Grevatt

To ensure students are fully supported to make progress through the new linear exams, OCR Gateway GCSE (9–1) Sciences was developed in consultation with assessment consultant, Dr Andrew Chandler-Grevatt. Andrew worked with the team to develop an assessment framework that supports students and teachers in tracking and promoting progress through Key Stage 3 and GCSE.

Andrew has a doctorate in school assessment, and a real passion for science teaching and learning. Having worked as a science teacher for ten years, of which five were spent as an AST, Andrew has a real understanding of the pressures and joys of teaching in the classroom. His most recent projects include *Activate for KS3 Science*, for which he developed a unique assessment framework to support schools in the transition away from levels.

## The new GCSE grading system (9–1)

With the new specifications and criteria comes a new grading system. The old system of grades A*–G, is being replaced with a numerical system with grades 9–1. Grade 9 is the highest, and is designed to award exceptional performance.

The new grades are not directly equivalent to the old A*–C system, although some comparisons can be drawn:

- Approximately the same proportion of students will achieve a grade 4 or above as currently achieve a grade C or above.
- Approximately the same proportion of students will achieve a grade 7 as above as currently achieve an A or above.
- The bottom of grade 1 will be aligned with the bottom of grade G.

A 'good pass' is considered to be a grade 5 or above.

Throughout the course, resources and assessments have been designed to help students working at different grades to make progress.

## 5-year assessment framework

### Purpose

The combination of the removal of levels, new performance measures, new grading system, and more demanding GCSEs makes it more important than ever to be able to track and facilitate progress from Year 7 and all the way through secondary. Assessment plays a key role in intervention and extension, and these are both vital in helping students of all abilities achieve their potential, and add value to their projected GCSE grade.

In the absence of levels, and as we learn more about the new GCSE grades, it is important that a framework is in place in order to inform learning, teaching, and assessment from Y7-Y11.

### Framework

Throughout the 5 years, it is useful to define three ability bands, which can be used to inform the design of learning outcomes, learning resources, and assessments. By defining three bands, realistic and valuable intervention and extension can be designed and implemented to help students of all abilities make progress, and improve their grade projection.

At KS3, the model is designed with the aim of encouraging every student to gain a 'secure' grasp of each concept and topic, so that they are ready to progress. These students will be on track to secure a 'good pass' (grade 5 or above) at GCSE.

In the KS3 course Activate three bands have been defined:

- **Developing**, in which students are able to know and understand a concept, and demonstrate their knowledge in simple and familiar situations.

- **Secure**, in which students are able to apply their knowledge and skills to familiar and some unfamiliar situations, undertake analysis, and understand more complex concepts.
- **Extending**, in which students are able to evaluate and create, apply their knowledge to complex and unfamiliar situations, and demonstrate advanced use of skills.

Using the framework throughout KS3 helps you to identify which students are ready to progress, and approximately what GCSE grades they should be aiming for.

At GCSE, students can then be differentiated into three bands, aiming for different grades.

- **Aiming for 4** is for students working at the lower grades 1–3, who would have been Developing at KS3, and aspiring to a Grade 4 at GCSE. Resources and assessments for these students are supportive, and focus on developing understanding of core concepts.
- **Aiming for 6** is for students working at grades 4–6, who would have been Secure at KS3. Resources and assessments for these students help to embed core concepts, by encouraging application and analysis, and beginning to explore more complex ideas and situations.
- **Aiming for 8** provides extension for students working at grades 7–9, who are able to grasp complex concepts, and demonstrate higher order skills, such as evaluation and creation in complex and unfamiliar situations.

The framework is summarised in the table below.

| Key stage 3 | Band | Developing | | Secure | | Extending | |
| --- | --- | --- | --- | --- | --- | --- | --- |
| | Level | 3 | 4 | 5 | 6 | 7 | 8 |
| GCSE | Band | Aiming for 4 | | | Aiming for 6 | | Aiming for 8 | | |
| | Grades | 1 | 2 | 3 | 4 | 5 | 6 | 7 | 8 | 9 |
| | Demand | Low | | | Standard | | | High | | |

## Informing learning outcomes

The assessment framework has informed the design of the learning outcomes throughout the course. Learning outcomes are differentiated, and there is a set of learning outcomes for every lesson for each ability band.

## The checkpoint assessment system

This series includes a checkpoint assessment system for intervention and extension, designed to help students of all abilities make continuous progress through the course. The system also helps you and your students to monitor achievement, and ensure all students are on-track and monitored through the new linear assessments.

Checkpoint assessments are provided in Kerboodle. These are Automarked objective tests with diagnostic feedback. Once students have completed their assessment, depending on their results, they will complete one of three follow up activities, designed for intervention and extension. Students are supported with activity sheets, and lesson plans and overviews are provided for the teacher. The three follow-up routes are:

1. **Aiming for 4** is for students who achieved low score. These resources support students by helping to develop and embed core concepts.
2. **Aiming for 6** is for students who achieved a medium score. These resources encourage students to embed and extend core concepts, and begin to apply their knowledge in more complex or unfamiliar situations.
3. **Aiming for 8** is for students who have achieved a high score. These resources encourage extensive use of more complex skills, in more complex and unfamiliar situations, helping them to reach for the top grades.

The diagram below provides an overview of how the system works.

# Differentiation and Skills

## Maths skills  and

With the introduction of the introduction of the new GCSE competence in maths, the support and development of maths skills in a scientific context will be vital for success.

The Student Books contain a maths skills reference section that covers all the maths required for the specification, explained in a scientific context and with a worked example for reference. Where maths skills are embedded within the scientific content, the maths is demonstrated in a Using Maths feature providing a worked example and an opportunity for students to have a go themselves.

In Kerboodle you will find maths skills interactives that are automarked and provide formative feedback. Calculation sheets provide opportunities for practice of the maths skills and links to MyMaths are shown in the Lesson Player and Teacher Handbook where additional resources exist that can be used to reinforce the maths skill. These include practice sheets and Invisi-pen worked examples.

## Literacy skills

Literacy skills enable students to effectively communicate their ideas about science and access the information they need. Though the marks allocated for QWC are no longer present in the new specifications, a good degree of literacy is required to read and answer longer, structured exam questions, to access the more difficult concepts introduced in the new GCSE Programme of Study, to be able to effectively interpret and answer questions.

The Student Books flag opportunities to develop and practice literacy skills through the use of the pen icon. Key words are identified in the text and a glossary helps students get to grips with new scientific terms.

In Kerboodle, you will find Literacy Skills Interactives that help assess literacy skills, including the spelling of key words. Additional Literacy worksheets are available to reinforce skills learnt and provide practise opportunities.

The Teacher Handbook flags literacy suggestions and opportunities relating to the lesson. All of these features will help to develop well-rounded scientists able to access information and communicate their ideas effectively.

## Working Scientifically

Working Scientifically is new to the 2016 GCSE criteria. It is divided up into four areas and is integrated into the teaching and learning of Biology, Chemistry, and Physics. The four areas are:

1. Development of scientific thinking in which students need to be able to demonstrate understanding of scientific methods and the scientific process and how these may develop over time and their associated limitations
2. Experimental skills and strategies in which students ask scientific questions based on observations, make predictions using scientific knowledge and understanding, carry out investigations to test predictions, make and record measurements and evaluate methods
3. Analysis and evaluation in which students apply mathematical concepts and calculate results, present and interpret data using tables and graphs, draw conclusions and evaluate data, are able to accuracy, precision, repeatability and reproducibility
4. Scientific vocabulary, quantities, units, symbols and nomenclature in which students calculate results and manipulate data using scientific formulae using basic analysis, SI units and IUPAC chemical nomenclature where appropriate.

Working Scientifically is integrated throughout the Student Book with flagged Practical boxes, flagged Required Practical boxes, questions. A dedicated Working Scientifically reference chapter is also provided at the back of the Student Book to refer to during investigations, when answering Working Scientifically questions and to enable investigative skills to be developed.

In Kerboodle there are Practicals and Activities resources with their own Working Scientifically objectives, additional targeted Working Scientifically skills sheets as well as other resources such as simulations and Webquests to target specific skills areas. Questions are ramped in difficulty and opportunity to build up to and practice the practical based questions for the exam are provided.

For the Practical Activity Groups, the guidance provided to students acknowledges the differing degrees of support and independence required, with targeted support sheets to the key grade descriptors of Grade 4, 6, and 8, with a view to move the students over that Grade point onwards.

In the Teacher Handbook lessons will often have a Working Scientifically focus in mind for the activities in that lesson. Working Scientifically Learning Outcomes, where specified, are differentiated to show the expectations for the differing ability levels. Each Student Book and Teacher Handbook starts with a Working Scientifically chapter, to help introduce key skills before commencing the course.

For the purpose of the practical based questions in the examination, practicals are flagged and practice opportunities are provided through out the Student Book in the summary questions and exam-style questions.

## Differentiation
Building upon the principles of *Activate* at Key Stage 3.

### Differentiation using the checkpoint system
The end of chapter Checkpoint lessons will help you to progress students of every ability, targeting the key Grade boundaries of 4, 6, and 8 to enable students to review, consolidate and extend their understanding at each of the grade lesson points.

The tasks focused at students to become secure at Grades 4 and 6 are designed to help them become more secure in their understanding and consolidate the chapter. Teacher input will help them grasp important concepts from the chapter with the opportunity for some extension for Grade 6 students.

The tasks focused at students to become secure and extend at Grade 8 are designed to develop and challenge. Students will work more independently on these tasks to free up the teacher to be able to focus on those that found the chapter more challenging.

### Teacher Handbook
Lesson outcomes are differentiated and suggestions for activities throughout the lesson plans are accompanied by support and extension opportunities.

### Student Book
Summary questions per lesson are ramped with a darker shading indicating a more challenging question. In the end of chapter summary questions and exam style questions, ramping occurs within the question (as would be seen in a typical exam question).

### Practicals and Activities
All practicals and activities are differentiated. Where more complex areas are covered, additional support sheets may be provided to allow lower attaining students to access the activity.

For all Practical Activity Groups that may be assessed in an exam, specific support sheets are provided targeting the progression of students across the key Grades 4, 6, and 8.

Additional skills sheets may be used in conjunction with practicals to provide additional support in generic competencies such as constructing a graph etc.

### Interactive Assessments
All interactive assessments are ramped in difficulty and support is provided in the feedback directing students where they can improve. In chapters with both levels of content, Higher and Foundation versions of assessment are available.

### Written assessments
End of section tests and end of year tests have Foundation and Higher versions.

# Kerboodle

**OCR Gateway GCSE Sciences Kerboodle** is packed full of guided support and ideas for running and creating effective GCSE Science lessons, and for assessing and facilitating students' progress. It is intuitive to use and customisable.

Kerboodle is online, allowing you and your students to access the course anytime, anywhere.

**OCR Gateway GCSE Sciences Kerboodle** consists of:
- lessons, resources, and assessment
- access to *OCR Gateway GCSE Science* Student Books for both teachers and students.

## Lessons, Resources, and Assessment

***OCR Gateway GCSE Sciences Kerboodle*** offers new, engaging lesson resources, as well as a fully comprehensive assessment package, written to match the *OCR Gateway GCSE (9–1) Science* specifications.

Kerboodle offers comprehensive and flexible support for the *OCR Gateway GCSE (9–1) Science* specifications, enabling you to follow our suggested lessons and schemes of work or to create your own lessons and schemes and share them with other members of your department.

You can **adapt** many of the resources to suit your students' needs, with all non-interactive activities available as editable Word documents. You can also **upload** your own resources so that everything is accessed from one location.

Set homework and assessments through the Assessment system and **track** progress using the Markbook.

## Lessons

Click on the **Lessons tab** to access the *OCR Gateway GCSE Science* lesson presentations and notes.

**Ready-to-play lesson presentations** complement every spread in the Teacher Handbook and Student Book. Each lesson presentation is easy to launch and features lesson objectives, starters, activity guidance, key diagrams, plenaries, and homework suggestions. The lesson presentations and accompanying note sections are 100% customisable. You can personalise the lessons by adding your own resources and notes, or build your own lesson plans using our resources.

Your lessons and notes can be accessed by your whole department and they are ideal for use in cover lessons.

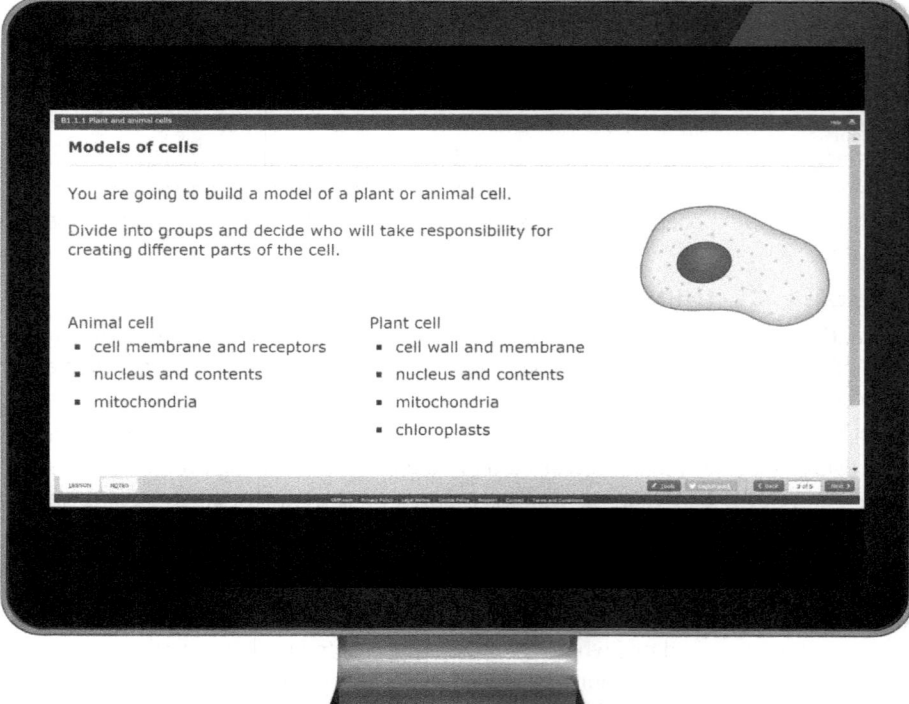

## Resources

Click on the Resources tab to access the full list of *OCR Gateway GCSE Science* resources. Use the navigation panel on the left hand side to find resources for any lesson, chapter, or topic.

Fully customisable content to cater to all your classes. Resources can be created using the create button.

Existing resources can be uploaded on to the platform using the upload button.

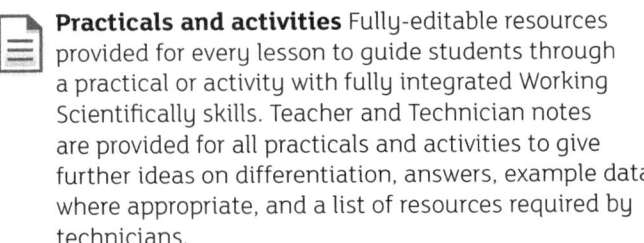

Navigation panel and search bar allow for easy navigation between resources by course and chapter.

Page navigator shows resources matching to particular pages in the Student Book.

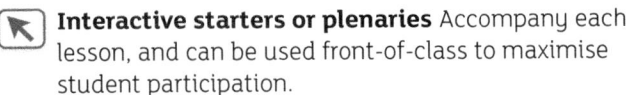

Resources matching every lesson in the *AQA GCSE Chemistry* series are shown here.

**Practicals and activities** Fully-editable resources provided for every lesson to guide students through a practical or activity with fully integrated Working Scientifically skills. Teacher and Technician notes are provided for all practicals and activities to give further ideas on differentiation, answers, example data where appropriate, and a list of resources required by technicians.

**Interactive starters or plenaries** Accompany each lesson, and can be used front-of-class to maximise student participation.

**Skills sheets** Editable worksheets that target Maths, Literacy, and Working Scientifically skills. They provide guidance and examples to help students whenever they need to use a particular skill.

**Skills interactives** Auto-marked interactive activities with formative feedback that focus on key maths and literacy skills. You can use these activities in your class to help consolidate core skills relevant to the lesson, or they can be assigned as homework by accessing them through the Assessment tab.

**Animations and videos** Help students to visualise difficult concepts or to learn about real-life contexts, with engaging visuals and narration. They are structured to clearly address a set of learning objectives and are followed by interactive question screens to help consolidate key points and to provide formative feedback.

**Simulations** Allow students to control variables and look at outcomes for experiments that are difficult to carry out in the classroom or focus on tricky concepts.

**Podcasts** Available for every chapter to help review and consolidate key points. The podcast presents an audio summary with transcript, followed by a series of ramped questions and answers to assist students in their revision.

**Targeted support sheets** Available for the full ability range and are provided to help students progress as they complete their GCSE. **Bump up your Grades** target common misconceptions and difficult topics to securely move students over the key boundaries of Grades 4, 6, and 8. Extensions activities provide opportunities for higher-ability students to apply their knowledge and understanding to new contexts, whilst **Go Further** worksheets aim to inspire students to consider the subject at A Level and beyond.

**WebQuests** Research-based activities set in a real-life context. WebQuests are fun and engaging activities that can be carried out individually or within a group and are ideal for peer-review.

**Checklists and chapter maps** Self-assessment checklists for students of the key learning points from each chapter to aid consolidation and revision. For teachers there is an additional chapter-map resource that provides an overview of the chapter, specific opportunities to support and extend, and information on tackling common misconceptions.

xi

## Assessment and markbook

All of the assessment material in Kerboodle has been quality assured by our expert Assessment Advisor. Click on the **Assessment tab** to find the wide range of assessment materials to help you deliver a varied, motivating, and effective assessment programme.

Once your classes are set up in Kerboodle, you can assign them assessments to do at home or in class individually or as a group.

A **Markbook** with reporting function helps you to keep track of your students' results. This includes both auto-marked assessments and work marked by you.

## Practice or test?

Many of the auto-marked assessment in the OCR Gateway GCSE Sciences Kerboodle is available in formative or summative versions.

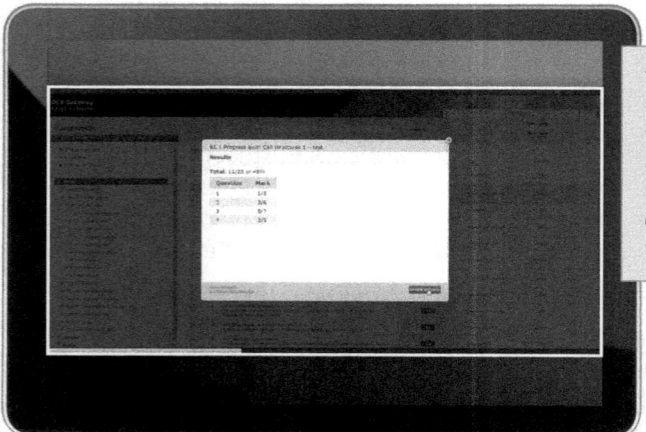

Test versions of the assessment provide feedback on performance at the end of the test. Students are only given one attempt at each screen but can review them and see which answers they get wrong after completing the activity. Marks are reported to the markbook.

Practice versions of the assessment provide screen-by-screen feedback, focusing on misconceptions, and provide hints for the students to help them revise their answer. Students are given the opportunity to try again. Marks are reported to the Markbook.

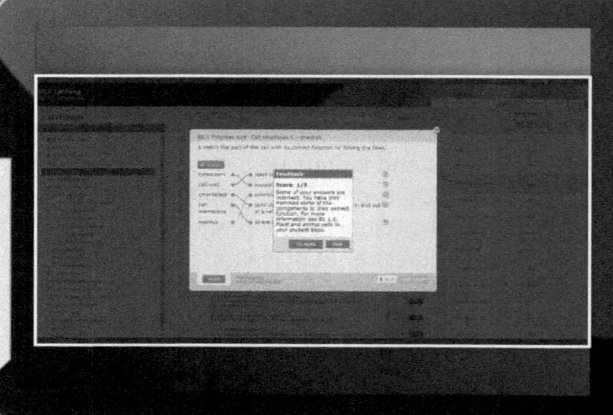

## Assessment per chapter

Through each chapter there are many opportunities for assessment and determining/monitoring progress.

 **Progress quizzes** Auto-marked assessments that focus on the content of the chapters. They are quick, engaging quizzes designed to be taken throughout the course to monitor progress and to focus revision.

**Checkpoint assessments** Auto-marked assessments designed to determine whether students have a secure grasp of concepts from the chapter. These assessments are ramped in difficulty and can be followed up by the differentiated Checkpoint Lesson activities.

 **On Your Marks** Improve students' exam skills by analysing questions, looking at other students' responses, interpreting mark schemes, and answering exam-style questions.

 **Homework activities** Auto-marked quizzes with ramped questions targeting the key Grades 4, 6, and 8 boundaries designed to help students apply and embed their knowledge and understanding from the classroom.

## Formal testing

 **End-of-chapter tests** Provide students with the opportunity to practise answering exam-style questions in a written format. There are differentiated Foundation and Higher versions, with separate options for the combined sciences and the separate sciences. Accompanied by a fully comprehensive mark scheme, data can be entered manually into the Markbook.

 **Mid-point and end-of-course written tests** Provide students with the opportunity to practise answering exam-style questions in a full-length paper. There are differentiated Foundation and Higher versions, with separate options for the combined sciences and the separate sciences. Accompanied by a fully comprehensive mark scheme, data can be entered manually into the Markbook.

## Kerboodle Book

The *OCR Gateway GCSE Science* Kerboodle Books are digital versions of the Student Books for you to use at the front of the classroom.

Access to the Kerboodle Book is automatically available as part of the Lessons, Resources, and Assessment package for both you and your students.

A set of tools is available with the Kerboodle Book so that you can personalise your book and make notes. Like all resources offered on Kerboodle, the Kerboodle Book can also be accessed using a range of devices.

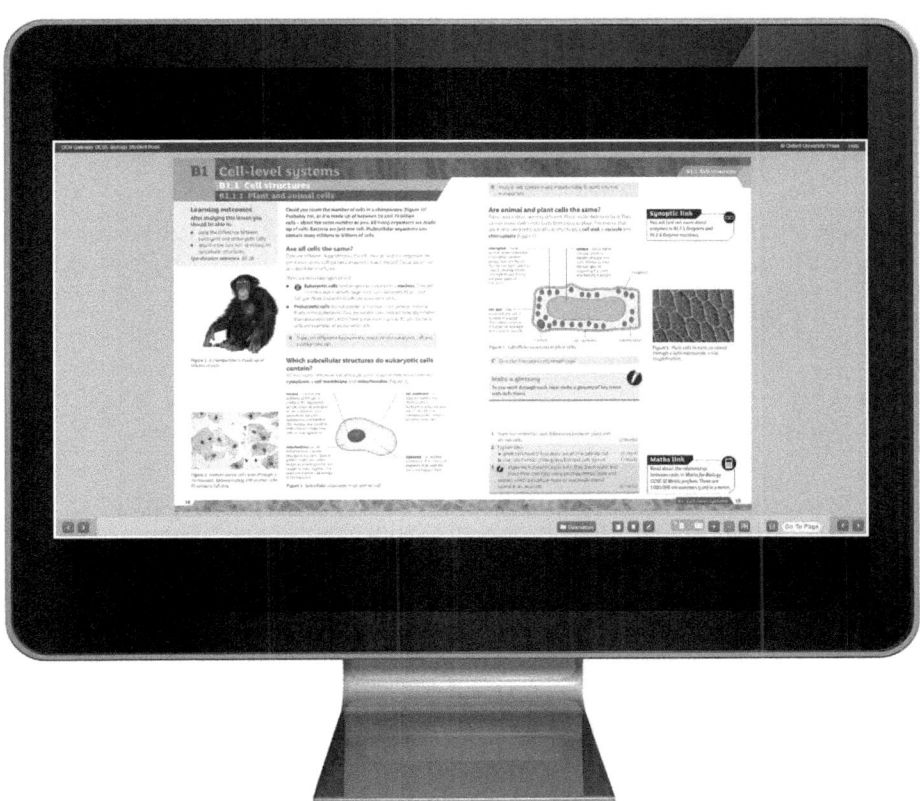

# Working Scientifically
## WS1 The power of science

**Specification links:**

WS1.1c Understand the power and limitations of science.

WS1.1d Discuss ethical issues arising from developments in science.

WS1.1e Explain everyday and technological applications of science.

WS1.1f Evaluate associated personal, social, economic, and environmental applications.

WS1.1g Make decisions based on the evaluation of evidence and arguments.

WS1.1h Evaluate risk both in practical science and the wider societal context.

| Target | Outcome | Checkpoint | |
|---|---|---|---|
| | | Question | Activity |
| **Aiming for GRADE 4** | State what technology is. | 1 | Starter 1 and 2, Plenary 1 |
| | Describe some implications of an application of science. | B | Main 1 and 2 |
| | Describe some hazards linked to an application of science. | | Main 1 and 2 |
| **Aiming for GRADE 6** | Describe some examples of technology. | A | Starter 1 and 2 |
| | Suggest personal, social, economic, environmental, and ethical implications of an application of science. | 3 | Main 2 |
| | Suggest hazards linked to an application of science and suggest how to minimise a given risk. | C, 2 | Main 2 |
| **Aiming for GRADE 8** | Suggest possible new technologies. | | Plenary 2 |
| | Evaluate in detail a wide range of implications of an application of science. | 4 | Main 1 and 2 |
| | Evaluate the hazards linked to an application of science and suggest how to minimise risk. | | Main 1 and 2 |

**Literacy**
Students write paragraphs to state and explain a decision.

**Key words**
economic impact, environmental impact, ethical issue, hazard, risk, technology

# Working scientifically

| Starter | Support/Extension | Resources |
|---|---|---|
| **What is technology?** (5 minutes) Display examples of technology, such as a mobile phone, a syringe to represent vaccines, bicycle oil. Student pairs work out definitions of technology – the definition used in the Student Book is *the application of science for practical purposes*.<br><br>**Vital technology** (10 minutes) Define technology as *the application of science for practical purposes*. Student pairs list as many examples of technology as possible. They create short radio adverts promoting technology, including examples and their benefits. | | |

| Main | Support/Extension | Resources |
|---|---|---|
| **Spanish solar thermal?** (20 minutes) Outline how a solar thermal power plant works and display pictures (see Student Book). Tell students a company wants to build a new solar thermal power plant in Spain. Students will decide whether or not it goes ahead.<br><br>Students sort cards outlining advantages and disadvantages in these categories: personal, social, economic, environmental, ethical. They also identify possible hazards. Small groups then evaluate the implications – do the advantages outweigh the disadvantages? – and make a decision. Individually, students each write a paragraph for the company, stating and explaining their decision. | **Support:** Select just a few cards for students to categorise. Provide a writing frame for students to communicate their decision.<br>**Extension:** Encourage students to suggest, or research, their own advantages and disadvantages. | **Activity:** Spanish solar thermal |
| **Phone implications** (20 minutes) Elicit some personal and social implications of mobile-phone use. Student pairs then use their own knowledge, and information provided on materials used to make mobile phones (including the extraction of coltan), to create posters showing the personal, social, environmental, and ethical implications of mobile-phone manufacture and use. They also use the information provided to outline hazards of mobile-phone use, and suggest how to reduce risks from these hazards. Student pairs then peer-assess each other's posters. | **Support:** Provide an outline poster for students to complete.<br>**Extension:** Students research implications for themselves, and suggest hazards based on prior knowledge. | **Activity:** Phone implications |

| Plenary | Support/Extension | Resources |
|---|---|---|
| **Key words** (5 minutes) Use the interactive activity in which students match key words from the lesson to their definitions.<br><br>**New technology** (10 minutes) Students suggest possible new technologies to solve a problem or enhance life. They share their ideas in pairs and identify possible implications. | **Support:** List the key words for students to choose from. | **Interactive:** Key words |

| Homework | | |
|---|---|---|
| Make a solar thermal oven, following and adapting any suitable method you find on the internet. Write down the advantages and disadvantages of using your oven, both at home and for someone who lives in a hot climate. | | |

# WS2 Methods, models, and communication

**Specification links:**

WS 1.1a Understand how scientific methods and theories develop over time, to include new technology allowing new evidence to be collected and changing explanations as new evidence is found.

WS1.1b Use models to solve problems, make predictions, and to develop scientific explanations and understanding of familiar and unfamiliar facts, to include representational, spatial, descriptive, computational, and mathematical models.

WS1.1i Recognise the importance of peer review of results and of communicating results to a range of audiences.

WS1.4a Use scientific vocabulary, terminology, and definitions.

M5b Visualise and represent 2D and 3D forms including 2D representations of 3D objects.

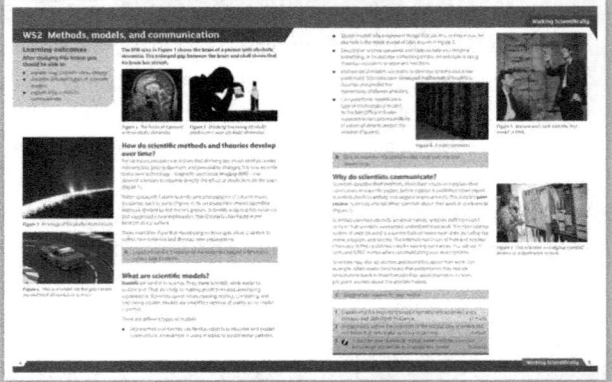

| Target | Outcome | Checkpoint | |
|---|---|---|---|
| | | Question | Activity |
| **Aiming for GRADE 4** ↓ | State one way in which new technology has allowed new evidence to be collected. | A | Starter 1 and 2 |
| | Describe different types of scientific model. | B | Main 1 |
| | State the meaning of peer review. | | Main 2 |
| **Aiming for GRADE 6** ↓ | Explain how new evidence might lead scientists to develop a new explanation. | 2 | Starter 1 and 2 |
| | Compare different types of scientific model. | | Main 1 |
| | Explain the purposes of peer review, and why scientists use internationally accepted units, symbols, and definitions. | C, 1 | Main 2 |
| **Aiming for GRADE 8** ↓ | Evaluate the contribution of a particular technology to the development of scientific explanations. | | Starter 2 |
| | Evaluate a scientific model. | 3 | Main 1 |
| | Suggest possible criteria for peer review. | | Plenary 2 |

**Maths**
Students evaluate 2D and 3D representations of objects.

**Literacy**
Students read and critique a scientific article.

**Key words**
model, peer review

# Working scientifically

| Starter | Support/Extension | Resources |
|---|---|---|
| **New technology, new science** (5 minutes) Display an MRI scan showing alcoholic dementia. Tell students that MRI is a relatively new technology. Students discuss what scientists might have learnt about alcoholic dementia from brain scans that they could not have learnt by direct observation. There are many examples of new technology that allow scientists to collect new evidence.<br><br>**Learning from microscopes** (10 minutes) Students observe cork cells through a microscope, as Robert Hooke did in the 1660s. Students list what we have learnt from microscopes (a new technology 400 years ago). | **Extension:** Students research examples to illustrate how new technology allows scientists to collect new evidence. | |

| Main | Support/Extension | Resources |
|---|---|---|
| **Models, models, models** (20 minutes) New technologies help scientists to collect new evidence and develop explanations. Scientists may also use models to help develop new explanations. Students read about models in the Student Book. They then evaluate models set up as a circus. For each model, they consider how it is like and unlike the real situation, and judge its usefulness. Suggestions for models:<br>• Marbles to represent water molecules<br>• Plastic models showing a red sphere joined to two white spheres to represent water molecules<br>• A physical model of the Solar System<br>• A word equation and a balanced symbol equation to model the burning reaction of methane, placed next to a lighted Bunsen burner<br>• A weather forecast animation set up on a computer (suggested search term: *forecast model animations*) | **Support:** Provide a writing frame for students to record and organise their model evaluations.<br>**Extension:** Students suggest how computer models compare to physical models. | **Activity:** Models, models, models |
| **Peer review** (20 minutes) Scientists publish new explanations in scientific journals. Some scientists recently published a paper saying that chocolate lowers the risk of stroke and heart disease. Is this true? Student pairs list questions they would like to ask the scientists about their work. Introduce peer review, in which other scientists review papers. Students read a simplified version of the paper, and look for answers to their questions. They then apply peer-review criteria to decide whether they think the paper should have been published. | **Support:** Provide straightforward questions for students to answer about the chocolate research.<br>**Extension:** Students suggest how the scientists could extend the study to support their claim. | **Activity:** Peer review |

| Plenary | Support/Extension | Resources |
|---|---|---|
| **What have I learnt?** (5 minutes) Students write down three things they have learnt in the lesson, as well as one thing they would like to learn more about.<br>**Peer review criteria** (10 minutes) Use the interactive activity in which students select appropriate criteria for peer review from a list of possible criteria. | | **Interactive:** Peer review criteria |

| Homework | | |
|---|---|---|
| Research how computer models are used to make predictions. Alternatively, find the answers to the questions posed in Plenary 1. | | |

# WS3 Asking scientific questions

**Specification links:**

WS1.2a Use scientific theories and explanations to develop hypotheses.

WS1.2b Plan experiments or devise procedures to make observations, produce or characterise a substance, test hypotheses, check data, or explore phenomena.

M4c Plot two variables from experimental or other data.

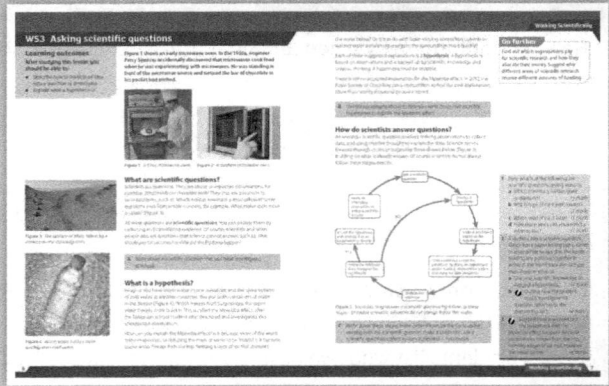

| Target | Outcome | Checkpoint | |
|---|---|---|---|
| | | Question | Activity |
| **Aiming for GRADE 4** ↓ | State what a scientific question is. | | Starter 1 and 2, Plenary 1 |
| | State what a hypothesis is. | | Plenary 1 |
| | Describe some steps in answering a scientific question. | | Main 1 |
| **Aiming for GRADE 6** ↓ | Recognise scientific questions and questions that are not scientific. | A, 1 | Starter 1 |
| | Identify statements that are hypotheses. | B | |
| | Explain a series of steps to answer a scientific question. | 2 | Main 1 and 2 |
| **Aiming for GRADE 8** ↓ | Suggest a scientific question to investigate. | | Starter 2 |
| | Suggest a hypothesis to explain an observation. | 2 | Main 1 |
| | Suggest how to test a given hypothesis to answer a scientific question. | 3 | Main 1, Plenary 2 |

**Maths**
Students plot variables from experimental data (M4c).

**Literacy**
Students write a paragraph to explain whether the evidence they collect in an investigation supports the hypothesis.

**Key words**
hypothesis, scientific question

# Working scientifically

| Starter | Support/Extension | Resources |
|---|---|---|
| **Scientific or not?** (5 minutes)  Tell students what a scientific question is. Then use the interactivity in which students identify questions that are scientific and those that are not. Suggested questions: How big is Pluto? How can we prevent meningitis? Who should pay for vaccines? What is made when petrol burns? <br><br> **Questions, questions** (10 minutes)  Tell students what a scientific question is. Demonstrate, but do not explain, the reaction of aluminium with iodine (see *Practical Chemistry* website). Student pairs list scientific questions that they would like to answer about what they have seen. | **Support:** Begin by giving scientific questions that they have previously investigated. <br><br> **Extension:** Students suggest their own scientific and non-scientific questions. | **Interactive:** Scientific or not? |

| Main | Support/Extension | Resources |
|---|---|---|
| **A question of volume** (35 minutes)  Pose a scientific question: What will happen to sea levels as a result of global warming? Gather initial responses — students will probably say that melting ice will make sea levels rise. Then remind students that many substances expand on heating; might this be the same for water? Tell students that they will follow the steps shown in Figure 5 in the Student Book to answer the scientific question. <br><br> Students use the Practical sheet to guide them in developing a hypothesis (e.g., on heating, particles in liquid water move faster and slightly apart from each other, resulting in an increase in volume) and making a prediction (e.g., heating a water sample will result in an increase in its volume). <br><br> They test their prediction by placing coloured water in a flask fitted with a bung with two holes. In one hole is a thermometer. In the other hole is a glass tube. Students heat the water and record in a table the height of the water column in the glass tube at different temperatures. <br><br> Students analyse the evidence by drawing a line graph. They then decide whether the evidence supports the hypothesis and write a paragraph to explain their decision. <br><br> **One step at a time** (5 minutes)  Students study Figure 5, and match what they did in the investigation to the steps shown. | **Support:** Provide a results table and graph axes. Provide a writing frame to help students record their decision. <br><br> **Extension:** Students suggest alternative methods for investigating this hypothesis. | **Practical:** A question of volume |

| Plenary | Support/Extension | Resources |
|---|---|---|
| **Key words** (5 minutes)  Students write definitions for the two key words of the lesson, and peer-assess one another's definitions. <br><br> **Matching steps** (10 minutes)  Return to one of the scientific questions posed in the starter. Students suggest what they would do for each step shown in Figure 5 to answer the question. | | |

| Homework | | |
|---|---|---|
| Choose a scientific question from the starter activity, or from the Student Book. Describe and explain what you would do for each step shown in Figure 5 to answer the question. | **Support:** Provide a simple question and writing frame to guide students in this task. | |

# WS4 Planning an investigation

**Specification links:**

WS1.1h Evaluate risks both in practical science and the wider societal context.

WS1.2b Plan experiments or devise procedures to make observations, produce or characterise a substance, test hypotheses, check data, or explore phenomena.

WS1.2c Apply a range of techniques, instruments, apparatus, and materials to select those appropriate to the experiment.

M4c Plot two variables from experimental or other data.

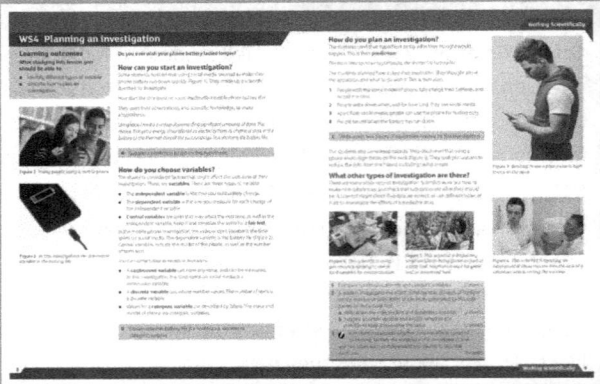

| Target | Outcome | Checkpoint | |
|---|---|---|---|
| | | Question | Activity |
| **Aiming for GRADE 4** ↓ | State what a variable is, and state the meanings of these terms: independent variable, dependent variable, control variable. | | Starter 1, Plenary 1 |
| | State examples of continuous, discrete, and categoric variables. | | Main 2 |
| | Describe the steps in a plan for an investigation to make observations, including making a prediction. | A, C | Main 1 |
| **Aiming for GRADE 6** ↓ | Explain whether given variables in an investigation are independent, dependent, or control variables. | | Main 1 |
| | Compare continuous, discrete, and categoric variables. | 1 | |
| | Describe and explain the steps in a plan for an investigation to make observations. | | Main 1 |
| **Aiming for GRADE 8** ↓ | Determine the variables to change, measure, and control when planning an investigation. | 2, 3 | Starter 2, Plenary 2 |
| | Determine whether given variables in an investigation are continuous, discrete, or categoric. | B, 3 | Main 2, Plenary 2 |
| | Justify decisions made in a plan for an investigation to make observations. | | Main 1 |

**Maths**
Students plot bar charts from their investigation data (M4c).

**Literacy**
Students define key words.

**Key words**
categoric variable, continuous variable, control variable, dependent variable, discrete variable, fair test, independent variable, prediction

# Working scientifically

| Starter | Support/Extension | Resources |
|---|---|---|
| **Defining variables** (5 minutes)  Students use Key Stage 3 knowledge to match key words (variable, independent variable, dependent variable, control variable) to their definitions.<br><br>**Phone variables** (10 minutes)  Display the scientific question *How does the time spent on social media affect mobile-phone battery life?* Students use Key Stage 3 knowledge to suggest the following variables for an investigation to answer this question: one independent variable, one dependent variable, two control variables. | **Support:** List variables for students to choose from.<br><br>**Extension:** Students write their own definitions of the key words. | **Interactive:** Defining variables |

| Main | Support/Extension | Resources |
|---|---|---|
| **Temperature and dissolving** (30 minutes)  Students plan and carry out an investigation to compare the temperature changes on dissolving different substances in water (e.g., ammonium chloride, ammonium nitrate, potassium nitrate, copper sulfate, potassium chloride, calcium chloride, sodium carbonate).<br><br>Students start by identifying variables (independent – substance; dependent – temperature change; control – starting temperature of water, amount of substance). They then consider the hazards, and how to minimise risks from these hazards (see CLEAPSS Student Safety Sheets).<br><br>Next, students decide what to do, and draw a results table, with the independent variable in the column on the left.<br><br>Students then carry out the investigation and collect data.<br><br>**Dissolving variables** (10 minutes)  Explain the differences between continuous, discrete, and categoric variables, including examples. Students categorise the variables in their investigation (substance – categoric; temperature change – continuous). Since one variable is categoric, they draw bar charts to display their results. | **Support:** Provide a writing frame to help students plan their investigation.<br><br>**Extension:** When planning their investigations, students justify each decision they make. They also explain how they know which type of variable is which.<br><br><br><br>**Support:** If time is short, focus on the variable categories only – do not ask students to draw bar charts. | **Practical:** Temperature and dissolving |

| Plenary | Support/Extension | Resources |
|---|---|---|
| **Variable quiz** (10 minutes)  Students make up a five-question quiz on variables. They swap quizzes and answer the questions.<br><br>**Swimming and shoe size** (5 minutes)  Students answer question 3 in the Student Book, and peer-assess each other's answers. In the peer assessment, they point out things that have been done well, and suggest any improvements or corrections. | | |

| Homework |
|---|
| Devise an investigation to answer the question *How does coffee drinking affect reaction time?* You may need to use the Internet for suggestions on how to measure reaction time. |

# WS5 Obtaining high-quality data

**Specification links:**

WS1.3c Carry out and represent mathematical and statistical analysis.

WS1.3g Evaluate data in terms of accuracy, precision, repeatability, and reproducibility.

WS1.4f Use an appropriate number of significant figures in calculation.

M2b Find arithmetic means.

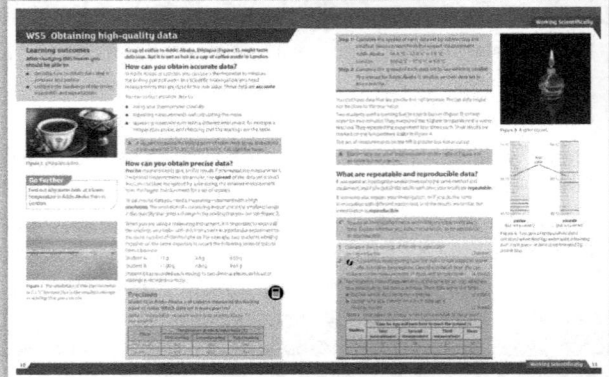

| Target | Outcome | Checkpoint | |
|---|---|---|---|
| | | Question | Activity |
| Aiming for GRADE 4 | State what is meant by accurate data and precise data. | | Starter 1, Main 1, Plenary 1 |
| | State the meanings of repeatable and reproducible. | C | Main 2, Plenary 1 |
| Aiming for GRADE 6 | Compare the meanings of accurate and precise when applied to data. | B, 3 | Main 1 |
| | Compare the meanings of repeatable and reproducible. | 1 | Main 2 |
| Aiming for GRADE 8 | Suggest how to maximise the accuracy and precision of data collected in an investigation. | A, 2 | Starter 2, Plenary 2 |
| | Suggest how to devise an investigation that is repeatable and reproducible. | | Plenary 2 |

**Maths**
Students calculate mean values for data sets (M2b), and give answers to a suitable number of significant figures (M2a).

**Literacy**
Students write paragraphs about the difference between accuracy and precision.

**Key words**
accurate, precise, repeatable, reproducible, resolution, spread

# Working scientifically

| Starter | Support/Extension | Resources |
|---|---|---|
| **How accurate?** (10 minutes) Demonstrate the volume change when salt dissolves in water by placing 300–400 g of salt in a 1 dm³ volumetric flask. Add enough water to cover the salt, swirl to wet it, and let air bubbles float to the top. Then add water to fill the flask to the mark. Shake to speed up dissolving. When no more salt dissolves, mark the new – lower – level of the solution. Ask student pairs to discuss how to get accurate data for the decrease in height. Answers: use the ruler carefully; repeat the procedure and calculate a mean; measure the height with a different instrument and check that the value is the same as for the ruler.<br><br>**Heart beat** (5 minutes) Students suggest how to get an accurate value for their resting pulse rate. Answers: place fingers on the pulse and count carefully; repeat and calculate a mean; use a pulse-rate monitor and check that the value is the same as for placing fingers on the pulse. | | |

| Main | Support/Extension | Resources |
|---|---|---|
| **Hand-span precision** (25 minutes) Elicit that accurate data is data that is close to the true value. State that precise has a different meaning – if data is precise, it has similar values.<br><br>In pairs, students measure each other's hand spans by marking the positions of the thumb and little finger on a piece of paper, and using a ruler to measure the distance between them. Each student repeats the procedure three times, records the measurements, and calculates the spread. In pairs, students compare their results: whose measurements are more precise? Students write a paragraph to explain the difference between accuracy and precision.<br><br>**Thumb width** (15 minutes) In pairs, students measure each other's thumb widths three times using a technique as for hand span. They swap partners and repeat. Finally, students return to their original partner and devise a different method for measuring thumb width, using callipers, for example. Students record all measurements.<br><br>Use the investigation to explain the difference between repeatability and reproducibility (see Student Book). Students complete a passage to explain the difference between the two terms. | **Support:** Supply results tables for students to complete. Supply a passage for students to complete to explain the difference between accuracy and precision.<br><br>**Extension:** Students write their own paragraphs to explain the difference between repeatability and reproducibility. | **Practical:** Hand-span precision |

| Plenary | Support/Extension | Resources |
|---|---|---|
| **Reproducibility and repeatability** (5 minutes) Students complete a paragraph to consolidate their understanding of reproducibility and repeatability.<br><br>**Accurate advice** (10 minutes) Students write instructions to a younger student to explain how to collect accurate and precise data. | **Extension:** Students write corrected versions of the false sentences. | **Interactive:** Reproducibility and repeatability |

| Homework | | |
|---|---|---|
| Make a small parachute from a handkerchief or similar item. Suspend a weight from it. Collect data on its time to fall to the ground from a given height. Explain what you did to collect precise and accurate data. Describe how you could find out if the data is repeatable and reproducible. | | |

# WS6 Presenting data

**Specification links:**

WS1.3a Present observations and other data using appropriate methods.

WS1.3b Translate data from one form to another.

M4c Plot two variables from experimental or other data.

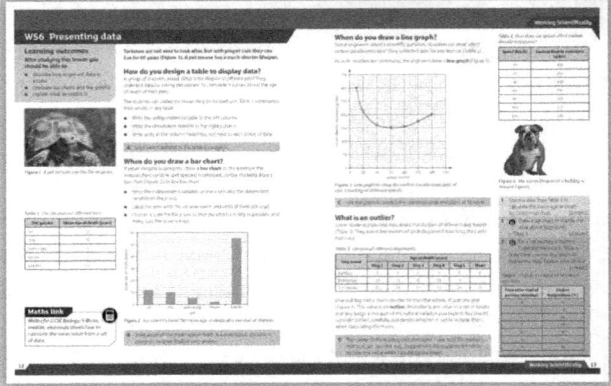

| Target | Outcome | Checkpoint | |
|---|---|---|---|
| | | Question | Activity |
| **Aiming for GRADE 4** | Draw a bar chart or line graph to present data, given fully labelled axes. | | Main 2 and 3 |
| | Identify the value of the dependent variable, given the value of the independent variable, from a bar chart. | | Main 2 |
| | State what an outlier is. | | Main 1 |
| **Aiming for GRADE 6** | Draw a bar chart or line graph to present data, including choosing which type of chart/graph to draw, labelling axes, and choosing suitable scales. | B, 2 | Starter 1 Main 2 and 3 |
| | Identify the value of the dependent variable, given a value of the independent variable, from a bar chart or line graph. | C | Plenary 1 and 2 |
| | Calculate the mean from a set of data. | 1 | Main 1 |
| **Aiming for GRADE 8** | Draw a bar chart or line graph to present data and justify the choice of bar chart or line graph. Decide which variables to place on which axes. | A, 3 | Starter 2 Main 2 |
| | Predict values for the dependent variable, given values for the independent variable, from a bar chart or line graph. | | Main 2 Plenary 2 |
| | Justify a decision to include or not to include an outlier when calculating the mean from a set of data. | D | Main 1 |

**Maths**
Students plot bar charts and line graphs (M4c).

**Literacy**
Students compose questions about their graphs.

**Key words**
bar chart, line graph

# Working scientifically

| Starter | Support/Extension | Resources |
|---|---|---|
| **Displaying dogs** (5 minutes) Display pictures of different dog breeds. Give values for the mean adult mass of dogs of each breed (Great Dane – 54 kg; Pekingese – 5 kg; Rottweiler – 39 kg). Ask whether this data is better displayed as a bar chart or line graph, and why. Answer – bar chart, since one variable is categoric. | **Support:** Point out that one of the variables (dog breed) is categoric. | |
| **Line graph or bar chart?** (10 minutes) Display tables showing different data sets. For each, students decide and justify whether the data should be presented as a bar chart or line graph. | **Extension:** Students suggest data sets for which bar charts or line graphs should be drawn. | **Interactive:** Line graph or bar chart? |

| Main | Support/Extension | Resources |
|---|---|---|
| **Means and outliers** (10 minutes) Give students the adult masses of six adult dogs of the same breed, including one outlier. Students calculate mean values. Point out the outlier. Discuss whether or not to include the outlier in calculating the mean. Tell students the outlier dog was ill, and could not eat enough. Have they changed their minds about whether to include this value in calculating the mean? (Suitable Great Dane values: 50, 54, 58, 56, 38, 50) | | |
| **Line graphs** (15 minutes) On the same axes, students use supplied data to plot growth curves for different puppy breeds (mass versus age). They peer-evaluate each other's graphs, checking that variables have been plotted on the correct axes, that the axes are labelled, that the scales are suitable, and that the curves for each dog breed are clearly labelled.  Students then make up questions about their graph and swap with a partner, who answers the questions. | **Support:** Provide labelled axes. Ask students to plot data for one dog breed only.  **Extension:** Students justify drawing a line graph for this data. | **Activity:** Line graphs and bar charts |
| **Bar charts** (15 minutes) Pass around equal-sized cuboids made from materials of different densities. Tell students that they will find out whether there is a link between the position of an element in the Periodic Table, and its density. Give data for six elements, as well as their relative positions in the Periodic Table. Students plot the data for the two groups on one bar chart. They then note any patterns in the data. Below is some suitable data for elements in adjacent groups of the periodic table: | **Support:** Supply labelled axes and ask students to plot data for one group only.  **Extension:** Students find the density for elements in other adjacent groups of the Periodic Table, and add this to their bar charts. | |

| Element | Density (g/cm$^3$) | Element | Density (g/cm$^3$) |
|---|---|---|---|
| cobalt | 8.9 | nickel | 8.9 |
| rhodium | 12.4 | palladium | 12.0 |
| iridium | 22.5 | platinum | 21.4 |

| Plenary | Support/Extension | Resources |
|---|---|---|
| **Emissions and car speed** (5 minutes) Students study the line graph in the Student Book. In pairs, they take turns to describe what it shows. They then answer in-text question C. | | |
| **Questions, questions** (10 minutes) Students make up questions about their bar charts and swap with a partner, who answers the questions. | | |

| Homework | | |
|---|---|---|
| Use the data provided to plot a bar chart or line graph. Justify your choice of graph type. | | |

# WS7 Interpreting data

**Specification links:**

WS1.3e Interpreting observations and other data.

WS1.3f Presenting reasoned explanations.

WS1.3g Evaluating data in terms of accuracy, precision, repeatability, and reproducibility.

M2g Use a scatter diagram to identify a relationship between two variables.

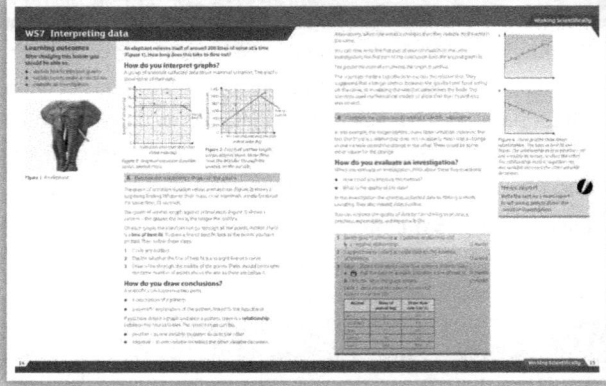

| Target | Outcome | Checkpoint | |
|---|---|---|---|
| | | Question | Activity |
| **Aiming for GRADE 4** | Draw a line of best fit on a simple graph. | | Main 2 |
| | Describe the relationship shown by a graph using non-specialist terms. | A | |
| | Describe one way of evaluating an investigation. | | Starter 1 |
| **Aiming for GRADE 6** | Draw a line of best fit on a graph that does not include outliers. | | Main 2 |
| | Describe the relationship shown by a graph using terms such as positive relationship. | A, 1, 3 | Starter 2 |
| | Explain at least two ways of evaluating investigations, including the quality of data. | 2 | Main 3 |
| **Aiming for GRADE 8** | Draw the line of best fit on a graph that includes outliers. | | Main 2 |
| | Describe in detail the relationship shown by a graph using technical terms. If appropriate, suggest and justify whether any relationship shown could be causal. | C, 3 | |
| | Suggest how to evaluate both the method and quality of data for a given investigation. | | Main 3 |

**Maths**
Students interpret scatter graphs.

**Literacy**
Students write conclusions for investigations.

**Key words**
line of best fit, relationship

# Working scientifically

| Starter | Support/Extension | Resources |
|---|---|---|
| **Urination duration** (10 minutes) Show a video of an animal such as an elephant urinating. Individually, students outline how they could collect high-quality data to compare the duration of urination for different mammal species. Each student shares their ideas with a partner, who evaluates their method, suggesting improvements that would enable them to collect more accurate data. Answers might include: make a video and then measure urination duration several times; find the mean of repeated readings. | **Support:** Suggest methods for students to evaluate. | |
| **What do graphs show?** (5 minutes) Use the interactive activity in which students have to identify, from graph sketches, whether a graph shows a positive relationship, a negative relationship, or no relationship. | | **Interactive:** What do graphs show? |

| Main | Support/Extension | Resources |
|---|---|---|
| **Urination duration – any relation?** (15 minutes) For several mammal species, provide data of urination duration and mean adult mass. Students plot the data as a scatter graph. Elicit that there is no relationship between the data – the data shows that, whatever the mass, urination duration is around 21 seconds. Students write conclusions for the investigation. | **Support:** Provide a writing frame for the conclusion. | **Activity:** Urination duration – any relation? |
| **Mass, urethra length, and lines of best fit** (15 minutes) For several species, provide data of mean adult mass and urethra length. Students plot the data as a scatter graph. Elicit that the data shows a positive relationship. Students write conclusions for the investigation. Provide further scatter graphs (some including outliers) so that students can practise drawing lines of best fit, as well as identifying whether each shows a positive relationship, a negative relationship, or no relationship. | **Support:** Provide a writing frame for the conclusion. **Extension:** Provide data so that students can sketch extra scatter diagrams of their own. | |
| **Evaluating an investigation** (10 minutes) If students did the activity in Starter 1, remind them how they evaluated the method. Now give further data for the urination experiment, and ask students to evaluate the data in terms of its precision. They can do this by calculating the spread of each data set. For which animal is the data most precise? | **Support:** Provide a series of questions to support students in evaluating the precision of the data. | |

| Plenary | Support/Extension | Resources |
|---|---|---|
| **Relationships** (5 minutes) Ask students to sketch graphs showing each of these relationships in turn – positive, negative, none. | | |
| **Evaluation** (10 minutes) Read out statements about evaluation, some true and some false. Students use mini-whiteboards to indicate which are true and which are false. | | |

| Homework | | |
|---|---|---|
| Make a poster to display your learning from the lesson. | | |

# WS8 Errors and uncertainties

**Specification links:**
WS1.3d Representing distribution of results and making estimations of uncertainty.

WS1.3h Identifying potential sources of random and systematic error.

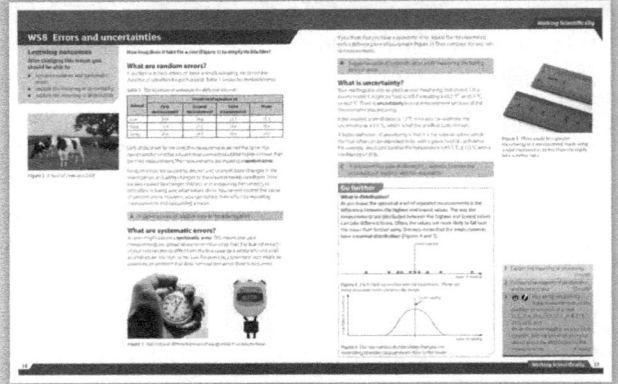

| Target | Outcome | Checkpoint | |
|---|---|---|---|
| | | Question | Activity |
| Aiming for GRADE 4 | State the meanings of random error and systematic error. | | Main 1<br>Plenary 2 |
| | State the scientific meaning of uncertainty. | 1 | Main 2<br>Plenary 2 |
| | State the meaning of the spread of a set of data. | | Main 3<br>Plenary 2 |
| Aiming for GRADE 6 | Compare random and systematic error and suggest causes of these types of error. | A, B, 2 | Starter 1 and 2<br>Main 1<br>Plenary 1 |
| | Estimate the uncertainty of a given measuring instrument using scale divisions. | C | Main 2 |
| | Recognise and sketch a plot showing normal distribution. | | Main 3 |
| Aiming for GRADE 8 | State whether a given error is random or systematic, and justify this choice. | | Main 1 |
| | Compare the uncertainties of two given measuring instruments using scale divisions. | | Main 2 |
| | Plot a blob diagram and explain what it shows about the distribution of measurements. | 3 | |

**Maths**
Students identify plots of normal distribution and explain what they mean.

**Literacy**
Students describe the difference between random and systematic errors.

**Key words**
normal distribution, random error, systematic error, uncertainty

# Working scientifically

| Starter | Support/Extension | Resources |
|---|---|---|
| **Timing errors I** (10 minutes)   Show a video clip of a 200m sprint. Students use stopwatches or other timing devices to measure the winning time. They then write down their results. Repeat the exercise twice more, so that each student has a set of three results. Ask students to compare their three results. Are they all the same? In pairs, students suggest reasons for any differences.<br><br>**Timing errors II** (5 minutes)   Ask students to think back to measuring urination duration. Imagine they watched a video of an animal urinating three times. Would they get the same measurements each time? If not, why not? | **Support:** Provide a table for recording results.<br><br>**Extension:** Tell students they will consider two types of error – random error, and systematic error. Can they suggest any differences in their meanings? | |

| Main | Support/Extension | Resources |
|---|---|---|
| **Boiling salty water** (20 minutes)   Students add four spatula measures of salt to approximately 100 cm$^3$ of water. They heat the solution in a beaker and measure and record its boiling temperature. They repeat this twice more, thus collecting a set of three results.<br><br>Students consider their results. Why might they be different? Introduce the idea of random errors, and state that these cannot be controlled, but that their effects can be reduced by repeating measurements and calculating a mean.<br><br>Then explain systematic errors. Gather mean values for the boiling temperature of salty water from all groups. Does it appear that one or more groups might have a systematic error? (Any group whose values are consistently lower or higher than those of other groups might have a systematic error.) Ask students to suggest what they might do about these errors. (Repeat with a different thermometer.)<br><br>**Uncertainty circus** (10 minutes)   Introduce the scientific meaning of uncertainty, and compare to the everyday meaning. Explain how to estimate the uncertainty of a measuring instrument as half of its smallest scale division. Set up a circus of measuring instruments. Students examine each and estimate the uncertainty in readings taken with the instrument.<br><br>**Distribution** (10 minutes)   Ask students to calculate the spread of their measurements for the boiling-water practical. Then take the results from the group with the biggest spread and draw a blob plot on the board. Explain that, for a given set of measurements, the measurements are likely to be distributed with more nearer the mean than further away. Students answer question 3 in the Student Book. | **Support:** Provide results tables and gap fill exercises for students to summarise their learning.<br><br>**Extension:** Students read about a second way of estimating uncertainty, as described in the Student Book. They also compare the uncertainties of two instruments for measuring the same quantity, such as time.<br><br><br><br><br><br><br><br><br><br><br><br>**Extension:** Point out the special case of a normal, or Gaussian, distribution, as shown in the Student Book. | **Practical:** Looking at errors |

| Plenary | Support/Extension | Resources |
|---|---|---|
| **Random versus systematic** (10 minutes)   Students write down the difference between random and systematic errors, and peer-assess.<br><br>**Key words** (5 minutes)   Read definitions of the key words, without saying which is which. Students write down the key words. | **Support:** Give key words for students to choose from. | **Interactive:** Key words |

| Homework | | |
|---|---|---|
| Answer all of the questions in the Student Book that you have not already answered. | | |

# B1 Cell-level systems
## B1.1 Cell structures
### B1.1.1 Plant and animal cells

**Specification links:**

B1.1b Explain how the main subcellular structures of eukaryotic cells (plants and animals) and prokaryotic cells are related to their functions. To include nucleus, genetic material, chromosomes, plasmids, mitochondria (contain enzymes for cellular respiration), chloroplasts (contain chlorophyll) and cell membranes (contain receptor molecules, provides a selective barrier to molecules).

WS1.4a Use scientific vocabulary, terminology and definitions.
WS2.a Carry out experiments.
WS2.b Make and record observations and measurements using a range of apparatus and methods.
WS2.c Present observations using appropriate methods.
WS2.d Communicate the scientific rationale for investigations, methods used, findings and reasoned conclusions.

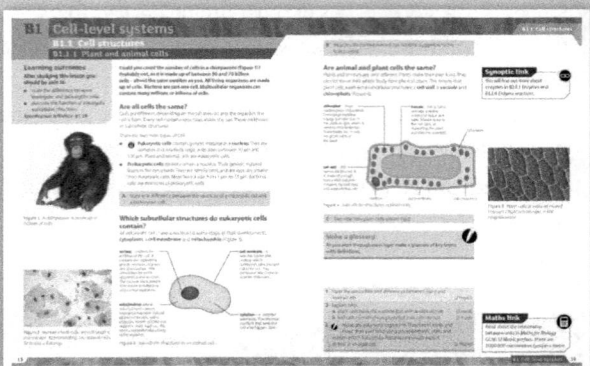

| Target | Outcome | Checkpoint | |
|---|---|---|---|
| | | Question | Activity |
| **Aiming for GRADE 4** | State the organelles (subcellular structures) present in a plant and animal cell. | B, 1, 2 | Starter 1 and 2<br>Main<br>Plenary 1 and 2 |
| | State the function of each of the main organelles present in a plant and animal cell. | B, C, 2 | Main<br>Plenary 1 and 2 |
| | Label the organelles in representational models of plant and animal cells. | | Plenary 1 and 2 |
| **Aiming for GRADE 6** | Compare the organelles present in plant and animal cells. | 1, 2 | Starter 2<br>Main<br>Plenary 2 |
| | Explain the function of the organelles, relating the structure and molecules present to the function of the organelles. | B, C, 2 | Main |
| | Explain how a model cell is similar to, and different from, a real cell. | | Main |
| **Aiming for GRADE 8** | Discuss the reasons for the presence or absence of organelles in different plant and animal cells. | 2, 3 | Plenary 1 and 2 |
| | Explain the roles of the molecules or structures within the organelles, such as the receptors in the cell membrane. | | Main |
| | Discuss the benefits and drawbacks of using a representational model to help in explaining the structures and functions of cell organelles. | | Main |

**Literacy**
Students communicate effectively orally, and produce coherent, well-structured and purposeful texts.

**Key words**
cell, cell membrane, cell wall, chloroplast, cytoplasm, eukaryotic cell, mitochondria, nucleus, prokaryotic cell, vacuole

## B1.1 Cell structures

| Starter | Support/Extend | Resources |
|---|---|---|
| **What are we made of?** (5 minutes)   Ask the class members to state a fact that they remember from Key Stage 3 about cells, whenever a soft ball is thrown at them.<br><br>**Cell theory** (10 minutes)   Show images of microscope sections through a few different tissues. Ensure that all images show clear cells, and that both plant and animal examples are included. Lead the class to identify the cells. Ask a student to draw a cell from a tissue type on the board, and ask the class to identify the parts in the cell. After looking at several tissues, draw the discussion to the point that all tissues are made of cells, and that they share many common parts. Finally ask students if they can identify any differences between plant and animal cells. Focus the discussion on the different organelles found in them. | **Support:** The ball is passed back to the teacher each time, allowing control of which student answers.<br><br>**Extend:** Establish the basic functions of the structures inside the cell.<br><br>**Support:** Start with tissues like cuboidal epithelia. Lead the class to look at one cell.<br><br>**Extend:** Show a single celled organism. | |

| Main | Support/Extend | Resources |
|---|---|---|
| **Build models of plant and animal cells** (20 minutes)   Divide class into groups of seven. Each group is divided into two subgroups (four students for the plant cell and three students for the animal cell). Ask students to use a variety of materials to build a model of a plant or animal cell. Within the groups, give each student responsibility for a different part of the cell. In the plant cell subgroup each student is responsible for one of the following: cell wall and membrane; the nucleus and contents; mitochondria; chloroplasts. In the animal cell subgroup each student is responsible for one of the following: the cell membrane and receptors; the nucleus and its contents; and the mitochondria. Students work individually to build their organelle, but coordinate so that the organelles can be placed in the finished model. Each person must be able to build the organelle, and describe its structure and function.<br><br>**Sharing knowledge** (20 minutes)   When the organelles are placed into the finished cell, students teach each other about the structure and role of the organelles. The plant and animal subgroups also share their final model. Finally, lead a class discussion to discuss the benefits and drawbacks of using a representational model to help to explain the structures and functions of cell organelles. | **Support:** Allocate organelles according to ability. Provide images of each organelle, and appropriate resources. Provide prompt questions for describing the structure and function. Possibly use a list of key words.<br><br>**Extend:** Organelles such as mitochondria and membrane receptors should be allocated to higher-attaining students. Place more emphasis on the functions of the organelles, and show some connection between the organelles. | **Activity:** Models of cells |

| Plenary | Support/Extend | Resources |
|---|---|---|
| **Plant and animal cells** (5 minutes)   Interactive showing an image of a cell with no labels. Students label the diagram.<br><br>**What goes where?** (10 minutes)   Create a table to list the organelles present in a plant cell and an animal cell. | **Extend:** Ask students to think of animal cells, which would have many mitochondria, and to explain why. Ask them which plant cells might lack chloroplasts, and explain why. | **Interactive:** Plant and animal cells |

| Homework | | |
|---|---|---|
| **Discovering cells** Research the discovery of cells. This should include answers to the following questions:<br>• Who first discovered cells?<br>• How did he discover cells?<br>• Who first realised that all living things are built out of cells?<br>• What is the cell theory? | **Extend:** Are viruses living things? Use the ideas of cell theory to justify your answer. | |

**kerboodle**
A Kerboodle highlight for this lesson is **Bump up your grade: Animal and plant cell features**. Refer to the **Content map** on Kerboodle for a full list of resources and assessment.

# B1.1.2 Bacterial cells

**Specification links:**

B1.1b Explain how the main subcellular structures of eukaryotic cells (plants and animals) and prokaryotic cells are related to their functions. To include nucleus, genetic material, chromosomes, plasmids, mitochondria (contain enzymes for cellular respiration), chloroplasts (contain chlorophyll), and cell membranes (contain receptor molecules, provides a selective barrier to molecules).

WS1.4a Use scientific vocabulary, terminology, and definitions.

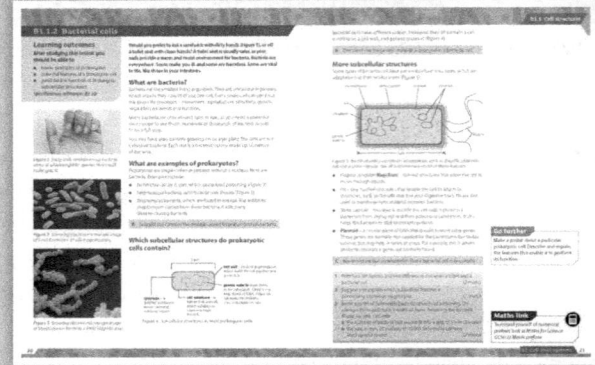

| Target | Outcome | Checkpoint | |
|---|---|---|---|
| | | Question | Activity |
| **Aiming for GRADE 4** | Name some examples of prokaryotes. | A | Starter 1, Main 2 |
| | State the main organelles present in a prokaryotic cell. | B, 2 | Starter 1, Main 2 |
| | Use a method, with some help to obtain results, working safely. | 1 | Main 1, Plenary 2 |
| **Aiming for GRADE 6** | Compare prokaryotic and eukaryotic cells. | 1 | Starter 2, Plenary 1 |
| | Explain the function of the organelles, relating the structure to the function of the organelles. | 2 | Main 2 |
| | Use a method independently to obtain results, noting some major hazards. | | Main 1, Plenary 2 |
| **Aiming for GRADE 8** | Discuss the reasons for the presence or absence of organelles in different prokaryotic cells. | C, 2 | |
| | Discuss how the organelles of the prokaryote can carry out all of the functions of the eukaryotic cell. | C, 2 | Main 1 |
| | Use a method independently to obtain results, justifying the steps to minimise risks. | | Main 1, Plenary 2 |

**Maths**
Students estimate the results of numbers of bacteria without using a calculator (M1d).

**Literacy**
Students communicate effectively orally, and produce coherent, well-structured and purposeful texts.

**Key words**
flagellum, plasmid

# B1.1 Cell structures

| Starter | Support/Extend | Resources |
|---|---|---|
| **Common bacteria** (5 minutes)  Display a newspaper headline about food poisoning caused by bacteria. Discuss what caused the poisoning. Then show images of common bacteria that students might have heard of, for example, *Escherichia coli, Salmonella,* MRSA and *Clostridium botulinum*. Ask what they know about them.<br><br>**The discovery of bacteria** (10 minutes)  Find a short film clip on the internet that introduces the discovery of bacteria by Pasteur, or the ideas of hygiene introduced by Semmelweis. Discuss how this opened biologists' minds to the previously unknown world of bacteria. | **Extend:** Show an electron microscope image of the internal structure of a bacterium, and ask students to identify differences to the cells they already know. | |

| Main | Support/Extend | Resources |
|---|---|---|
| **Streak plates for single colonies** (30 minutes)  Students follow a method, which might be used in a hospital lab or public health laboratory. They use aseptic technique to streak an agar plate to culture single colonies from milk or yoghurt. Discuss the hazards associated both with the technique and with handling the resulting plates, and how to minimise the risks from these hazards.<br><br>The students observe the results in the next lesson. Alternatively, use pre-prepared plates to show bacterial colonies.<br><br>**Drawing bacterial cells** (10 minutes)  Draw and label a bacterial cell and indicate the structures present that are different to those in a plant or animal cell. Indicate why they might be different, and their functions. | **Support:** Provide a risk assessment writing frame to structure the responses.<br><br>**Extend:** Students use CLEAPSS Student Safety Sheet (SSS001 Microorganisms) for the growth of bacteria to obtain information about risk management.<br><br>**Support:** Provide an outline of the bacterial cell.<br><br>**Extend:** Students discover how prokaryotic cells and plasmids are used in genetic engineering by tackling the tasks on the Go Further sheet. | **Practical:** Streak plates |

| Plenary | Support/Extend | Resources |
|---|---|---|
| **Eukaryotes and prokaryotes** (5 minutes)  Students sort the statements into those that refer to eukaryotic cells and those that refer to prokaryotic cells.<br><br>**Grime busters** (10 minutes)  Show the students a picture of a busy restaurant kitchen. Suggest that they imagine they work for a public health laboratory. Ask them what they would want to test in the kitchen to check for bacteria, and how they would do the test. Ask them why there is no clear evidence of bacteria. | **Extend:** If only two bacteria were present and divided approximately every 20 minutes, estimate how many bacteria there would there be after twenty four hours, without using a calculator. | **Interactive:** Eukaryotic and prokaryotic cells |

| Homework | | |
|---|---|---|
| Create a table of the differences between prokaryotic and eukaryotic cells. | | |

*kerboodle*

A Kerboodle highlight for this lesson is **Go further: Eukaryotic and prokaryotic cells**. Refer to the **Content map** on Kerboodle for a full list of resources and assessment.

# B1.1.3 Light microscopy

**Specification links:**

B1.1a Describe how light microscopes and staining can be used to view cells. To include lenses, stage, lamp, use of slides and coverslips, and the use of stains to view colourless specimens or to highlight different structures/tissues and calculation of magnification.

WS1.2c Apply knowledge of a range of techniques, instruments, apparatus, and materials to select those appropriate to the experiment.

WS1.4c Use SI units and IUPAC chemical nomenclature unless inappropriate.

WS1.4d Use prefixes and powers of ten for orders of magnitude (tera, giga, mega, kilo, deci, centi, milli, micro, and nano).

WS1.4e Interconvert units.

BM1.1i Demonstrate an understanding of number, size, and scale, and the quantitative relationship between units (M2a, M2h).

BM1.1ii Use estimations and explain when they should be used (M1b).

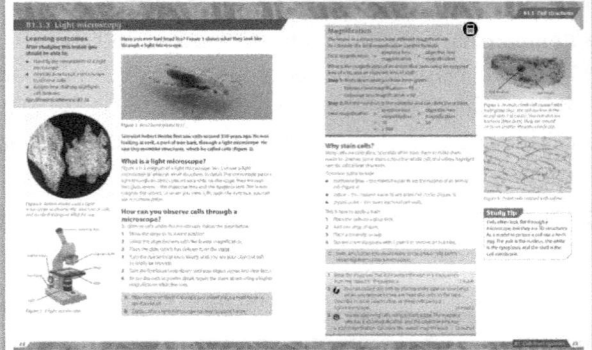

| Target | Outcome | Checkpoint | |
|---|---|---|---|
| | | Question | Activity |
| **Aiming for GRADE 4** ↓ | Identify the components of the light microscope. | A, B, 1, 2 | Starter 1 and 2 |
| | Describe how to use a microscope to observe cells. | A, B, 2 | Starter 1 and 2 |
| | Use a microscope to observe and draw a cell. | | Main |
| **Aiming for GRADE 6** ↓ | Explain the role of each part of the microscope. | A, B | Starter 2, Plenary 1 |
| | Explain why stains are used to highlight cell features. | C | Main, Plenary 2 |
| | Draw an accurate representation of a cell and calculate the magnification used to make the drawing. | 2 | Main |
| **Aiming for GRADE 8** ↓ | Discuss why different lenses on the microscope are needed. | A, B | Plenary 1 |
| | Discuss why different stains might be required when viewing different cells or tissues. | C | Main, Plenary 2 |
| | Calculate specimen size, image size, and magnification by substituting values into an equation, rearranging when necessary. | | Main |

**Maths**
Students will use an appropriate number of significant figures (M2a), and estimate orders of magnitude (M2h).

**Literacy**
Students will communicate effectively producing coherent, well structured and purposeful text in response to questions.

# B1.1 Cell structures

| Starter | Support/Extend | Resources |
|---|---|---|
| **Parts of a microscope** (5 minutes) Use the interactive, in which students label the parts of the light microscope. Students also order the steps used to view a sample using a light microscope.<br><br>**Labelling your microscope** (10 minutes) Provide each group with a microscope, and a set of sticky notes with the names of the key parts of the microscope. Students attach each label to the correct part of the microscope. Then give out a second colour sticky note, on which the students write an explanation of the part's function. Students feed back to the rest of the class. | **Support:** Provide the second set of sticky notes with the functions already written, or carry out the task verbally. | **Interactive:** The light microscope |

| Main | Support/Extend | Resources |
|---|---|---|
| **Observation of animal cells under a microscope** (25 minutes) Students observe animal (cheek) cells using a light microscope and draw images. The slides can either be prepared or students can make their own. They carry out magnification calculations.<br>SAFETY: Follow CLEAPSS advice when handling cheek cells.<br><br>**Other cells** (15 minutes) Students look at other prepared slides, such as *Amoeba, Paramecium, Spirogyra,* yeasts, and moulds like *Penicillium*. They look at several slides and draw and label some parts of at least one of the cells. | **Support:** Provide support to make the slide and focus the microscope. Use projected images of the cell to model how to draw a cell from the slide.<br><br>**Extend:** Students calculate the magnification used and ensure that they draw parts of the cell in the correct proportions. They also tackle the magnification questions on the Extension sheet. | **Practical:** Observation of cells under a microscope<br><br>**Extension:** Microscopes and magnification |

| Plenary | Support/Extend | Resources |
|---|---|---|
| **Magnifications for the job** (10 minutes) Show images of three or four different specimens, such as bacteria, blood, *Amoeba*, epithelial cells, and an insect's leg. Students arrange them in order of actual size. Then ask what magnification they might use to observe such cells/tissues.<br><br>**Colour vision** (5 minutes) Project an image of a TS section of a stem, but in black and white (turn normal image to greyscale). Ask the students to see if they can locate different tissues in the image. Ask how the task could be made easier. Then show a colour image of the slide. Ask students to list the advantages and disadvantages of stains, how many stains might have been used in the stained stem. | **Support:** Restrict the number of images.<br><br>**Extend:** Ask students to justify their selection.<br><br>**Extend:** Link to any slides students might have used in Main 2. Discuss how many stains might have been used and how they know. | |

| Homework | | |
|---|---|---|
| Write a newspaper report, which explains how a biomedical technician used a microscope to identify the cause of death as the bacterial infection tuberculosis in human lung tissue. | **Support:** Either provide a list of key words to help the students structure their report, or a writing frame, such as:<br>1. Obtain a sample of lung tissue from the patient…<br>2. Make a microscope slide…<br>3. Stain…<br>4. Observe, using the microscope… | |

**kerboodle**
The Kerboodle highlight for this lesson is **Working Scientifically: Interconverting units**. Refer to the **Content map** on Kerboodle for a full list of resources and assessment.

The Practical Skills lesson for PAG 1 Microscopy could follow this lesson.

# B1.1.4 Electron microscopy

**Specification links:**

B1.1c Explain how electron microscopy has increased our understanding of subcellular structures, to include increased resolution in TEM.

WS1.1a Understand how scientific methods and theories develop over time.

WS1.4c Use SI units and IUPAC chemical nomenclature unless inappropriate.

WS1.4d Use prefixes and powers of ten for orders of magnitude (tera, giga, mega, kilo, deci, centi, milli, micro, and nano).

BM1.1i Demonstrate an understanding of number, size, and scale, and the quantitative relationship between units.

BM1.1iii Calculate with numbers written in standard form (M1b).

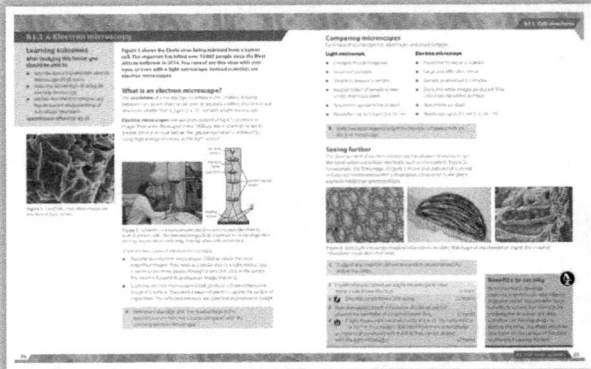

| Target | Outcome | Checkpoint | |
|---|---|---|---|
| | | Question | Activity |
| **Aiming for GRADE 4** | Describe simply how a transmission electron microscope (TEM) works. | 2 | Main |
| | State an advantage of using an electron microscope. | A, B, 1 | Starter 1 and 2<br>Main<br>Plenary 1 and 2 |
| | State the resolution achieved by an electron microscope in SI units using the correct order of magnitude. | | Main<br>Plenary 1 |
| **Aiming for GRADE 6** | Explain how electron microscopy has increased understanding of subcellular structures. | 1 | Starter 1 and 2<br>Main<br>Plenary 2 |
| | Describe the advantages of using the electron microscope compared with the light microscope. | C | Starter 1 and 2<br>Main<br>Plenary 1 |
| | Compare the increase in resolution, in standard form, of an electron microscope with that of a light microscope. | C, 1 | Main<br>Plenary 1 |
| **Aiming for GRADE 8** | Discuss how useful the electron microscope has been in medicine and biology. | | Main<br>Plenary 2 |
| | Evaluate the relative advantages and disadvantages of using an electron microscope compared with a light microscope. | 1, 3 | Main<br>Plenary 1 and 2 |
| | Calculate how many times greater the resolution of an electron microscope is compared with a light microscope. | 4 | Main |

**Maths**
Students recognise expressions in standard form (M1b). They will also make order-of-magnitude calculations (M2h).

**Literacy**
Whilst completing the task, students will summarise and evaluate text with accuracy. They will also produce coherent, well-structured and purposeful texts.

**Key words**
electron microscope, resolution

# B1.1 Cell structures

| Starter | Support/Extend | Resources |
|---|---|---|
| **Design your own microscope** (10 minutes)  So far, students have only been taught about light microscopes. Divide the class into groups of three. Set the task of designing a new microscope that would be of more use to biologists than the light microscope. Students need to list three characteristic features or properties that the new microscope would have that would make it more useful. Class feedback and discussion should focus on being able to see an image in more detail. | **Support:** Show students images taken using electron microscopes, showing greater magnification, to help give ideas to the students. | |
| **Can you see the point?** (10 minutes)  Project a low resolution image of any cell or cell structure. Discuss the usefulness of seeing a structure in more detail. Lead students to talk about magnifying the image. Then, enlarge the image to magnify. Ask students if this achieves the aim. They should reach the conclusion that greater magnification alone is not enough. Introduce the idea of resolution. | **Extend:** Students should be asked to explain and justify their microscope's properties. | |

| Main | Support/Extend | Resources |
|---|---|---|
| **Electron microscopes** (30 minutes)  Students work in pairs. Each pair has a set of three information cards, one for each type of microscope to be studied (light, SEM, and TEM). Each card describes the major features of its type of microscope. It includes: the resolution achieved; advantages and disadvantages; brief detail of how the microscope is used; examples of its uses in medical studies; and the images that can be produced with it. Students find the answers to the following questions:<br>• What is the resolution of the microscope?<br>• How does the microscope work?<br>• What are the advantages of the microscope?<br>• What are the disadvantages of the microscope?<br>• What is the microscope used for?<br>Allow 10 minutes to complete each card. Circulate the cards in a carousel fashion until each student pair has completed a card for each microscope. | **Support:** Simplify the cards. | **Activity:** Electron microscopes |
| **Feedback** (10 minutes)  Students put together a proposal for the school management to buy an electron microscope. The pitch could include ideas about cost, uses, and advantages. | **Extend:** Ask students to calculate how many times greater the resolution of the EM is compared with the light microscope. | |

| Plenary | Support/Extend | Resources |
|---|---|---|
| **Light and electron microscopes** (5 minutes)  Drag and drop interactive, where students sort characteristic features, resolutions, advantages, and disadvantages for each type of microscope. | | **Interactive:** Light and electron microscopes |
| **Medical microscopy** (5 minutes)  Show students an electron micrograph of a virus responsible for any recent headline-grabbing infection. Ask students what type of microscope was used to take the image, and why. Then ask students to give three reasons to explain why the electron microscope was used. | **Extend:** Ask students to suggest problems with using the electron microscope, and justify its use. | |

| Homework | | |
|---|---|---|
| Write a television script for the TV news in 1950. It explains the invention of a new type of microscope called the electron microscope. The script should suggest how useful this type of microscope might be to biologists and doctors in the future. You can also make a video of the news item.<br><br>Alternatively, compare the sizes of various objects and think about what kind of microscope is needed in each case. The Activity sheet helps you to do this, and gives you practice with standard form. | | |

**kerboodle**

A Kerboodle highlight for this lesson is **Webquest: Microscopes through the ages**. Refer to the **Content map** on Kerboodle for a full list of resources and assessment.

# Checkpoint
## B1.1 Cell structures

### Overview of B1.1 Cell structures

In this chapter, students have studied cells in plants, animals, and single celled organisms. They should be able to distinguish between these types of cell based on their different features, and should also be able to recognise the similarities.

Students should be able to describe the main cell structures, including the nucleus, cell membrane, cytoplasm, and mitochondria, with the addition of the cell wall, chloroplasts, and vacuoles in plant and algal cells. They should be aware that not all plant cells contain chloroplasts, and link this to work on specialised cells in B2.1 *Supplying the cell*. They should be able to recall differences between eukaryotic and prokaryotic cells along with information about the specialised subcellular structures of bacteria – flagella, pili, slime capsules, and plasmids.

In their studies of microscopy, students should have used light microscopes in practical lessons, and studied the structures of plant cells, animal cells, and single celled organisms.

Students should be aware that electron microscopes are commonly used in laboratories because they offer much greater resolution and magnification than light microscopes. They should be able to compare the advantages and disadvantages of light microscopes and electron microscopes.

You can find additional support for the maths skills covered in this chapter on **MyMaths**, including making estimations of populations of bacteria without using a calculator, using an appropriate number of significant figures, and estimating orders of magnitude.

### PAGs

All students are expected to have carried out the PAG *1 Microscopy*. A full lesson plan for each PAG is provided in the Practical skills chapter. PAG *1 Microscopy* should be completed after lesson B1.1.3 *Light microscopy*.

### kerboodle

For this chapter, the following assessments are available on Kerboodle:
B1.1 Checkpoint quiz: Cell structures
B1.1 Progress quiz: Cell structures 1
B1.1 Progress quiz: Cell structures 2
B1.1 On your marks: Cell structures
B1.1 Exam-style questions and mark scheme: Cell structures

### Checkpoint follow-up lesson

A student's route through this lesson can be determined using the Checkpoint assessment. Percentage pass marks are supplied in the Checkpoint teacher notes.

For each successive route through it is assumed that the student can perform to their current route as well as previous routes. For example, students working at Aiming for 6 are assumed to be secure in Aiming for 4 knowledge and understanding and working towards achieving all the learning objectives for Aiming for 6.

# B1.1 Cell structures

|  | Aiming for 4 | Aiming for 6 | Aiming for 8 |
|---|---|---|---|
| **Learning outcomes** | Label the parts and functions of animal and plant cells. | Describe parts of animal, plant, and bacterial cells and their functions. | Compare the parts and functions of animal, plant, and bacterial cells. |
|  | Demonstrate correct use of a light microscope. | Describe how to use a light microscope. | Explain how to use a light microscope. |
|  | State some differences between a light microscope and an electron microscope. | State some differences between a light microscope and an electron microscope. | Describe some differences between an electron and light microscope. |
| **Starter** | **Animal, plant, or bacteria? (5 minutes)** Show pictures of animal, plant, and bacterial cells. Ask questions, such as – how do we know what these cells are and what they do? | | |
| **Differentiated checkpoint activity** | **Activity 1 Animal, plant, and bacterial cells (20 minutes)** Students complete question 1 on the differentiated worksheets, to label plant and animal cells, give the functions of the cell parts, and compare different types of cell. You may need to explain the functions of parts of the cell for Aiming for 4 students. Students will need pencils, rulers, and access to the Student Book. Aiming for 8 students work independently to prepare a visual summary. They will need A3 paper. | | |
|  | The Aiming for 4 sheet provides questions about plant and animal cells. Give a brief introduction to question 1. Students work in pairs to answer part (d) and then rotate to ask and answer questions. You may need to prompt students to move on to the next part. | The Aiming for 6 sheet provides questions about plant cells, animal cells, and bacterial cells. Students should not require any introduction to start question 1. Students work in pairs to answer part (c) and then rotate to ask and answer questions. You may need to prompt students to move on to the next part. | The Aiming for 8 sheet asks students to prepare a visual summary about plant cells, animal cells, and bacterial cells. They should be able to complete the activity with no introduction from the teacher. |
|  | **Activity 2 How to use a light microscope (5 minutes)** Demonstrate how to safely use a light microscope and the parts of the microscope for Aiming for 4 and Aiming for 6 students, in preparation for Activity 3. Aiming for 8 students could complete Activity 1 or start Activity 3. | | |
|  | **Activity 3 Cell structures (20 minutes)** Students answer question 2 on the differentiated worksheets, and work in groups to observe prepared slides using a light microscope. They will require pencils, rulers, calculators, access to microscopes, and a range of prepared slides. | | |
|  | The Aiming for 4 sheet gives a series of instructions for students to use a light microscope and make drawings. Students are prompted to calculate the magnification and provided with the formula to use. | The Aiming for 6 sheet asks students to use a light microscope and make drawings. Students are prompted to calculate the magnification and provided with the formula to use. | Aiming for 8 students are asked to provide labelled drawings and to include the magnification. |
|  | **Kerboodle resource:** B1.1 Checkpoint follow-up: Aiming for 4, B1.1 Checkpoint follow-up: Aiming for 6, B1.1 Checkpoint follow-up: Aiming for 8 | | |
| **Plenary** | **Light or electron? (5 minutes)** First show pictures of cells again from the starter. Can students now identify all of them? | | |
|  | Provide each student with two different coloured cards. Read a series of statements – students hold up one coloured card if the statement is about light microscopy and the other colour if it is about electron microscopy. | | |
| **Progression** | The Aiming for 4 activity is highly structured. You could check answers or provide answers for students to check each other's work. | The Aiming for 6 activity is fairly structured. You should check answers or provide answers for students to check each other's work. You could provide a less structured brief for students to model a plant cell, an animal cell, or a single celled organism. | The Aiming for 8 sheet has very little structure, and students work independently. |
|  | Some students may have made model cells during Key Stage 3. You could extend this and ask students to model a plant cell or an animal cell, and provide a choice of options, for example, vacuole or no vacuole, large surface area or small surface area. |  | Students might benefit from a more complex brief to model a cell, with less guidance and asking for more explanation of how a cell might be specialised for a certain role. |

# B1.2 What happens in cells?
## B1.2.1 DNA

**Specification links:**

B1.2a Describe DNA as a polymer.

B1.2b Describe DNA as being made up of two strands forming a double helix.

B1.2c Describe that DNA is made from four different nucleotides; each nucleotide consisting of a common sugar and phosphate group with one of four different bases attached to the sugar. To include the pairs of complementary bases. **H**

WS1.4a Use scientific vocabulary, terminology, and definitions.

WS2a Carry out experiments with due regard to the correct manipulation of apparatus, the accuracy of measurements, and health and safety considerations, and following written instructions.

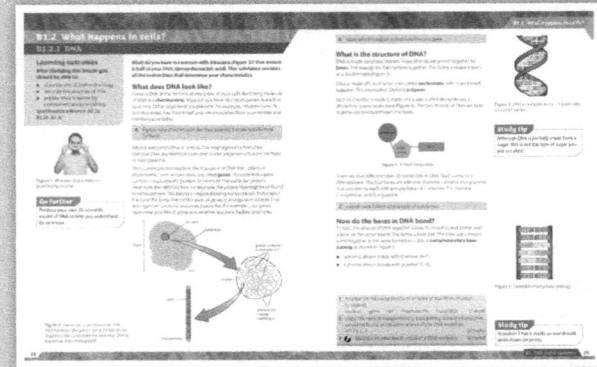

| Target | Outcome | Checkpoint | |
|---|---|---|---|
| | | Question | Activity |
| **Aiming for GRADE 4** | Describe the structure of DNA. | C, 3 | Starter 1 and 2<br>Main<br>Plenary 1 and 2 |
| | State the role of DNA. | A | Starter 1 |
| | Use the correct apparatus to follow a method with help. | | Main |
| **Aiming for GRADE 6** | Describe the structure of the nucleotide as the building block of DNA. | C, 3 | Starter 1 and 2<br>Plenary 2 |
| | Describe the role of a gene. | A | Starter 1 |
| | Use a method to carry out an experiment appropriately and independently, having due regard for the correct manipulation of apparatus. | | Main |
| **Aiming for GRADE 8** | Explain what is meant by complementary base pairing. | 2, 3 | Plenary 1 and 2 |
| | Explain the relationship between DNA, genes, and chromosomes. | B, 1 | |
| | Use a method to carry out an experiment appropriately and independently, with due regard to the correct manipulation of apparatus and the accuracy of measurements. | | Main |

**Literacy**
Follow straightforward instructions carefully to carry out an experiment.

**Key words**
chromosome, complementary base pairing, DNA, DNA base, gene, nucleotide

# B1.2 What happens in cells?

| Starter | Support/Extend | Resources |
|---|---|---|
| **True or false?** (5 minutes) Show a newspaper headline or film clip of a TV news item describing the importance of DNA in current medical issues. Briefly discuss the story and its relevance. Students have a red (false) and green (true) card. The teacher then makes a number of statements and the students vote true or false. The statements cover:<br>• The structure of DNA.<br>• The role of DNA.<br>• The location of DNA.<br>**What is DNA?** (5 minutes) Students complete the interactive by matching the following words to the correct definitions: gene, chromosome, DNA bases, and nucleotides. Students then select true or false in a series of statements. | **Support:** Focus statements on the role of DNA and simple structure of DNA.<br>**Extend:** Statements include structure of nucleotides and the role of genes. | **Interactive:** DNA |

| Main | Support/Extend | Resources |
|---|---|---|
| **Extracting DNA from kiwi fruits** (40 minutes) Follow a practical method for the extraction of DNA from a kiwi fruit or similar.<br>The practical sheet guides students in reviewing the procedure they have just carried out, including justifying some of its stages. | **Support:** Break the method into three stages. Explain each stage to the class and get the class to complete each stage together, before moving onto the next section. | **Practical:** Extracting DNA from kiwi fruits |

| Plenary | Support/Extend | Resources |
|---|---|---|
| **Human DNA** (5 minutes) Issue each student a sheet of paper with a letter (A, T, C, or G). Ask them to make an appropriate pairing, and then link the pairs together to build a DNA molecule.<br>**Describing DNA** (5 minutes) Students work in pairs. Each pair sit back to back. Student one is issued with an image of a nucleotide or DNA molecule (see the Student Book, Figures 3 and 4). Student 2 has a pen and paper. Student 1 then describes the structure of either the nucleotide or DNA and student 2 has to draw the molecule. Student 2 reveals the result and they discuss the actual structure. | **Extend:** Students explain why they have linked together in such a fashion. | |

| Homework | | |
|---|---|---|
| Build a card model of DNA.<br>Alternatively, produce a fully annotated drawing of the DNA molecule. | | |

# GCSE BIOLOGY ONLY — HIGHER TIER
## B1.2.2 Transcription and translation

**Specification links:**

B1.2d Recall a simple description of protein synthesis. To include the unzipping of the DNA molecule around the gene, copying to mRNA in nucleus (transcription), (translation) of the nucleotide sequence, in the cytoplasm.

B1.2e Explain simply how the structure of DNA affects the proteins made in protein synthesis. To include triplet code and its use to determine amino acid order.

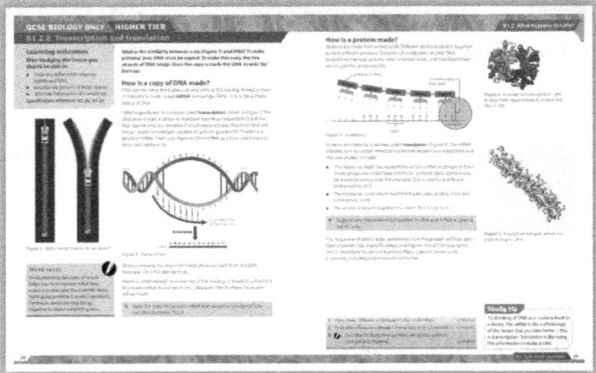

| Target | Outcome | Checkpoint | |
|---|---|---|---|
| | | Question | Activity |
| **Aiming for GRADE 6** | Compare the difference in structure between mRNA and DNA. | A, 1 | Starter 2<br>Main |
| | Describe the process of protein synthesis; to include transcription and translation. | A, B, 2, 3 | Starter 1<br>Main<br>Plenary 1 and 2 |
| | Summarise and evaluate with accuracy and clear understanding. | | Main |
| **Aiming for GRADE 8** | Distinguish between the roles of mRNA and DNA in the process of protein synthesis. | 3 | Starter 2<br>Main<br>Plenary 1 and 2 |
| | Explain how the base sequence in the DNA molecule determines the amino acid sequence in the protein. | B, 3 | Main<br>Plenary 1 and 2 |
| | Summarise and critically evaluate with detailed and perceptive understanding. | | Main |

**Literacy**
During the activity, students will summarise and critically evaluate with detailed and perceptive understanding.

**Key words**
mRNA, transcription, translation

# B1.2 What happens in cells?

| Starter | Support/Extend | Resources |
|---|---|---|
| **Central dogma sequence game** (10 minutes)  Students work in groups of three. Issue each group with a series of six cards each with a statement describing a step in the process of protein synthesis. Students are given 2–3 minutes to put the statements in the correct order. | **Support:** Tell students the first card.  **Extend:** The statements can be tailored to the class. | **Interactive:** Transcription and translation |
| **Transcription and translation** (5 minutes)  Students use the interactive to select the bases found in mRNA and then to sort statements about DNA and mRNA. | | |

| Main | Support/Extend | Resources |
|---|---|---|
| **Protein synthesis marketplace**  **Stage 1 Becoming experts** (15 minutes)  Split the class into groups of three. Supply each group with one of three information cards, a large sheet of paper (flip chart paper), and pens. Students have 20 minutes to become experts on the information on their card. To do this, they read the card and make drawings to illustrate the information from the card, but you should limit the number of words the groups can use. Then, collect in the cards.  The cards describe:  • The structure of DNA and mRNA.  • The process of transcription.  • The process of translation.  **Stage 2 Gathering information** (10 minutes)  One member of each group stays in place and acts as a teacher, using the drawings their group has made. The other two move to separate groups, and learn about the other two topics.  **Stage 3 Sharing learning** (15 minutes)  Students return to their home group and share the information learnt with the other team members. Each student should have learnt about the entire process of protein synthesis. | **Support:** The information cards could be differentiated. Increase the word limit. The students who gather information could use a frame to record the information they learn, which could include questions, or an indication of the stages in the process.  **Extend:** Increase the difficulty of Stage 1 by limiting students to 10 words to accompany their pictures. | **Activity:** Protein synthesis marketplace |

| Plenary | Support/Extend | Resources |
|---|---|---|
| **DNA to protein** (5 minutes)  Students fill in the gaps to complete a paragraph about how DNA and protein are connected. | **Extend:** Students explain how triplets are codes for amino acids, and therefore explain how changing the sequence of DNA bases would change the amino acid sequence. | **Interactive:** DNA to protein |
| **Making mRNA** (10 minutes)  Issue students with two sheets of different coloured A4 paper. Ask them to make simple paper strip models to illustrate how mRNA is made in the nucleus. | | |

| Homework |
|---|
| Imagine you are a scientist giving a presentation to a sports coaching group about how athletes develop muscle protein. Produce a PowerPoint presentation to show the process of protein synthesis. |

**kerboodle**

A Kerboodle highlight for this lesson is **Homework: DNA**. Refer to the **Content map** on Kerboodle for a full list of resources and assessment.

# B1.2.3 Enzymes

**Specification links:**

B1.2g Explain the mechanism of enzyme action. To include the role of enzymes in metabolism, the role of the active site, enzyme specificity (lock and key hypothesis), and factors affecting the rate of enzyme-controlled reactions (pH, temperature, substrate, and enzyme concentration).

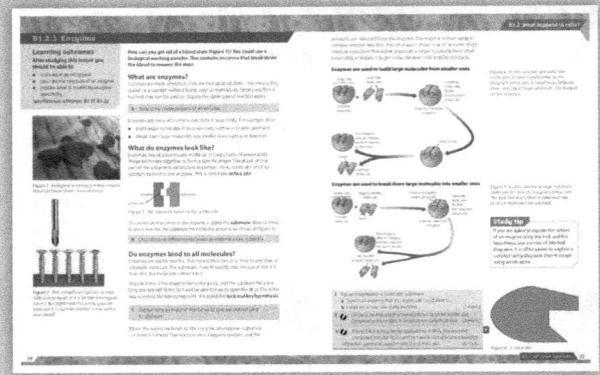

| Target | Outcome | Checkpoint | |
|---|---|---|---|
| | | Question | Activity |
| **Aiming for GRADE 4** | State what an enzyme is. | A, B | Starter 1 and 2<br>Main<br>Plenary 1 |
| | Describe simply how an enzyme works. | A | Starter 1 and 2<br>Main |
| | Describe how an enzyme works by communicating simply and with some clarity for the audience. | | Main |
| **Aiming for GRADE 6** | Describe the structure of an enzyme. | B, 1 | Starter 2<br>Main<br>Plenary 2 |
| | Explain how an enzyme works. | C, 2 | Starter 2<br>Main<br>Plenary 1 and 2 |
| | Illustrate how an enzyme works by communicating effectively, sustaining the audience's interest. | | Main |
| **Aiming for GRADE 8** | Explain what is meant by enzyme specificity. | C, 1, 2, 3 | Starter 2 (extension)<br>Main<br>Plenary 2 |
| | Explain in detail how an enzyme interacts with its substrate to catalyse a reaction. | C, 2, 3 | Main |
| | Interpret how an enzyme works by communicating, with impact and influence. | | Main |

**Literacy**

During the main task, students will need to communicate effectively, using scientific vocabulary, sustaining the interest of an audience.

**Key words**

active site, enzymes, lock and key hypothesis, substrate

# B1.2 What happens in cells?

| Starter | Support/Extend | Resources |
|---|---|---|
| **Mystery agents** (10 minutes) Tell students that we produce a toxic waste in cells called hydrogen peroxide, which must be removed. Carry out a simple demonstration to show what happens to the waste substance. Take three test tubes with hydrogen peroxide (about 5 cm³ at 1.8 mol dm⁻³). Add a small piece of liver to one test tube; it will fizz rapidly. To the second, add a piece of potato; there will be the same response, but less dramatic. Finally, add something non-living, for example, a marble. The key features to draw out from the students are:<br>• The process occurs in living tissues and it is speeded up by an enzyme.<br>• It is rapid.<br>• It is a chemical reaction.<br>Introduce enzymes as the vital component. | | |
| **Nuts and bolts** (5 minutes) Use one spanner, and a nut and bolt combination. Demonstrate that the spanner can be used to take apart the nuts and bolts. Referring to learning from Key Stage 3, draw an analogy to enzyme structure, the active site, substrate, and simple enzyme function. | **Extend:** Using a different nut or bolt would allow the idea of specificity to be explored. | |

| Main | Support/Extend | Resources |
|---|---|---|
| **How does an enzyme work?** (40 minutes) Students produce a cartoon to explain how an enzyme works. This could be achieved by providing the students with a storyboard template or, alternatively, they could produce a stop-motion cartoon by photographing modelling clay models or drawings. Students could use tablets, phones or cameras.<br>The cartoon should include text and images, as well as the definition of an enzyme. | **Support:** Provide sub-headings for different stages in the action of the enzyme (probably four stages).<br>**Extend:** Encourage students to use scientific vocabulary correctly, and to explain what 'specificity' is. | **Activity:** Storyboard template |

| Plenary | Support/Extend | Resources |
|---|---|---|
| **Metabolism** (5 minutes) Provide a simple list of enzyme systems, for example, enzymes involved in breaking starch into sugars, or enzymes responsible for building sugars from carbon dioxide and water. Ask students to identify where these systems operate, the name of the life process they are involved in, and what would happen if the organism did not have the enzymes. | | |
| **Use of enzymes** (10 minutes) Students complete an interactive activity where they complete a series of paragraphs summarising the key points of enzymes. They then identify true and false statements about enzymes. | | **Interactive:** Enzymes |

| Homework | | |
|---|---|---|
| Produce the back panel for a biological washing powder packet, which explains how the enzymes in the product work to digest stains. | **Extend:** Consider the effect of temperature, and the advantages and disadvantages of biological washing powders. | |

*kerboodle*
The Kerboodle highlight for this lesson is **Animation: Enzyme action**. Refer to the **Content map** on Kerboodle for a full list of resources and assessment.

# B1.2.4 Enzyme reactions

**Specification links:**

B1.2f Describe experiments that can be used to investigate enzymatic reactions.

B1.2g Explain the mechanism of enzyme action, to include the role of enzymes in metabolism, the role of the active site, enzyme specificity (lock and key hypothesis), and factors affecting the rate of enzyme-controlled reactions (pH, temperature, substrate, and enzyme concentration).

WS1.1h Evaluate risks both in practical science and the wider societal context.

WS1.2b Plan experiments or devise procedures to make observations, produce or characterise a substance, test hypotheses, check data, or explore phenomena.

WS1.2c Apply a knowledge of a range of techniques, instruments, apparatus, and materials to select those appropriate to the experiment.

WS1.3a Present observations and other data using appropriate methods.

WS1.3b Translate data from one form to another.

WS1.3c Carry out and represent mathematical and statistical analysis.

WS1.3d Represent distributions of results and make estimations of uncertainty.

WS1.3e Interpret observations and other data.

WS1.3f Present reasoned explanations, including relating data to hypotheses.

WS2a Carry out experiments.

WS2b Make and record observations and measurements using a range of apparatus and methods.

BM1.2i Carry out rate calculations for chemical reactions (M1a, M1c).

BM1.2ii Understand and use simple compound measures, such as the rate of a reaction (M1a, M1c).

| Target | Outcome | Checkpoint | |
|---|---|---|---|
| | | Question | Activity |
| **Aiming for GRADE 4** | State the factors that affect enzyme-controlled reactions. | A | Starter 1 and 2 Main |
| | State what is meant by denaturation. | B | Main Plenary 1 |
| | Record observations from an experimental procedure, using a range of apparatus. | | Starter 2 Main |
| **Aiming for GRADE 6** | Describe the effect of a factor on the rate of an enzyme-controlled reaction. | C, 2, 3 | Starter 1 and 2 Main |
| | Describe what happens when an enzyme is denatured. | B, 3 | Main Plenary 1 |
| | Record measurements from an experimental procedure, and plot a simple graph having been given the axes. | | Main |
| **Aiming for GRADE 8** | Explain how different factors affect the rate of an enzyme-controlled reaction. | | Plenary 2 |
| | Explain how denaturation affects the rate of an enzyme-controlled reaction. | 3 | Main Plenary 1 |
| | Record accurate measurements from an experimental procedure, plotting an accurate rate graph. | | Main |

# B1.2 What happens in cells?

**Maths**
During the analysis of experimental data, students will recognise and use expressions in decimal form (M1a); and use ratios, fractions, and percentages (M1c).

**Literacy**
Students will read text and make valid responses.

**Key words**
denatured

| Starter | Support/Extend | Resources |
|---|---|---|
| **Factors affecting enzyme reactions** (5 minutes)   Ask students to suggest factors that might affect enzyme reactions. Then use the interactive to decide what factors affect enzyme action and answer questions about a graph.<br>**Hot and cold** (5 minutes)   Reuse the mystery agents idea from the previous lesson. This time have the hydrogen peroxide prepared by placing one tube in ice and one in warm water. Add a cube of liver to each, and ask the students what the difference is. Ask them to suggest a relationship between temperature and the rate of enzyme-controlled reactions. | | **Interactive:** Enzyme reactions |

| Main | Support/Extend | Resources |
|---|---|---|
| **Investigating the effect of temperature on enzyme reactions** (40 minutes)   Students plan an experiment to investigate how pH or temperature affect the rate of amylase activity. Students should be guided to choose a suitable range for the independent variable and to use control variables. Students use their data to plot a line graph and answer questions in order to draw conclusions from the data and evaluate the method. Students should swap data with a group that investigated the other variable from them.<br>Students plot a graph of rate on the *y*-axis against temperature on the *x*-axis. Include a series of questions to encourage students to describe and explain the action of temperature on the enzyme action.<br>SAFETY: Avoid enzyme dust when preparing solutions. | **Support:** Break the practical activity into a series of steps that the class complete together. Provide a results table and axes for the graph.<br>**Extend:** Students plan their own investigation into the effect of pH on enzyme reactions by identifying the independent, dependent, and control variables, and planning a suitable procedure (with guidance). | **Practical:** Factors that affect the rate of enzyme-controlled reactions |

| Plenary | Support/Extend | Resources |
|---|---|---|
| **Mystery agents yet again** (5 minutes)   Return to the second starter. To a final tube of peroxide add some boiled liver. Nothing happens. Ask students to explain what might have happened to the enzyme.<br>**Explaining the graphs** (5 minutes)   Divide the class into pairs. Give each group one of four sketch graphs showing the effect of different factors on the rate of enzyme reaction (temperature, pH, substrate concentration, and enzyme concentration); only the axes are labelled. Students annotate the graph they have been given to explain what is happening at the key points on the graph. | **Extend:** Discuss how heat changes the shape of the molecule.<br>**Support:** Provide key words on the graph margin for students to use in their annotation. | |

| Homework | | |
|---|---|---|
| Write a plan to test the effect of pH on the rate of reaction of amylase. Include the following points:<br>What variables will be changed;<br>What variables will be recorded;<br>What variables will be kept the same;<br>Improving repeatability. | | **Working Scientifically:** The effect of temperature on an enzyme-controlled reaction |

**kerboodle**
A Kerboodle highlight for this lesson is **Maths skills: Enzymes and rates**. Refer to the **Content map** on Kerboodle for a full list of resources and assessment.

The Practical Skills lesson for PAG 4 Rates of enxyme-controlled reactions could follow this lesson.

# Checkpoint

## B1.2 What happens in cells?

### Overview of B1.2 What happens in cells?

In this chapter students have studied DNA as the molecule that caries the information that determines an organism's characteristics. They should understand that DNA is arranged into sections called genes, and that each gene codes for a specific protein.

Students should be able to describe the structure of DNA as a polymer made of two strands that form a double helix. They should know that DNA is made from four different nucleotides that are each made of a sugar, a phosphate group, and one of four different bases. Students should be able to describe complementary base pairing between the four bases and know that it holds the two strands of DNA together. Higher-tier GCSE Biology students have studied how the information stored on DNA is transcribed and translated into proteins.

Students have studied enzymes, and should be able to state their functions as well as the factors that affect enzyme-controlled reactions. They should be able to describe the mechanism of enzyme action using the lock and key hypothesis, and understand the importance of the active site for specificity.

Students should understand that the rates of enzyme-controlled reactions are affected by many factors, including temperature, pH, substrate concentration, and enzyme concentration. They should be able to explain how changes in these factors affect the rate of a reaction. Students should be able to describe what happens when an enzyme is denatured.

You can find additional support for the maths skills covered in this chapter on **MyMaths**, including recognising and using expressions in decimal form, using ratios, fractions, and percentages, and working with graphs.

### PAGs

All students are expected to have carried out the PAG *4 Rates of enzyme-controlled reactions*. A full lesson plan for each PAG is provided in the Practical skills chapter. PAG *4 Rates of enzyme-controlled reactions* should be completed after lesson B1.2.4 *Enzyme reactions*.

### kerboodle

For this chapter, the following assessments are available on Kerboodle:
B1.2 Checkpoint quiz: What happens in cells?
B1.2 Progress quiz: What happens in cells? 1
B1.2 Progress quiz: What happens in cells? 2
B1.2 On your marks: What happens in cells?
B1.2 Exam-style questions and mark scheme: What happens in cells?

### Checkpoint follow-up lesson

A student's route through this lesson can be determined using the Checkpoint assessment. Percentage pass marks are supplied in the Checkpoint teacher notes.

For each successive route through it is assumed that the student can perform to their current route as well as previous routes. For example, students working

## B1.2 What happens in cells?

at Aiming for 6 are assumed to be secure in Aiming for 4 knowledge and understanding and working towards achieving all the learning objectives for Aiming for 6.

|  | Aiming for 4 | Aiming for 6 | Aiming for 8 |
|---|---|---|---|
| **Learning outcomes** | State what DNA is. | Describe the structure of DNA. | Explain the structure of DNA. |
|  | Describe simply how proteins are synthesised. | Describe how proteins are synthesised. | Explain how proteins are synthesised. |
|  | State the effects of temperature on enzyme activity. | Describe the effects of temperature on enzyme activity. | Explain the effects of temperature on enzyme activity. |
| **Starter** | **Modelling DNA (5 minutes)** You will need a card or piece of paper with one letter A, G, C, or T on it for each student. Give each student one card and see if the class can line up in two lines, each paired with their complementary base, to make a human DNA chain. Ask – how is the structure of DNA different from the human model we have made? |||
| **Differentiated checkpoint activity** | **Activity 1 Modelling protein synthesis (25 minutes)** Students take part in the teacher-led activity to model protein synthesis. You will need cards for student roles as described below:<br>• 12 students represent six pairs of complementary DNA bases<br>• six students represent six mRNA bases complementary to the DNA bases<br>• six students represent six bases to make two amino acids<br>• any further students can form the ribosome and nuclear membrane.<br>Assign different areas of the classroom to be the nucleus and the cell cytoplasm. Give out the role cards. To model protein synthesis, the DNA bases line up in a double strand with complementary bases paired. The two strands separate and the mRNA bases face their complementary DNA base on one of the DNA strands. They line up to form an mRNA strand. The mRNA strand leaves the nucleus (two students can form a gateway) and enters the cytoplasm area of the classroom. Here the mRNA strand enters the ribosome, which is formed by at least two students. At the ribosome complementary bases pair with mRNA bases, and join in threes to form two amino acids. These two amino acids are joined in the ribosome to form a protein.<br><br>Students then each answer question 1 on the differentiated worksheets about protein synthesis. |||
|  | Aiming for 4 students are given statements and prompted to draw a diagram for each one to build up a diagram showing protein synthesis. | Aiming for 6 students are guided to draw a series of diagrams to show the sequence. | Aiming for 8 students draw a step by step sequence of protein synthesis. |
|  | **Activity 2 Demonstrating enzyme activity (5 minutes)** Demonstrate putting liver into hydrogen peroxide. You will need hydrogen peroxide solution, a piece of liver, a boiling tube, and a splint. Test the gas produced with a lighted splint to show it is oxygen. Explain that liver contains catalase, which is an enzyme. Ask – what is happening in this reaction? Is it exothermic? What are the products?<br>**Activity 3 Enzyme activity (15 minutes)** Students answer question 2 on the differentiated worksheets, which is data analysis on enzyme activity. They will require pencils, rulers, calculators, and graph paper. |||
|  | Aiming for 4 students are prompted to draw a graph of enzyme activity against temperature and answer structured questions about the optimum temperature. | Aiming for 6 students plot a graph of enzyme activity against temperature and answer more detailed questions about the optimum temperature. | Aiming for 8 students are asked to plot a graph and choose the axes themselves. They answer more in-depth and open-ended questions about the effect of temperature on enzyme activity. |
|  | **Kerboodle resource:** B1.2 Checkpoint follow-up: Aiming for 4, B1.2 Checkpoint follow-up: Aiming for 6, B1.2 Checkpoint follow-up: Aiming for 8 |||
| **Plenary** | **Enzyme action (5 minutes)** Student pairs will need mini-whiteboards and pens. Ask pairs to draw enzyme activity graphs on mini-whiteboards, one for temperature and one for pH. Check understanding by asking them to explain their graphs. Aiming for 8 students could also draw graphs for enzyme concentration and substrate concentration. |||
| **Progression** | The Aiming for 4 activity is highly structured. Students may need extra guidance to complete the sheet. It is important that they understand that genetic material is contained in the chromosomes found in every cell in the body, and be able to explain that a gene is a length of DNA, and that genes determine our characteristics. | The Aiming for 6 activity is reasonably structured. Students should be able to start these questions without any guidance from the teacher. You may need to review answers or provide answers for students to peer assess each other's work. | The Aiming for 8 sheet has very little structure. Students should be able to complete the activity without introduction from the teacher.<br><br>Students should be introduced to the structure of DNA, and can move on to looking at transcription and translation. |

# B1.3 Respiration
## B1.3.1 Carbohydrates, proteins, and lipids

**Specification links:**

B1.3d Explain the importance of sugars in the synthesis and breakdown of carbohydrates. To include use of the terms monomer and polymer.

B1.3e Explain the importance of amino acids in the synthesis and breakdown of proteins. To include the use of the terms monomer and polymer.

B1.3f Explain the importance of fatty acids and glycerol in the synthesis and breakdown of lipids.

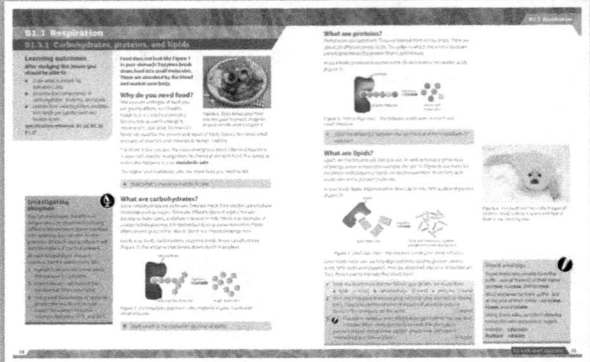

| Target | Outcome | Checkpoint | |
|---|---|---|---|
| | | Question | Activity |
| **Aiming for GRADE 4** | Describe the components of carbohydrates, proteins, and lipids. | B, 1 | Starter 1<br>Main 2<br>Plenary 1 and 2 |
| | State what is meant by metabolic rate. | A | Starter 2<br>Main 1 |
| | Use scientific vocabulary, terminology, and definitions, with limited accuracy in spelling, punctuation, and grammar. | | Main 2 |
| **Aiming for GRADE 6** | Explain how carbohydrates, proteins, and lipids are synthesised and broken down. | C, 1, 3 | Starter 1<br>Main 2<br>Plenary 2 |
| | Describe the relationship between metabolic rate, activity levels, and food intake. | | Starter 2<br>Main 1 |
| | Use scientific vocabulary, terminology, and definitions accurately with occasional errors in spelling, punctuation, and grammar. | | Main 2 |
| **Aiming for GRADE 8** | Distinguish between monomers and polymers in biological molecules. | B, 3 | Main 2<br>Plenary 2 |
| | Explain that metabolic reactions can be divided into different groups. | C | Main 1 |
| | Use scientific vocabulary, terminology, and definitions accurately and error-free in spelling, punctuation, and grammar. | | Main 2 |

**Literacy**

During the tasks, the students will be expected to read, summarise, and evaluate information in the text, and use scientific vocabulary, terminology, and definitions.

**Key words**

metabolic rate

The Practical Skills lesson for PAG 2 Testing for biological molecules would work well following this lesson.

# B1.3 Respiration

| Starter | Support/Extend | Resources |
|---|---|---|
| **Transformations** (10 minutes) Issue small cubes made of about 20 lego blocks. Ask students to transform the cube into a pyramid, allowing 2 minutes only. Discuss quickly how they achieved this, by taking the cube apart and rebuilding a pyramid. Then show students a protein drink. Ask why people drink these (to build muscle). Then ask them how that might be achieved, linking it to the lego exercise. | | |
| **Being active** (5 minutes) Ask a student to jog on the spot for about a minute. Measure the forehead temperature before and after the exercise using a thermometer strip. Use an image of a lazy cartoon character doing nothing, and discuss why the temperature of the active person would be higher. Where does the heat come from? What could you predict about the number of reactions in the muscles of the active person compared with the inactive person? Finally, link metabolic rate to the rate of reactions inside cells. | | |

| Main | Support/Extend | Resources |
|---|---|---|
| **Metabolism** (15 minutes) Show a random series of metabolic reactions that can be grouped. (Show reactions suggested here only – not the groups). Such as:<br>• Digestion: Starch is broken down into sugars, protein is broken down into amino acids, etc.<br>• Synthesis: Glucose is built up into glycogen, glucose is built from carbon dioxide and water, etc.<br>• Respiration: Glucose is broken down to release lactic acid, glucose is broken down into carbon dioxide and water, etc.<br>Students study the reactions and form groups of reactions that are similar. Discuss what the reactions represent. Define metabolism, and outline the relationship between metabolic rate, activity levels, and food intake. | **Support** or **Extend** can be achieved by controlling the number and types of reactions given. | |
| **Carbohydrates, fats, and proteins** (25 minutes) Issue a series of cards with facts about the features of biological molecules. The cards include information on:<br>• the building blocks of carbohydrates, lipids, and proteins (i.e. sugars, fatty acids, glycerol, and amino acids)<br>• how they are joined together<br>• their uses in the body<br>• the enzymes used to break them down.<br>Students sort them and put the information into a table.<br>Then lead a discussion to point out that fats, proteins and some carbohydrates are examples of polymers. They are made up of substances with much smaller molecules, called monomers. | **Support:** Provide a table template. | **Practical:** Carbohydrates, fats, and proteins |

| Plenary | Support/Extend | Resources |
|---|---|---|
| **Biochemical facts** (5 minutes) Use the interactive by linking lines between the biochemical groups to either their building blocks or the function of the group. | | **Interactive:** Biochemical facts |
| **Building models** (10 minutes) Provide students with paper or molymodels and ask them to build starch from sugar blocks or proteins from amino acid blocks. | **Extend:** Establish which units are monomers or polymers, and decide on a definition for the terms. | |

| Homework |
|---|
| Create a crossword using as many words from the lesson as possible. |

**kerboodle**
A Kerboodle highlight for this lesson is **Practical: Food tests**. Refer to the **Content map** on Kerboodle for a full list of resources and assessment.

# B1.3.2 Aerobic respiration

**Specification links:**

B1.3a Describe cellular respiration as a universal chemical process, continuously occurring, that supplies ATP in all living cells.

B1.3b Describe cellular respiration as an exothermic reaction.

WS1.2a Use scientific theories and explanations to develop hypotheses.

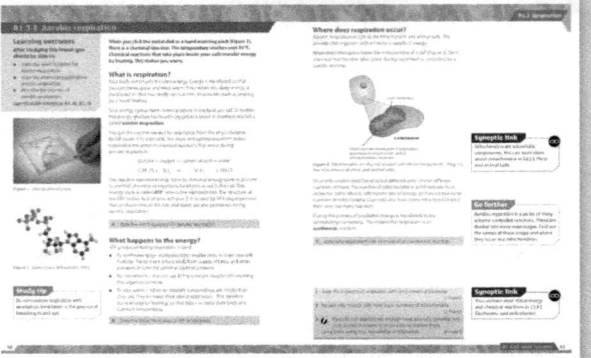

| Target | Outcome | Checkpoint | |
|---|---|---|---|
| | | Question | Activity |
| **Aiming for GRADE 4** ↓ | State the word equation for respiration. | A | Starter 1 and 2 |
| | State that respiration transfers energy. | C | Starter 1 and 2, Main |
| | Plot a graph of data from experiments. | | Main |
| **Aiming for GRADE 6** ↓ | State the chemical equation for respiration. | 1 | Starter 1, Main |
| | Describe the process of aerobic respiration as an exothermic reaction. | B, C, 2 | Starter 2, Main, Plenary 1 and 2 |
| | Plot an appropriate line graph of two variables from experimental data. | | Main |
| **Aiming for GRADE 8** ↓ | Discuss the use by the body of the energy transferred in respiration. | B, 2, 3 | Starter 2, Plenary 1 and 2 |
| | Explain how ATP is produced during aerobic respiration. | | Main |
| | Plot an appropriate accurate line graph of two variables from experimental data, and interpret the data to draw conclusions. | | Main |

**Maths**
During the main task students will translate information between graphical and numeric form (M4a), and plot two variables from experimental or other data (M4c).

**Literacy**
During the main task students will be expected to produce coherent and purposeful responses to questions.

**Key words**
aerobic respiration, ATP, exothermic

# B1.3 Respiration

| Starter | Support/Extend | Resources |
|---|---|---|
| **Aerobic respiration introduction** (5 minutes) Use the interactive, which shows a drawing of a cell. Students drag and drop the raw materials for respiration, and the products produced, into the correct places. Students also complete the balanced equation for aerobic respiration. | **Extend:** Produce a word/balanced chemical equation from the screen. | **Interactive:** Aerobic respiration |
| **Energy in food** (10 minutes) Demonstrate burning a food, such as sugar or custard powder. Do this by sprinkling it into a Bunsen flame. Students may have seen this before, so ask the students to explain what has happened and why. Build the names of the key reactants and products (glucose, oxygen, carbon dioxide, and water) into the discussion. Then link to the ideas of energy stores in food being the source of energy for the body. | | |

| Main | Support/Extend | Resources |
|---|---|---|
| **Respiration of peas** (5 minutes) Demonstrate the respiration of peas inside a thermos flask to the class. Use two flasks, one with living, respiring peas, and one with dead peas. Explain that respiration transfers energy to the surroundings, resulting in a temperature rise in the surroundings. | | |
| **Question sheet** (35 minutes) Provide students with a worksheet containing data from a similar experiment. The sheet has data from three experiments: <br> • living, respiring peas, which have been washed in disinfectant <br> • living, respiring peas, which are unwashed and thus contain bacteria <br> • boiled (dead, non-respiring) peas. <br> Students plot the three lines on a graph and answer questions about respiration (including the balanced symbol equation for aerobic respiration), the production of ATP, and the transfer of energy to the surroundings by heating (including the term exothermic). <br> Return to the demonstration to observe any change in temperature. | **Support:** Students can plot just two sets of data; omit the set of data for unwashed peas. Also they can plot on separate graphs, or you supply axes. <br> **Extend:** Students answer extension questions about ATP. | **Activity:** Graphing respiration |

| Plenary | Support/Extend | Resources |
|---|---|---|
| **Energy tally for different organisms** (5 minutes) Provide students with the images of about six different organisms, for example, athlete, physical worker, earthworm, plant, sedentary person, and arctic explorer. Ask students to list what the organisms might need energy for. Try to estimate the relative amount of energy each will transfer in a typical day. | **Support:** Make the examples more obvious and give fewer types. | |
| **Minute cartoons** (10 minutes) Divide the class into pairs. Issue each pair with an envelope containing cards. Each one has a word related to the transfer of energy in the body, such as body temperature, movement, growth, and so on. One student reads the card and, without talking, does a drawing to illustrate the word. Allow 1 minute for each word. The other student guesses the word. | | |

| Homework | | |
|---|---|---|
| Imagine you are a sports scientist and write a leaflet to explain how an athlete can obtain energy from a carbohydrate diet. | **Extend:** Include an explanation of the role of ATP. | |

**kerboodle**
A Kerboodle highlight for this lesson is **Go further: Respiration balance**. Refer to the **Content map** on Kerboodle for a full list of resources and assessment.

# B1.3.3 Anaerobic respiration

**Specification links:**

B1.3c Compare the processes of aerobic respiration and anaerobic respiration. To include in plants, fungi, and animals, and the different conditions, substrates, products, and relative yields of ATP.

WS1.2c Apply a knowledge of a range of techniques, instruments, apparatus, and materials to select those appropriate to the experiment.

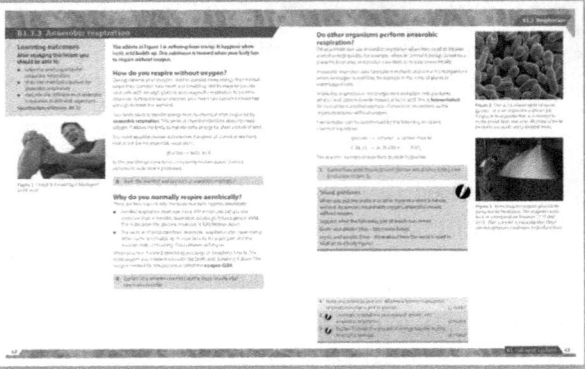

| Target | Outcome | Checkpoint | |
|---|---|---|---|
| | | Question | Activity |
| **Aiming for GRADE 4** | State the word equation for anaerobic respiration. | A | Starter 1<br>Main 2 |
| | State that there are different types of anaerobic respiration in different organisms. | 1 | Starter 1 and 2<br>Plenary 2 |
| | Use the correct apparatus to follow a method with help. | | Main |
| **Aiming for GRADE 6** | State a chemical equation for anaerobic respiration. | | Main 2 |
| | Describe the different processes of anaerobic respiration and where they occur. | B, 1, 2, 3 | Starter 1 and 2<br>Main 2<br>Plenary 2 |
| | Use a method to carry out an experiment appropriately and independently, giving due regard to the correct manipulation of apparatus. | | Main 1 |
| **Aiming for GRADE 8** | Compare the processes of aerobic and anaerobic respiration in terms of energy yield. | 2, 3 | Main 2<br>Plenary 2 |
| | Explain the consequences of anaerobic respiration in muscles in terms of oxygen debt. | B, C, 3 | Starter 1<br>Main 2<br>Plenary 2 |
| | Use a method to carry out an experiment appropriately and independently, giving due regard to the correct manipulation of apparatus and the accuracy of measurements. | | Main 1 |

**Literacy**
During the main task students will be expected to produce coherent and purposeful responses to questions.

**Key words**
anaerobic respiration, fermentation, oxygen debt

# B1.3 Respiration

| Starter | Support/Extend | Resources |
|---|---|---|
| **Why do we get a stitch?** (5 minutes) Show a cartoon of a runner demonstrating pain from a stitch or cramp. Pose the question 'Why have I got cramp?' Either open this to discussion or put a few possible comments on the cartoon to prompt debate, such as:<br>the muscles are making lactic acid<br>the muscles are over-stretched<br>the muscles are tired.<br>**Making alcohol** (10 minutes) Start with images of making alcohol for example, beer-making or wine-making, or show demijohns and describe the functions of the jar. Ask students if they can explain how alcohol is made: what are the raw materials? Lead discussion to yeasts. Ask questions such as: What is the name of the process that makes the alcohol? What is the starting substance? Where does the starting material come from? | **Support:** Include few, obvious comments.<br>**Extend:** Include more open comments. | |

| Main | Support/Extend | Resources |
|---|---|---|
| **Investigating fermentation in yeast** (30 minutes) Provide students with a method for the fermentation of yeast to make alcohol and carbon dioxide. They accurately measure out the volumes of the starting substances, and add them to the apparatus. Students then observe the carbon dioxide turning lime water milky.<br>**Comparing anaerobic and aerobic respiration** (10 minutes) Students use the student book to note down three differences between anaerobic and aerobic respiration, including the word equations and symbol equation for aerobic respiration. Students should also include reference to the relative yields of ATP. Students should also note the meaning of the term 'oxygen debt'. | | **Practical:**<br>Anaerobic respiration |

| Plenary | Support/Extend | Resources |
|---|---|---|
| **Respiration definitions** (5 minutes) Tackle the interactive activity in which students match words and phrases to their definitions.<br>**Respiration and athletics** (10 minutes) Show the class a short film clip of a 200 m or 400 m sprint race. Ask questions such as:<br>How does the runner feel at the end of the race?<br>Why does he or she feel like this?<br>What substance has been produced in the runner's muscles? | **Extend:** Ask students to write the chemical equations on the board.<br>**Extend:** Identify the type of respiration occurring before, during, and after the race, or compare different types of race, for example, sprint and distance races. | **Interactive:**<br>Anaerobic respiration |

| Homework | | |
|---|---|---|
| Create a flow chart to describe the process of wine production. The flow chart of steps can be found on the internet or in books, but you need to add descriptions of how the conditions for anaerobic respiration are established, and explain the process of fermentation, including equations. | **Extend:** Explain the extra steps needed to produce a sparkling wine like champagne. | |

*kerboodle*
A Kerboodle highlight for this lesson is **Bump up your grade: Anaerobic respiration in animals and in plants**. Refer to the **Content map** on Kerboodle for a full list of resources and assessment.

# Checkpoint
## B1.3 Respiration

### Overview of B1.3 Respiration

In this chapter, students have been introduced to the idea of metabolic rate and how organic molecules are needed by the body as a source of energy. Building on B1.2 *What happens in cells?*, they have looked at carbohydrates, proteins, and lipids, and their synthesis and breakdown.

Respiration is one of the most important processes in living cells. Students have studied aerobic respiration and written equations to represent this process. They have looked at mitochondria as the site of respiration, and considered examples of living processes that use the energy released by respiration. They should have studied aerobic respiration as an exothermic process, and be able to compare rates of respiration using this concept. They should also have investigated the effect of exercise on the heart rate and breathing rate, and considered how this is linked to respiration.

Building on this study of aerobic respiration, students have gone on to study anaerobic respiration, first in mammalian muscles. They should understand the importance of this process in muscle fatigue and the oxygen debt. Second, they should appreciate that anaerobic respiration occurs in yeast cells and some plant cells, as the process of fermentation. Finally they should be able to compare aerobic and anaerobic respiration.

Students should appreciate the link between the process of respiration *releasing* energy and the various processes in living things that *require* energy. They should link their knowledge of enzymes from B1.2 *What happens in cells?* to their studies of respiration.

### MyMaths

You can find additional support for the maths skills covered in this chapter on **MyMaths**, including plotting graphs.

### PAGs

All students are expected to have carried out the PAG *2 Testing for biological molecules*. A full lesson plan for each PAG is provided in the Practical skills chapter. PAG *2 Testing for biological molecules* should be completed after lesson B1.3.1 *Carbohydrates, proteins, and lipids*.

For this chapter, the following assessments are available on Kerboodle:
B1.3 Checkpoint quiz: Respiration
B1.3 Progress quiz: Respiration 1
B1.3 Progress quiz: Respiration 2
B1.3 On your marks: Respiration
B1.3 Exam-style questions and mark scheme: Respiration

### Checkpoint follow-up lesson

A student's route through this lesson can be determined using the Checkpoint assessment. Percentage pass marks are supplied in the Checkpoint teacher notes.

For each successive route through it is assumed that the student can perform to their current route as well as previous routes. For example, students working at Aiming for 6 are assumed to be secure in Aiming for 4 knowledge and understanding and working towards achieving all the learning objectives for Aiming for 6.

# B1.3 Respiration

|  | Aiming for 4 | Aiming for 6 | Aiming for 8 |
|---|---|---|---|
| **Learning outcomes** | Give the word equation for aerobic respiration. | Give the word equations for aerobic and anaerobic respiration. | Give the word and symbol equations for aerobic and anaerobic respiration. |
|  | State the effects of exercise on respiration. | Describe the effects of exercise on respiration. | Explain the effects of exercise on respiration |
|  | State the uses of energy released from respiration. | Describe the uses of energy released from respiration. | Explain how energy released from respiration is used. |
|  | State the differences between aerobic and anaerobic respiration. | Describe the differences between aerobic and anaerobic respiration. | Explain the differences between aerobic and anaerobic respiration. |
| **Starter** | **Exercise and respiration (5 minutes)** Students run on the spot for 1 minute. Ask – what could you feel happening to your heart and breathing rate? Can you explain why? What does respiration have to do with it? | | |
| **Differentiated checkpoint activity** | **Activity 1 Respiration circus (20 minutes)** Provide a brief introduction before all students complete the respiration circus in small groups, spending 3 minutes at each of five stations, and each completing question 1 on the differentiated worksheets. The following resources are required:<br><br>• station 1 – mirrors that have been kept in fridge<br>• station 2 – boiling tubes, limewater, straw and goggles<br>• station 3 – two conical flasks with cress seeds on cotton wool suspended from a bung, one of the flasks containing pyrogallol solution<br>• station 4 – two thermos flasks with thermometers, one containing germinating peas and one containing boiled peas<br>• station 5 – a beaker containing respiring yeast or bread dough.<br>After this activity, review the equations for aerobic and anaerobic respiration on the board. | | |
|  | Aiming for 4 students answer structured questions about their observations at each station. | Aiming for 6 students are asked to describe and explain their observations at each station. | Aiming for 8 students are asked to describe and explain their observations, and to write a conclusion for each station. |
|  | **Activity 2 Respiration revision visual summary/exam question (25 minutes)** Students complete question 2 on the differentiated worksheets. Aiming for 4 and Aiming for 6 students make a visual summary on A3 paper to revise respiration. Aiming for 8 students write an exam question and provide feedback. | | |
|  | Provide an introduction to this question. Aiming for 4 students work individually, using the Student Book. | Provide an introduction to this question. Aiming for 6 students work individually to answer this question. They may use the Student Book to check their work. | Aiming for 8 students work in pairs, one of each pair writing an exam question on aerobic respiration and the other on anaerobic respiration. They write a mark scheme. They swop questions, answer their partner's question and then swop back and provide feedback. |
|  | **Kerboodle resource:** B1.3 Checkpoint follow-up: Aiming for 4, B1.3 Checkpoint follow-up: Aiming for 6, B1.3 Checkpoint follow-up: Aiming for 8 | | |
| **Plenary** | **True or false quiz (5 minutes)** Read out some true or false statements about respiration to check students' understanding. Students could either write down their answers, or show one coloured card for true and a different coloured one for false. In this case, each student will need two cards of different colours. | | |
| **Progression** | Students may need additional guidance to complete question 1 of the Aiming for 4 activity. The activity is highly structured and students can write their answers directly on the sheet. These students may require help to check their answers. | Students may need additional guidance to complete question 1 of the Aiming for 6 activity. The activity is fairly structured and students can write their answers directly on the sheet. These students could use the Student Book to check their own work. | The Aiming for 8 activity has little structure and students can write their answers on the sheet or on paper. These students peer assess each other's work. |

# B1.4 Photosynthesis
## B1.4.1 Photosynthesis

**Specification links:**

B1.4a Describe photosynthetic organisms as the main producers of food and therefore biomass for life on Earth.

B1.4b Describe the process of photosynthesis. To include reactants and products, location of the reaction (in the chloroplasts).

B1.4c Describe photosynthesis as an endothermic reaction.

WS1.3a Presenting observations and other data using appropriate methods

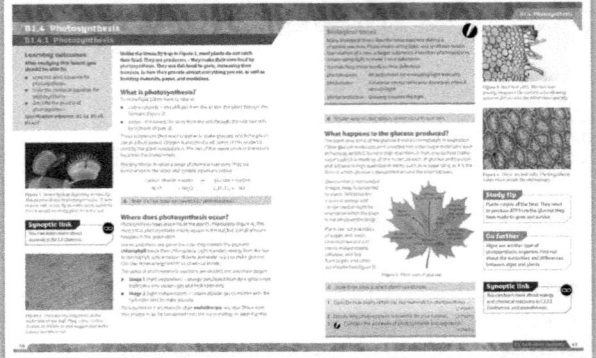

| Target | Outcome | Checkpoint | |
|---|---|---|---|
| | | Question | Activity |
| **Aiming for GRADE 4** | State the word equation for photosynthesis. | A, 3 | Starter 1 and 2  Main |
| | State that sunlight energy is required for the process of photosynthesis. | B, 3 | Starter 1 and 2  Main  Plenary 2 |
| | State basic facts (about photosynthesis), communicating simply and with some clarity. | 3 | Starter 1  Main |
| **Aiming for GRADE 6** | State the chemical equation for photosynthesis. | 3 | Main  Plenary 1 |
| | Describe the process of photosynthesis as an endothermic reaction. | B, 1, 2, 3 | Starter 1 and 2  Main |
| | Illustrate the process of photosynthesis using labelled diagrams that communicate effectively, making coherent statements. | | Main |
| **Aiming for GRADE 8** | Discuss the fate of the products of photosynthesis. | C | Main  Plenary 2 |
| | Explain that photosynthesis is a two-stage process, and where those stages occur. | | Main |
| | Annotate diagrams to explain the process of photosynthesis in detail, communicating coherently and with impact. | | Main |

**Literacy**

During the completion of the main task students will need to communicate ideas clearly and coherently, in well-structured statements.

**Key words**

biomass, chlorophyll, endothermic, photosynthesis, producer

# B1.4 Photosynthesis

| Starter | Support/Extend | Resources |
|---|---|---|
| **Sorting out photosynthesis** (10 minutes)  Give each group a plant pot with a number of card leaves, each with one word written on it. Some of the words are about the process of photosynthesis, for example, water, chlorophyll, sunlight, glucose, etc. Some of the words name plant parts involved in photosynthesis, for example, leaf, roots, etc. Some of the words are not relevant to photosynthesis, for example, flower, bee, etc. Students sort the leaves, rejecting irrelevant words. They then sort the relevant words to start to explain what happens in photosynthesis and where it occurs. | **Support:** Remove the irrelevant words. And suggest two categories to sort into.  **Extend:** Generate a word equation. | |
| **Feeding plants** (5 minutes)  Place a pot plant on each table. Ask students to discuss how the plant feeds itself. What substances does it need to feed itself, and where does it get them? What waste substances does it produce? Students feedback their ideas to the rest of the class. | **Extend:** Name the process and try to generate a word equation. | |

| Main | Support/Extend | Resources |
|---|---|---|
| **Photosynthesis poster** (30 minutes)  Give students 10 minutes to read about photosynthesis.  Student pairs then produce posters stating why photosynthesis is important, and giving details of the process, including raw materials, products, a word and symbol equation, and where in plants it occurs. Posters should also describe photosynthesis as an endothermic reaction.  Before students start making their posters, share success criteria with the class. Students will use these to peer-evaluate each others' posters. | **Extend:** Research into the early experiments that show an increase in mass. | **Activity:** Photosynthesis poster |
| **Growing cress** (10 minutes)  Provide groups with a beaker, cotton wool pads, cress seeds, and cling film. Recreate the Van Helmont experiment. Place the seeds on the pad, add water, and cover the top in cling film. Measure the mass of the seeds and return to these in about 2–3 days; re-measure the seeds and record the increase in mass. | | |

| Plenary | Support/Extend | Resources |
|---|---|---|
| **Photosynthesis** (5 minutes)  Use the interactive, where students sort the reactants and products of photosynthesis and then type in missing words to complete sentences about photosynthesis. | | **Interactive:** Photosynthesis |
| **Peer evaluation** (10 minutes)  Each group peer-assesses the posters produced by two other groups, using the given success criteria. Students point out where the posters meet the success criteria, and make suggestions for improvement. | | |

| Homework | | |
|---|---|---|
| Draw a palisade cell. Annotate the drawing as fully as possible to show the raw materials entering the cell, where the reactions will occur (including the two stages, if appropriate), and the fate of the products made. | | |

**kerboodle**
A Kerboodle highlight for this lesson is **Bump up your grade: Learning the photosynthesis equation off by heart**. Refer to the **Content map** on Kerboodle for a full list of resources and assessment.

# B1.4.2 Photosynthesis experiments

**Specification links:**

B1.4d Describe experiments to investigate photosynthesis.

WS1.1h Evaluate risks both in practical science and the wider societal context.

WS1.2c Apply a knowledge of a range of techniques, instruments, apparatus, and materials to select those appropriate to the experiment.

WS1.3a Presenting observations and other data using appropriate methods

WS1.3e Interpreting observations and other data.

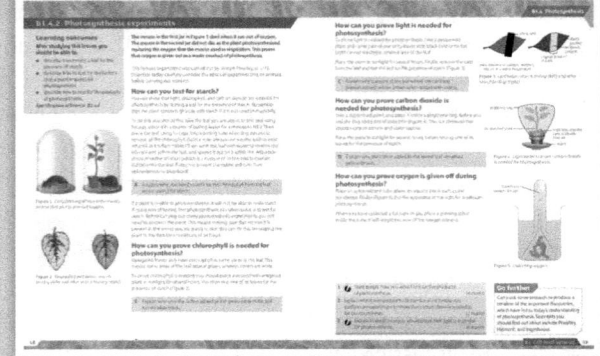

| Target | Outcome | Checkpoint | |
|---|---|---|---|
| | | Question | Activity |
| **Aiming for GRADE 4** | Describe how to test a leaf for the presence of starch. | 1 | Starter 1 and 2<br>Main<br>Plenary 1 |
| | Use the correct apparatus to follow a method with help, having due regard for some health and safety considerations. | | Starter 2<br>Main |
| | State a simple conclusion from a scientific observation. | | Starter 1<br>Main |
| **Aiming for GRADE 6** | Explain how to use the starch test to investigate the factors that affect whether or not photosynthesis occurs. | B, C, D, 1, 2, 3 | Main<br>Plenary 1 and 2 |
| | Follow a method to carry out an experiment appropriately and independently, having due regard for most health and safety considerations. | | Starter 2<br>Main |
| | Interpret experimental observations, drawing a valid conclusion. | | Main |
| **Aiming for GRADE 8** | Justify the use of each of the steps in the test for starch. | A, 2 | Main<br>Plenary 1 |
| | Follow a method to carry out an experiment appropriately and independently, having due regard for the correct manipulation of apparatus and all health and safety considerations. | | Starter 2<br>Main<br>Plenary 1 |
| | Interpret fully all experimental observations, to provide a detailed conclusion. | | Main<br>Plenary 2 |

**Literacy**

During the task students will be required to produce coherent and well-structured responses to questions.

# B1.4 Photosynthesis

| Starter | Support/Extend | Resources |
|---|---|---|
| **Iodine and starch** (5 minutes)  Have ready a piece of potato or bread and some iodine. Elicit that one of the products of photosynthesis is glucose. Point out that in plants some glucose molecules join together to form starch, which plants store in roots and seeds. Ask how we can show that starch is present — students might have covered this at Key Stage 3. Demonstrate the colour change when adding iodine to potato or bread, and tell students that the blue-black colour shows that starch is present. | **Extend:** Remind students that starch will not affect water potential, so ask them to explain the advantages of storing glucose as starch. | |
| **Risk assess** (5 minutes)  Provide the method for the practical in the main activity. Students do a simple risk assessment, identifying hazards and risk levels, and suggesting how to minimise risks from the hazards. | **Extend:** Use hazcards. | |

| Main | Support/Extend | Resources |
|---|---|---|
| **Light in photosynthesis** (40 minutes)  Use the practical sheet (or a standard method) to investigate the need for light in photosynthesis, using a leaf that has been partly covered with foil or card for two days. Then follow the method for the starch test using iodine.<br><br>Include questions about the procedure, and health and safety, and ask students to write a conclusion for the experiment. | **Extend:** Ask students to suggest a reason for each step in the method. This is best done after they have completed the method and can see what has happened. | **Practical:** Testing for starch |

| Plenary | Support/Extend | Resources |
|---|---|---|
| **Why all the steps?** (5 minutes)  Use the interactive where students put sentences in order to show how you test a leaf for starch and then match the step to why it is done. | | **Interactive:** Photosynthesis experiments |
| **Dinosaur extinction** (5 minutes)  One theory for the extinction of dinosaurs is that herbivorous dinosaurs ran out of food. (The meteor hit the Earth, creating a massive dust cloud: this prevented photosynthesis, due to the light being blocked. The plants died and this then had an effect on the food chain.)<br><br>Student pairs discuss how today's experiment provides evidence to support this theory. | **Support:** Discuss the events of a meteor strike and its impact first. | |

| Homework | | |
|---|---|---|
| Design an experiment to investigate if another factor (e.g. the wavelength of light or presence of chlorophyll) might be important for photosynthesis. Suggest a method and predict an outcome. | | |

*kerboodle*
A Kerboodle highlight for this lesson is **Extension: Measuring photosynthetic output**. Refer to the **Content map** on Kerboodle for a full list of resources and assessment.

# B1.4.3 Factors affecting photosynthesis

**Specification links:**

B1.4e Explain the effect of temperature, light intensity, and carbon dioxide concentration on the rate of photosynthesis.

WS1.2e Evaluate methods and suggest possible improvements and further investigations.

WS1.3a Present observations and other data using appropriate methods.

WS1.3b Translate data from one form to another.

WS1.4c Use SI units and IUPAC chemical nomenclature unless inappropriate.

WS2a Carry out experiments.

WS2b Make and record observations and measurements using a range of apparatus and methods.

BM1.4i Understand and use simple compound measures, such as the rate of a reaction (M1a, M1c).

BM1.1.4iii Plot and draw graphs, selecting appropriate scales and axes (M4a, M4c).

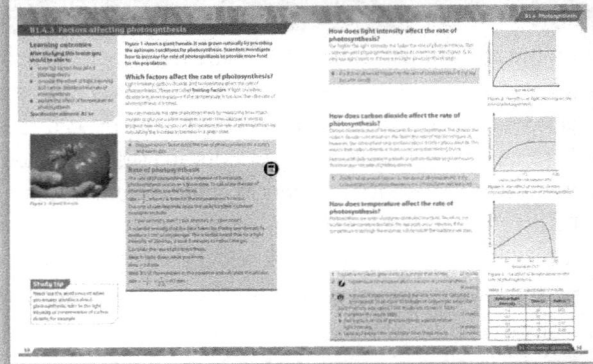

| Target | Outcome | Checkpoint | |
|---|---|---|---|
| | | Question | Activity |
| **Aiming for GRADE 4** | State the factors affecting the rate of photosynthesis. | A | Starter 1 and 2 Main Plenary 2 |
| | Record data from an experiment in the table provided. | | Main |
| | State any difficulties encountered carrying out this method. | | Main Plenary 1 |
| **Aiming for GRADE 6** | Describe the effect of light intensity, carbon dioxide concentration, and temperature on the rate of photosynthesis. | B, C | Starter 1 and 2 Main Plenary 2 |
| | Calculate a class average (mean) from data collected in an experiment. | | Main |
| | Suggest how any difficulties have affected the repeatability of the results. | | Main Plenary 1 |
| **Aiming for GRADE 8** | Explain the effect of light intensity, carbon dioxide concentration, and temperature on the rate of photosynthesis. | 1, 2, 3c | Main Plenary 2 |
| | Calculate the mean rate of photosynthesis from data collected in an experiment, and plot a rate graph as a line graph. | 3a, 3b | Main |
| | Evaluate the method, discussing the impact upon the validity of the results, and suggest improvements. | | Main Plenary 1 |

**Maths**

In the practical activity students collect data and calculate mean values (M2b) and reaction rates, working with compound measures (rate in bubbles per minute). They will also plot and draw graphs (M4d).

**Literacy**

In their conclusions, students will need to produce coherent, well-structured responses, and support their comments with evidence.

**Key words**

limiting factor

# B1.4 Photosynthesis

| Starter | Support/Extend | Resources |
|---|---|---|
| **Three factors** (5 minutes)  Use the interactive where students select a series of true or false sentences that describe the effect of the three factors on the rate of photosynthesis.<br><br>**Growth spurt** (10 minutes)  Show the class a plant and ask them to suggest ways in which the plant could be made to grow faster on a farm. They will suggest factors like light, but might need prompting to suggest increasing the temperature and adding extra carbon dioxide. Ask them to describe the relationship between the factor and the rate of photosynthesis. Ask students why it is important to obtain maximum growth rates in crops on farms or plant nurseries, focusing on two contrasting examples: rice (a staple food in many parts of the world) and cut flowers (a luxury product). | **Extend:** Try to identify the factors as independent variables, and the rate of photosynthesis measurement as the dependent variables. | **Interactive:** Factors affecting photosynthesis |

| Main | Support/Extend | Resources |
|---|---|---|
| **How does light intensity affect the rate of photosynthesis?**<br>(40 minutes)  Follow a standard method to measure the effect of changing the light intensity on the rate of photosynthesis. Use *Elodea* or *Cabomba* and change the distance of the pondweed from a lamp, recording the time taken to produce a set number of bubbles of oxygen. It is vital to test the experiment beforehand in order to gauge the number of bubbles likely to be produced, which will vary with time of year, type of pondweed and so on.<br><br>As students work through the experiment, encourage them to discuss which variables are independent, dependent, and which are control variables.<br><br>Results should give: distance between light and pondweed; time to produce a set number of bubbles. You might like to calculate a class value of the mean time to produce a set number of bubbles.<br><br>Plot a graph of distance against rate (1/time).<br><br>Students write a conclusion to their investigation.<br><br>SAFETY: *Cabomba* may be an invasive species: do not dispose of in rivers or ponds. | **Support:** Provide a results table. Limit the number of distance readings to every 20 cm. If students plot a rate graph, suggest that the values should be $1/\text{time} \times 1000$.<br><br>**Extend:** Students evaluate the method and the validity of the results. They suggest improvements.<br><br>**Extend:** Discuss how to modify the experiment to show the effects of carbon dioxide levels and temperature on the rate. | **Practical:** Light intensity and rate of photosynthesis |

| Plenary | Support/Extend | Resources |
|---|---|---|
| **How good was my experiment?** (5 minutes)  Provide each group with a series of cards that contain words connected to the experiment, for example, temperature; bubbles; time; distance; carbon dioxide; light. Ask the class to decide if each variable was controlled, independent (changed), or dependent (recorded). Ask them to identify a problem that each variable might have caused in the experiment.<br><br>**Photosynthesis chain game** (10 minutes)  Divide the class into groups of six. Issue each group nine sheets of A4 card. Within each group of six one pair writes a factor that affects the rate of photosynthesis on each of the three cards (a different factor on each card). Another pair writes a quick description of the relationship between each of these factors and the rate (one on each of the three cards). The third pair writes a quick explanation for each relationship, again on three separate cards. Then the teacher selects a group and asks them to hold up a card with a factor. The group nominates a new group, who hold up and read the description of the relationship. If they are right, they nominate a third group who hold up the explanation. Repeat until all factors have been discussed. | **Extend:** Rank how seriously they feel any of the errors might have been and suggest improvements.<br><br><br><br>**Support:** Identify the factors.<br>**Extend:** Provide the explanation. | |

| Homework | | |
|---|---|---|
| Plan an experiment, based on the method you have used in class, to investigate whether or not another factor, such as wavelength of light, might affect the rate of photosynthesis. Plan a results table. | | |

**kerboodle**

A Kerboodle highlight for this lesson is **Go further: An oxygen detective story**. Refer to the **Content map** on Kerboodle for a full list of resources and assessment.

# HIGHER TIER

## B1.4.4 Interaction of limiting factors

**Specification links:**

B1.4f Explain the interaction of these factors in limiting the rate of photosynthesis.

WS1.3a Present observations and other data using appropriate methods.

WS1.3b Translate data from one form to another.

WS1.3c Carry out and represent mathematical and statistical analysis.

WS1.3e Interpret observations and other data.

WS1.3f Present reasoned explanations including relating data to hypotheses.

WS1.4e Interconvert units.

BM1.7 Translate information between graphical and numeric form.

BM1.4iv Extract and interpret information from charts, graphs, and tables (M2c, M4a).

BM1.4v Understand and use inverse proportion – the inverse square law and light intensity in the context of factors affecting photosynthesis (M1c).

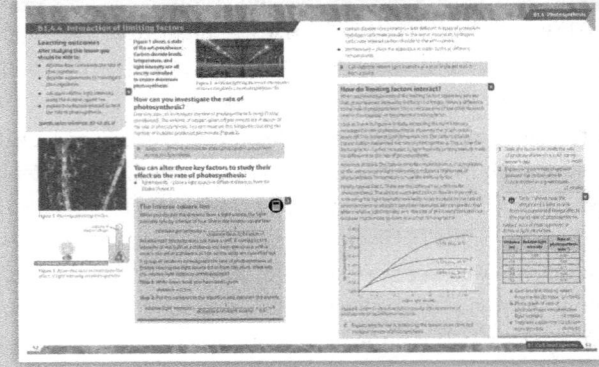

| Target | Outcome | Checkpoint | |
|---|---|---|---|
| | | Question | Activity |
| **Aiming for GRADE 6** | Explain the concept of a limiting factor. | C, 1 | Starter 2<br>Main 2 |
| | Calculate relative light intensity using the inverse square law. | B, 3a | Starter 1<br>Main 1 |
| | Describe how light intensity, carbon dioxide concentration, and temperature can be controlled. | 2 | Main 2<br>Plenary 1 and 2 |
| **Aiming for GRADE 8** | Explain how factors interact to limit the rate of photosynthesis. | 2 | Starter 2<br>Main 2<br>Plenary 2 |
| | Explain the relationship between light intensity and distance from a lamp. | 3c | Starter 1<br>Main 1 |
| | Discuss how controlling the factors that affect the rate of photosynthesis can affect the yield of a plant crop. | 2 | Main 2<br>Plenary 1 and 2 |

**Maths**
During the first main activity students transform data by substituting data collected from an experiment, using an algebraic equation (M3c). They will then need to plot this information in a graph (M4c).

**Literacy**
During the second main activity students will be expected to produce coherent, well-structured, and purposeful texts.

# B1.4 Photosynthesis

| Starter | Support/Extend | Resources |
|---|---|---|
| **Spreading it thin** (5 minutes)  Shine a torch light held by a student on a sheet of paper. Record the distance between the torch and paper, and estimate the proportion of the page lit. Ask students to predict what will happen if you increase the distance. Then double the distance and again estimate the area lit: it should have increased four-fold. Link this to a decrease in the light intensity. | **Support:** Draw 1 cm$^2$ squares on the paper and count the squares.  **Extend:** Deduce a mathematical relationship between distance and area covered. | |
| **Limiting production** (10 minutes)  Divide the class into groups of three (or use three students in a demonstration). Each group builds one tower from four coloured bricks, starting when you tell them to. Person 1 joins a red brick to a white brick and passes to person 2; who adds a blue brick and passes to person 3; who adds a yellow brick to complete the process. Now, limit one of the individuals, by slowing them in some way. Ask about the overall effect on the process of slowing down just one student. Explain the idea of limiting factors. | **Extend:** Explain why speeding up one factor has no effect on the overall process. | |

| Main | Support/Extend | Resources |
|---|---|---|
| **Inverse square law** (20 minutes)  Using data collected from the pondweed experiment in B1.4.3, calculate the relative light intensity for each distance value using the formula light intensity = 1/distance$^2$. Use this data to plot a graph of rate of photosynthesis (*y*-axis) against relative light intensity (*x*-axis). Remember to plot in terms of increasing light intensity, because, as the distance increases, the light intensity will decrease. Students identify the relationship between light intensity and rate. | | |
| **Greenhouse economics** (20 minutes)  Introduce to students how greenhouses can be used to increase the growth of plants and therefore profits for growers. Link each feature of a greenhouse to the limiting factors of photosynthesis. Students are then presented with data looking at the costs of running a greenhouse and the potential profits. They use the data to decide on the cost-effectiveness of adding extra carbon dioxide, heat, and light to the greenhouse. | | **Activity:** Using greenhouses |

| Plenary | Support/Extend | Resources |
|---|---|---|
| **Increasing yield** (5 minutes)  Use the interactive where students look at a graph and decide which factor is affecting the rate of photosynthesis, and how certain conditions will affect the rate of photosynthesis. | | **Interactive:** Interaction of limiting factors |
| **Gardeners' world problem page** (10 minutes)  Give each group a problem involving poor plant growth that they offer a solution for, such as: 'Why do the plants at the centre of my field grow slower during a warm summer day?' 'My house plants don't grow well in the centre of my room.' 'An old gardener told me to heat my greenhouse with a paraffin heater instead of an electric heater. Why?' 'I have a plant in sunny porch, why doesn't it grow in winter?' | **Extend:** Why do the tomato plants grow well in spring, but then die in summer in my greenhouse? | |

| Homework | | |
|---|---|---|
| Write an account or draw an annotated design of a greenhouse to explain how it can be used to control the rate of photosynthesis in plants. | | |

**kerboodle**
A Kerboodle highlight for this lesson is **Homework: Photosynthesis**. Refer to the **Content map** on Kerboodle for a full list of resources and assessment.

The Practical Skills lesson for PAG 5 Photosynthesis could follow this lesson.

# Checkpoint
## B1.4 Photosynthesis

### Overview of B1.4 Photosynthesis

In this chapter, students have studied photosynthesis, and should be able to write an equation for the process. They should know that photosynthesis is an endothermic reaction that requires sunlight energy and, building on knowledge from B1.1 *Cell structures*, that the process occurs in the chloroplasts of plant cells.

In studying the reactants and products of photosynthesis, students should have considered how plants obtain the raw materials and what happens to the glucose produced. In preparation for B4.1 *Ecosystems*, they should understand that plants are producers. They should be aware of the link between respiration and photosynthesis, and that while photosynthesis occurs in sunlight in plant cells, respiration occurs throughout the day and night in all living cells.

Students should have investigated the factors needed for photosynthesis to occur, using the iodine test for starch on de-starched leaves. They should have calculated the rate of photosynthesis and considered the effect on this of light intensity, temperature, and concentration of carbon dioxide. They should link their knowledge of enzymes from B1.2 *What happens in cells?* to their studies of photosynthesis and temperature.

Finally, higher-tier students should have studied the interaction between limiting factors, and have calculated light intensity using the inverse square law.

You can find additional support for the maths skills covered in this chapter on **MyMaths**, including calculating means and rates and plotting graphs.

### PAGs

All students are expected to have carried out the PAG *5 Photosynthesis*. A full lesson plan for each PAG is provided in the Practical skills chapter. PAG *5 Photosynthesis* should be completed after lesson B1.4.4 *Interaction of limiting factors*.

For this chapter, the following assessments are available on Kerboodle:
B1.4 Checkpoint quiz: Photosynthesis
B1.4 Progress quiz: Photosynthesis 1
B1.4 Progress quiz: Photosynthesis 2
B1.4 On your marks: Photosynthesis
B1.4 Exam-style questions and mark scheme: Photosynthesis

### Checkpoint follow-up lesson

A student's route through this lesson can be determined using the Checkpoint assessment. Percentage pass marks are supplied in the Checkpoint teacher notes.

For each successive route through it is assumed that the student can perform to their current route as well as previous routes. For example, students working at Aiming for 6 are assumed to be secure in Aiming for 4 knowledge and understanding and working towards achieving all the learning objectives for Aiming for 6.

# B1.4 Photosynthesis

| | Aiming for 4 | Aiming for 6 | Aiming for 8 |
|---|---|---|---|
| **Learning outcomes** | State the results of investigations carried out on plants kept in different conditions. | Describe the results for an investigation testing plants kept in different conditions. | Explain the results for an investigation testing plants kept in different conditions. |
| | State the uses of glucose in the plant. | Describe the uses of glucose in the plant. | Explain the uses of glucose in the plant. |
| | State and describe the factors that affect photosynthesis | Describe the factors that affect photosynthesis. | Explain the factors that affect photosynthesis. |
| **Starter** | **Reactants and products of photosynthesis (10 minutes)** In small mixed-ability groups, students look at a picture of a plant and add Post-it notes to show what is needed and produced during photosynthesis. Each group will need photocopied pictures of plants including the roots and soil, and arrow Post-it notes. Build up the word equation on the board together. | | |
| **Differentiated checkpoint activity** | **Activity 1 Photosynthesis (25 minutes)** Briefly introduce the activity. In small groups, students carry out starch testing on four previously prepared leaves and then each answer question 1 on the differentiated worksheets. The following resources are required: a water bath, ethanol, boiling tubes, white tiles, tweezers, iodine, and four pre-prepared leaves per group:<br><br>• leaf A – from a plant kept in normal (light) conditions<br>• leaf B – from a plant kept in dark conditions<br>• leaf C – a variegated leaf from a plant kept in light conditions<br>• leaf D – from a plant deprived of carbon dioxide by placing it in a plastic bag with soda lime. | | |
| | The Aiming for 4 activity sheet is highly structured for students to record their results and complete a conclusion. | Aiming for 6 students draw a results table and write a one-sentence conclusion on the sheet. | Aiming for 8 students draw a results table and write a detailed conclusion. |
| | **Activity 2 What happens to the glucose? (5 minutes)** After a brief introduction, working in small mixed-ability groups, students have a competition to write down all the uses of glucose in a plant they can remember in 3 minutes. Each group will need a sheet of A3 paper. Compare the groups' answers and summarise the uses of glucose on the board. | | |
| | **Activity 3 Greenhouse advice (10 minutes)** Students give advice to a greenhouse owner who is new to horticulture on how to improve the yield of their crops by answering question 2 on the differentiated worksheets. | | |
| | Aiming for 4 students answer structured questions on the sheet. They may require the Student book or teacher prompts to help them check their answers. | Aiming for 6 students write a short pamphlet. They are given headings to structure their work. They may use the Student book to check their work. | Aiming for 8 students write a short letter. They are given some suggestions as to what they might include. |
| | **Kerboodle resource:** B1.4 Checkpoint follow-up: Aiming for 4, B1.4 Checkpoint follow-up: Aiming for 6, B1.4 Checkpoint follow-up: Aiming for 8 | | |
| **Plenary** | **True or false quiz (5 minutes)** Read out some true or false statements about photosynthesis to check students' understanding. Students could either write down their answers, or show one coloured card for true and a different coloured one for false. In this case, each student will need two cards of different colours. | | |
| **Progression** | Aiming for 4 students may need additional guidance to complete the practical and question 1. The activity is highly structured and students can write their answers directly on the sheet. | Aiming for 6 students may need additional guidance to complete the practical and question 1. The activity is fairly structured and students can write their answers directly on the sheet. | The Aiming for 8 activity has little structure. These students can peer assess each other's work.<br><br>Higher-tier students could research how many factors are controlled in a greenhouse. A possible research task for these students is to find out more about the light-dependent and light-independent stages of photosynthesis. |

# B1 Cell-level systems: Topic summary

**B1.1** Cell structures
**B1.2** What happens in cells (and what do cells need)?
**B1.3** Respiration
**B1.4** Photosynthesis

| Spec ref | Statement | Book spreads |
| --- | --- | --- |
| B1.1a | Describe how light microscopes and staining can be used to view cells. | B1.1.3 |
| B1.1b | Explain how the main sub-cellular structures of eukaryotic cells (plants and animals) and prokaryotic cells are related to their functions. | B1.1.1, B1.1.2 |
| B1.1c | Explain how electron microscopy has increased our understanding of sub-cellular structures | B1.1.4 |
| B1.2a | Describe DNA as a polymer. | B1.2.1 |
| B1.2b | Describe DNA as being made up of two strands forming a double helix. | B1.2.1 |
| B1.2c | Describe that DNA is made from four different nucleotides; each nucleotide consisting of a common sugar and phosphate group with one of four different bases attached to the sugar. | B1.2.1 |
| **B1.2d** | **Recall a simple description of protein synthesis.** | **B1.2.2** |
| **B1.2e** | **Explain simply how the structure of DNA affects the proteins made in protein synthesis.** | **B1.2.2** |
| B1.2f | Describe experiments that can be used to investigate enzymatic reactions. | B1.2.3, B1.2.4 |
| B1.2g | Explain the mechanism of enzyme action. | B1.2.3, B1.2.4 |
| B1.3a | Describe cellular respiration as a universal chemical process, continuously occurring in all cells that supply ATP. | B1.3.2 |
| B1.3b | Describe cellular respiration as an exothermic reaction | B1.3.2 |
| B1.3c | Compare the processes of aerobic and anaerobic respiration. | B1.3.3 |
| B1.3d | Explain the importance of sugars in the synthesis and breakdown of carbohydrates. | B1.3.1 |
| B1.3e | Explain the importance of amino acids in the synthesis and breakdown of proteins. | B1.3.1 |
| B1.3f | Explain the importance of fatty acids and glycerol in the synthesis and breakdown of lipids. | B1.3.1 |
| B1.4a | Describe photosynthetic organisms as the main producers of food and therefore biomass for life on Earth. | B1.4.1 |
| B1.4b | Describe the process of photosynthesis. | B1.4.1 |
| B1.4c | Describe photosynthesis as an endothermic reaction. | B1.4.1 |
| B1.4d | Describe experiments to investigate photosynthesis. | B1.4.2 |
| B1.4e | Explain the effect of temperature, light intensity, and carbon dioxide concentration on the rate of photosynthesis. | B1.4.3 |
| **B1.4f** | **Explain the interaction of these factors in limiting the rate of photosynthesis.** | **B1.4.4** |

**Bold** denotes higher tier

*Maths*

| Specification | | Book spread | |
| --- | --- | --- | --- |
| Spec ref | Statement | Main content | Maths chapter |
| BM1.1i | Demonstrate an understanding of number, size, and scale, and the quantitative relationship between units (M2a and M2h). | B1.1.3, B1.1.4 | 1, 3, 12 |
| BM1.1ii | Use estimations and explain when they should be used (M1b). | B1.1.3 | 4, 7, 10 |
| BM1.1iii | Calculate with numbers written in standard form (M1b). | B1.1.4 | 2, 4, 5, 12 |
| BM1.2i | Carry out rate calculations for chemical reactions (M1a and M1c). | B1.2.4 | 14 |
| BM1.2ii | Understand and use simple compound measures, such as the rate of a reaction (M1a and M1c). | B1.2.4 | 14 |
| BM1.4i | Understand and use simple compound measures, such as the rate of a reaction (M1a and M1c). | B1.4.3 | 14 |
| BM1.4ii | Translate information between graphical and numeric form. | B1.4.4 | 13, 14 |
| BM1.4iii | Plot and draw graphs, selecting appropriate scales and axes (M4a and M4c). | B1.4.3 | 6, 13, 14 |
| BM1.4iv | Extract and interpret information from charts, graphs, and tables (M2c and M4a). | B1.4.4 | 6, 13, 14 |
| BM1.4v | Understand and use inverse proportion – the inverse square law and light intensity in the context of factors affecting photosynthesis (M1c). | B1.4.4 | |

## Working scientifically

| Specification | | Book spread | |
|---|---|---|---|
| Spec ref | Statement | Main content | WS chapter |
| WS1.1a | Understand how scientific methods and theories develop over time. | B1.1.4 | WS2 |
| WS1.1h | Evaluate risks both in practical science and the wider societal context. | B1.2.4, B1.4.2, WS1, | WS1 |
| WS1.2a | Use scientific theories and explanations to develop hypotheses. | B1.3.2 | WS3, WS4, WS7 |
| WS1.2b | Plan experiments or devise procedures to make observations, produce or characterise a substance, test hypotheses, check data, or explore phenomena. | B1 2.4 | WS4 |
| WS1.2c | Apply knowledge of a range of techniques, instruments, apparatus, and materials to select those appropriate to the experiment. | B1.1.3, B1.2.4, B1.3.3, B1.4.2, B1.4.3 | WS4 |
| WS1.2d | Recognise when to apply a knowledge of sampling techniques to ensure any samples collected are representative. | B1.2.4 | |
| WS1.3a | Presenting observations and other data using appropriate methods | B1.2.4, B1.4.1, B1.4.2, B1.4.3, B1.4.4 | WS6 |
| WS1.3b | Translating data from one form to another. | B1.2.4, B1.4.3, B1.4.4, B1.4.4 | WS7 |
| WS1.3c | Carrying out and representing mathematical and statistical analysis. | B1.2.4 | |
| WS1.3d | Representing distributions of results and make estimations of uncertainty. | B1.2.4 | WS8 |
| WS1.3e | Interpreting observations and other data | B1.2.4, B1.4.2, B1.4.4 | WS7 |
| WS1.3f | Presenting reasoned explanations, including relating data to hypotheses. | B1.2.4, B1.4.4 | WS7 |
| WS1.4a | Use scientific vocabulary, terminology and definitions | B1.1.1, B1.1.2, B1.2.1 | WS2 |
| WS1.4c | Use SI units and IUPAC chemical nomenclature unless inappropriate. | B1.1.3, B1.1.4, B1.4.3 | WS2 |
| WS1.4d | Use prefixes and powers of ten for orders of magnitude (e.g. tera, giga, mega, kilo, centi, milli, micro, and nano). | B1.1.3, B1.1.4 | WS2 |
| WS1.4e | Interconvert units. | B1.1.3, B1.4.4 | |
| WS2a | Carry out experiments. | B1.2.1, B1.2.4, B1.4.3 | |
| WS2b | Make and record observations and measurements using a range of apparatus and methods. | B1.2.4, B1.4.3 | WS5 |
| WS2e | Evaluate methods and suggest possible improvements and further investigations. | B1.4.3 | WS7, WS8 |

# B2 Scaling up

## B2.1 Supplying the cell
### B2.1.1 Diffusion

**Specification links:**

B2.1a Explain how substances are transported into and out of cells through diffusion, osmosis, and active transport. To include examples of substances moved, direction of movement, concentration gradients, and use of the term water potential (no mathematical use of water potential required).

WS1.1b Use models to solve problems, make predictions, and to develop scientific explanations and understanding of familiar and unfamiliar facts.

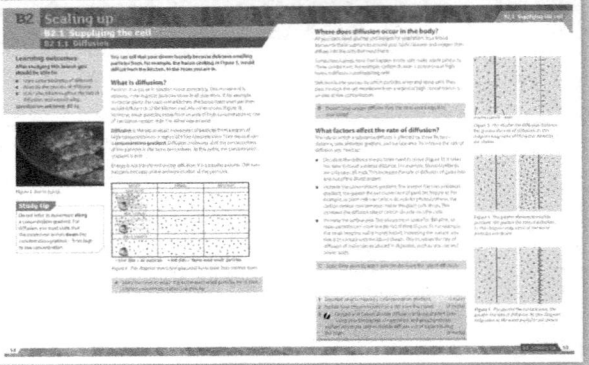

| Target | Outcome | Checkpoint | |
|---|---|---|---|
| | | Question | Activity |
| **Aiming for GRADE 4** | State some examples of diffusion. | A | Starter 1 and 2<br>Main 1 and 2<br>Plenary 2 |
| | State factors that affect the rate of diffusion. | C | Main 1 and 2<br>Plenary 1 and 2 |
| | Describe by communicating simply, producing text with basic structure and familiar vocabulary. | | Main 1 and 2 |
| **Aiming for GRADE 6** | Describe the process of diffusion. | B, 1 | Starter 1 and 2<br>Main 1 and 2 |
| | Describe the effect of factors on the rate of diffusion. | 1, 3 | Main 1 and 2<br>Plenary 1 and 2 |
| | Describe by communicating effectively, producing coherent text, which is well structured, and use some appropriate scientific vocabulary. | | Main 2 |
| **Aiming for GRADE 8** | Explain fully at a molecular level the process of diffusion. | B, 2 | Starter 1 and 2<br>Main 1 and 2 |
| | Explain the reasons for the effects of factors on the rate of diffusion. | 3 | Main 1 and 2<br>Plenary 2 |
| | Describe by communicating with impact, producing effectively-structured texts, using a full range of precise scientific vocabulary. | | Main 2 |

**Literacy**

During the main tasks, students will be asked to orally (Main 1), and in writing (Main 2), produce coherent text to describe and explain a complex idea. This involves the use of complex scientific vocabulary.

**Key words**

concentration gradient, diffusion

# B2.1 Supplying the cell

| Starter | Support/Extend | Resources |
|---|---|---|
| **Demonstrating diffusion** (5 minutes)  Use a large beaker of cold tap water and carefully add a large crystal or a very small spatula measure of potassium manganate(VII) down the side of the beaker, and ask the class to describe what they observe. The effect is improved if you can place the beaker on an overhead projector (OHP). Students have learnt about diffusion at Key Stage 3, so they should use the correct vocabulary. | **Extend:** Encourage the explanation of the random movement of molecules. | |
| **Diffusion drama** (10 minutes)  The class all stand at one end of the laboratory. One student acts as a narrator, and reads a script, which is made of a series of statements. These statements describe the process of diffusion, whilst giving instructions for the students to move in a random way to spread out around the lab. | **Support:** Identify key words and list them on the board.  **Extend:** Avoid reading the key words on the script, and ask students to supply them. | |

| Main | Support/Extend | Resources |
|---|---|---|
| **Investigating diffusion** (30 minutes)  Students carry out the practical investigation. They look at diffusion and one of the factors that affects the rate of diffusion – temperature. They also look at diffusion across a membrane to embed the idea that diffusion can occur across cell membranes. | **Support:** Students may need some help understanding why iodine can diffuse through the membrane, but starch cannot (starch molecules are too big). | **Practical:** Diffusion |
| **Explaining diffusion** (10 minutes)  Show the students a picture of a red blood cell. State that oxygen enters the red blood cell when the cell is in the lungs and exits when it is in the tissues.  Ask students to produce an extended written explanation of the diffusion of oxygen in and out of the cell. The explanation should include details of the three factors discussed during the lesson. Give communication-based success criteria. | **Support:** Ask students to describe only the movement of oxygen into the red blood cell. | |

| Plenary | Support/Extend | Resources |
|---|---|---|
| **Linking factors** (5 minutes)  Use the interactive in which students decide which factors affect the rate of diffusion and then sort statements as to whether they would increase or decrease the rate of diffusion in the body. | | **Interactive:** Diffusion |
| **The alveolus** (10 minutes)  Show students the standard image of an alveolus with a blood capillary wrapped around it, but remove all labels. Remind students that oxygen is taken up into the blood in the alveolus. Give students 2–3 minutes to discuss, in their groups, why diffusion is so efficient in the lungs. Ask some groups to present their views to the class. Their explanations should refer to surface area and concentration gradients. | **Extend:** Ask students to explain how gas exchange occurs in fish. Ask them to speculate about diffusion rates in cold water fish and tropical fish | |

| Homework | | |
|---|---|---|
| Design an experiment to show the effect of temperature on the diffusion of the brown colour from tea bags in a glass of water. | | |

**kerboodle**

A Kerboodle highlight for this lesson is **Working Scientifically: Concentration**. Refer to the **Content map** on Kerboodle for a full list of resources and assessment.

# B2.1.2 Osmosis

**Specification links:**

B2.1a Explain how substances are transported into and out of cells through diffusion, osmosis, and active transport. To include examples of substances moved, direction of movement, concentration gradients, and use of the term water potential (no mathematical use of water potential required).

WS1.3a Present observations and other data using appropriate methods.

BM2.1i Use percentiles, and calculate percentage gain and loss of mass (M1c).

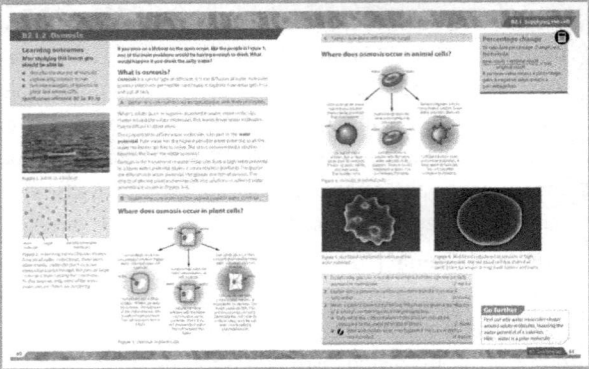

| Target | Outcome | Checkpoint | |
|---|---|---|---|
| | | Question | Activity |
| **Aiming for GRADE 4** ↓ | State that osmosis is the movement of water molecules into or out of cells. | | Starter 1 and 2<br>Main<br>Plenary 2 |
| | State that osmosis is a type of diffusion. | | Starter 1 and 2<br>Main |
| **Aiming for GRADE 6** ↓ | Describe the process of osmosis. | A, C, 3 | Starter 1 and 2<br>Main<br>Plenary 1 and 2 |
| | Explain why osmosis occurs. | 1, 2, 3 | Starter 2<br>Main<br>Plenary 2 |
| **Aiming for GRADE 8** ↓ | Explain the effect of osmosis on potato cells. | C, 3 | Main<br>Plenary 1 and 2 |
| | Explain, in terms of water potential, why osmosis occurs. | B, 3 | Starter 1 and 2<br>Main |

**Maths**
During the main activity, students will calculate percentage change in mass (M1c) and plot two variables collected from experimental data (M4c). Extension work requires students to determine the intercept of a linear graph (M4d).

**Literacy**
During the main activity, students will need to produce coherent answers to questions.

**Key words**
osmosis, water potential

## B2.1 Supplying the cell

| Starter | Support/Extend | Resources |
|---|---|---|
| **Explaining osmosis** (5 minutes) Issue each group with a sheet of A4 paper, with a semi-permeable membrane drawn down the middle. Also issue two sets of paper discs, some larger than the pore size and labelled sugar; others smaller than the pore size labelled water. Allow students to explore the possible movement of the molecules across the membrane. Draw the diagram on the board and model the process of osmosis, eliciting responses from the class to help tell the story. | **Support:** There are many animations available to help students to visualise molecular movement. **Extend:** Introduce the concept of water potential. | |
| **The osmometer** (10 minutes) Set up a standard osmometer as a demonstration. Ensure the sugar solution is coloured with food dye and is very concentrated (exact value is unimportant) – this will cause visible and quick movement. Describe and explain what is happening as you set up the experiment. Finish with a definition of osmosis. | | |

| Main | Support/Extend | Resources |
|---|---|---|
| **Osmosis in potato chips** (40 minutes) Students investigate osmosis in potato cylinders. During this lesson, the students set up the experiment and make predictions for the test, such as what will happen to the potatoes in each solution and why. They also answer questions about the method, such as what variables are they controlling, what are the dependent and independent variables, and so on. Follow a standard method for placing cylinders of potatoes (chips) in five sugar solutions of different concentrations between 0.25 mol/dm³ and 1.25 mol/dm³ glucose. In this lesson, students record initial mass and set up the experiment. The experiment needs to run for 24 hours. (The set-up can be left for up to two days, but not longer. You may need to make alternative arrangements for the collection of results outside the lesson, or you could supply data.) There will be time in the next lesson for students to write a conclusion, to describe and explain what has happened. | **Support:** Cut the potato cylinders using a borer in advance. Students find it difficult to record the correct mass of the potato for each solution. You could label the tubes; or different groups can do different concentrations; or set up one concentration, stop, then set up the second, etc. Only predict for the two extreme values of glucose. **Extend:** Ask questions referring to the concept of water potential. | **Practical:** Osmosis in potato chips |

| Plenary | Support/Extend | Resources |
|---|---|---|
| **Osmosis and plant and animal cells** (10 minutes) Use the interactive activity in which students identify the correct definition of osmosis, and link words connected with osmosis in plant and animal cells (plasmolysis, flaccid, osmosis, turgor) to their meanings. | | **Interactive:** Osmosis |
| **Osmosis in catering** (5 minutes) Provide students with small lengths (about 2–3 cm) of salad onions. They cut down the shaft of the onion for about 1 cm, using a scalpel and tile, then place in water. Ask students what will happen. Then show one prepared earlier, which will have splayed open. Explain why this has happened. The onion cells absorb water by osmosis, increasing their size, causing the strips to bend outwards. | **Extend:** Repeat for a glucose solution. Use the term water potential. | |

| Homework | | |
|---|---|---|
| Write a training manual for paramedics to explain why you need to bathe kidneys being used for transplants in saline solution, not water, during transport from a donor to a recipient. This could include labelled drawings. | | |

*kerboodle*
A Kerboodle highlight for this lesson is **Bump up your grade: Osmosis**. Refer to the **Content map** on Kerboodle for a full list of resources and assessment.

The Practical Skills lesson for PAG 8 Transport in and out of cells could follow this lesson.

# B2.1.3 Active transport

**Specification links:**

B2.1a Explain how substances are transported into and out of cells through diffusion, osmosis, and active transport. To include examples of substances moved, direction of movement, concentration gradients, and use of the term water potential (no mathematical use of water potential required).

WS1.1b Use models to solve problems, make predictions, and to develop scientific explanations and understanding of familiar and unfamiliar facts.

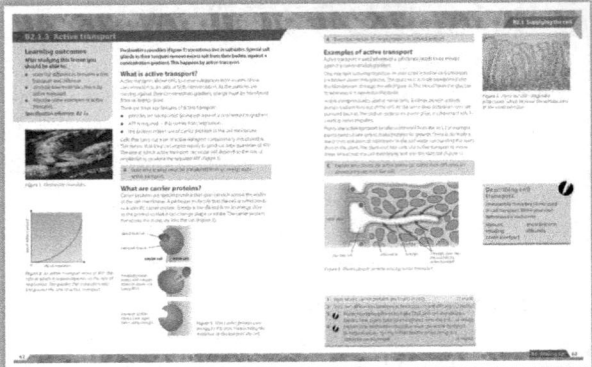

| Target | Outcome | Checkpoint | |
|---|---|---|---|
| | | Question | Activity |
| **Aiming for GRADE 4** | State some examples of active transport. | 3 | Main 2<br>Plenary 1 |
| | State the differences between active transport and diffusion. | 2 | Plenary 1 and 2 |
| | Record measurements from an experimental method, and calculate a change in mass. | | Starter 2<br>Main 2<br>Plenary 1 |
| **Aiming for GRADE 6** | Describe examples of active transport in plants and animals. | C | Main 2<br>Plenary 1 |
| | Describe how molecules move by active transport. | A, B, 1, 3 | Starter 1 and 2<br>Main 2<br>Plenary 2 |
| | Record measurements from an experimental method, and calculate a percentage change in mass. | | Starter 2<br>Main 2 |
| **Aiming for GRADE 8** | Explain the importance of active transport in plants and animals. | C, 4 | Plenary 1 |
| | Explain how carrier proteins function in the process of active transport. | A, B, 3 | Starter 1 and 2<br>Main 2<br>Plenary 2 |
| | Record measurements from an experimental method, calculate a percentage change in mass, and plot the data to determine the concentration that is equal to the cell. | | Starter 2<br>Main 2 |

**Maths**
Some students will carry out Main 1, which uses the maths skills outlined in B2.1.2.

**Literacy**
During Main 2, students will be asked to read text and communicate their ideas effectively, either in writing or orally, to sustain interest.

**Key words**
active transport

## B2.1 Supplying the cell

| Starter | Support/Extend | Resources |
|---|---|---|
| **Revolving door** (5 minutes) Remind students of diffusion and osmosis. Tell students that there is a third method called active transport. Then set up a kinaesthetic model. Arrange the desks with a gap between two tables. This represents the membrane. Then ask three or four students to form a wheel in the gap, with arms extended acting as spokes – this is the carrier protein. Arrange the other students with most of them on one side of the membrane (table). There should be space between the 'spokes' (arms) to fit a student (who represents a molecule). The wheel then rotates and the molecule student moves across the membrane. | **Extend:** Ask students to identify differences between this method and diffusion or osmosis. | |
| **The problems of getting sugar into cells** (10 minutes) Have a drawing of a cell membrane on the board. Ask if there are glucose molecules in the cell. Students should reply that there is. Draw sugar on one side of the membrane. Ask how it got there. They then need to explore the reasons why diffusion and osmosis cannot explain this. Tell them there is a third way. Ask them to discuss in groups how it could work. At short intervals ask for ideas, or provide additional hints, for example, draw a carrier protein in the membrane. | | |

| Main | Support/Extend | Resources |
|---|---|---|
| **Investigating osmosis results analysis** (20 minutes) Obtain results from the osmosis experiment in B2.1.2. Calculate the percentage change in mass, then plot this against concentration on a graph. Students write a short conclusion to explain what has happened. | | **Practical:** Osmosis in potato chips |
| **Modelling active transport** (20 minutes) Students work in small groups to carry out a model of active transport. Ask for a couple of groups to demonstrate their model, while the rest evaluate its effectiveness and comment on possible improvements. | | **Activity:** Modelling active transport |

| Plenary | Support/Extend | Resources |
|---|---|---|
| **Which route?** (10 minutes) Provide students with a list of substances (oxygen, carbon dioxide, water, glucose, sodium ions, nitrate ions, etc.) Ask which method is used for the substance to enter or leave the cell. Then ask student pairs to spend a minute or so discussing similarities and differences between active transport and diffusion, and explaining the importance of both in plants and animals. | **Extend:** Ask the students to justify their selection. | |
| **Conditions for active transport** (5 minutes) Use the interactive activity in which students select true or false for statements about active transport. | | **Interactive:** Active transport |

| Homework | | |
|---|---|---|
| You are a pathologist investigating a case where a patient has died from a poison that stops respiration in cells. Explain why this has caused death due to a failure of active transport mechanisms in nerves and the gut, and not from diffusion or osmosis. | | |

**kerboodle**
A Kerboodle highlight for this lesson is **Go Further: Cell membrane adaptation for transport**. Refer to the **Content map** on Kerboodle for a full list of resources and assessment.

# B2.1.4 Mitosis

**Specification links:**

B2.1b Describe the process of mitosis in growth, including the cell cycle, to include the stages of the cell cycle such as DNA replication, movement of chromosomes, followed by the growth of the cell.

WS1.1b Use models to solve problems, make predictions, and to develop scientific explanations and understanding of familiar and unfamiliar facts.

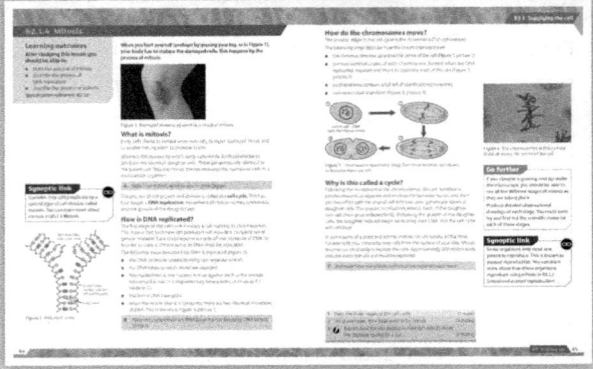

| Target | Outcome | Checkpoint | |
|---|---|---|---|
| | | Question | Activity |
| **Aiming for GRADE 4** | State the stages of the cell cycle. | 1 | Starter 1 Main |
| | State the purpose of mitosis. | A, C, 2 | Starter 2 Main |
| | Use a model to illustrate the major steps in the cell cycle. | | Starter 1 Main |
| **Aiming for GRADE 6** | Describe the key features of each stage of the cell cycle. | 3 | Starter 1 Main Plenary 1 and 2 |
| | Describe the process of mitosis. | 3 | Main Plenary 1 and 2 |
| | Use a representational model to describe the key events during the cell cycle. | | Starter 1 Main |
| **Aiming for GRADE 8** | Explain the process of DNA replication in the cell cycle. | B | Main Plenary 1 and 2 |
| | Explain the process of mitosis in terms of the movement of chromosomes. | 3 | Main Plenary 1 and 2 |
| | Use a representational model to develop scientific explanations of all of the events during the cell cycle. | | Main |

**Literacy**

During the main activity, students will be expected to communicate effectively, sustaining the listeners' interest.

**Key words**

cell cycle, DNA replication, mitosis

## B2.1 Supplying the cell

| Starter | Support/Extend | Resources |
|---|---|---|
| **Role play of cell cycle** (10 minutes) Create a circular walkway around the class, with three sections called: DNA replication, mitosis, and cell growth. One student with one length of string (DNA) starts a walk around the cycle at the end of the cell growth sector. As they move into DNA replication, they are given a second length of string. This represents DNA replication. As they move into mitosis, they 'divide' by a second student joining the walk, and being given one of the lengths of string. They then enter cell growth. The process continues. Before continuing with the lesson, check that students can state the purpose of mitosis.<br>**Growth** (5 minutes) Pose the question to the class in groups: 'How do we grow?' Elicit any responses. List ideas on the board. Show any short film that shows cell growth of a shoot tip or embryo as a process of cell division. Ask students to describe what they have seen in the film. | **Support:** Teacher narrates what is happening as the students walk around the room.<br>**Extend:** Teacher asks students to describe the events in the cell being illustrated. | |

| Main | Support/Extend | Resources |
|---|---|---|
| **Wall chart of the cell cycle and mitosis** (40 minutes) Teacher draws an outline of the cell cycle to show outlines of a cell in Stage 1: DNA replication, up to four cells in Stage 2: Movement of chromosomes (Mitosis), and the two product cells in Stage 3: Cell growth.<br>Give students some wool (2-ply), scissors, and sellotape. Using information in the Student Book, use the wool to create the chromosomes in a cell with two chromosomes. Each outline represents the cell at the various stages of the cell cycle. Gives students some wool, scissors, and sellotape. Using information in the Student Book, use the wool to create the chromosomes in a cell with two chromosomes. Each outline represents the cell at the various stages of the cell cycle. Complete the poster by adding annotations, ensuring that the purpose of mitosis is included.<br>Each group looks at a poster produced by another group and points out one thing about the poster that helps them to understand the cell cycle, and suggests one improvement. | **Support:** Use fewer stages during mitosis.<br>**Extend:** Include more cells during mitosis to elicit more detail. Introduce chromosome pairs of different sizes.<br>Students could illustrate unzipping of the DNA by unravelling the 2-ply wool. | **Activity:** Modelling mitosis |

| Plenary | Support/Extend | Resources |
|---|---|---|
| **Drag and drop sort** (5 minutes) Use the interactive which asks students to select the correct events that happen during mitosis and then match the event to the correct stage of mitosis.<br>**Jumbled statements** (10 minutes) Produce the statements from the Student Book on 'How is DNA replicated' or 'How do the chromosomes move?' as separate statements on separate cards. Student groups sort the cards into the right sequence. If there is time, swap the card sets between groups to complete both processes. | **Support:** Tell students the start card.<br>**Extend:** Shuffle both packs together. | **Interactive:** Mitosis |

| Homework | | |
|---|---|---|
| You work in the orthopaedics department of a busy hospital. You have been asked to put together an information leaflet to explain to patients with broken limbs how their bones are repairing. This requires you to describe and explain the cell cycle that the bone cells are going through to produce new bone tissue rapidly. | | |

**kerboodle**
A Kerboodle highlight for this lesson is **Extension: Stages of mitosis**. Refer to the **Content map** on Kerboodle for a full list of resources and assessment.

# B2.1.5 Cell differentiation

**Specification links:**

B2.1c Explain the importance of cell differentiation. To include the production of specialised cells allowing organisms to become more efficient and examples of specialised cells.

WS1.3a Present observations and other data using appropriate methods.

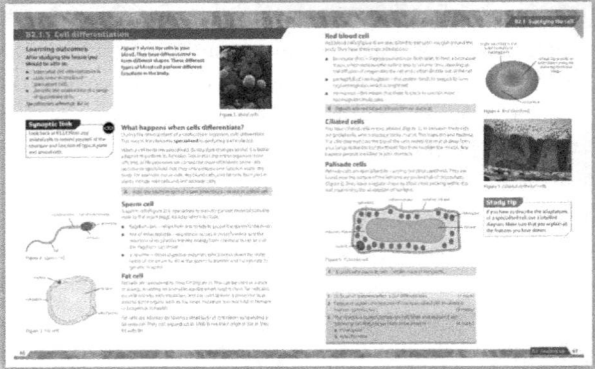

| Target | Outcome | Checkpoint | |
|---|---|---|---|
| | | Question | Activity |
| **Aiming for GRADE 4** | State what is meant by cell differentiation. | 1 | Starter 1 and 2<br>Main<br>Plenary 1 |
| | State some examples of specialised cells. | A, 2 | Starter 1<br>Main<br>Plenary 1 |
| | Use text to be able to describe features with some accuracy. | | Main |
| **Aiming for GRADE 6** | Explain why cells become differentiated. | B, C | Starter 2<br>Main<br>Plenary 1 and 2 |
| | Describe the adaptations of a range of specialised cells. | B, C, 2, 3 | Main<br>Plenary 2 |
| | Summarise text, with accuracy, to show clear understanding of cell features. | | Main |
| **Aiming for GRADE 8** | Explain the need for cellular differentiation in multicellular organisms. | | Starter 2<br>Main<br>Plenary 2 |
| | Explain the link between the adaptation of each specialised cell and its function. | B, C, 2, 3 | Main<br>Plenary 2 |
| | Summarise text showing detailed and perceptive understanding of cell features and functions. | | Main |

**Literacy**

During the Main, students will be asked to read scientific texts, and summarise the text with accuracy and clear understanding.

**Key words**

differentiated, specialised

## B2.1 Supplying the cell

| Starter | Support/Extend | Resources |
|---|---|---|
| **The fate of cells** (10 minutes)   Ask students to create an epigenetic landscape model (look up the model on the internet). They do this by building a branching series of channels, using long cylinders of modelling clay on a tray. It starts at the top of the tray with one trough between two cylinders, which branch several times as you descend the tray. At the end of every branch are the names of different types of cell in the human body. Using a marble as a cell, hold it at the top of the initial branch and allow it to roll down the tray. It will roll into one channel, illustrating that it becomes a differentiated cell. Link this to events in the body as cells differentiate. (To save time, the models could be made beforehand). | **Extend:** Discuss how this model represents the specialisation of the cell into a special cell. | |
| **Why specialise?** (5 minutes)   Divide the class into small groups. Issue some groups with a small set of plain Lego bricks, whilst other groups will have a selection of Lego bricks, doors, wheels and so on. Ask the groups to build something. Elicit that the groups with the selection of Lego pieces could build more complicated models because they had specialised bricks. Link this to the idea of cell differentiation. | | |

| Main | Support/Extend | Resources |
|---|---|---|
| **Special cells for special jobs** (15 minutes)   Set up a carousel of microscopes around the lab with slides of ciliated epithelium, adipose (fat) cells, red blood cells, and palisade cells, (or images from the internet). Also have the Student Book open for students to read about the cell they are looking at. Students make notes about the special features of the cells, the functions of cells, and the role of the special part in carrying out the function. Lead a brief discussion to elicit some benefits of cell differentiation, including the need for cellular differentiation in multicellular organisms. | **Support:** Identify the special parts for each cell type. | **Activity:** Specialised cells for specialised jobs |
| **Using the knowledge** (25 minutes)   Student pairs create a quiz/crossword based on the special cells (names, special parts, and their functions). This could be done using IT. The finished task is passed to the neighbouring pair, who attempt to answer. The answering pair checks that the clues and answers are correct, and suggests improvements to the puzzle or quiz. | **Support:** Quiz, wordsearch or game might be easier to construct than a crossword. | |

| Plenary | Support/Extend | Resources |
|---|---|---|
| **Landscapes revisited** (10 minutes)   Return to the epigenetic landscape model built at the start of the lesson. Ask students if the cells can swap channels. The answer is no. Then ask why. Students should point out, using what they have learnt from the main activity, that the cells have developed special parts for one function. These parts cannot be unmade. | **Extend:** Discuss limitations of the use of models like this.<br><br>Or: What has caused the cells to develop special parts? The idea of gene activity. | |
| **Parts to functions** (5 minutes)   Use the interactive, which asks students to match specialised cells with their functions and then to decide which adaptations belong to which type of specialised cell. | | **Interactive:** Cell differentiation |

| Homework | | |
|---|---|---|
| Make a model of a specialised cell. Label the special parts and describe how each part contributes to its function. | | |

*kerboodle*

A Kerboodle highlight for this lesson is **Extension: The human eye.** Refer to the **Content map** on Kerboodle for a full list of resources and assessment.

# B2.1.6 Stem cells

**Specification links:**

B2.1d Recall that stem cells are present in embryonic and adult animals, and in meristems in plants.

B2.1e Describe the functions of stem cells. To include division to produce a range of different cell types for development, growth, and repair.

B2.1f Describe the difference between embryonic and adult stem cells in animals.

WS1.1e Explain everyday and technological applications of science.

WS1.1f Evaluate associated personal, social, economic, and environmental implications.

WS1.1h Evaluate risks both in practical science and the wider societal context.

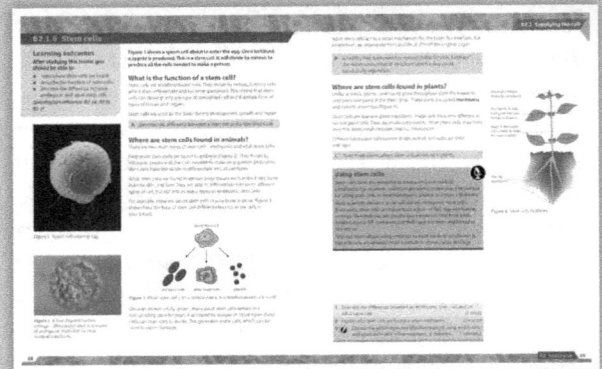

| Target | Outcome | Checkpoint | |
|---|---|---|---|
| | | Question | Activity |
| **Aiming for GRADE 4** | State where stem cells are found. | C | Starter 1 and 2<br>Main<br>Plenary 1 |
| | State some uses of stem cells. | 2 | Starter 1 and 2<br>Main<br>Plenary 1 |
| | Use general references to scientific texts to support their comments and opinions. | | Main |
| **Aiming for GRADE 6** | Describe the difference between a stem cell and a differentiated cell. | A | Starter 1 and 2<br>Main<br>Plenary 1 |
| | Describe the function of stem cells. | 2 | Starter 1 and 2<br>Main<br>Plenary 1 |
| | Use appropriate references to scientific texts to support their understanding and opinions. | | Main |
| **Aiming for GRADE 8** | Explain the difference between embryonic and adult stem cells. | 1 | Starter 2<br>Main<br>Plenary 2 |
| | Evaluate the advantages and disadvantages of using stem cells in medicine. | 3 | Main<br>Plenary 2 |
| | Justify their understanding and opinions with illuminating use of references to scientific texts. | | Main |

**Literacy**
During the main activity, students will be required to read scientific texts to use references that will support written explanations, showing understanding and opinions.

**Key words**
meristem, stem cell

# B2.1 Supplying the cell

| Starter | Support/Extend | Resources |
|---|---|---|
| **What do you want to know?** (5 minutes) State that the lesson is about stem cells and show an image of a newspaper headline about stem cell research. Issue each student with a sticky note. Allow them a few minutes to discuss in pairs what they know about stem cells, and ask them to write a question on the sticky note that they want to learn about in this lesson. Place the questions on a board for the end of the lesson. | | |
| **Stem cells** (10 minutes) Use the interactive activity in which students read statements about stem cell research and select whether they think the statement agrees or disagrees with stem cell research. | | **Interactive:** Stem cells |

| Main | Support/Extend | Resources |
|---|---|---|
| **Writing scientifically with stem cells** (35 minutes) Students are provided with example articles on stem cells. (Alternatively, provide students with short examples of science articles printed from websites or cut out from magazines.) Ask them to discuss in pairs what they think about the articles – how did the articles capture their attention and hold it? Did the articles explain the science well? Did the articles leave them wanting to know more? Go through the main points of how to write a science article with the class. Students then research how stem cells are used to help medical conditions and use the information to write their own article on stem cells.<br><br>Students should include the following in their articles:<br>1. State what is meant by a stem cell, and describe a difference between a stem cell and a differentiated cell.<br>2. List three sources of stem cells.<br>3. What medical conditions are stem cells used to treat?<br>4. For one named condition describe briefly how stem cells are used.<br>5. Describe some arguments that can be used in favour of stem cell research.<br>6. Describe some arguments that can be used against stem cell research. | **Extend:** Explain the difference between embryonic and adult stem cells. | **Activity:** Writing scientifically with stem cells |

| Plenary | Support/Extend | Resources |
|---|---|---|
| **What have we learnt?** (5 minutes) Return to the question board from Starter 1. Select a few questions from the board and ask students for the answers. | | |
| **Advantages and disadvantages of the types of stem cells** (10 minutes) Use the interactive, which asks students to drag and drop statements into one of three categories (adult stem cells, embryonic stem cells, plant stem cells). These statements are a selection of advantages and disadvantages of using stem cells in medical treatments. | **Extend:** Discuss the ethical issues associated with some of the statements. | |

| Homework | | |
|---|---|---|
| Write an extended newspaper article that discusses the advantages and disadvantages of using stem cell technology. The article could argue for or against the technology. | **Extend:** The article should contain an evaluation and justification of the technology, including consideration of ethical issues. | |

**kerboodle**
A Kerboodle highlight for this lesson is **Webquest: Stem cell research**. Refer to the **Content map** on Kerboodle for a full list of resources and assessment.

# Checkpoint

## B2.1 Supplying the cell

### Overview of B2.1 Supplying the cell

In this chapter, students have studied diffusion, including where it occurs in the body and factors that affect its rate. They should make links to the diffusion of glucose, oxygen, and carbon dioxide in B1.3 *Respiration* and B1.4 *Photosynthesis*. This topic also links with B2.2 *The challenges of size* where factors affecting the rate of diffusion are considered, and transport of substances in a range of organisms.

Students have also looked at osmosis and the concept of water potential. They should have studied the effect of changing the water potential of a solution on animal cells and plant cells. They have experimented with potato chips immersed in different concentrations of sugar solution, and measured the percentage change in mass and length. They have also studied active transport, and should be able to give examples of this process in plants and animals.

Students should understand the link between osmosis, active transport, and cell specialisation in considering how water and mineral ions are taken up by root hair cells in plants. They have studied the cell cycle including mitosis, along with its role in growth and repair. Linked to this is an understanding of cell differentiation, and how the adaptations of each cell are linked to its function.

Finally students should be able to describe what is special about stem cells, where they are found in plants and animals, and their potential future uses in medicine.

You can find additional support for the maths skills covered in this chapter on **MyMaths**, including calculating percentages and plotting graphs.

### PAGs

All students are expected to have carried out the PAG 8 *Transport in and out of cells*. A full lesson plan for each PAG is provided in the Practical skills chapter. PAG 8 *Transport in and out of cells* should be completed after lesson B2.1.2 *Osmosis*.

For this chapter, the following assessments are available on Kerboodle:
B2.1 Checkpoint quiz: Supplying the cell
B2.1 Progress quiz: Supplying the cell 1
B2.1 Progress quiz: Supplying the cell 2
B2.1 On your marks: Supplying the cell
B2.1 Exam-style questions and mark scheme: Supplying the cell

### Checkpoint follow-up lesson

A student's route through this lesson can be determined using the Checkpoint assessment. Percentage pass marks are supplied in the Checkpoint teacher notes.

For each successive route through it is assumed that the student can perform to their current route as well as previous routes. For example, students working at Aiming for 6 are assumed to be secure in Aiming for 4 knowledge and understanding and working towards achieving all the learning objectives for Aiming for 6.

# B2.1 Supplying the cell

|  | **Aiming for 4** | **Aiming for 6** | **Aiming for 8** |
|---|---|---|---|
| **Learning outcomes** | State what happens during diffusion, osmosis, and active transport. | Describe what happens during diffusion, osmosis, and active transport. | Explain what happens during diffusion, osmosis, and active transport. |
|  | State what mitosis is needed for. | Describe what occurs at each stage of the cell cycle. | Explain what occurs at each stage of the cell cycle. |
|  | State what occurs at each stage of the cell cycle. | Describe differences between animal and plant stem cells. | Explain differences between animal and plant stem cells. |
| **Starter** | **Demonstrating diffusion and osmosis (5 minutes)** Demonstrate some examples of diffusion and osmosis. Spray perfume, and show a potato tuber that has been in distilled water and one that has been in concentrated salt or sugar solution. Ask targeted questions, such as – what process is this? What is happening? How can we make it faster? | | |
| **Differentiated checkpoint activity** | **Activity 1 Transport of substances (10 minutes)** Students each answer question 1 about diffusion, osmosis, and active transport on the differentiated worksheets. They may use the Student book to check their understanding. | | |
|  | The Aiming for 4 activity sheet is highly structured for students to fill in the gaps to define diffusion, add arrows to labelled diagrams of osmosis, and answer true or false questions about active transport. | Aiming for 6 students are prompted to complete particle diagrams and write definitions of diffusion. They add arrows and label diagrams of osmosis, and write two ways in which active transport is different from diffusion and osmosis. | Aiming for 8 students draw detailed diagrams to explain the process of diffusion, and complete a data analysis exercise on osmosis. They will require a calculator. They write a paragraph about how active transport differs from diffusion and osmosis. |
|  | **Activity 2 Specialised cells (5 minutes)** Working in pairs or small groups, students name all the specialised cells they can remember in 2 minutes. Recap on the board and note which are plant cells and which are animal cells. | | |
|  | **Activity 3 The cell cycle (15 minutes)** Introduce the activity by showing a picture of skin with a graze or cut. Suitable images should be readily available on the Internet. Ask – what happens to the graze? How do we produce new skin? Are the new skin cells identical? Students then answer question 2 on the differentiated worksheets, drawing a flow chart to explain what happens in the cell cycle. The sheets provide progressive levels of support for Aiming for 4, 6, or 8 students. Students can complete the cell cycle in their books or on A3 paper. | | |
|  | Aiming for 4 students complete a structured table to compare differences between animal and plant stem cells using the Student book. | Aiming for 6 students draw a table to compare differences between animal and plant stem cells. They may require the Student book to help them. | Aiming for 8 students draw a table to compare differences between animal and plant stem cells. They may require the Student book to help them. |
|  | **Kerboodle resource:** B2.1 Checkpoint follow-up: Aiming for 4, B2.1 Checkpoint follow-up: Aiming for 6, B2.1 Checkpoint follow-up: Aiming for 8 | | |
| **Plenary** | **Cell transport and the cell cycle (10 minutes)** Students work in small groups, each group with three cards – one for diffusion, one for osmosis, and one for active transport. Read out statements about the movement of substances for students to show the appropriate card. Examples might include: needs ATP; is the movement of water. Provide targeted prompts to support students. | | |
|  | Then write the first stage of the cell cycle on the board. Choose students to come and add more until the cell cycle is complete. | | |
| **Progression** | Aiming for 4 activities comprise highly structured questions. Students may need a brief introduction from the teacher before tackling each question. Teachers will need to check student's answers or provide them with answers to check each other's work. A debate about the use of stem cells would be suitable for all abilities. | Aiming for 6 activities are reasonably structured. Teachers will need to check student's answers or provide them with answers to check each other's work. Question 3 may need a brief introduction from the teacher. | The Aiming for 8 activities have very little structure, including a data analysis question. Students should be able to complete all the activities without introduction from the teacher. Students can peer assess their work. More able students could find out why adding sugar to water lowers the water potential of the solution. They could be asked to make the link between rate of respiration and rate of active transport, and to recognise the difference between the rate of diffusion and the rate of active transport. |

# B2.2 The challenges of size
## B2.2.1 Exchange and transport

**Specification links:**

B2.2a Explain the need for exchange surfaces and a transport system in multicellular organisms in terms of surface area:volume ratio. To include surface area, volume and diffusion distances.

B2.2b Describe some of the substances transported into and out of a range of organisms in terms of the requirements of those organisms. To include oxygen, carbon dioxide, water, dissolved food molecules, mineral ions, and urea.

WS1.3e Interpret observations and other data.

WS1.4d Use prefixes and powers of ten for orders of magnitude.

WS1.4e Interconvert units.

WS1.4f Use an appropriate number of significant figures in calculation.

BM2.2i Calculate surface area:volume ratios (M1c).

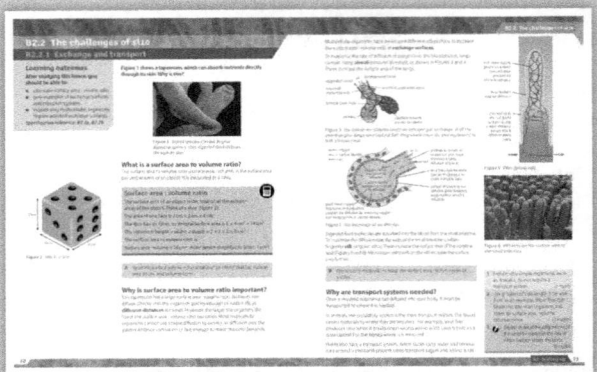

| Target | Outcome | Checkpoint | |
|---|---|---|---|
| | | Question | Activity |
| **Aiming for GRADE 4** | State some examples of exchange surfaces and transport systems. | | Plenary 1 and 2 |
| | Calculate the surface area or volume of an object. | 2 | Starter 1 and 2, Main |
| | Describe simple observations made during an experiment. | | Main |
| **Aiming for GRADE 6** | Describe the features of an efficient exchange surface. | B, 1, 3 | Plenary 1 and 2 |
| | Calculate the surface area : volume ratio. | A, 2 | Starter 1 and 2, Main |
| | Interpret observations and data made during an experiment. | | Main |
| **Aiming for GRADE 8** | Explain why multicellular organisms require adapted exchange surfaces. | 1 | Plenary 1 and 2 |
| | Compare the relationship between the surface area : volume ratio and the size of an organism or cell. | 2 | Starter 1 and 2, Main |
| | Interpret observations and data obtained during an experiment, identifying patterns and drawing conclusions. | | Main |

**Maths**
During the main activity, students will be expected to calculate surface area:volume ratios (M1c).

**Literacy**
During the main activity, students will be expected to produce coherent and well-structured responses to questions.

**Key words**
alveoli, diffusion distance, exchange surface, villi

72

## B2.2 The challenges of size

| Starter | Support/Extend | Resources |
|---|---|---|
| **Changing the surface area** (5 minutes)   Use a square biscuit, and calculate the surface area of the top and bottom. Then place the biscuit into a plastic bag and crush it. Spread the crumbs out in a tray and estimate the surface area. Ask students what has happened to the surface area as the size of the structures has decreased. | **Extend:** Ask students to link these observations to the amount of uptake in the two extremes. | |
| **Demonstrating surface area and volume** (10 minutes)   Use two wooden cubes, one small (1 cm³) and one larger, for example, 5 cm³. Ask class to help calculate the surface area. Then place the cube in a eureka can, and collect and measure the volume. These should give surface area : volume ratios close to those that could be calculated mathematically. | **Extend:** This can be done with a small and large plastic animal. To calculate surface area, ask students to draw around the shape on graph paper and count the number of squares. Use as many surfaces as possible. | |

| Main | Support/Extend | Resources |
|---|---|---|
| **Investigating efficient uptake by different-sized cells** (40 minutes)   Students cut cubes of gelatine of different sizes, 1 cm³, 2 cm³, 5 cm³. The gel will have been stained with universal indicator before the lesson.<br><br>They place these cubes into dilute hydrochloric acid for a fixed time, then remove, and slice through the middle. Students measure the depth into the cube that the colour has changed.<br><br>Students create a results table, which lists the side length, surface area, volume, and surface area : volume ratio. They observe the change of colour.<br><br>Questions to link to efficiency of exchange, and the need for the development of specialised exchange surfaces. | **Support:** Provide a blank results table for the students. Students only make observations of the extent of colour change.<br><br>**Extend:** Students measure the extent of colour change, calculate the proportion of change by working out the unchanged volume, and calculate this as a percentage. | **Practical:** Investigating efficient uptake by different-sized cells |

| Plenary | Support/Extend | Resources |
|---|---|---|
| **Surface area in the gut** (10 minutes)   Provide each student with a sheet of A4 and A5 paper. The A5 paper when rolled into a cylinder represents a small length of the gut. The students take the A4 paper and fold it concertina style, and then roll that up inside the tube. The students should recognise that a larger surface area caused by the foldings, which represent the villi, is present in the same length and diameter of tube. Ask students to suggest how this would increase the efficiency of uptake. | | |
| **Exchange and transport** (5 minutes)   Use the interactive in which students fill in the blanks in the sentences. The paragraph describes how oxygen moves from the air into the alveoli. | | **Interactive:** Exchange and transport |

| Homework | | |
|---|---|---|
| On an outline of a human body or a leaf, label the drawing with the name of a substance that moves into and out of the body or leaf, and describe how the exchange is achieved. | **Support:** Name the substances. | |

*kerboodle*
A Kerboodle highlight for this lesson is **Maths skills: Surface area: volume ratio**. Refer to the **Content map** on Kerboodle for a full list of resources and assessment.

# B2.2.2 Circulatory system

## Specification links:

**B2.2c** Describe the human circulatory system. To include the relationship with the gaseous exchange system, the need for a double circulatory system in mammals, and the arrangement of vessels.

**B2.2d** Explain how the structure of the heart and the blood vessels are adapted to their functions. To include the structure of the mammalian heart with reference to valves, chambers, cardiac muscle, and the structure of blood vessels with reference to thickness of walls, diameter of lumen, presence of valves.

**WS1.4a** Use scientific vocabulary, terminology, and definitions.

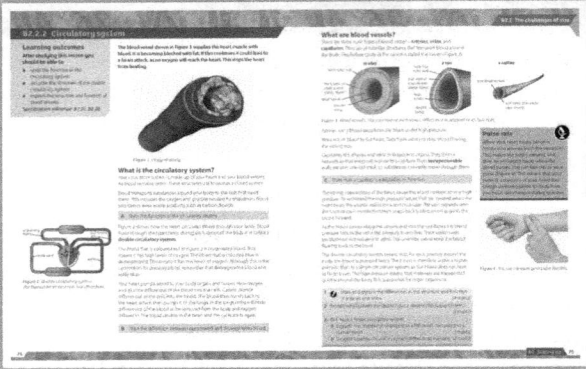

| Target | Outcome | Checkpoint | |
|---|---|---|---|
| | | Question | Activity |
| **Aiming for GRADE 4** ↓ | State the function of the circulatory system. | A | Starter 1<br>Main<br>Plenary 2 |
| | Name the different types of blood vessels found in a circulatory system. | | Starter 2<br>Main<br>Plenary 1 and 2 |
| | Use familiar vocabulary to some effect to describe the circulatory system. | | Starter 1 and 2<br>Main |
| **Aiming for GRADE 6** ↓ | Describe the structure of the double circulatory system. | 3 | Main |
| | Describe the structure of the blood vessels. | C, 1 | Main<br>Plenary 1 and 2 |
| | Use vocabulary appropriate to purpose and effect to describe the structure of the circulatory system. | | Main |
| **Aiming for GRADE 8** ↓ | Explain the need for a double circulatory system in mammals. | 2, 3 | Main |
| | Explain the link between the structure and function of the different types of blood vessels. | 1 | Main<br>Plenary 1 |
| | Use a wide range of well-selected and precise vocabulary to enhance impact when explaining the functioning of the circulatory system. | | Main |

### Literacy
During the main task, students are asked to communicate information about the structure and function of the circulatory system. To do this they will need to use appropriate scientific vocabulary.

### Key words
artery, capillary, double circulatory system, heart, semipermeable, vein

# B2.2 The challenges of size

| Starter | Support/Extend | Resources |
|---|---|---|
| **Parts of the circulatory system** (10 minutes) Issue sets of nine cards to pairs of students. The students have to sort the cards into three sets. Each set contains the name of a component of a circulatory system, the human/mammal example, and the function.<br>Cards:<br>Pump, heart, causes the blood to move, tubes, blood vessels, takes the fluid to and from the organs, fluid, blood, contains substances and is moved around the body.<br>**Circulation role play** (5 minutes) The teacher plays the part of the heart. At the opposite side of the class will be a group of about six students who are muscle cells. A second group of students act as blood. The teacher directs the students to walk clockwise around the room, from teacher to the muscle and back. Introduce the idea of circulation. Repeat, but this time students hold up cards with the name artery, capillary, and vein at the correct position. | **Support:** Could have three colours, one for component, one for the human example, one for the function. Tell students that they need one of each colour in each statement.<br><br>**Extend:** Remove the human example and ask students to insert this.<br>**Extend:** Have a figure of eight movement and introduce lungs into the circulation. | |

| Main | Support/Extend | Resources |
|---|---|---|
| **Exploring circulation** (40 minutes) Divide the class into groups of eight, and subdivide these groups into pairs. Within the group of eight, each pair is given the task to research a section of the circulatory system. (15 minutes)<br>1. What happens in the right side of the heart (no details of heart are needed), focusing on the veins in and arteries out?<br>2. What happens in the lungs?<br>3. What happens in the left side of the heart?<br>4. What happens in the tissues, including details of the capillaries?<br>The groups of eight then reform and pool their information around a diagram of the human circulatory system. (10 minutes)<br>Then give each student their own diagram of the human circulatory system. Students annotate their diagrams to cover the points they have learnt, including the following: the function of the circulatory system, how blood circulates, different types of blood vessels, oxygenated and deoxygenated blood. (20 minutes) | **Support:** Provide a scaffold, for example, name the blood vessels, type of blood, etc.; students describe the blood vessel structure, and process that might occur; explain what is happening and link to description.<br><br>**Extend:** Ask students to find out about, and explain, the need for a double circulatory system in mammals. | **Activity:** Exploring circulation |

| Plenary | Support/Extend | Resources |
|---|---|---|
| **Features of blood vessels** (5 minutes) Use the interactive in which students drag and drop descriptions about blood vessels into the correct blood vessel category.<br>**Discovering circulation** (10 minutes) Show the class an image of one of Harvey's classic experiments providing evidence for the circulation of the blood. Give a brief description of what Harvey did, and ask students to explain what has happened. You can demonstrate this using a blood vessel in your hand/arm (no need to use a tourniquet). | **Support:** Use the demonstration in the hand/arm rather than Harvey images. | **Interactive:** Features of blood vessels |

| Homework |
|---|
| **First Aid** You are teaching a group of students basic first aid. You need to produce a leaflet or PowerPoint presentation to describe the difference observed if a patient has cut an artery or a vein. You need to include an explanation of why there would be a difference. |

**kerboodle**
A Kerboodle highlight for this lesson is **Extension: Blood vessels**. Refer to the **Content map** on Kerboodle for a full list of resources and assessment.

The Practical Skills lesson for PAG 6 Physiology, responses, respiration could follow this lesson.

# B2.2.3 Heart and blood

**Specification links:**

B2.2d Explain how the structure of the heart and the blood vessels are adapted to their functions. To include the structure of the mammalian heart with reference to valves, chambers, cardiac muscle; and the structure of blood vessels with reference to thickness of walls, diameter of lumen, presence of valves.

B2.2e Explain how red blood cells and plasma are adapted to their transport functions in the blood.

WS1.4a Use scientific vocabulary, terminology, and definitions.

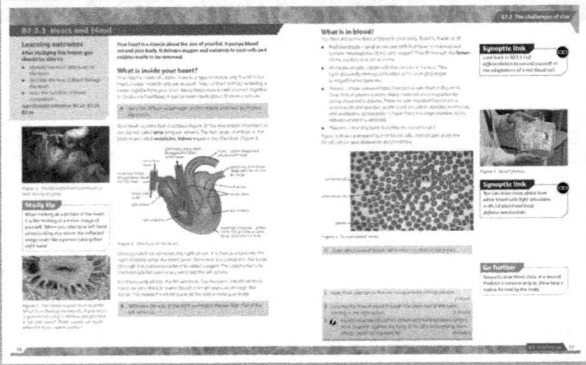

| Target | Outcome | Checkpoint | |
|---|---|---|---|
| | | Question | Activity |
| **Aiming for GRADE 4** | Identify the components of the blood. | C | Starter 1 and 2<br>Main 1 |
| | Identify the main structures in the heart. | A, 2 | Main 2<br>Plenary 1 and 2 |
| | State the names of the major parts of the heart and blood. | 2 | Starter 1<br>Main 1 and 2<br>Plenary 1 and 2 |
| **Aiming for GRADE 6** | Describe the functions of the main components of the blood. | 1, 3 | Starter 2<br>Main 1 |
| | Describe the flow of blood through the heart. | B, 2 | Main 2<br>Plenary 1 and 2 |
| | Use the correct names of the parts of the heart and blood when describing their function. | | Starter 1 and 2<br>Main 1 and 2<br>Plenary 1 and 2 |
| **Aiming for GRADE 8** | Explain the adaptations of the red blood cell that enable it to carry out its function. | | Starter 2<br>Main 1 |
| | Explain how the thickness of the chambers of the heart are related to their function. | B | Main 2 |
| | Use an appropriate range of scientific vocabulary and terminology when explaining the functions of the blood and heart. | | Main 1 and 2 |

**Literacy**

During the Main tasks, students will be required to make their own comments about the blood and heart. This will require the use of appropriate scientific vocabulary.

**Key words**

lumen

# B2.2 The challenges of size

| Starter | Support/Extend | Resources |
|---|---|---|
| **What can you see in blood?** (5 minutes) Show an image of a blood smear, either by projecting it onto a screen directly from a microscope or from the internet. Ask students to identify the types of cell they can see, and their names. Ask the name of the liquid the cells are suspended in. | | |
| **Functions of the blood** (10 minutes) Write a series of questions on cards and place them in envelopes. Divide the class into groups, and give each group a complete set of the questions. Give them 4–5 minutes to discuss the questions and suggest answers. Then ask groups to offer their answers. Discuss feedback.<br>Questions:<br>Why does the blood need to be a liquid?<br>Why does the blood contain different components?<br>Why should the plasma be a good solvent?<br>What is haemoglobin for? | **Extend:** You may wish to demonstrate the fact that blood contains solids in a liquid, by placing animal blood from a piece of tissue in a centrifuge and spinning it until it separates. | |

| Main | Support/Extend | Resources |
|---|---|---|
| **The blood** (15 minutes) Tell students that red blood cells and plasma are involved in transport. Students model a red blood cell out of modelling clay and discuss how it is adapted to transport oxygen efficiently (large surface area, small size, contains haemoglobin). Quickly describe plasma as a liquid able to carry soluble substances. Create a table, linking the adaptations of plasma and red blood cells to their functions. | **Support:** Have models of red blood cells ready-made. Create a table for the students, which they complete. | |
| **Heart dissection** (25 minutes) This can be done as a demonstration or grouped practical. Students should draw a simplified and labelled diagram of the heart from viewing the dissection. Students who do not wish to be involved with the practical due to religious or moral objections can complete the questions on the corresponding Student Book spread then complete the Bump up your grade worksheet to understand the role of valves in controlling the direction of the blood flow in the heart. The information for this should come from the teacher-led dissection. | **Extend:** Ask students to annotate the diagram to explain the thicknesses of the walls, the role of the valves, role of the coronary artery, etc. | **Practical:** Sheep heart dissection |

| Plenary | Support/Extend | Resources |
|---|---|---|
| **Functions of the parts of the heart** (5 minutes) Use the interactive to get students to label a diagram of the heart and then match up blood vessels to the correct function. | | **Interactive:** Heart and blood |
| **Cardiology ward** (10 minutes) Divide the class into groups of six. Each group splits into pairs that quickly research one of three heart conditions. They explain to the rest of the group what the condition is and how it affects the basic functioning of the heart. Suggested conditions: heart attack, hole in the heart, and valve failure. | **Extend:** Introduce angina and ask students to explain the difference between angina and a heart attack. | |

| Homework | | |
|---|---|---|
| You work in a cardiology ward. You are writing an information leaflet for patients with heart conditions. Write a description of the flow of blood through the heart. Select any one heart condition suggested in Plenary 2 and explain how it affects the functioning of the heart. | | |

*kerboodle*

A Kerboodle highlight for this lesson is **Bump up your grade: Valves and blood flow**. Refer to the **Content map** on Kerboodle for a full list of resources and assessment.

# B2.2.4 Plant transport systems

**Specification links:**

B2.2g Describe the processes of transpiration and translocation. To include the structure and function of the stomata.

B2.2h Explain how the structure of the xylem and phloem are adapted to their functions in the plant.

WS1.4a Use scientific vocabulary, terminology, and definitions.

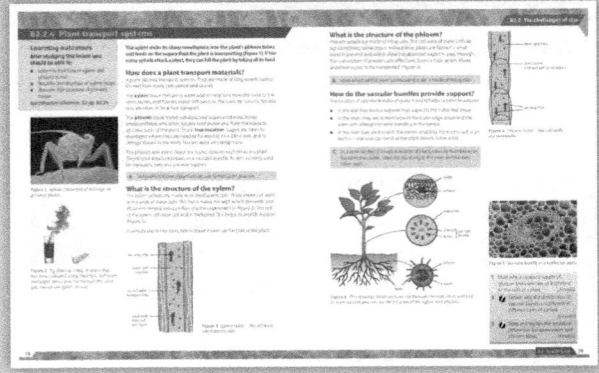

| Target | Outcome | Checkpoint | |
|---|---|---|---|
| | | Question | Activity |
| **Aiming for GRADE 4** ↓ | State the function of xylem. | 1 | Starter 1 and 2<br>Main 1<br>Plenary 1 and 2 |
| | State the function of phloem. | A, 1 | Starter 1 and 2<br>Main 2<br>Plenary 1 and 2 |
| | Label diagrams using simple sentence structure and familiar vocabulary. | | Main 1 and 2 |
| **Aiming for GRADE 6** ↓ | Describe the function and distribution of xylem tissue. | C | Starter 1<br>Main 1<br>Plenary 1 and 2 |
| | Describe the function and distribution of phloem tissue. | B, C | Starter 1<br>Main 2<br>Plenary 1 and 2 |
| | Annotate diagrams using varied sentence types and appropriate scientific vocabulary. | | Main 1 and 2 |
| **Aiming for GRADE 8** ↓ | Explain how the structure and distribution of xylem tissue is related to its function. | 2, 3 | Main 1<br>Plenary 1 and 2 |
| | Explain how the structure and distribution of phloem tissue is related to its function. | 2, 3 | Main 2<br>Plenary 1 and 2 |
| | Annotate diagrams using a wide range of sentence types, including precise and appropriate scientific vocabulary. | | Main 1 and 2 |

**Literacy**

During the main activity, students will be expected to produce coherent notes to annotate a diagram, using appropriate scientific vocabulary.

**Key words**

phloem, translocation, xylem

# B2.2 The challenges of size

| Starter | Support/Extend | Resources |
|---|---|---|
| **Demonstrate uptake of water** (10 minutes)   Have prepared a cutting of celery or a Busy Lizzy, standing in coloured water. Demonstrate the set-up of this experiment, then remove the prepared sample, and cut the stem a little way up to show that the coloured dye has moved into the stem – but only in the vascular bundles. Name the cell types involved and the process shown. Then remind students about photosynthesis and ask them how sugars would be transported to the roots. Name the phloem and the process. | | |
| **Features of xylem and phloem** (5 minutes)   Use the interactive in which students type in answers to complete sentences about xylem and phloem, and then sort statements into whether they describe xylem or phloem. | | **Interactive:** Plant transport systems |

| Main | Support/Extend | Resources |
|---|---|---|
| **Movement through the xylem** (20 minutes)   Supply students with celery sticks that have been left overnight in ink. They cut the sticks to see how the dye has stained the xylem walls. Students then answer a series of questions on the structure and function of xylem that review knowledge of specialised cells, and draw an annotated diagram of xylem tissue. | **Extend:** Students can suggest how celery left in ink could be used to measure the rate of flow of water up a stem, for example, by measuring how far up the ink has reached in four hours. | **Practical:** Movement through the xylem |
| **Transport in the phloem** (20 minutes)   Show the class a video that shows how sap is tapped from trees in order to make maple syrup. Discuss with the class where the sugars in the tree trunk (stem) come from and how they are transported, or translocated, in the phloem. Ask students to explain how phloem cells are adapted for their function and to draw an annotated diagram of phloem tissue. | | |

| Plenary | Support/Extend | Resources |
|---|---|---|
| **Plant transport game** (10 minutes)   Divide the class in half. Select a student from one half who names a feature about the structure or distribution of xylem or phloem that helps it function. They select a student from the other team to give a reason why the feature helps. If the second student gets the answer correct they can then ask the next question. And so on. | | |
| **Four words** (5 minutes)   Issue mini white boards. Ask a series of questions to which there are only four possible answers, xylem, phloem, transpiration, or translocation. Students write the answer to each question on the white board. | **Extend:** Ask students to explain why they have selected the answer. | |

| Homework | | |
|---|---|---|
| Design a web page for an online revision course. The page should show the distribution of xylem and phloem in a stem and root. The web page should have some way (e.g. hyperlinks) to link to other websites (which do not need to be developed), in order to explain the function of the tissues. | | |

# B2.2.5 Transpiration stream

**Specification links:**

B2.2f Explain how water and mineral ions are taken up by plants, relating the structure of the root hair cells to their function.

B2.2g Describe the processes of transpiration and translocation. To include the structure and function of the stomata.

WS1.3f Present reasoned explanations.

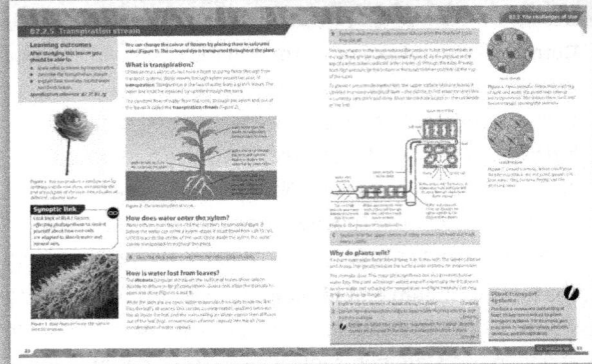

| Target | Outcome | Checkpoint | |
|---|---|---|---|
| | | Question | Activity |
| **Aiming for GRADE 4** ↓ | State what is meant by transpiration. | 1 | Main 2<br>Plenary 2 |
| | State the location of most stomata in a plant. | | Starter 1<br>Main 2<br>Plenary 1 |
| | Describe the observations made during each experiment. | | Main 1 and 2 |
| **Aiming for GRADE 6** ↓ | Describe the transpiration stream. | A, 1 | Starter 2<br>Main 2<br>Plenary 1 and 2 |
| | Describe the structure of a stoma. | | Starter 1 and 2<br>Main 2 |
| | Explain the observations made during each experiment. | | Main 1 and 2 |
| **Aiming for GRADE 8** ↓ | Explain the mechanisms by which water is moved through the plant. | B, 2 | Main 1 and 2<br>Plenary 1 and 2 |
| | Explain how stomata control water loss from leaves. | C, 3 | Main 2 |
| | Relate the findings of both experiments to one another, to explain how water is lost from the plant. | | Main 1 and 2 |

**Maths**
During the main task, students will need to record data to an appropriate number of significant figures (M2a).

**Literacy**
During the main task, students will need to produce explanations using coherent, well-structured sentences.

**Key words**
stomata, transpiration, transpiration stream

## B2.2 The challenges of size

| Starter | Support/Extend | Resources |
|---|---|---|
| **Balloon stoma** (5 minutes) Inflate two long, thin balloons (but do not knot them), to represent guard cells. Place a length of sticky tape along one edge. The two taped edges should be lined up as the inner edge of the stoma. Blow a small amount of extra air into both balloons – they will curve, causing the stoma to open. Demonstrate this as explaining the situation in the leaf.<br>**Cells for the job** (10 minutes) Give each group in the class an outline drawing of a root hair cell (and possibly a xylem cell). Ask them to add labels to the diagram to suggest how the cell is adapted and what it does. | **Extend:** Provide a drawing of a stoma, and ask students to label this structure and explain how it might work. | |

| Main | Support/Extend | Resources |
|---|---|---|
| **Weight potometer** (15 minutes) Follow a suitable method to set up a weight potometer. Use a potometer with a plant and one without a plant as the control. Record the initial weight of each set-up. Students predict the outcome. Either have results from a previously set-up experiment, or collect the results at the start of the next lesson.<br>Questions focus on uptake by roots and transport of water through the plant, and connect to previous lessons. | **Extend:** Ask the students to consider the concept of control experiments in a conclusion. | |
| **Investigating stomata** (25 minutes) Demonstrate how you can carry out an epidermal peel to view stomata under the microscope. Ask students to discuss in small groups what you could investigate about the stomata using this method and how they would do so. Examples include comparing the number of stomata on different types of plant, different leaves on one plant, and different areas of the leaf. Discuss the use of sampling to study different leaves and different areas on the leaf. Students then carry out the practical in small groups. They count the number of stomata in several fields of view before calculating a mean and writing a conclusion. | **Support:** Students can just count the number of stomata they can see in the field of view.<br>**Support:** Students can practise the skill by completing the Calculation sheet.<br>**Extend:** Students can calculate the area of the field of view to estimate the number of stomata on the whole leaf. | **Practical:** Investigating stomata |

| Plenary | Support/Extend | Resources |
|---|---|---|
| **Taking a cutting** (10 minutes) Demonstrate taking a cutting from a plant like a geranium. Emphasise that the plant has lost its roots. Then, break off the lower leaves and place the cutting into wet soil. Ask students to explain the importance or significance of each of these points.<br>**Transpiration stream** (5 minutes) Use the interactive to place a series of statements, which give the sequence of events in the transpiration stream, into the correct order. | **Support:** Pick up key words for each step to guide their thinking. | **Interactive:** Transpiration stream |

| Homework | | |
|---|---|---|
| **Recycling in the rainforest** There is high humidity in the canopy of the rainforest, which leads to condensation of water, which runs into the soil. A scientist claimed that this water was constantly being recycled through the trees. Describe and explain how transpiration could recycle the water. | | |

**kerboodle**

A Kerboodle highlight for this lesson is **Calculation sheet: Transpiration data**. Refer to the **Content map** on Kerboodle for a full list of resources and assessment.

# B2.2.6 Factors affecting transpiration

**Specification links:**

B2.2i Explain the effect of a variety of environmental factors on the rate of water uptake by a plant. To include light intensity, air movement, and temperature.

B2.2j Describe how a simple potometer can be used to investigate factors that affect the rate of water uptake.

WS1.2c Apply a knowledge of a range of techniques, instruments, apparatus, and materials to select those appropriate to the experiment.

WS1.2e Evaluate methods, and suggest possible improvements and further investigations.

WS1.3a Present observations and other data using appropriate methods.

WS1.3b Translate data from one form to another.

WS1.3c Carry out and represent mathematical and statistical analysis.

WS1.3d Represent distributions of results and make estimations of uncertainty.

WS1.3e Interpret observations and other data.

WS1.3f Present reasoned explanations.

WS1.3g Evaluate data in terms of accuracy, precision, repeatability, and reproducibility.

WS2a Carry out experiments.

WS2b Make and record observations and measurements using a range of apparatus and methods.

BM2.2ii Use simple compound measures, such as rate (M1a, M1c).

BM2.2iii Carry out rate calculations (M1a, M1c).

BM2.2iv Plot, draw, and interpret appropriate graphs (M4a, M4b, M4c, M4d).

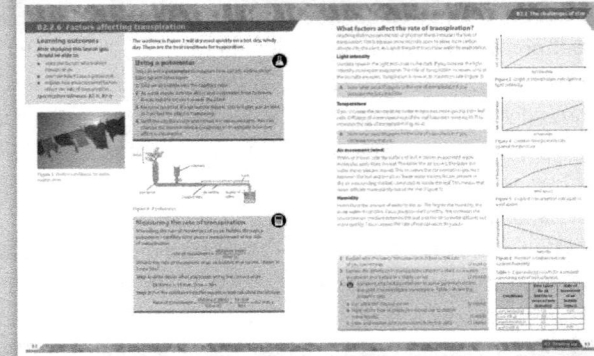

| Target | Outcome | Checkpoint | |
|---|---|---|---|
| | | Question | Activity |
| **Aiming for GRADE 4** | State the factors that affect the rate of transpiration. | A, B, C | Starter 1 and 2<br>Main<br>Plenary 2 |
| | State what a potometer measures. | 2 | Main |
| | State a limitation found with the method. | | Main<br>Plenary 1 |
| **Aiming for GRADE 6** | Describe the relationship between a given factor and the rate of transpiration. | A, B, C | Starter 1 and 2<br>Main<br>Plenary 2 |
| | Describe how to use a potometer. | | Main<br>Plenary 1 |
| | Discuss a range of limitations with this method, which might affect the results. | | Main<br>Plenary 1 |
| **Aiming for GRADE 8** | Explain how environmental factors affect the rate of transpiration. | 1, 2, 3 | Main<br>Plenary 2 |
| | Explain how to calculate the rate of transpiration using a potometer. | 3 | Main |
| | Discuss a range of limitations with this method, which might affect the results, suggesting a series of improvements. | | Main<br>Plenary 1 |

# B2.2 The challenges of size

**Maths**
During the Main task, students will collect data and use the data to calculate the rate of transpiration. They may calculate a mean value of their data, and their calculations of means (M2b) and rates should be to an appropriate number of significant figures (M2a). Students will then plot two variables from experimental data.

**Literacy**
During the main activity, students will need to use coherent well-structured sentences to explain their findings and evaluate the method.

**Key words**
potometer

| Starter | Support/Extend | Resources |
|---|---|---|
| **Affecting the rate** (10 minutes)  Provide the student groups with a set of six cards with terms written on them (sunny day, dull day, windy day, still day, warm day, and cold day). Students sort the cards into two groups, showing which conditions would produce rapid transpiration and which would lead to slow transpiration. Name the three factors. | **Extend:** Suggest an explanation for their decisions for each condition. | |
| **Environments** (5 minutes)  Hold up a card with the title of a type of environment (for example, desert, sand dune, woodland, school field, tropical rainforest). Ask students to say which environment has the fastest/slowest rate of transpiration. Ask them to state the factor that leads them to their decision. | **Extend:** Explain why they think the factor would have that effect. | |

| Main | Support/Extend | Resources |
|---|---|---|
| **Factors affecting transpiration** (40 minutes)  Explain to students that the rate of evaporation increases as the temperature increases, humidity decreases, and air flow increases. Demonstrate how a mass potometer and a moving bubble potometer can be used to measure the uptake of water by the plant. Discuss how leaving the equipment in different conditions would affect the rate of water uptake and why. Mention why light intensity increases rate of transpiration (it does not affect evaporation). Ask students to draw diagrams of the equipment and to describe briefly how they work. Students then make a prediction and plan a fair test to investigate one of the factors that affects the movement of water through a plant by transpiration. | **Support:** Help with the set-up of the potometer, or have them already set up.  Provide a results table outline and the axes of the graph.  **Extend:** Use a range of different distances between the potometer and the hair drier. This will allow students to plot a line graph. | **Activity:** Factors affecting transpiration |

| Plenary | Support/Extend | Resources |
|---|---|---|
| **Evaluating the potometer** (10 minutes)  Show an image of the potometer set-up on the board. Ask students to list any limitations they found with the experiment. Ask them to explain why they found this to be a limitation. Did it affect the results? | **Extend:** Suggest improvements that might eliminate some of the limitations. | |
| **Factors affecting transpiration** (5 minutes)  Use the interactive in which students link statements about transpiration with the correct explanation. | | **Interactive:** Factors affecting transpiration |

| Homework | Support/Extend | Resources |
|---|---|---|
| **Florists** Consider the ideal conditions in a florist shop. Describe the relationship between each condition and the health of the cut flowers, that is, reduced transpiration (no wilting). | **Extend:** Explain why people should cut the base off cut flowers after they have transported them home. | |

*kerboodle*
A Kerboodle highlight for this lesson is **Calculation sheet: Pie charts of gases**. Refer to the **Content map** on Kerboodle for a full list of resources and assessment.

# Checkpoint
## B2.2 The challenges of size

### Overview of B2.2 The challenges of size

In this chapter, students have studied exchange and transport in organisms. They should understand the need for multicellular organisms to have specialised exchange surfaces and transport systems. They should be able to calculate surface area : volume ratios and be able to cite the alveoli and villi as two examples of increasing the surface area for exchange. Students should link this with work on diffusion in B2.1 *Supplying the cell*, and with respiration in B1.3 *Respiration*, and understand that exchange surfaces and transport systems are needed to provide glucose and oxygen to all cells so that they can respire. Students should appreciate the distinction between the size of an organism and the surface area : volume ratio of an organism or exchange surface. They should understand that the alveolus wall is one cell thick, and be able to distinguish between the alveolus wall and the cell wall of a plant cell.

Students have studied the circulatory system, including the double circulatory system, the functioning of the heart, and the different types of blood vessel, focusing on their structure and function. They should understand that the large network of capillaries gives them a large total cross-sectional area. They should be able to state the components of blood, and link this with specialised cells from B2.1 *Supplying the cell*.

Students have also studied plant transport systems, and should be familiar with the structure of xylem and phloem tissue, and the processes of transpiration and translocation. They should be aware that liquid water does not diffuse out of the stomata, as water evaporates within the leaf into water vapour. Again there are links with B2.1 *Supplying the cell*, which covered the root hair cell as an example of a specialised cell and the role of active transport in transporting mineral ions into the root hair cell.

You can find additional support for the maths skills covered in this chapter on **MyMaths**, including calculating surface area : volume ratios and calculating to an appropriate number of significant figures.

### PAGs

All students are expected to have carried out the PAG *6 Physiology, responses, and respiration*. A full lesson plan for each PAG is provided in the Practical skills chapter. PAG *6 Physiology, responses and respiration* should be completed after lesson B2.2.2 *Circulatory system*.

For this chapter, the following assessments are available on Kerboodle:
B2.2 Checkpoint quiz: The challenges of size
B2.2 Progress quiz: The challenges of size 1
B2.2 Progress quiz: The challenges of size 2
B2.2 On your marks: The challenges of size
B2.2 Exam-style questions and mark scheme: The challenges of size

# B2.2 The challenges of size

# Checkpoint follow-up lesson

A student's route through this lesson can be determined using the Checkpoint assessment. Percentage pass marks are supplied in the Checkpoint teacher notes.

For each successive route through it is assumed that the student can perform to their current route as well as previous routes. For example, students working at Aiming for 6 are assumed to be secure in Aiming for 4 knowledge and understanding and working towards achieving all the learning objectives for Aiming for 6.

| | Aiming for 4 | Aiming for 6 | Aiming for 8 |
|---|---|---|---|
| **Learning outcomes** | State the names of parts of the heart. | State the names of parts of the heart. | Describe the functions of parts of the heart. |
| | Give the names of the blood vessels. | Describe the structure and function of the blood vessels. | Explain how the structure of the blood vessels is related to their functions. |
| | State the factors that affect transpiration. | Describe the factors that affect transpiration. | Explain how factors affect transpiration. |
| | State how light intensity affects transpiration. | Describe how light intensity affects transpiration. | Explain how light intensity affects transpiration. |
| **Starter** | **Dissecting the heart (10 minutes)** Demonstrate the dissection of a heart. You will need a sheep's heart and dissection instruments. Ask targeted questions to review the names and functions of parts of the heart and blood vessels. | | |
| **Differentiated checkpoint activity** | **Activity 1 The heart and blood vessels (20 minutes)** Students each answer question 1 about the circulatory system on the differentiated worksheets. You may need to set time limits to ensure that students move on to the next part question. | | |
| | Introduce Aiming for 4 students to the task. They first complete a labelling activity on the heart, in pairs or individually. They will need a glue stick and scissors. Students may need help from the teacher or access to the Student book. They then complete a table comparing different types of blood vessel. They will need diagrams of an artery, a vein, and a capillary. | Aiming for 6 students should be able to start this activity without an introduction, but may need access to the Student book. This activity can be carried out in pairs or individually. Students write labels on a diagram of the heart, and make a table to compare different types of blood vessel. They will need diagrams of an artery, a vein, and a capillary. | Aiming for 8 students should be able to be complete the activity without introduction from the teacher. Students work individually but will need access to the Student book. They describe the pathway of blood as it travels around the body. |
| | **Activity 2 Transpiration (20 minutes)** First demonstrate a potometer. Ask targeted questions – what is this used to measure? What factors will affect the movement of water? Working in pairs or small groups, students then answer question 2 on the differentiated worksheets. | | |
| | The Aiming for 4 activity comprises data analysis on the effect of light intensity on the rate of transpiration. Students will need graph paper, rulers, and pencils. For those needing extra support, the axis can be already drawn on graph paper. Students should need minimal instruction but the teacher should review the answers. | Aiming for 6 students can work in pairs or small groups. They should be able to start this activity without guidance from the teacher. Students plan an investigation about the effect of light intensity on the rate of transpiration, using headings provided on the sheet. They write a prediction and consider other factors that might affect the investigation. | Aiming for 8 students can work in pairs or small groups. Students plan an investigation about the effect of light intensity on the rate of transpiration. They write a prediction and consider other factors that might affect the investigation. An evaluation of why a potometer only estimates transpiration rate would be a good extension activity. |
| | **Kerboodle resource:** B2.2 Checkpoint follow-up: Aiming for 4, B2.2 Checkpoint follow-up: Aiming for 6, B2.2 Checkpoint follow-up: Aiming for 8 | | |
| **Plenary** | **Blood vessels and rate of transpiration (5 minutes)** Show pictures of blood vessels and ask students to name them. Suitable pictures should be readily available on the Internet. Then give each student two cards of different colours. Say a range of different environmental stimuli, such as increasing temperature. Ask students to raise one coloured card if the factor will increase the rate of transpiration in plants, and another colour if it will decrease it. | | |
| **Progression** | The Aiming for 4 activities are highly structured, though students may need some guidance. Students may need to be reminded of the parts of the heart and blood vessels and their functions, and may need extra guidance to complete the sheet. | The Aiming for 6 activities about the heart and blood vessels are reasonably structured. | The Aiming for 8 activities about the pathway of blood around the body and factors affecting transpiration have very little structure. Aiming for 8 students could go on to compare the differences between a single and double circulatory system. |

# B2 Scaling up: Topic summary

B2.1 Supplying the cell
B2.2 The challenges of size

| Spec ref | Statement | Book spreads |
|---|---|---|
| B2.1a | Explain how substances are transported into and out of cells through diffusion, osmosis and active transport | B2.1.1, B2.1.2, B2.1.3 |
| B2.1b | describe the process of mitosis in growth, including the cell cycle | B2.1.4 |
| B2.1c | Explain the importance of cell differentiation | B2.1.5 |
| B2.1d | Recall that stem cells are present in embryonic and adult animals and meristems in plants | B2.1.6 |
| B2.1e | Describe the functions of stem cells | B2.1.6 |
| B2.1f | Describe the difference between embryonic and adult stem cells in animals | B2.1.6 |
| B2.2a | Explain the need for exchange surfaces and a transport system in multicellular organisms in terms of surface area : volume ratio | B2.2.1 |
| B2.2b | Describe some of the substances transported into and out of a range of organisms in terms of the requirements of those organisms | B2.2.1 |
| B2.2c | Describe the human circulatory system | B2.2.2 |
| B2.2d | Explain how the structure of the heart and the blood vessels are adapted to their functions | B2.2.2, B2.2.3 |
| B2.2e | Explain how red blood cells and plasma are adapted to their transport functions in the blood | B2.2.3 |
| B2.2f | Explain how water and mineral ions are taken up by plants, relating the structure of the root hair cells to their function | B2.2.5 |
| B2.2g | Describe the processes of transpiration and translocation | B2.2.4, B2.2.5 |
| B2.2h | Explain how the structure of the xylem and phloem are adapted to their functions in the plant | B2.2.4 |
| B2.2i | Explain the effect of a variety of environmental factors on the rate of water uptake by a plant | B2.2.6 |
| B2.2j | Describe how a simple potometer can be used to investigate factors that affect the rate of water uptake | B2.2.6 |

## Maths

| Specification | | Book spread | |
|---|---|---|---|
| Spec ref | Statement | Main content | Maths chapter |
| BM2.1i | Use percentiles and calculate percentage gain and loss of mass | B2.1.2 | 3 |
| BM2.2i | Calculate surface area : volume ratios | B2.2.1 | 3, 15 |
| BM2.2ii | Use simple compound measures such as rate | B2.2.6 | 14 |
| BM2.2iii | Carry out rate calculations | B2.2.6 | 14 |
| BM2.2iv | Plot, draw and interpret appropriate graphs | B2.2.6 | 13, 14 |

## Working scientifically

| Specification | | Book spread | |
|---|---|---|---|
| Spec ref | Statement | Main content | WS chapter |
| WS1.1b | Use models to solve problems, make predictions, and to develop scientific explanations and understanding of familiar and unfamiliar facts. | B2.1.1, B2.1.3, B2.1.4 | WS2 |
| WS1.1e | Explain everyday and technological applications of science. | B2.1.6 | WS1 |
| WS1.1f | Evaluate associated personal, social, economic, and environmental implications. | B2.1.6 | WS1 |
| WS1.1h | Evaluate risks both in practical science and the wider societal context. | B2.1.6 | WS1, WS4 |
| WS1.2c | Apply a knowledge of a range of techniques, instruments, apparatus, and materials to select those appropriate to the experiment. | B2.2.6 | |
| WS1.2e | Evaluate methods, and suggest possible improvements and further investigations. | B2.2.6 | |
| WS1.3a | Presenting observations and other data using appropriate methods. | B2.1.2, B2.1.5, B2.2.6 | WS6 |
| WS1.3b | Translating data from one form to another. | B2.2.6 | WS6 |
| WS1.3c | Carrying out and representing mathematical and statistical analysis. | B2.2.6 | WS5 |
| WS1.3d | Representing distributions of results and make estimations of uncertainty. | B2.2.6 | WS8 |
| WS1.3e | Interpreting observations and other data. | B2.2.1, B2.2.6 | WS7 |
| WS1.3f | Presenting reasoned explanations. | B2.2.5, B2.2.6 | WS7 |
| WS1.3g | Evaluating data in terms of accuracy, precision, repeatability, and reproducibility. | B2.2.6, B2.2.6 | WS5, WS7 |
| WS1.4a | Use scientific vocabulary, terminology, and definitions. | B2.2.2, B2.2.3, B2.2.4 | WS2 |
| WS1.4d | Use prefixes and powers of ten for orders of magnitude. | B2.2.1 | |
| WS1.4e | Interconvert units. | B2.2.1 | |
| WS1.4f | Use an appropriate number of significant figures in calculation. | B2.2.1 | |
| WS2a | Carry out experiments. | B2.2.6 | |
| WS2b | Make and record observations and measurements using a range of apparatus and methods. | B2.2.6 | |

# B3 Organism-level systems
## B3.1 The nervous system
### B3.1.1 Nervous system

**Specification links:**

B3.1a Describe the structure of the nervous system. To include Central Nervous System, sensory and motor neurones, and sensory receptors.

B3.1b Explain how the components of the nervous system can produce a coordinated response. To include that it goes to all parts of the body, has many links, has different sensory receptors, and is able to coordinate responses.

WS1.3c Carry out and represent mathematical and statistical analysis.

WS1.3f Present reasoned explanations.

WS1.3h Identify potential sources of random and systematic error.

WS2a Carry out experiments.

WS2b Make and record observations and measurements using a range of apparatus and methods.

WS2c Present observations using appropriate methods.

WS2d Communicate the scientific rationale for investigations, methods used, findings, and reasoned conclusions.

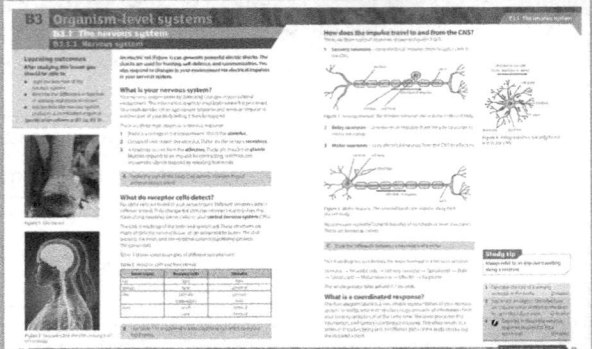

| Target | Outcome | Checkpoint | |
|---|---|---|---|
| | | Question | Activity |
| Aiming for GRADE 4 | State the function of the nervous system. | A | Starter 1 and 2, Plenary 2 |
| | State the difference between a nerve and a neurone. | C | Plenary 2 |
| | State that the reaction time measured is controlled by the nervous system. | | Main |
| Aiming for GRADE 6 | Describe the pathway taken by an impulse in a nervous reaction. | B, 1, 2 | Starter 2, Main, Plenary 1 and 2 |
| | Describe the different types of neurone in the nervous system. | 1 | Starter 1 and 2, Main, Plenary 1 and 2 |
| | Identify reasons for reaction times measured, by describing the pathway taken by the impulse. | | Main |
| Aiming for GRADE 8 | Explain how the nervous system produces a coordinated response. | B, 3 | Starter 2, Main, Plenary 2 |
| | Explain the difference in function of sensory and motor neurones. | 3 | Starter 2, Main, Plenary 2 |
| | Explain the reasons for different reaction times between dominant and non-dominant hands. | | Main |

**Maths**
During the Main, students will collect data and calculate means (M2b). They will use the means to plot histograms (M2c).

**Literacy**
During the main activity, students will be required to produce coherent, well-structured, and purposeful text in their conclusions, using appropriate vocabulary.

**Key words**
central nervous system, effectors, glands, motor neurone, receptors, relay neurone, sensory neurone, stimulus

# B3.1 The nervous system

| Starter | Support/Extend | Resources |
|---|---|---|
| **The senses** (5 minutes)  In groups of five, allow two minutes to identify the five senses, the sense organs that contain the receptors for those senses, and the stimulus that the receptor cells detect. Then elicit from students the function of the nervous system.<br><br>**Catching the ball** (10 minutes)  Throw a sponge or paper ball to a member of the class. Tell the class that events have happened in the body to enable that student to catch the ball. Ask what has happened in the body, and collect initial ideas. Students then create a sequence of events in the body. Lead the class in stating the function of the nervous system, and then in naming all the steps involved in a nervous reaction. | **Extend:** Ask the class why it is important to detect any stimulus.<br><br>**Support:** Lead the discussion by asking focused questions to build the sequence. | |

| Main | Support/Extend | Resources |
|---|---|---|
| **Measuring reaction times** (40 minutes)  Students drop rulers to investigate whether their reaction time is quicker with the dominant or non-dominant hand.<br><br>One student acts as the experimenter, the other as the subject. The experimenter drops the ruler between the subject's fingers, and the subject catches the ruler and measures the drop distance. Repeat at least three times.<br><br>Students swap roles and repeat. They then collect data from two other students. They calculate the mean drop distance for each hand for each student.<br><br>The shorter the drop distance, the quicker the reaction time. Students then display their data on a histogram.<br><br>Students explain in their conclusion how different parts of the nervous system, including motor and sensory neurones, were involved in the reaction. They evaluate their data, identifying causes of error. | **Support:** Provide a blank results table to record results.<br><br>**Extend:** Students attempt to explain why there are differences in reaction times, and draw a conclusion about hand dominance and reaction time. | **Practical:** Measuring reaction times |

| Plenary | Support/Extend | Resources |
|---|---|---|
| **Nervous reactions** (5 minutes)  Use the interactive to drag and drop statements into the correct order to describe the key steps in the sequence of a nervous reaction.<br><br>**Nervous poetry** (10 minutes)  Divide the class into pairs. Each pair writes a short poem about either a sensory neurone, motor neurone, nerves, or senses. The poem should be four lines long. It should include:<br><br>Line 1 – a name<br>Line 2 – a description<br>Line 3 – a function<br>Line 4 – a summary.<br><br>Students read their poems to the class. | | **Interactive:** Nervous system |

| Homework |
|---|
| Build a model of a neurone. Use tags to label the parts of the neurone. Also, provide a short description of the function of the cell. |

**kerboodle**

A Kerboodle highlight for this lesson is **Working scientifically: Increasing accuracy**. Refer to the **Content map** on Kerboodle for a full list of resources and assessment.

# B3.1.2 Reflexes

**Specification links:**

B3.1c Explain how the structure of a reflex arc is related to its function.

WS1.2b Plan experiments or devise procedures to make observations, produce or characterise a substance, test hypotheses, check data, or explore phenomena.

WS2a Carry out experiments.

WS2b Make and record observations and measurements using a range of apparatus and methods.

WS2c Present observations using appropriate methods.

WS2d Communicate the scientific rationale for investigations, methods used, findings, and reasoned conclusions.

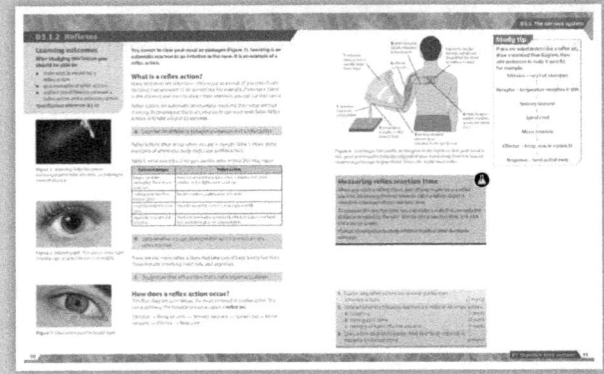

| Target | Outcome | Checkpoint | |
|---|---|---|---|
| | | Question | Activity |
| **Aiming for GRADE 4** | State what is meant by a reflex action. | | Starter 1 and 2, Main |
| | List examples of reflex actions. | B, C, 2 | Starter 1 and 2, Main, Plenary 1 and 2 |
| ↓ | Plan a simple experiment to make a basic observation of the iris reflex. | | Main |
| **Aiming for GRADE 6** | Describe the pathway of the impulse in the reflex arc during a reflex action. | 3 | Starter 2, Main, Plenary 2 |
| | Describe the difference between a reflex action and a voluntary action. | A | Plenary 1 |
| ↓ | Plan a series of simple experiments to make observations of the iris reflex. | | Main |
| **Aiming for GRADE 8** | Explain how a specific example of a reflex action occurs. | 3 | Starter 2, Main |
| | Explain why a reflex action is faster than a voluntary action. | 1 | |
| ↓ | Plan a systematic series of experiments to fully investigate the iris reflex. | | Main |

**Literacy**
During the main activity, students will need to produce coherent, well-structured, and purposeful text to explain their findings.

**Key words**
reflex action, reflex arc

## B3.1 The nervous system

| Starter | Support/Extend | Resources |
|---|---|---|
| **The knee jerk** (5 minutes)  Demonstrate the knee jerk response, by asking students to carry it out (or find a video clip.) Then ask students to describe what has happened. Elicit that the response was rapid, protective, involuntary (automatic), and always the same (stereotypical). Name this response as a reflex action. | | |
| **Types of reflexes** (10 minutes)  Ask students to quickly describe what happens when: a flash light fires, you step on a toy building brick, you see a ball coming toward your face, and so on. Elicit that the common features of these reflexes are that they are rapid, protective, and so on. Then issue a set of cards containing the names of the steps in the pathway of a reflex arc. Ask students to arrange the names in order and then describe what is happening in their body during one of the examples given. | **Extend:** Ask students if they think reflexes can be over-ridden. Present the example of holding a hot object; the reflex can be over-ridden if needed. | |

| Main | Support/Extend | Resources |
|---|---|---|
| **Investigating reflexes** (40 minutes)  Students could either investigate a number of reflex actions, using the Reflexes Activity, or investigate the iris reflex in more depth: Students plan one or more experiments to observe the iris reflex. They record the basic plan as a statement. Tests could include:<br>• Observe iris when lit.<br>• Observe iris when dark.<br>• Observe the two irises, one illuminated and one dark.<br>• Observe changes after having been blindfolded for 5 minutes.<br>• Observe the irises independently.<br>• Observe irises using different intensities of light (move lamp away from eye).<br>Carry out experiments and record observations. Students could film the iris response.<br>Class discussion of findings, followed by a written conclusion. In the discussion, include reference to the reflex arc pathway; the rapid, automatic, and protective nature; the type of protection it affords.<br>SAFETY: Check student suitability. Make sure that light is not too bright and keep objects that could damage the eye well away. | **Support:** Suggest two or three methods – the earlier ones from the list.<br><br>**Extend:** Encourage thinking about the later, more systematic investigations.<br>**Extend:** Students may produce conclusions independently. | **Activity:** Reflexes |

| Plenary | Support/Extend | Resources |
|---|---|---|
| **Voluntary and reflex** (5 minutes)  Use the Simple interactive to drag and drop a list of responses into either reflex or voluntary actions. | | **Interactive:** Voluntary and reflex |
| **Descriptions** (10 minutes)  Divide the class into groups of three to five. Give each group a set of cards containing key words from the lesson, such as the parts of the reflex arc. In turn, one student draws a card. They have one minute to describe the word on their card, without actually using the word. The rest of the team guesses the word. | **Extend:** Increase the number of banned words that cannot be used during the description. List these on the card. | |

| Homework |
|---|
| Draw and fully label a diagram to show the path taken by the impulse in any reflex action that you have learnt about this lesson. You will need to find out what these diagrams look like. |

**kerboodle**

A Kerboodle highlight for this lesson is **Literacy sheet: pass the zap**. Refer to the **Content map** on Kerboodle for a full list of resources and assessment.

# GCSE BIOLOGY ONLY
## B3.1.3 The eye

**Specification links:**

B3.1d Explain how the main structures of the eye are related to their functions. To include cornea, iris, pupil, lens, retina, optic nerve, ciliary body, and suspensory ligaments.

B3.1e Describe common defects of the eye and explain how some of these problems may be overcome. To include colour blindness, short-sightedness, and long-sightedness.

WS1.1b Use models to solve problems, make predictions, and to develop scientific explanations and understanding of familiar and unfamiliar facts.

WS1.1e Explain everyday and technological applications of science.

WS2a Carry out experiments.

WS2b Make and record observations and measurements using a range of apparatus and methods.

WS2c Present observations using appropriate methods.

WS2d Communicate the scientific rationale for investigations, methods used, findings, and reasoned conclusions.

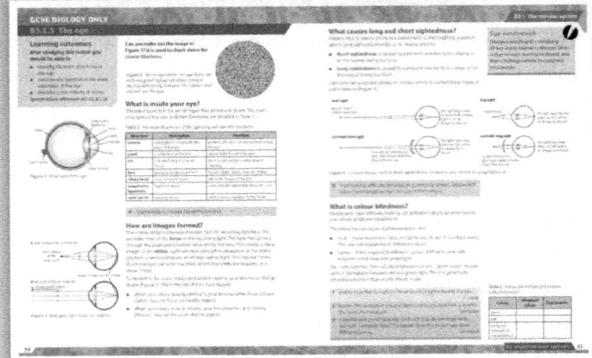

| Target | Outcome | Checkpoint | |
|---|---|---|---|
| | | Question | Activity |
| **Aiming for GRADE 4** | Identify the main structures of the eye. | A, B | Starter 1 and 2<br>Main<br>Plenary 1 |
| | Name some defects of vision. | C | Main<br>Plenary 2 |
| | Use a model to observe how light travels through the eye. | | Starter 1 and 2<br>Main |
| **Aiming for GRADE 6** | Describe the function of each of the main structures in the eye. | 1 | Starter 1 and 2<br>Main<br>Plenary 1 and 2 |
| | Describe some defects of vision. | C, 3 | Main<br>Plenary 2 |
| | Use a model to describe how the structures of the eye focus light on the retina. | | Main |
| **Aiming for GRADE 8** | Explain how the eye focuses light on the retina. | 2 | Main |
| | Explain how common defects of vision can be corrected. | c | Plenary 2 |
| | Use a model to explain how changes in the lens shape would result in accommodation of light rays. | 2 | Main |

**Literacy**
During the main activity, students will need to produce coherent, well-structured, and purposeful texts as they describe the functions of the parts of the eye, and as they explain their findings.

**Key words**
ciliary body, colour blindness, focus, cornea, iris, lens, long-sightedness, optic nerve, pupil, retina, short-sightedness, suspensory ligaments

## B3.1 The nervous system

| Starter | Support/Extend | Resources |
|---|---|---|
| **Pin-hole camera demonstration** (5 minutes)  Use a pin-hole camera to show how light travels through a hole in one side of the box and forms an image on the back of the box. Link this to the structures in the eye.  **Eye dissection or model** (10 minutes)  Use either a model or a dissection to identify the main parts of the eye. Briefly outline the functions of the parts observed. | **Extend:** Notice properties of the image – it is upside down and smaller. | |

| Main | Support/Extend | Resources |
|---|---|---|
| **Refraction** (40 minutes)  Students have an outline drawing of a cross section of the eye. (The drawing needs to be an appropriate size for the second part of this activity. This needs to be determined in advance, and will depend on the lenses available. There are commercial kits that will achieve these aims.) Students label each part of the drawing with the name of the part and a description of its function, including rods and cones. Colour blindness could be mentioned at this point.  Place the drawing on the table and place a convex lens in the correct position. Using two ray boxes parallel to each other, students focus the light rays on the retina in the drawing. Add lines showing these rays onto the diagram of the eye.  Demonstrate short- and long-sightedness using these models. Indicate that the focus point will be before or behind the retina.  Students write a conclusion to explain focusing in the eye. It should describe the path of light rays from outside the eye, through the lens, and onto the retina. | **Support:** Draw lines (outside the eye drawing) to indicate the position of the ray boxes.  **Extend:** Use different shaped convex lenses to demonstrate accommodation. | **Practical:** Refraction |

| Plenary | Support/Extend | Resources |
|---|---|---|
| **Labelling the eye** (5 minutes)  Use the interactive in which students label an image of the eye and match descriptions and functions of parts of the eye to the correct name. | | **Interactive:** The eye |
| **Visiting the optician** (10 minutes)  Discuss what happens during a visit to an optician, including a video clip. Ask students about short-sightedness and long-sightedness. Show an image of two outlines of the eye, with the light rays focused on one in front of the retina in another behind the retina. Ask how this would be corrected and elicit some explanation of a change in the amount of refraction. | **Extend:** Find a few images of a colour blindness test. Allow students to read the numbers if they can. Discuss how they work and link to problems with cones leading to colour blindness. | |

| Homework | | |
|---|---|---|
| Describe similarities and differences between a diagram of the eye and the camera. | | |

**kerboodle**
A Kerboodle highlight for this lesson is **Webquest: Defects of the eyes**. Refer to the **Content map** on Kerboodle for a full list of resources and assessment.

# GCSE BIOLOGY ONLY
## B3.1.4 The brain

**Specification links:**

B3.1f Describe the structure and function of the brain. To include cerebrum, cerebellum, medulla, hypothalamus, and pituitary.

B3.1g Explain some of the difficulties of investigating brain function. To include the difficulty in obtaining and interpreting case studies and the consideration of ethical issues. **H**

WS1.1d Discuss ethical issues arising from developments in science.

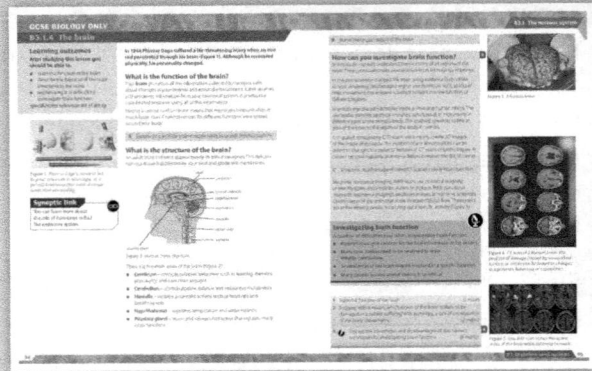

| Target | Outcome | Checkpoint | |
|---|---|---|---|
| | | Question | Activity |
| Aiming for GRADE 4 ↓ | Name the main structures in the brain. | B | Main<br>Plenary 1 and 2 |
| Aiming for GRADE 6 | Describe the location of the main structures of the brain. | | Main<br>Plenary 1 |
| | Describe some of the different techniques used to investigate brain function. | C, 3 | Starter 2<br>Main<br>Plenary 2 **H** |
| ↓ | Describe a range of practical and ethical concerns in scientific research. | C, 3 | Starter 2<br>Main<br>Plenary 2 |
| Aiming for GRADE 8 | Describe the function of the main structures in the brain. | A, 1, 2 | Starter 1<br>Main<br>Plenary 1 and 2 |
| | Explain why it is difficult to investigate brain function. | C, 3 | Main<br>Plenary 2 **H** |
| ↓ | Justify decisions about the ethics of scientific research methods. | | Main<br>Plenary 2 |

**Literacy**

During the main activities, students will need to produce coherent, well-structured, and purposeful texts as they describe the functions of the parts of the brain, and as they discuss issues arising from brain research. Students will support their understanding and opinions with apt references, informed by their wider reading.

**Key words**

brain, cerebrum, cerebellum, hypothalamus, medulla, pituitary gland

94

## B3.1 The nervous system

| Starter | Support/Extend | Resources |
|---|---|---|
| **What do you want to find out about the brain?** (5 minutes) Ask students to produce a question that they would like to be answered about the brain during the lesson. These can be written on sticky notes and stuck on the board. | | |
| **Activities** (10 minutes) Select about five students to come to the front. Issue each student with a card containing a different task, each using a different area of the brain (e.g. balance on one leg, read something, smell something, pick something up, listen to something). The students then carry out the action, or mime it. Ask the class to describe what the students at the front are doing. Continue by asking them to explain what is happening in their nervous systems, and finally focus on the brain. Tell students that different areas of the brain are involved in the different functions, so establishing the idea of regionalisation of function. | **Extend:** Ask students how they think scientists can tell which area of the brain is involved in any particular function. | |

| Main | Support/Extend | Resources |
|---|---|---|
| **Functions of regions of the brain** (15 minutes) Issue students with an outline of the brain, and display an image or a model so that they can name the regions of the brain. Then issue cards, each of which describes a patient case with a defect in an area of the brain, and the effect it has on the body. Students deduce the role of that region of the brain. | **Support:** Extend the amount of time. | |
| **Brain research** (25 minutes) Identify at least three methods by which researchers have learnt about the functioning of the brain. Discuss the information students think that each method might provide. Ask them to suggest issues arising from the techniques, such as ethical issues, cost, hazards from radiation, and so on. Students could quickly research the techniques using tablets or similar (if available). Students then take on the role of the director of a medical research centre carrying out research into brain function. Write a policy statement that outlines what types of research might be carried out, what might be learnt from each type of research, and any issues that might be involved with the research methods. | **Support:** Reduce the amount of time allowed for this as it is really a higher tier component. Lower-attaining students need not attempt the last section. **Extend:** Students make justified decisions about the policy for the department regarding the limits they might apply to the research. | **Activity:** Brain research  **H** |

| Plenary | Support/Extend | Resources |
|---|---|---|
| **Areas of the brain** (5 minutes) Use the interactive activity in which students link the names of the different parts of the brain to their function. | | **Interactive:** Areas of the brain |
| **Question board** (10 minutes) Return to the questions on the board from the first starter. Select a few of the questions and ask the students to answer them. You may select some questions that have not been answered, which the students might be able to extend their knowledge to answer; or they might be able to suggest what studies would be needed to answer the questions. Alternatively, these questions might prompt more input from the teacher. | **Support:** Select questions mainly about structure and function. **Extend:** Ask students how the scientific community discovered the answers to the questions. | |

| Homework |
|---|
| You are a GP. One of your patients has been asked to volunteer to go to the hospital for a CT scan. The hospital is carrying out research into which areas of the brain are active during certain common processes, such as reading. You need to explain to your patient what a CT scan is, what might happen, and what the images will show. **H** |

**kerboodle**
A Kerboodle highlight for this lesson is **Literacy interactive: The brain**. Refer to the **Content map** on Kerboodle for a full list of resources and assessment.

# GCSE BIOLOGY ONLY — HIGHER TIER
## B3.1.5 Nervous system damage

**Specification links:**

B3.1h Explain some of the limitations in treating damage and disease in the brain and other parts of the nervous system. To include limited ability to repair nervous tissue, irreversible damage to the surrounding tissues, and difficulties with accessing parts of the nervous system.

WS1.1e Explain everyday and technological applications of science.

WS1.1f Evaluate associated personal, social, economic, and environmental implications.

WS1.1h Evaluate risks both in practical science and the wider societal context.

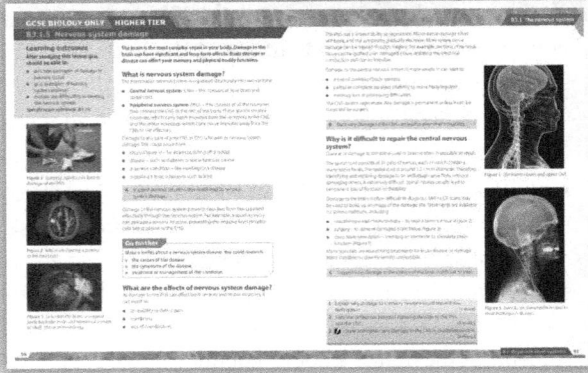

| Target | Outcome | Checkpoint | |
|---|---|---|---|
| | | Question | Activity |
| **Aiming for GRADE 6** | Describe examples of damage to nervous tissue. | A | Starter 1 and 2 Main Plenary 2 |
| | Describe some methods used to treat damage to the nervous system. | 2 | Main Plenary 2 |
| | Describe some of the personal implications to the patient of treatments for damage to the nervous system. | | Main Plenary 1 |
| **Aiming for GRADE 8** | Explain how damage to nervous tissue has an effect on the functioning of the body. | B, 1 | Starter 1 and 2 Main Plenary 2 |
| | Explain the difficulties in treating the nervous system. | C, 3 | Main Plenary 1 and 2 |
| | Evaluate the personal implications to the patient of treatments for damage to the nervous system. | | Main Plenary 1 |

**Literacy**
During the main activity, students will need to summarise and evaluate text with accuracy and clear understanding. They will also need to support their understanding and opinions with apt references to texts.

**Key words**
central nervous system, peripheral nervous system

# B3.1 The nervous system

| Starter | Support/Extend | Resources |
|---|---|---|
| **Seeing stars** (5 minutes) Show a cartoon image of a character being hit on the back of the head and seeing stars. Ask students to describe what they see and to try to suggest a scientific reason for why this might actually happen. | | |
| **Types of nervous damage** (10 minutes) Ask students to identify as many different types of damage to the nervous system as they can. (Strokes, tumours, physical damage, poisons, and infections). Then ask them to suggest an explanation for the damaging effects on the nervous tissue. | **Support:** Supplement their list if it is too brief. The teacher can also support with clues to the explanation. | |

| Main | Support/Extend | Resources |
|---|---|---|
| **Media review** (20 minutes) Select a variety of newspaper articles (or TV clips) that discuss recent examples of treatments for nervous tissue damage. Examples could include:<br>• limb grafts<br>• eye/ear implants<br>• radiotherapy for brain tumours<br>• brain surgery.<br>Give different articles to different groups.<br>Students read their article and select key pieces of scientific information. They should be able to contribute their own knowledge about the problems with treating nerve damage. They may need to do further research on the internet.<br>Students should:<br>• describe the type of neural damage<br>• describe the personal effect on the patient<br>• describe the treatment<br>• identify advantages and disadvantages of the treatment from the article.<br>**Feedback to the class** (20 minutes) Each group presents their findings to the class. | **Extend:** Evaluate the benefits and drawbacks of the treatment for the patient. | **Activity:** Media review |

| Plenary | Support/Extend | Resources |
|---|---|---|
| **Treatments – pros and cons** (5 minutes) Use the interactive activity in which students draw lines to link each treatment type to one advantage and one disadvantage.<br>**Frankenstein's monster** (10 minutes) Project an image of Frankenstein's monster. Ensure that students understand the story. Groups then discuss what problems would have occurred in the nervous tissue, and why this monster could not actually be made. | | **Interactive:** Treatments – pros and cons |

| Homework | | |
|---|---|---|
| You are a scientific journalist. Write a letter of application to write articles for TV or newspapers on breakthrough treatments for neuroscience. The letter should outline what you think is important in such articles. | | |

*kerboodle*
A Kerboodle highlight for this lesson is **Progress quiz: The nervous system 2**. Refer to the **Content map** on Kerboodle for a full list of resources and assessment.

# Checkpoint

## B3.1 The nervous system

### Overview of B3.1 The nervous system

In this chapter, students have studied the structure and function of the human nervous system. They should be familiar with the structure of sensory and motor neurones. Students should link this with work on diffusion in B2.1 *Supplying the cell*, which covered the differentiation of cells such as nerve cells. They should understand the pathway of a reflex arc and be able to give examples of common reflexes. They should be able to use the term electrical impulse when describing the nervous system, and should understand that receptors detect a change in stimulus.

Students should be able to describe the structure and function of the human eye. Aiming for 8 students should understand the process of accommodation, including the contraction of the ciliary muscles. They should understand that light enters the eye and is detected by photoreceptors in the retina, forming an image which is interpreted by the brain. Students should be familiar with common defects of the eye including colour blindness, short sight, and long sight, and how these conditions can be treated.

In studying the brain, students should be able to link each feature with its function. They should be aware of the links between their studies of the brain in this chapter and the role of the pituitary gland in the brain in B3.2 *The endocrine system*, and the control of body temperature and water balance in B3.3 *Maintaining internal environments*.

Higher-tier students should be able to outline the structure of the nervous system in terms of the central nervous system (CNS) and peripheral nervous system (PNS), and be aware of common causes of damage and the likely effects of such damage. They should appreciate why damage to the CNS is difficult to repair, and be able to describe how the brain may be investigated and how brain damage may be treated.

### MyMaths

You can find additional support for the maths skills covered in this chapter on **MyMaths**, including collecting data, calculating means, and plotting histograms of reaction times.

For this chapter, the following assessments are available on Kerboodle:
B3.1 Checkpoint quiz: The nervous system
B3.1 Progress quiz: The nervous system 1
B3.1 Progress quiz: The nervous system 2
B3.1 On your marks: The nervous system
B3.1 Exam-style questions and mark scheme: The nervous system

### Checkpoint follow-up lesson

A student's route through this lesson can be determined using the Checkpoint assessment. Percentage pass marks are supplied in the Checkpoint teacher notes.

For each successive route through it is assumed that the student can perform to their current route as well as previous routes. For example, students working at Aiming for 6 are assumed to be secure in Aiming for 4 knowledge and understanding and working towards achieving all the learning objectives for Aiming for 6.

## B3.1 The nervous system

| | **Aiming for 4** | **Aiming for 6** | **Aiming for 8** |
|---|---|---|---|
| **Learning outcomes** | State how a reflex action is coordinated. | Describe how a reflex action is coordinated. | Explain how a reflex action is coordinated. |
| | State the structure and function of the parts of the eye. | Describe the structure and function of the parts of the eye. | Explain the changes to the eye when focusing on near and distant objects. |
| | State the structure and function of parts of the brain. | Describe the structure and function of parts of the brain. | Explain structure and function of the parts of the brain. |
| **Starter** | **Impulses and reflexes (10 minutes)** Ask the class to hold hands in a big circle. One person squeezes the hand of their neighbour, and as soon as they feel this they pass the squeeze along. Time the 'impulse' passing using a stopwatch. | | |
| | Then make an unexpected loud sound such as ringing a bell or shouting. If students jump, explain this is a reflex action. Ask students in pairs to write down as many reflex actions as they can think of, then compare with a neighbouring pair. | | |
| **Differentiated checkpoint activity** | **Activity 1 Describing a reflex action (10 minutes)** Students each answer question 1 on the differentiated worksheets, which asks them to describe a reflex action. They may need access to the Student book. The sheets provide varying degrees of support – the Aiming for 4 sheet provides prompt words to help students describe the reflex arc, while the Aiming for 6 sheet provides the start and end of the pathway and the main terminology, and the Aiming for 8 sheet asks for a detailed flowchart with no prompts. | | |
| | **Activity 2 Eye test (10 minutes)** In pairs or small groups, students test each other's eyesight using an eye test chart. These are readily available on the Internet. If there is time they should test both eyes together, then the right, then the left, before testing another student. | | |
| | **Activity 3 The eye (10 minutes)** Students each answer question 2 on the differentiated worksheets about the structure and functions of the parts of the eye. | | |
| | The Aiming for 4 sheet provides the labels for students to label a diagram of the eye. They match each part of the eye with its function. | Aiming for 6 students label a diagram of the eye and draw a table to show the function of each labelled part. | Aiming for 8 students label a diagram of the eye and draw diagrams to explain accommodation. |
| | **Activity 4 Question time (10 minutes)** Ask targeted questions about the brain and nervous system damage, such as – what is the CNS? What is the function of the brain? How can we check brain function? What happens if the CNS is damaged? Students then complete question 3 on the differentiated worksheets about the structure and function of the brain. They will need access to the Student book. | | |
| | The Aiming for 4 activity provides the labels for students to use to label a diagram of the brain. They match each part of the brain with its function. | Aiming for 6 students label a diagram of the brain and draw a table to show the function of each labelled part. | Aiming for 8 students label a diagram of the brain and draw a table to show the function of each area of the brain. |
| | **Kerboodle resource:** B3.1 Checkpoint follow-up: Aiming for 4, B3.1 Checkpoint follow-up: Aiming for 6, B3.1 Checkpoint follow-up: Aiming for 8 | | |
| **Plenary** | **True or false? (5 minutes)** Read out a series of statements about this topic. Ask students to raise one coloured card for true, and another coloured card for false. Students will each need two cards of different colours. | | |
| **Progression** | The Aiming for 4 activities provide highly structured questions. Students may need a brief introduction from the teacher. Teachers will need to check student's answers or provide them with answers to check each other's work. The investigation on reaction times could challenge all abilities. | The Aiming for 6 activities are reasonably structured. Question 1 may need a brief introduction from the teacher. Questions 2 and 3 should not require any introduction from the teacher. Teachers will need to check student's answers or provide them with answers to check each other's work. | The Aiming for 8 activities have very little structure. Students should be able to complete all the activities with no introduction from the teacher. More able students could be extended by practising interpreting and drawing ray diagrams for accommodation and sight defects. To support the higher-tier statements about brain studies, students could research studies of brain injury. |

# B3.2 The endocrine system
## B3.2.1 Hormones

**Specification links:**

B3.2a Describe the principles of hormonal coordination and control by the human endocrine system. To include use of chemical messengers, transport in blood, endocrine glands, and receptors.

B3.2c Describe the role of hormones in human reproduction including the control of the menstrual cycle. To include oestrogen, progesterone, FSH, and testosterone.

WS1.4a Use scientific vocabulary, terminology, and definitions.

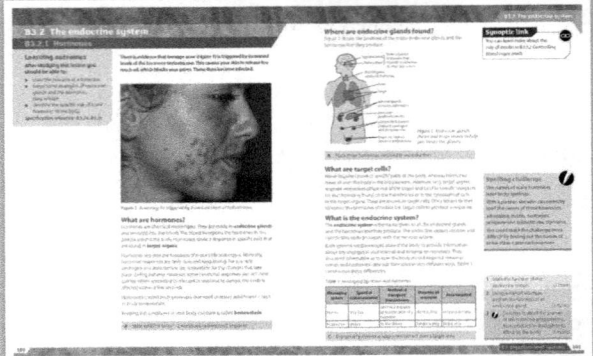

| Target | Outcome | Checkpoint | |
|---|---|---|---|
| | | Question | Activity |
| **Aiming for GRADE 4** | Name examples of endocrine glands and the hormones they release. | B, 2 | Starter 2<br>Main<br>Plenary 1 |
| | State the function of a hormone. | B, 1 | Starter 1 and 2<br>Main<br>Plenary 1 |
| | Use simple sentence types and familiar vocabulary, limited to scientific names, when producing texts. | | Main |
| **Aiming for GRADE 6** | Describe how a hormone reaches its target organ. | A, C, 2, 3 | Main<br>Plenary 2 |
| | Describe the specific roles of some hormones in the body. | | Starter 2<br>Main<br>Plenary 1 |
| | Use a variety of sentence types and vocabulary appropriate to purpose when describing the actions of hormones. | 2, 3 | Main |
| **Aiming for GRADE 8** | Explain how a hormone acts as a chemical messenger. | C, 2 | Main<br>Plenary 2 |
| | Explain how named hormones bring about homeostatic regulation in the body. | 2 | Main |
| | Use a wide range of well-selected sentence types and precise vocabulary when explaining the action of hormones. | 3 | Main |

**Literacy**

During the main activity, students will need to use a range of sentence types and a large range of scientific vocabulary to describe and explain the action of hormones in the body.

**Key words**

endocrine gland, endocrine system, hormone, homeostasis, target organ

# B3.2 The endocrine system

| Starter | Support/Extend | Resources |
|---|---|---|
| **Messages** (5 minutes) Arrange a line of at least 10 students. First activity: students link hands and you signal to the student at one end of the line. That student then gently squeezes the hand of the next student and this continues until it reaches the last student, who raises their hand. Record the time. Second activity: release hands and pass the first student a ball of paper. This ball is passed from student to student until it reaches the last in line, who opens the paper to read a message stating 'hormone – raise your hand.' Again record time. Draw out differences between nervous response (activity 1) and hormonal response (activity 2). | | |
| **Rollercoasters** (10 minutes) Show a short film of someone on a rollercoaster ride. Ask the students what is happening to the person – they will probably use terms like *adrenaline rush* and list changes to the body, such as heart rate increases, breathing increases, more alert/active, etc. Elicit that adrenaline is a chemical messenger and that it has long lasting effects, over many organs. | **Extend:** Discuss the effects of adrenaline and why they are important. | |

| Main | Support/Extend | Resources |
|---|---|---|
| **Webpage on hormones** (40 minutes) Supply students with an outline of a body for them to draw on the endocrine glands, which they can label with the name and function. They can use the information from the Student Book to do this. Then, set a series of questions looking at the hormones that these glands produce, how hormones travel to their target organs, and the differences between hormonal and nervous control. Students use this information to design a webpage for a GCSE internet revision site to cover the topic of hormones. The page should contain:<br>• at least 5 key facts about hormones, including how hormones reach their target organ<br>• a diagram of the human body showing the position of the endocrine glands<br>• labels of the major endocrine glands.<br>Each gland is annotated, or hyperlinked to a section that names the hormones produced in the gland, and explains the function of the hormone. They should also include a second link for each organ, giving a medical example of a problem caused by lack or excess of the hormone. | **Support:** Divide the task into short steps.<br><br><br><br><br><br><br><br>**Extend:** The explanations should explain how each hormone brings about homeostatic control of a body function (where appropriate). | **Activity:** Endocrine glands |

| Plenary | Support/Extend | Resources |
|---|---|---|
| **The endocrine system** (5 minutes) Use the interactive that contains an image of the endocrine glands in the body. Students match glands to the hormones that they produce. | | **Interactive:** The endocrine system |
| **Post or e-mails** (10 minutes) Ask students in groups to list the similarities between the nervous system and e-mails; and between the endocrine system and letters in the post. | **Extend:** Students need to be able to use the terms 'endocrine gland' and 'target organ' correctly in the comparison. | |

| Homework |
|---|
| Write an entry for an online encyclopaedia about a hormone of your choice. All of the scientific words that need a hyperlink need to be highlighted. |

**kerboodle**

A Kerboodle highlight for this lesson is **Bump up your grade: The endocrine system**. Refer to the **Content map** on Kerboodle for a full list of resources and assessment.

**B3 Organism-level systems**

# HIGHER TIER
## B3.2.2 Negative feedback

**Specification links:**

B3.2b Explain the roles of thyroxine and adrenaline in the body, including thyroxine as an example of a negative feedback system.

WS1.1b Use models to solve problems, make predictions, and to develop scientific explanations and understanding of familiar and unfamiliar facts.

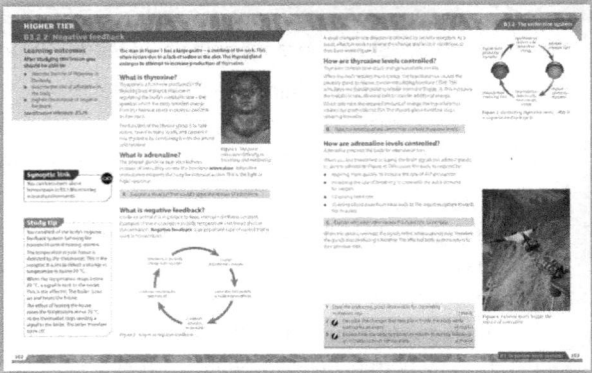

| Target | Outcome | Checkpoint | |
|---|---|---|---|
| | | Question | Activity |
| **Aiming for GRADE 6** ↓ | Describe the role of thyroxine and adrenaline in the body. | A, 1, 2 | Starter 1 and 2<br>Main<br>Plenary 1 |
| | Describe how negative feedback occurs. | 3 | Starter 1 and 2<br>Main<br>Plenary 1 and 2 |
| | Use a model to describe how negative feedback occurs. | | Main<br>Plenary 2 |
| **Aiming for GRADE 8** ↓ | Explain how the roles of thyroxine and adrenaline are brought about by a number of responses in the body. | C, 3 | Starter 1 and 2<br>Main<br>Plenary 1 |
| | Explain the purpose of negative feedback. | 3 | Starter 2<br>Main<br>Plenary 2 |
| | Use a model to explain how negative feedback brings about control. | | Main<br>Plenary 2 |

**Literacy**

During the main activity, students will be required to produce coherent, well-structured sentences, using appropriate scientific vocabulary.

**Key words**

adrenaline, negative feedback, thyroxine

## B3.2 The endocrine system

| Starter | Support/Extend | Resources |
|---|---|---|
| **Feeling nervous?** (5 minutes) Ask students to describe as many changes that happen in their bodies when they are stressed as they can. Link this to adrenaline. Ask students if these sensations last. Suggest that a system in the body stops the effects. | **Extend:** Repeat for thyroxine. | |
| **Thermostats** (10 minutes) Introduce the idea of thermostats and ask students to suggest how they work. Establish that they switch off the heating system. Ask why this is important. Now, refer to the human body and ask if such a system might be useful. | **Support:** Adrenaline is a better known system. | |

| Main | Support/Extend | Resources |
|---|---|---|
| **Negative feedback flow diagrams** (40 minutes) Divide the class into pairs. Half of the pairs will work on thyroxine and the other half will work on adrenaline.<br><br>Each group researches one hormone and how it acts in the body, using ICT or the Student Book. They create/complete a flow diagram to explain the action of the hormone in regulating the body's function, including an indication of the process of negative feedback, in the case of thyroxine.<br><br>Each pair shares their learning so that all students learn about both hormones. | **Support:** For the flow diagram, provide students the following as prompts in a frame.<br>• Change in the body's condition.<br>• Detection.<br>• Hormone released.<br>• Corrective mechanisms used.<br>Indicate how this system is controlled (negative feedback). | **Activity:** Effects of hormones |

| Plenary | Support/Extend | Resources |
|---|---|---|
| **Sequence of events** (5 minutes) Use the interactive activity in which students drag and drop a series of statements into the correct order, therefore describing the series of events in the action of one of the hormones. | | **Interactive:** Sequence of events |
| **Other negative feedback systems** (10 minutes) Ask student groups to think of other situations in the body where we need to keep the level in the body controlled and therefore might use a negative feedback system. | **Support:** Suggest the case of insulin and blood sugar control.<br>**Extend:** Students could explain how they think the negative feedback system works, and what might happen if the system fails. | |

| Homework | | |
|---|---|---|
| Research the lack of production of thyroxine in a condition called goitre. Describe and explain the causes and effects of the condition. Suggest why negative feedback does not work well in this condition. Finally, describe the treatments. | | |

*kerboodle*

A Kerboodle highlight for this lesson is **Literacy sheet: Adrenaline and thyroxine**. Refer to the **Content map** on Kerboodle for a full list of resources and assessment.

# B3.2.3 The menstrual cycle

**Specification links:**

B3.2c Describe the role of hormones in human reproduction, including the control of the menstrual cycle. To include oestrogen, progesterone, FSH, and testosterone.

B3.2d Explain the interactions of FSH, LH, oestrogen, and progesterone in the control of the menstrual cycle. **H**

WS1.3e Interpret observations and other data.

BM3.2i Extract and interpret data from graphs, charts, and tables (M2c).

BM3.2ii Translate information between numerical and graphical forms (M4a).

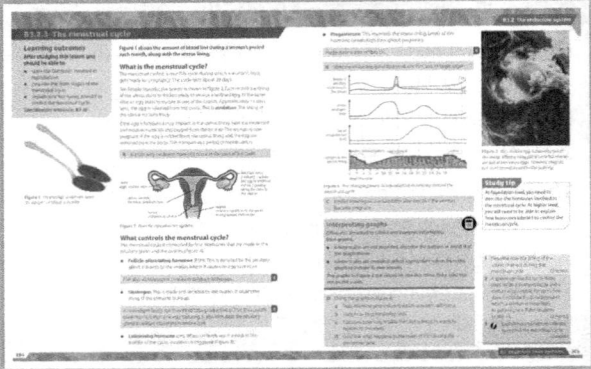

| Target | Outcome | Checkpoint | |
|---|---|---|---|
| | | Question | Activity |
| **Aiming for GRADE 4** | State the hormones involved in the menstrual cycle. | | Starter 2 Main Plenary 2 |
| | Describe the main stages of the menstrual cycle. | A, 1, 2 | Starter 1 Main Plenary 1 and 2 |
| | State simple factual statements based on data and observations from texts. | B | Main Plenary 1 and 2 |
| **Aiming for GRADE 6** | Describe how the levels of the hormones change during the menstrual cycle. | C | Main Plenary 1 and 2 |
| | Describe how hormones cause the changes that occur at the different stages of the menstrual cycle. | A | Main Plenary 1 and 2 |
| | Use data and observations from texts to describe processes in detail. | | Main |
| **Aiming for GRADE 8** | Explain how some hormones control the level of production of other hormones during the menstrual cycle. | 3 | Main Plenary 1 and 2 |
| | Explain how hormones interact to control the menstrual cycle. | 3 | Main Plenary 1 and 2 |
| | Interpret data and observations from texts to explain how changes in the menstrual cycle are related to patterns in the hormone levels. | | Main |

**Maths**
During the main activity, students will need to extract and interpret information from line graphs. They will need to read their graphs to make valid statements (M4a).

**Literacy**
During the main activity, students will need to communicate effectively to sustain interest.

**Key words**
follicle-stimulating hormone (FSH), luteinising hormone (LH), oestrogen, ovulation, period, progesterone

# B3.2 The endocrine system

| Starter | Support/Extend | Resources |
|---|---|---|
| **Planting a seed** (10 minutes)  Ask two or three students to help in a demonstration. Give them a plant pot, compost, and a packet of pea seeds. Ask them to plant a seed. They will follow a precise sequence to do this task. Then ask them why they have used a sequence. State that the control of reproduction is precise. Repeat the task, but now link it to the menstrual cycle.<br>• Placing the compost in the pot is like the uterus thickening<br>• Taking the seed out of the packet represents ovulation<br>• Placing the seed in the compost is like implantation.<br>Emphasise the control of the steps.<br>**The menstrual cycle** (5 minutes)  Use the interactive to drag and drop from a list of words those that are relevant to the menstrual cycle, and those that are not. Words include hormones, organs of the body, and processes. | | **Interactive:** The menstrual cycle |

| Main | Support/Extend | Resources |
|---|---|---|
| This is the first of three lessons on reproductive biology. The aim of the series of lessons is to produce a TV programme (or script) about reproductive biology.<br>**Episode 1 – the menstrual cycle** (40 minutes)  Create a 10 minute TV programme (or script) that explains the events and control of the menstrual cycle. The TV programme is aimed at a specific audience, such as school students. Remind students that the programme should be appropriate.<br>Start the lesson by researching the cycle, using the Activity sheet to ensure that all of the main points are covered. The TV programme should explain the changes in the uterine wall and include graphs showing the changing hormone levels throughout the cycle.<br>Students use tablets or computers to produce the film. | **Support:** Provide a running order to act as a writing frame.<br>**Extend:** The programme should include explanations of how the hormones interact, and inhibit production of some hormones. [H] | **Activity:** Hormones and the menstrual cycle |

| Plenary | Support/Extend | Resources |
|---|---|---|
| **Flash cards** (5 minutes)  Have a series of four flash cards each of which gives the name of one of the four main hormones involved in the menstrual cycle. Hold the cards up one at a time and ask individuals for a fact about the hormone. The cards can be held up several times.<br>**Pregnancy** (10 minutes)  Ask students to discuss in groups what might happen to the menstrual cycle, and hormone levels, if the woman becomes pregnant. Feedback to the class and establish an accurate picture of the event. | **Extend:** Higher-attaining students should be able to describe how hormones interact with each other.<br><br>**Support:** Focus on progesterone levels and the uterine wall.<br>**Extend:** Discuss FSH and lack of further ovulation. | |

| Homework |
|---|
| Annotate a diagram of the changes in the thickness of the uterine wall. The notes should describe the changes in the hormone levels, and explain how this leads to the changes in the uterine wall and other events in the menstrual cycle, such as ovulation. |

*kerboodle*

A Kerboodle highlight for this lesson is **Calculation sheet: Interpreting a menstrual cycle diagram**. Refer to the **Content map** on Kerboodle for a full list of resources and assessment.

# B3.2.4 Controlling reproduction

**Specification links:**

B3.2e Explain the use of hormones in contraception and evaluate hormonal and non-hormonal methods of contraception. To include relative effectiveness of the different forms of contraception.

WS1.1d Discuss ethical issues arising from developments in science.

WS1.1e Explain everyday and technological applications of science.

WS1.1f Evaluate associated personal, social, economic, and environmental implications.

| Target | Outcome | Checkpoint | |
|---|---|---|---|
| | | Question | Activity |
| **Aiming for GRADE 4** | State some examples of contraception. | A | Starter 1 and 2<br>Main |
| | Name the different types of hormone-based contraception. | | Starter 1 and 2<br>Main |
| | State that applications of science have helped humans control their reproduction. | 1 | Starter 1<br>Main |
| **Aiming for GRADE 6** | Describe how the different methods of contraception work. | A, B, 1, 3 | Starter 1 and 2<br>Main<br>Plenary 1 |
| | Explain how hormones are used in contraception. | | Main<br>Plenary 1 |
| | Discuss how knowledge of reproduction allowed scientists to develop applications to control reproduction. | 2 | Main |
| **Aiming for GRADE 8** | Evaluate different methods of contraception. | 2, 3 | Main<br>Plenary 2 |
| | Evaluate hormonal contraception methods compared with non-hormonal contraception. | 2 | Main<br>Plenary 2 |
| | Explain the need for scientists to evaluate reproductive applications of science, in order to inform the public. | 2, 3 | Main<br>Plenary 2 |

**Maths**
During the main activity, students will need to compare effectiveness of the contraceptive methods by comparing percentages (M1c).

**Literacy**
During the main activity, students will need to communicate effectively to sustain interest.

**Key words**
contraception

# B3.2 The endocrine system

| Starter | Support/Extend | Resources |
|---|---|---|
| **Knowledge of contraception** (10 minutes)   Provide each group with a set of cards with the name of one type of contraception on each card. Ask a series of questions, and get the students to divide the cards into groups. This can be followed by a brief class discussion.<br>Groups:<br>Hormonal or non-hormonal.<br>Barrier method or not.<br>Required a knowledge of the menstrual cycle to develop.<br>Old method or more recent method.<br>**Contraception** (5 minutes)   Ask students if they know what the word contraception means. Then ask groups to list different types of contraception. | **Support:** Structure the order of the questions.<br>**Extend:** Add a question about effectiveness.<br><br><br><br><br><br>**Extend:** Can they suggest how some of the types of contraception work? | |

| Main | Support/Extend | Resources |
|---|---|---|
| This is the second of three lessons on reproductive biology. The aim of the series of lessons is to produce a TV programme (or script) about reproductive biology.<br>**Episode 2 – Controlling reproduction** (40 minutes)   Create a 10 minute TV programme (or script) that considers the different methods scientists have developed to help us control our reproductive biology.<br>This should describe the different types of contraception, explain how they prevent pregnancy, and how a knowledge of the menstrual cycle allowed scientists to develop some of the modern techniques.<br>Students use data from scientific surveys (given in the Student Book) to compare the effectiveness of the methods. When using scientific data from a survey, students need to consider how reliable the data is. Was the survey well organised, unbiased, and based on a sufficiently large sample size? | **Support:** Provide a running order to act as a writing frame.<br>**Extend:** The programme should include an evaluation of the effectiveness of different types of contraception, as well as a consideration of their side effects. There should also be an explanation of the purposes of evaluating reproductive technologies. | **Activity:** Controlling reproduction |

| Plenary | Support/Extend | Resources |
|---|---|---|
| **Controlling reproduction** (5 minutes)   Use the interactive to link the name of a contraceptive method to a description of how it works.<br>**Scientific method** (10 minutes)   Pose the question 'How might scientists obtain valid and reliable results in studies about the effectiveness of contraceptive techniques?'<br>Through group discussion or as a class activity, lead students to the following:<br>• Large numbers of participants.<br>• Consideration of factors, such as participant age, time period.<br>• Analysis of statistics. | **Support:** Provide the method points and ask why they might be used.<br>**Extend:** Ask why scientists need to do these studies, and how they communicate with the public. | **Interactive:** Controlling reproduction |

| Homework | | |
|---|---|---|
| You work in a biological research institute looking at reproductive biology. Write a letter of application for a grant for further research. The letter needs to explain how research has been of benefit to society. Use the control of reproduction as your example. | | |

# HIGHER TIER
## B3.2.5 Using hormones to treat infertility

**Specification links:**

B3.2f Explain the use of hormones in modern reproductive technologies to treat infertility.

WS1.1d Discuss ethical issues arising from developments in science.

WS1.1e Explain everyday and technological applications of science.

WS1.1f Evaluate associated personal, social, economic, and environmental implications.

WS1.1g Make decisions based on the evaluation of evidence and arguments.

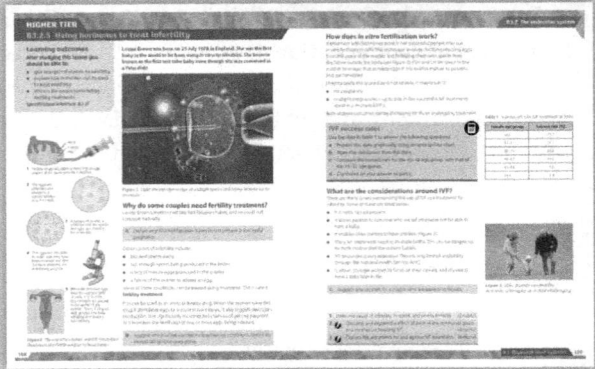

| Target | Outcome | Checkpoint | |
|---|---|---|---|
| | | Question | Activity |
| **Aiming for GRADE 6** | Describe some causes of infertility. | A, B, 1 | Starter 2 / Main |
| | Describe the process of *in vitro* fertilisation (IVF). | 2 | Starter 1 / Main / Plenary 2 |
| | Use evidence to support or reject the use of IVF. | 3 | Main / Plenary 1 |
| **Aiming for GRADE 8** | Discuss issues surrounding fertility treatment. | C, 3 | Starter 1 / Main / Plenary 1 |
| | Explain how hormones can be used to treat infertility. | 2 | Main / Plenary 2 |
| | Justify decisions about the suitability of IVF based on an evaluation of the evidence and arguments about the technique. | 3 | Main |

**Literacy**

During the main activity, students will need to communicate effectively to sustain interest.

**Key words**

fertility treatment

## B3.2 The endocrine system

| Starter | Support/Extend | Resources |
|---|---|---|
| **Test tube babies** (10 minutes) Show a cartoon image of students talking about IVF, including captions designed to initiate discussion, for example:<br>• Test tube babies grow and develop in test tubes.<br>• Fertilisation takes place in a test tube.<br>• Test tube babies are fertilised in a Petri dish.<br>• The fertilised egg is implanted into the mother.<br>**Causes of problems** (5 minutes) Provide groups with diagrams of both male and female reproductive systems. Ask them to indicate possible areas that might cause infertility. Feedback to the class. | **Support:** Teacher leads discussion one point at a time.<br>**Extend:** Why do we use IVF? Are there any issues with using IVF? | |

| Main | Support/Extend | Resources |
|---|---|---|
| This is the third of three lessons on reproductive biology. The aim of the series of lessons is to produce a TV programme (or script) about reproductive biology.<br>**Episode 3 – fertility treatment** (40 minutes) Create a 10 minute TV programme (or script) that describes and explains the process of *in vitro* fertilisation (IVF). Students should use the Activity sheet to ensure that all of the main points are covered. The programme needs to outline the causes of infertility, to give a brief history of IVF, and to describe the steps in the process of IVF, including reference to the hormones involved.<br>The programme should discuss some of the pros and cons of the process, including ethical considerations. | **Support:** Provide a running order to act as a writing frame.<br>**Extend:** The programme should include a consideration about how people make decisions about the use of IVF having evaluated the pros and cons. | **Activity:** Solving fertility problems |

| Plenary | Support/Extend | Resources |
|---|---|---|
| **Pros and cons of IVF** (5 minutes) Use the interactive to drag and drop statements into one of two columns – one for advantages and one for disadvantages of IVF.<br>**Hormones in reproductive biology** (10 minutes) Write the names of the four hormones (FSH, LH, oestrogen, and progesterone) on the board. Ask students to write a comment about the role of each hormone in the normal menstrual cycle, a description of the use of any of the hormones in contraception, and a description of the use of any of the hormones in IVF treatment. | **Support:** Just ask for any statements about each hormone.<br>**Extend:** Expand discussion to include how the hormones might be involved during a pregnancy. | **Interactive:** Pros and cons of IVF |

| Homework | | |
|---|---|---|
| Write a summary for a TV listings magazine that outlines the content of the TV programmes produced in the last three lessons. | | |

**kerboodle**

A Kerboodle highlight for this lesson is **Extension: What do you do with the rest?**. Refer to the **Content map** on Kerboodle for a full list of resources and assessment.

# GCSE BIOLOGY ONLY
## B3.2.6 Plant hormones

**Specification links:**

B3.2g Explain how plant hormones are important in the control and coordination of plant growth and development, with reference to the role of auxins in phototropisms and gravitropisms. To include unequal distribution of auxin.

WS1.2a Use scientific theories and explanations to develop hypotheses.

WS2a Carry out experiments.

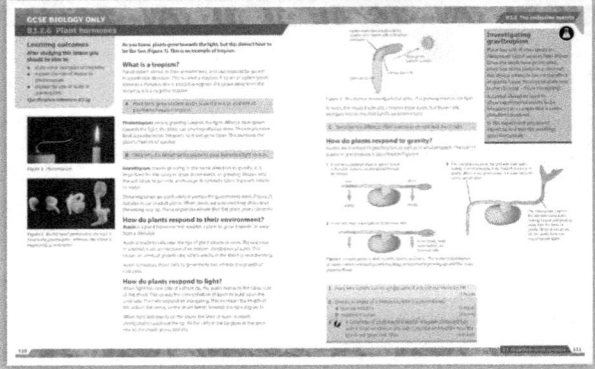

| Target | Outcome | Checkpoint | |
|---|---|---|---|
| | | Question | Activity |
| **Aiming for GRADE 4** ↓ | Name the process by which plants respond to light. | 1, 2 | Starter 1 and 2<br>Main<br>Plenary 2 |
| | Name the process by which plants respond to gravity. | 2 | Starter 2<br>Main<br>Plenary 1 and 2 |
| | Use scientific facts to develop a method, given a hypothesis. | | Starter 2<br>Main<br>Plenary 1 |
| **Aiming for GRADE 6** ↓ | Describe the process of phototropism. | B, 1, 3 | Starter 1 and 2<br>Main<br>Plenary 2 |
| | Describe the process of gravitropism. | | Starter 2<br>Main<br>Plenary 1 and 2 |
| | Use scientific theories to develop a hypothesis. | | Main |
| **Aiming for GRADE 8** ↓ | Explain the role of auxins on phototropism. | C, 3 | Main<br>Plenary 2 |
| | Explain the role of auxins in gravitropism. | C | Main<br>Plenary 1 and 2 |
| | Use scientific theories to develop a hypothesis that clearly links a dependent and independent variable. | | Main |

**Literacy**

During the main activity, students will need to produce coherent, well-structured responses to questions.

**Key words**

auxin, gravitropism, phototropism, tropism

## B3.2 The endocrine system

| Starter | Support/Extend | Resources |
|---|---|---|
| **Responses in plants** (5 minutes)   Show a short film of time lapse of plant growth as a stimulus for discussion. There are good examples of bramble-growing. Ask students what the plants are doing. Are they responding to light? How do they respond? Why? (If you are concerned the film is too close to your main activity, avoid any commentary on the film, or simply ask 'Do plants respond to the environment?') | **Extend:** Link to photosynthesis. | |
| **Crooked plants** (10 minutes)   Use examples of plants in your lab window. Most pot plants will have their leaves angled toward the light. Discuss why this has happened. What has the plant responded to? Why has the plant done this? What will happen if you turn the plant around? How will the plant achieve this? How long will it take? | **Extend:** Ask students what they think might happen in the roots. | |

| Main | Support/Extend | Resources |
|---|---|---|
| **Tropisms** (20 minutes)   Introduce to students the concepts of phototropism and gravitropism. Build on the Starter activities to discuss why it is important for plant growth that plant shoots grow upwards and towards light, and for roots to grow downwards. Supply students with unlabelled diagrams of the seedlings, and ask them to annotate the diagrams, writing captions in their own words to explain what is happening. | **Support:** Supply students with a range of key words that they must include (phototropism, light, gravitropism, gravity). | |
| **Investigating newly germinated shoots** (20 minutes)   Students work in small groups to write a hypothesis on the effect of light on the growth of seedlings and then plan a method to allow them to investigate it. They may need reminding to set one or more controls so that they can accurately describe the effect of the independent variable. After checking their method, allow students to set up their investigation and leave it for at least five days for the seedlings to grow. | **Support:** Students can simply set up an experiment using germinated cress seeds in a box with a hole cut in the side to investigate the effect of light from one direction.   **Extend:** They should also write a scientific prediction. | **Practical:** Investigating newly germinated shoots |

| Plenary | Support/Extend | Resources |
|---|---|---|
| **Plants in space** (10 minutes)   Either show images of gravitropism experiments carried out in space, or talk about the experiments. Ask the students to describe and explain what has happened. What type of tropism was being investigated? Why have these results occurred? | **Extend:** Ask students why it might be important for us to be able to grow plants in space. | |
| **Seedlings in space** (5 minutes)   Use the interactive in which students complete a multiple choice activity about the growth of seedlings in space. | | **Interactive:** Seedlings in space |

| Homework | | |
|---|---|---|
| Your teacher will give you an image of several classic experiments investigating tropisms and auxins, for example, use of agar block, mica plates, covering shoot tips, etc. In each case, predict what might happen and why. | | |

**kerboodle**

A Kerboodle highlight for this lesson is **Working scientifically: Does light affect the germination of seedlings?** Refer to the **Content map** on Kerboodle for a full list of resources and assessment.

# GCSE BIOLOGY ONLY
## B3.2.7 Uses of plant hormones

**Specification links:**

B3.2h Describe some of the variety of effects of plant hormones, relating to auxins, gibberellins, and ethene. **H**
To include controlling growth, controlling germination, fruit ripening, flower opening, and shedding of leaves.

B3.2i Describe some of the different ways in which people use plant hormones to control plant growth. To include selective herbicides, root cuttings, seedless fruit (parthenocarpic fruit development), and altering dormancy. **H**

WS1.1e Explain everyday and technological applications of science.

WS1.1f Evaluate associated personal, social, economic, and environmental implications.

WS2a Carry out experiments.

WS2b Make and record observations and measurements using a range of apparatus and methods.

WS2c Present observations using appropriate methods.

WS2d Communicate the scientific rational for investigations, methods used, findings, and reasoned conclusions.

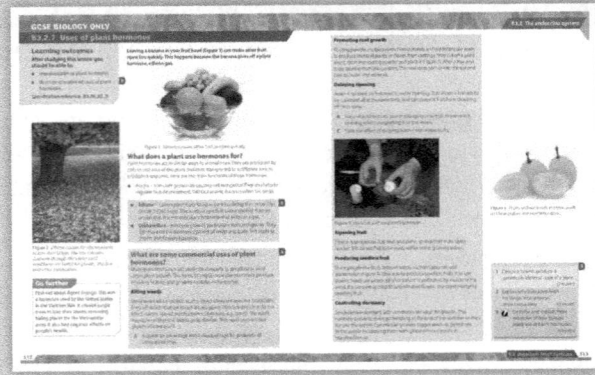

| Target | Outcome | Checkpoint | |
|---|---|---|---|
| | | Question | Activity |
| **Aiming for GRADE 4** | Give an example of a plant hormone. | B, 1, 3 | Starter 1<br>Main<br>Plenary 1 |
| | State one advantage of the use of plant hormones. | 3 | Starter 1<br>Main<br>Plenary 2 |
| **Aiming for GRADE 6** | Describe some of the effects of plant hormones on the plant. | B, C, 1, 2, 3 | Starter 1 and 2<br>Main<br>Plenary 1 and 2 |
| | Describe commercial uses of plant hormones. | A, B, 2, 3 | Starter 1 and 2<br>Main<br>Plenary 1 | **H** |
| | Describe some impacts on society of the use of plant hormones. | A, 3 | Starter 1<br>Main |
| **Aiming for GRADE 8** | Explain how plant hormones have their effects on plants. | 2, 3 | Main<br>Plenary 2 |
| | Explain the commercial advantages of using plant hormones. | A, 2, 3 | Starter 1<br>Main | **H** |
| | Evaluate the economic and other benefits to society of the commercial use of plant hormones. | | Main<br>Plenary 2 |

**Literacy**
During the main activity, students will be required to summarise texts with accuracy, and to demonstrate understanding.

**Key words**
ethene, gibberellins

# B3.2 The endocrine system

| Starter | Support/Extend | Resources |
|---|---|---|
| **Hormonal benefits** (10 minutes) Provide groups of students with a series of statements about the effects of use of hormones, for example, fruit ripening at the same time, seedless fruit produced, weed killers, rooting powders, controlling dormancy, or germination. Student groups discuss why we might use hormones for these reasons. They describe the advantage and explain why it is of benefit. | **Support:** Filter the statements to the statements relevant to auxins. **Extend:** Consider the negative effects. | |
| **Weed killers** (5 minutes) Show a short TV advert for a weed-killer. Ask the class how they think it works. Elicit the following ideas: Most weeds in a crop field are broad-leaved. Plants absorb weed-killers mainly through the leaves. Broad-leaved weeds absorb more weed-killer. Narrow-leaved plants are able to breakdown the weed-killer. Then surprise students with the fact that many weed-killers contain the plant hormone auxin. | **Extend:** Ask class to suggest why auxin might kill the weeds. | **H** |

| Main | Support/Extend | Resources |
|---|---|---|
| **Results** (15 minutes) Record observations of the effect of light on seedlings seen in the experiment set up in the previous lesson. Students explain what has happened, why it happened, and what has caused the growth pattern. | **Support:** More time can be given to this first task if needed. Provide a table to indicate what observations to record. | |
| **Uses of hormones** (25 minutes) Create a table, which students complete, to state which hormones are involved in the different processes, and explain how they work. Suggested column headings: Name of the hormone Actions of the hormone Commercial uses of the hormones Economic benefits of the uses. | **Support:** Only required to consider auxins, and do not need to consider the economic benefits. **Extend:** Add a column to evaluate the advantages and disadvantages. | **Activity:** Uses of hormones  **H** |

| Plenary | Support/Extend | Resources |
|---|---|---|
| **Uses of plant hormones** (5 minutes) Use the interactive activity in which students drag and drop the uses of plant hormones to sort them into hormone categories. | **Extend:** State the other hormones that would control the non-auxin-controlled effects. | **Interactive:** Uses of plant hormones  **H** |
| **Rotten bananas** (10 minutes) State that bananas release ethene as they ripen. Ask the class to discuss in pairs the implications of this fact on the transport of the fruit to shops and the home, and the storage of the fruit in shops and the home. | **Extend:** Why do growers store and transport bananas in cool conditions, but not cold? | |

| Homework | | |
|---|---|---|
| Create an advert for a gardening magazine to promote any product that uses plant hormones. The advert should be attractive, appealing, and include scientific detail. | | |

**kerboodle**
A Kerboodle highlight for this lesson is **Go further: More plant hormones**. Refer to the **Content map** on Kerboodle for a full list of resources and assessment.

# Checkpoint
## B3.2 The endocrine system

### Overview of B3.2 The endocrine system

In this chapter, students have studied hormones as chemical messengers, endocrine glands and target organs, and how hormones work to control body processes. They should be able to link this work with homeostasis in B3.3 *Maintaining internal environments*. Students should know where the main glands are located and be able to compare the action of the nervous system with that of the endocrine system. Higher-tier students should be able to explain the process of negative feedback, as applied to thyroxine and adrenaline.

Students should know about the menstrual cycle and its hormonal control. They should be able to state the four main hormones involved the responses they initiate. Higher-tier students should be able to interpret a graph of changing hormone levels through the month, and be able to explain how the hormones control the menstrual cycle. They should be able to describe the interactions between the menstrual cycle hormones in terms of negative feedback processes.

Students should be able to evaluate hormonal and non-hormonal methods of contraception. Higher-tier students should be able to describe the use of hormones to treat infertility and give examples of the use of hormones for treatment, including IVF.

Students should be able to outline the action of plant hormones and plant tropisms including phototropism and gravitropism. They should understand the action of auxin in terms of its unequal distribution and how it causes cell elongation. Higher-tier students should be able to describe commercial uses of plant hormones including auxins, gibberellins, and ethene.

You can find additional support for the maths skills covered in this chapter on **MyMaths**, including extracting and interpreting information from line graphs, and comparing percentages.

For this chapter, the following assessments are available on Kerboodle:
B3.2 Checkpoint quiz: The endocrine system
B3.2 Progress quiz: The endocrine system 1
B3.2 Progress quiz: The endocrine system 2
B3.2 On your marks: The endocrine system
B3.2 Exam-style questions and mark scheme: The endocrine system

### Checkpoint follow-up lesson

A student's route through this lesson can be determined using the Checkpoint assessment. Percentage pass marks are supplied in the Checkpoint teacher notes.

For each successive route through it is assumed that the student can perform to their current route as well as previous routes. For example, students working at Aiming for 6 are assumed to be secure in Aiming for 4 knowledge and understanding and working towards achieving all the learning objectives for Aiming for 6.

## B3.2 The endocrine system

|  | **Aiming for 4** | **Aiming for 6** | **Aiming for 8** |
|---|---|---|---|
| **Learning outcomes** | State some of the functions of the hormones of the endocrine system. | Describe some of the functions of the hormones of the endocrine system. | Describe some of the functions of the hormones of the endocrine system. |
|  | State what happens during the menstrual cycle. | Describe what happens during the menstrual cycle. | Explain what happens during the menstrual cycle. |
|  | State some uses of plant hormones. | Describe some uses of plant hormones. | Explain some uses of plant hormones. |
| **Starter** | **Hormones (5 minutes)** Ask students in pairs to write down as many hormones in the body as they can think of, then compare with a neighbouring pair. Summarise the hormones they have listed on the board. | | |
| **Differentiated checkpoint activity** | **Activity 1 The endocrine system (15 minutes)** Students each answer question 1 on the differentiated worksheets, which asks them to label a diagram of the endocrine system and state the functions of hormones. | | |
|  | The Aiming for 4 sheet provides the labels for students to use. These students will complete a table of the functions of hormones. | The Aiming for 6 sheet provides the hormones for students to use to label the diagram, but not the glands. Students draw a table of the functions of the named hormones. Students can check each others' answers. | Aiming for 8 students write the labels for the glands and hormones. They draw a table of the functions of the hormones they have labelled. |
|  | **Activity 2 The menstrual cycle (15 minutes)** Ask questions to establish how much students can remember about the menstrual cycle, such as – when does ovulation occur? How long does the period last? What hormones are involved? Students then complete question 2 about the menstrual cycle on the differentiated worksheets. They may need access to the Student book. The sheets offer varying levels of support, with the Aiming for 4 sheet asking structured questions, the Aiming for 6 sheet asking more detailed structured questions, and the Aiming for 8 sheet asking for explanations of the cycle. | | |
|  | **Activity 3 Plant hormones and their uses (15 minutes)** You will need a plant that has been growing towards light from one direction. Show the plant and ask targeted questions about what has happened to the plant and why. Students then complete question 3 on the differentiated worksheets. | | |
|  | The Aiming for 4 activity provides hormone labels for students to cut out and match with their uses. Students will need access to scissors and glue sticks. | Aiming for 6 students make a visual summary of the uses of some named plant hormones. They can check each other's work through peer assessment or using the Student book. | Aiming for 8 students make a visual summary of the uses of plant hormones without any prompts. They can check each other's work through peer assessment or using the Student book. |
|  | **Kerboodle resource:** B3.2 Checkpoint follow-up: Aiming for 4, B3.2 Checkpoint follow-up: Aiming for 6, B3.2 Checkpoint follow-up: Aiming for 8 | | |
| **Plenary** | **Hormone card sort (5 minutes)** Each small groups of students will need a set of cards with hormone names. Ask students to sort the cards into groups, selecting appropriate cards for each grouping, for example, plant and animal hormones, hormones released by the pituitary gland, menstrual hormones, the hormone that causes eggs to mature. | | |
| **Progression** | The Aiming for 4 activities provide highly structured questions. Teachers will need to check students' answers. Aiming for 4 students may benefit from seeing models of the human body showing the gland positions. To help them understand the hormones of the menstrual cycle, they could use different colours to track the changes in level of each hormone on a graph. | The Aiming for 6 activities are reasonably structured. The questions should not require any introduction from the teacher. A debate about the advantages and disadvantages of fertility treatment would allow all abilities to put over their points of view on this higher-tier topic. | The Aiming for 8 activities have very little structure. Students should be able to complete the activities without introduction. Aiming for 8 students can produce a graph showing how the concentrations of the menstrual cycle hormones change. An extension task for these students might be to research how hormones work in terms of their interaction with DNA and protein synthesis. There are opportunities for practical work on plant hormones to be extended to investigate other factors. |

# GCSE BIOLOGY ONLY
# B3.3 Maintaining internal environments
## B3.3.1 Controlling body temperature

**Specification links:**

B3.3a Explain the importance of maintaining a constant internal environment in response to internal and external change. To include allowing metabolic reactions to proceed at appropriate rates.

B3.3b Describe the function of the skin in the control of body temperature. To include detection of external temperature, sweating, shivering, change to blood flow.

B3.3j Explain the response of the body to different temperature and osmotic challenges. **H**

WS1.4a Use scientific vocabulary, terminology, and definitions.

WS2a Carry out experiments. WS2b Make and record observations and measurements using a range of apparatus and methods. WS2c Presenting observations using appropriate methods. WS2d Communicating the scientific rational for investigations, methods used, findings, and reasoned conclusions.

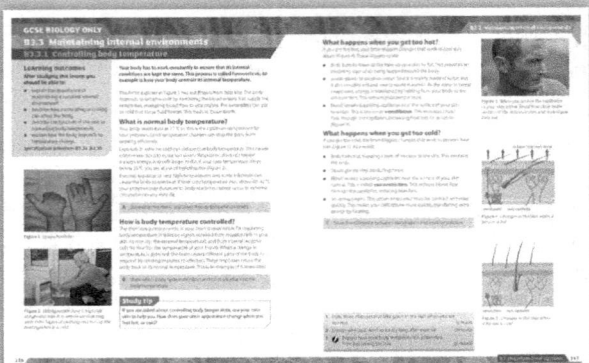

| Target | Outcome | Checkpoint | |
|---|---|---|---|
| | | Question | Activity |
| **Aiming for GRADE 4** ↓ | State some of the changes that occur in the skin at high or low temperatures. | 1 | Starter 1 and 2<br>Main<br>Plenary 1 and 2 |
| | State what is meant by homeostasis. | | Starter 2<br>Main<br>Plenary 1 and 2 |
| | Make and record measurements from an experiment. | | Main |
| **Aiming for GRADE 6** ↓ | Describe the function of the skin in controlling body temperature. | C, 2, 3 | Starter 1 and 2<br>Main<br>Plenary 1 |
| | Describe how overheating or cooling can affect the body. | A, B, 3 | Starter 2<br>Main<br>Plenary 1 and 2 **H** |
| | Make and record accurate measurements in a clear table. | | Main |
| **Aiming for GRADE 8** ↓ | Explain in detail the body's responses to temperature change. | 2, 3 | Main<br>Plenary 2 **H** |
| | Explain the importance of maintaining a constant internal environment. | 3 | Starter 2<br>Plenary 2 |
| | Make and record accurate, repeated measurements systematically in a well-organised table with clear headings and units. | | Main |

**Maths**
During the main activity, students will collect data from an experiment, find the arithmetic means for the data (M2b), and plot two variables (M4c).

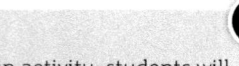

**Literacy**
During the main activity, students will need to produce coherent, well-structured statements to explain the findings of their experiment.

**Key words**
homeostasis, vasoconstriction, vasodilation

116

## B3.3 Maintaining internal environments

| Starter | Support/Extend | Resources |
|---|---|---|
| **Structure of the skin** (10 minutes)  Show an unlabelled image of a section through the skin. Ask students to identify it; name the major structures; and describe what each structure does. Ensure that you cover the structures used in temperature control. | **Support:** Have the functions of the parts either on a board, or on cards, and have students match the function to a part during the discussion. | |
| **In balance** (5 minutes)  Ask a student to hold a piece of trunking in balance. Place a marble in the middle. Ask the student to try to keep the marble in balance throughout the activity. Tell them that many things in the body are kept in balance. Ask them to suggest some and focus on temperature control. Then add a weight to one end of the trunking, this is an increase in body temperature. The student will counter balance to bring the marble back to the middle. Explain that, similarly, the body will counter balance to maintain a constant internal body temperature. This is an example of homeostasis. Repeat for as many temperature examples as time permits. | **Extend:** Ask students to suggest ways the body will respond to counter the increase in temperature, etc. Also, ask students what the implications are to the body of not correcting the temperature. | |

| Main | Support/Extend | Resources |
|---|---|---|
| **Investigating the effect of wind chill on body temperature** (30 minutes)  Students set up two retort stands 100 cm apart. Place a hair dryer in one stand. Fill a boiling tube with warm water (37 °C). This represents a model of the human body. Attach a paper towel around the outside, and keep moist throughout the experiment. This represents sweating. Place a thermometer inside the water tube.<br>When the temperature is stable, start the hair dryer running on a cool setting. Record the initial temperature and the temperature after a fixed period of time (5 minutes).<br>Record the temperature drop. Repeat three times with fresh warm water. Repeat using the distances 80 cm, 60 cm, 40 cm and 20 cm.<br>As the experiment is time-consuming, allocate one distance to each group and collate class results.<br>Calculate the average (mean) temperature drop for each distance. Plot a graph of temperature drop against distance.<br>Students write a conclusion, including a description of the pattern shown by the results and an evaluation of the usefulness of the model.<br>SAFETY: Take care to keep water and mains electricity apart. | **Support:** Provide a table format.<br>**Extend:** Consider what other factors could be investigated using this model. | **Practical:** Wind chill |
| **Over or under** (10 minutes)  Divide the class into groups. Half the groups will need to explain hypothermia, the other half heat stroke. To help them, give all groups a series of cards that contain one of the following prompts: temperature, enzymes, chemical reactions, respiration.<br>The students need to try to explain the two situations using the prompts. | **Support:** Issue the cards one at a time in a logical sequence to help students frame a response.<br>**Extend:** Issue fewer cards. | |

| Plenary | Support/Extend | Resources |
|---|---|---|
| **Controlling body temperature** (5 minutes)  Use the interactive to drag and drop statements about changes in the body in response to temperature into two columns, entitled 'Keeping warm' and 'Cooling down'.<br>**Extending the experiment** (10 minutes)  Ask students in groups to suggest modifications to the basic experimental method that they have carried out, which would allow them to investigate some of the other factors mentioned above that affect temperature control, for example, hair/clothing, body size, etc. | | **Interactive:** Controlling body temperature |

| Homework |
|---|
| Write what a sports manufacturer has to consider when designing clothes for warm weather sports like tennis, or cold weather sports like skiing. |

**kerboodle**
A Kerboodle highlight for this lesson is **Working Scientifically: Body temperature frequency diagram**. Refer to the **Content map** on Kerboodle for a full list of resources and assessment.

**B3 Organism-level systems** 117

# B3.3.2 Controlling blood sugar

**Specification links:**

B3.3c Explain how insulin controls blood sugar levels in the body.

B3.3d Explain how glucagon interacts with insulin to control blood sugar levels in the body. **H**

B3.3e Compare type 1 and type 2 diabetes, and explain how they can be treated.

WS1.1e Explain everyday and technological applications of science.

WS1.3e Interpret observations and other data.

WS2a Carry out experiments.

WS2b Make and record observations and measurements using a range of apparatus and methods.

WS2c Present observations using appropriate methods.

WS2d Communicate the scientific rational for investigations, methods used, findings, and reasoned conclusions.

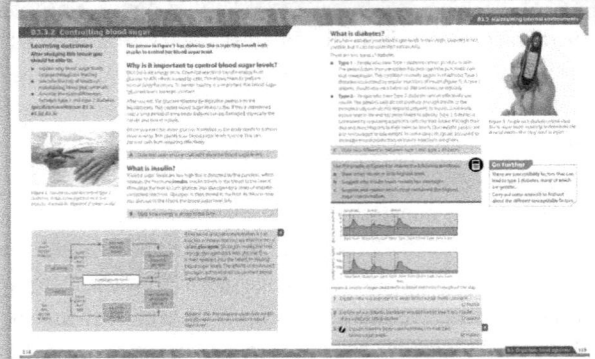

| Target | Outcome | Checkpoint | |
|---|---|---|---|
| | | Question | Activity |
| **Aiming for GRADE 4** | Name a hormone involved in blood sugar control. | | Starter 2<br>Main<br>Plenary 1 and 2 |
| | State why blood sugar levels change throughout the day. | A | Starter 1 and 2<br>Main<br>Plenary 2 |
| | State basic observations about blood sugar levels obtained in an experiment. | | Main |
| **Aiming for GRADE 6** | Explain the role of insulin in maintaining blood glucose levels. | B, 1, 3 | Starter 2<br>Main<br>Plenary 1 and 2 |
| | Describe the main differences between type 1 and type 2 diabetes. | C | Starter 2<br>Main<br>Plenary 1 |
| | Interpret data, obtained in an experiment, to describe the changes in blood glucose levels. | | Main |
| **Aiming for GRADE 8** | Explain the role of glucagon and insulin in maintaining blood glucose levels. | 3 | Main<br>Plenary 2 |
| | Explain the differences between the treatments for type 1 and type 2 diabetes. | | Main<br>Plenary 1 |
| | Interpret data, obtained in an experiment, to explain the changes in blood glucose levels and compare with other data. | | Main |

**Maths**
During the main activity, students will be required to plot two variables from experimental data (M4c).

**Literacy**
During the main activity, students will need to produce coherent, well-structured statements to explain the findings of their experiment.

**Key words**
diabetes, glucagon, insulin

# B3.3 Maintaining internal environments

| Starter | Support/Extend | Resources |
|---|---|---|
| **Balancing sugar** (5 minutes)  Remind students of the balancing analogy used in the previous lesson (Starter 2). State that we also need to balance our blood sugar/glucose. Ask how we get sugar into our body (students usually mention diet) and how we can reduce our blood glucose (they usually mention exercise). Then introduce the role of the liver. | **Extend:** Ask students what would happen during a lack of food. | |
| **Key words** (10 minutes)  Provide groups of students with a series of key words, all connected to the control of blood glucose. Ask students in their groups to write a short sentence that uses the word correctly in relation to blood glucose control. Feed back to the class. Correct any errors and provide an explanation for any unknown key words. | **Support:** Only use words applicable to the foundation tier (not glucagon). **Extend:** Include glucagon. **H** | |

| Main | Support/Extend | Resources |
|---|---|---|
| **Investigating glucose levels in urine** (40 minutes)  Use a suitable method that includes the following instructions: a series of five synthetic urine samples supposedly taken from a patient at regular time intervals (15 minutes) following a sugary meal. A second set of tubes should be used supposedly from a person with diabetes. Students use Clinistix to measure the amount of glucose present. To do this they dip the stick into the urine for 10 seconds, remove from the urine, and wipe the excess urine from the stick with paper. Allow a further 10 seconds for the reaction to take place, and compare the colour to the colour chart and record the amount of glucose in mmol/l. Record the results in a table and plot a line graph showing both normal and diabetic results. Students answer questions explaining the role of insulin in controlling the blood glucose level, and the difference in a person with diabetes. In type 1 diabetes, the insulin levels do not rise, so students should explain the impact on blood glucose. However, in type 2 diabetes, the insulin levels do rise, so students need to explain the lack of a response. | **Support:** Do the two sets of tests separately. Provide a results table. **Extend:** Ask students to explain what would happen following a period of starvation and the role of glucagon. **H** | **Practical:** Investigating glucose levels in urine |

| Plenary | Support/Extend | Resources |
|---|---|---|
| **Diabetes** (5 minutes)  Use the drag and drop sorting interactive to decide whether statements are about type 1 or type 2 diabetes. | | **Interactive:** Diabetes |
| **Negative feedback** (10 minutes)  Remind students about negative feedback and control mechanisms. Then issue groups with a large sheet of paper (flip chart, if possible) and ask them to draw an annotated flow chart to illustrate negative feedback in the action of insulin. | **Support:** Provide a series of statements on cards for students to construct the flow chart. **Extend:** Repeat the task for glucagon. | **H** |

| Homework | | |
|---|---|---|
| Write an information leaflet or a page from a medical book, aimed at young people aged 10–14, who have been diagnosed with type 1 diabetes. The text should explain clearly, but in suitable language, what has happened in their body and how they can manage the condition. | | |

**kerboodle**
A Kerboodle highlight for this lesson is **Literacy interactive: Glucose, glycogen, and glucagon**. Refer to the **Content map** on Kerboodle for a full list of resources and assessment.

# GCSE BIOLOGY ONLY
## B3.3.3 Maintaining water balance

**Specification links:**

B3.3f Explain the effect on cells of osmotic changes in body fluids. To include higher, lower, or equal water potentials leading to lysis or shrinking (no mathematical use of water potentials required).

B3.3g Describe the function of the kidneys in maintaining the water balance of the body. To include varying the amount and concentration of urine and hence water excreted.

WS1.1b Use models to solve problems, make predictions, and to develop scientific explanations and understanding of familiar and unfamiliar facts.

WS2a Carry out experiments.

WS2b Make and record observations and measurements using a range of apparatus and methods.

WS2c Present observations using appropriate methods.

WS2d Communicate the scientific rational for investigations, methods used, findings, and reasoned conclusions.

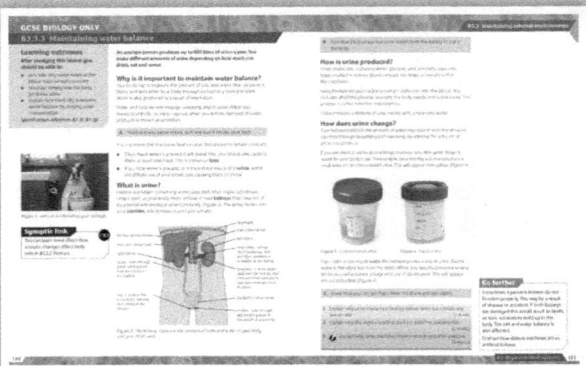

| Target | Outcome | Checkpoint | |
|---|---|---|---|
| | | Question | Activity |
| **Aiming for GRADE 4** | State the ways in which water enters and leaves the body. | A, B | Starter 1 and 2<br>Main<br>Plenary 2 |
| | State that water moves into and out of a cell by osmosis. | | Starter 2<br>Main<br>Plenary 1 |
| | Use a model to make observations of osmosis in cells. | | Main |
| **Aiming for GRADE 6** | Describe how the water level in the blood is maintained by the production of urine. | B, C | Starter 1<br>Plenary 2 |
| | Describe the effect of osmosis on cells. | | Starter 2<br>Main<br>Plenary 1 |
| | Use a model to describe the effect of osmosis on cells. | | Main |
| **Aiming for GRADE 8** | Explain how the body maintains water balance by varying urine concentration. | 2, 3 | Starter 1<br>Main<br>Plenary 2 |
| | Explain the movement of water into and out of cells down a water potential gradient. | | Starter 2<br>Main<br>Plenary 1 |
| | Use models to explain the significance of water potential gradients in scientific applications. | | Main |

**Literacy**
During the main activity, students will be required to write coherent, succinct, and well-structured texts.

**Key words**
bladder, kidneys, lysis, urine, solute

# B3.3 Maintaining internal environments

| Starter | Support/Extend | Resources |
|---|---|---|
| **Water balance** (5 minutes) Show an image of a person standing in the middle of a see-saw. State that we keep water levels balanced in the body. Ask students to suggest ways that water gets into our body and ways that it gets out, and to write these on either side of the image on the board. Then elicit from students that the body maintains water balance by varying urine concentration and volume. | **Extend:** Focus on the idea of balance, for example, why do we vary the amount we drink or urinate? | |
| **Dehydration** (10 minutes) Give each group in the class a sheet of A4 paper with four boxes drawn on it. Ask the class a series of four questions, for example, what is dehydration? Describe the symptoms of dehydration. Explain what they think the effect will be inside the body, especially to our cells, for example, dehydration of brain cells leads to headaches, etc. Ask why dehydration is dangerous. The students write key words in the box for each question. Then feed back to class. | **Support:** Remind the class about osmosis when talking about the effects.<br>**Extend:** Consider over-hydration. | |

| Main | Support/Extend | Resources |
|---|---|---|
| **Investigating osmosis**<br>1. **Creating model cells** (10 minutes) Set up two model cells, using Visking tubing, both containing a sugar solution. One of the cell models will be placed in dilute sugar solution (1%), the other into concentrated (saturated) sugar solution. Leave them for 20 minutes.<br>2. **Osmosis and animal cells** (25 minutes) Provide students with a diagram showing a diagrammatic animal cell, and showing one placed in dilute solution or water and one placed in a more concentrated solution. These solutions can represent the plasma. Ask students a series of questions at short, timed intervals at which times they annotate the diagram. For example:<br>• Describe what you think will happen to the cells in each case.<br>• Give an example of when excess water might get into the body, creating a dilute plasma around the cells.<br>• Give an example of when excess water might leave the body, creating a concentrated plasma around the cells.<br>• Indicate the direction of movement of the water molecules for each animal cell.<br>• Explain why the water moves in each case.<br>3. **Model cells results** (5 minutes) Look at the results of the model cells. Write observations and relate this to the real cells on the annotated diagrams. | **Support:** Provide key words or discuss each question as a class before they write a response.<br><br>**Extend:** Include the following:<br>• Give an example of this in the body.<br>• Suggest where it might occur during medical treatments.<br>• Suggest how the body might maintain a more constant plasma concentration. | **Practical:** Investigating osmosis |

| Plenary | Support/Extend | Resources |
|---|---|---|
| **Water in and out of cells** (5 minutes) Use the gap fill interactive, which describes and explains how water moves into and out of cells, down water potential gradients.<br>**Five steps of separation** (10 minutes) Starting with normal blood water levels, students write five statements that describe how they will return to normal blood water level, if they have drunk a litre of water. Repeat for dehydration, if time allows. | | **Interactive:** Water in and out of cells |

| Homework |
|---|
| Write an explanation for a survival manual that explains the statement 'you can only survive three days without water'. |

*kerboodle*
A Kerboodle highlight for this lesson is **Bump up your grade: Osmosis**. Refer to the **Content map** on Kerboodle for a full list of resources and assessment.

# GCSE BIOLOGY ONLY
## B3.3.4 Inside the kidney

**Specification links:**

B3.3g Describe the function of the kidneys in maintaining the water balance of the body. To include varying the amount and concentration of urine, and hence water, excreted. **H**

B3.3h Describe the gross structure of the kidney and the structure of the kidney tubule.

B3.3i Describe the effect of ADH on the permeability of the kidney tubules. To include amount of water reabsorbed and negative feedback. **H**

WS1.4a Use scientific vocabulary, terminology, and definitions.

WS2a Carry out experiments.

WS2b Make and record observations and measurements using a range of apparatus and methods.

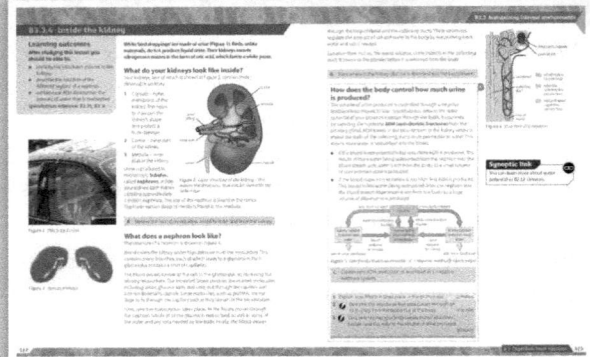

| Target | Outcome | Checkpoint | |
|---|---|---|---|
| | | Question | Activity |
| **Aiming for GRADE 4** ↓ | Identify the structures present in the kidney. | A, B, 2 | Starter 1 and 2 |
| | State that the concentration of urine can change. | | Main, Plenary 1 |
| | Use some scientific vocabulary when discussing the structure or function of the kidney. | 2 | Starter 1 and 2, Main |
| **Aiming for GRADE 6** ↓ | Describe the function of the different regions of a nephron. | B, 1 | Main, Plenary 1 and 2 |
| | Describe how the kidney can produce varying amounts of urine depending upon the body's level of hydration. | 3 | Main, Plenary 1 **H** |
| | Use appropriate scientific vocabulary when describing the function of the nephron. | 1, 2 | Main |
| **Aiming for GRADE 8** ↓ | Explain ultrafiltration and selective reabsorption in the nephron. | 1 | Main, Plenary 1 and 2 |
| | Explain how ADH determines the amount of water that is reabsorbed. | C 3 | Main **H** |
| | Use a full range of scientific vocabulary and terminology to explain the functioning of the nephron. | 1 | Main |

**Maths**
During the main activity, students will use ratios, fractions, and percentages (M1c).

**Literacy**
During the main activity, students will be required to write coherent, succinct, and well-structured texts.

**Key words**
ADH (anti-diuretic hormone), nephron, tubule

122

## B3.3 Maintaining internal environments

| Starter | Support/Extend | Resources |
|---|---|---|
| **Kidney dissection** (10 minutes) Remind the class of the function of the kidney. Then, either as a demonstration or in groups, dissect the kidney to reveal the outer cortex (refer to capsule), the medulla, and the pelvis.<br>**Parts of the kidney** (5 minutes) Use the interactive which asks students to label a diagram of a kidney. Please note – this is used as a teaching (not consolidating) activity. | **Extend:** Indicate the basic functions of these zones. | **Interactive:** Parts of the kidney |

| Main | Support/Extend | Resources |
|---|---|---|
| **The function of the nephron** (40 minutes) Divide the class into about four or five groups, and clear areas of lab floor or large table areas. Provide each group with a 2 m sheet of wallpaper onto which the students will draw a nephron outline with a blood vessel (in glomerulus at least, but around tubule, if possible).<br>Provide the students with a bag of plastic counters, which represent the contents of the blood. [Large red, large white, (which represent red and white blood cells); medium-sized orange counters (proteins); small blue counters (water molecules), small yellow counters (urea), small green counters (sugar), and small purple counters (salts).]<br>Students place all the blood contents into the blood vessel in the glomerulus. The teacher reads a script that describes the process of ultrafiltration: larger discs (red, white, and orange) cannot be filtered, so students will need to create pores for the filtration. Next, describe reabsorption by active transport (sugar) or osmosis (water), or active transport/diffusion (salts). Students then move the counter along the nephron as the teacher narrates the process. | **Support:** Pre-draw the nephron. Remove salts from the bag of counters.<br>**Extend:** Ask students to explain how ADH determines the amount of water that is reabsorbed. [H] | **Activity:** The function of the nephron |

| Plenary | Support/Extend | Resources |
|---|---|---|
| **Higher or lower?** (5 minutes) Play a gameshow-style activity with the class. Start with the concentration of any one of the relevant substances in the blood as it enters the kidney. As the substance moves into the next part of the nephron, students call out whether the concentration is higher or lower.<br>**Present or not?** (10 minutes) Have a series of synthetic solutions set up labelled blood plasma, glomerular filtrate, urine. Tell the students that you will test the solutions for proteins (biuret) and glucose (Clinistix). They predict whether or not protein or glucose will be present in each sample. They can also predict for urea and salts. | **Support:** Avoid salts and water.<br><br>**Extend:** How will the results be different for someone with diabetes or kidney damage? | |

| Homework | | |
|---|---|---|
| Research kidney dialysis machines and either write an account or draw a labelled diagram to show how the machine replaces the function of the kidney. This could be in the form of a leaflet explaining the function of the machine to new users. | | |

**kerboodle**

A Kerboodle highlight for this lesson is **Extension: The role of ADH**. Refer to the **Content map** on Kerboodle for a full list of resources and assessment.

# GCSE BIOLOGY ONLY — HIGHER TIER
## B3.3.5 Responding to osmotic challenges

**Specification links:**

B3.3j Explain the response of the body to different temperature and osmotic challenges. To include high sweating and dehydration, excess water intake, high salt intake. Responses to include mechanism of kidney function, thirst.

WS2a Carry out experiments.

WS2b Make and record observations and measurements using a range of apparatus and methods.

WS2c Present observations using appropriate methods.

WS2d Communicate the scientific rational for investigations, methods used, findings, and reasoned conclusions.

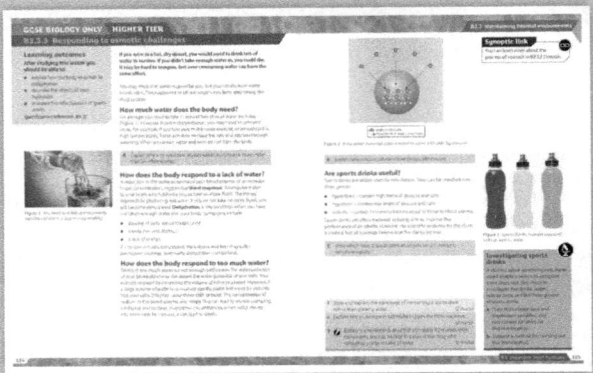

| Target | Outcome | Checkpoint | |
|---|---|---|---|
| | | Question | Activity |
| **Aiming for GRADE 6** ↓ | Describe the effects of over- and under-hydration on the body. | A, B | Starter 1<br>Plenary 2 |
| | Describe the constituents of different types of sports drinks. | C | Starter 2<br>Main<br>Plenary 1 and 2 |
| | Communicate findings from experiments and provide a basic conclusion. | | Main |
| **Aiming for GRADE 8** ↓ | Explain how the body responds to dehydration and over-hydration. | A, B, 2, 3 | Starter 1 |
| | Evaluate the effectiveness of sports drinks. | C, 1 | Main<br>Plenary 1 and 2 |
| | Communicate findings and give a reasoned conclusion based on scientific understanding. | | Main |

**Literacy**
During the main activity, students will need to produce coherent, well-structured sentences when explaining their findings.

**Key words**
dehydration, thirst response

# B3.3 Maintaining internal environments

| Starter | Support/Extend | Resources |
|---|---|---|
| **Over- or under-hydrated?** (10 minutes)  Provide groups with a sheet of paper with four empty boxes on it. Tell students that half the groups will consider over-hydration, the other half of the groups will consider under-hydration. Pose four questions and give the groups a minute to write down a response. The questions are: What do we mean by over-or under-hydration? What causes the condition? What are the responses of the body to this condition? Why is it dangerous to the body? Then have feedback, so that all groups learn from each other. | **Extend:** The last two questions should involve explanations. | |
| **Sports drinks** (5 minutes)  Use the interactive to link the component of a sports drink with its function in the body. | **Extend:** Explain how the component has the effect. | **Interactive:** Sports drinks |

| Main | Support/Extend | Resources |
|---|---|---|
| **Making sports drinks** (10 minutes)  Make up 250 cm³ of three different sports drinks, as follows: | **Support:** Have the drinks made-up beforehand, or use the real drinks. | **Practical:** Sports drinks |

| Drink | Glucose (g) | Electrolyte (g) | Water (cm³) |
|---|---|---|---|
| Hypotonic | 2.5 | 0.5 | 250 |
| Isotonic | 8.7 | 0.5 | 250 |
| Hypertonic | 22.0 | 0 | 250 |

| | | |
|---|---|---|
| **Testing sports drinks** (30 minutes)  Set up three osmometers. Each osmometer is filled with liquid that is at the same concentration as would be expected in the human body. (This should be the same concentration as in the isotonic drink.) Fill three beakers, one each with the three different drinks made. Suspend the Visking tubing in the beakers of different drinks. Observe the direction and extent of movement of the fluid in the tubing during the 20–30 minutes of the activity. Conclusion questions focus on the movement of the water into or out of body cells, and the impact that this will have on body cells. Suggest which of the drinks might be used at different stages of a sport. | **Support:** Make up the Visking tubing bags in advance.  **Extend:** Consider the effect if the body is under-hydrated before you drink. | |

| Plenary | Support/Extend | Resources |
|---|---|---|
| **Ingredients list** (10 minutes)  Either provide students with ingredients labels from sports drinks or project them. Ask students to go through the list and decide what is essential for function, what is desirable for sales, and what is not needed. If different drinks are used, then this could be done in groups, and students could feed back to the class about these. | **Extend:** Suggest which components contribute to heart function, muscle function, and temperature regulation. | |
| **Tour de France** (5 minutes)  You are in the back-up team for the cycle race. Suggest which type of drink you will give the cyclists at different points in the day and explain why. | | |

| Homework | | |
|---|---|---|
| You are a St John's Ambulance worker at an all-day pop concert. A patient is suffering from headaches, confusion, dizziness, lack of energy, and a high temperature. Diagnose what has happened to the person and suggest some treatments. | | |

**kerboodle**

A Kerboodle highlight for this lesson is **Working Scientifically: Sweat-beater: Fake or real?** Refer to the **Content map** on Kerboodle for a full list of resources and assessment.

# Checkpoint
## B3.3 Maintaining internal environments

### Overview of B3.3 Maintaining internal environments

In this chapter, students begin their study of homeostasis with the control of body temperature. They should be able to explain why and how we regulate body temperature, and outline the responses of the body to an increase or decrease in core temperature, and the consequences if body temperature rises too high or falls too low. They should understand that it is the blood vessels leading to the capillaries that constrict or dilate, not the capillaries themselves, that blood is diverted to the skin surface or kept near the core, and that temperature receptors respond to a change in temperature.

Students should understand how blood glucose concentration is controlled, including the role of insulin and, for higher-tier students, glucagon. Students should distinguish between type 1 and type 2 diabetes.

In studying the control of water balance and why this is important, students should be able to outline what urine is and how it is produced. They should understand that urine composition changes in response to the water content of the blood, and link this with osmosis from B2.1 *Supplying the cell*.

Students should be able to describe the structure of the kidney and of the nephron. They should understand how the kidneys filter the blood, and that many substances such as glucose are reabsorbed in selective reabsorption. They should link this with diffusion, osmosis, and active transport in B2.1 *Supplying the cell*. Higher-tier students should be familiar with the hormone ADH and the process of negative feedback in the homeostatic control of blood water content, linking with work in B3.2 *The endocrine system*.

Higher-tier students should be able to discuss how the body responds to dehydration and over-hydration, and the thirst response in humans. They should have carried out an evaluation on the effectiveness of sports drinks, linked with B2.1 *Supplying the cell* on osmosis and the consequences to animal cells when water potential is changed.

You can find additional support for the maths skills covered in this chapter on **MyMaths**, including finding the mean, plotting graphs, and working with ratios, fractions, and percentages.

For this chapter, the following assessments are available on Kerboodle:
B3.3 Checkpoint quiz: Maintaining internal environments
B3.3 Progress quiz: Maintaining internal environments 1
B3.3 Progress quiz: Maintaining internal environments 2
B3.3 On your marks: Maintaining internal environments
B3.3 Exam-style questions and mark scheme: Maintaining internal environments

### Checkpoint follow-up lesson

A student's route through this lesson can be determined using the Checkpoint assessment. Percentage pass marks are supplied in the Checkpoint teacher notes.

## B3.3 Maintaining internal environments

A student's route through this lesson can be determined using the Checkpoint assessment. Percentage pass marks are supplied in the Checkpoint teacher notes.

For each successive route through it is assumed that the student can perform to their current route as well as previous routes. For example, students working at Aiming for 6 are assumed to be secure in Aiming for 4 knowledge and understanding and working towards achieving all the learning objectives for Aiming for 6.

|  | Aiming for 4 | Aiming for 6 | Aiming for 8 |
|---|---|---|---|
| **Learning outcomes** | State the body's response to hot and cold conditions. | Describe the body's response to hot and cold conditions. | Explain the body's response to hot and cold conditions. |
|  | State the body's response to high blood glucose concentrations. | Describe the body's response to high and low blood glucose concentrations. | Explain the body's response to high and low blood glucose concentrations. |
|  | State the differences between type 1 and type 2 diabetes. | Describe the differences between type 1 and type 2 diabetes. | Explain the differences between type 1 and type 2 diabetes. |
|  | State the body's response to high and low water concentration in the blood. | Describe the body's response to high and low water concentration in the blood. | Explain the body's response to high and low water concentration in the blood. |
| **Starter** | **Controlling the body (5 minutes)** Ask students in pairs to write down as many conditions in the body that they can think of that need to be controlled, then compare with a neighbouring pair. Summarise their work on the board. | | |
| **Differentiated checkpoint activity** | **Activity 1 Temperature control (10 minutes)** Show pictures of someone in hot and cold conditions on screen. Ask – what can you see that tells you that they are cold/hot? Aiming for 4 and Aiming for 6 students complete question 1 on the differentiated worksheets, while Aiming for 8 students to complete question 1(a). | | |
|  | The Aiming for 4 sheet is a cut and paste exercise on the body's response when it is too hot or too cold. Students will need access to scissors and glue sticks. | The Aiming for 6 sheet asks students to list changes in the body under the headings too hot and too cold. | Aiming for 8 students spend the lesson building up a large visual summary to show how the body controls temperature, the glucose concentration of the blood, and the water concentration of the blood. |
|  | **Activity 2 Control of glucose concentration of the blood (20 minutes)** You will need a bag of sweets. Show the sweets and ask students targeted questions about digestion, such as – what happens to the sugar in the sweets inside the body? Where does glucose go in the body? Aiming for 4 and Aiming for 6 students complete question 2 on the differentiated worksheets, while Aiming for 8 students complete question 1(b). | | |
|  | The Aiming for 4 sheet provides statements for students to order to describe what happens to glucose in the body, followed by a table comparing type 1 and type 2 diabetes for them to complete. | Aiming for 6 students use the Student book to draw flow charts about what happens to glucose in the body, and what happens if someone has not eaten for a long time. They then draw a table comparing type 1 and type 2 diabetes. | Aiming for 8 students continue building up their visual summary. |
|  | **Activity 3 Kidney dissection demonstration (15 minutes)** You will need a kidney and dissection instruments. Carry out the dissection and ask targeted questions about what the kidney is for, the parts of the kidney, and the structures inside the kidney. Aiming for 4 and Aiming for 6 students complete question 3 on the differentiated worksheets, while Aiming for 8 students to complete question 1(c). | | |
|  | The Aiming for 4 sheet is a cut and paste exercise to produce a flow chart showing the body's response to drinking lots of water. These students will need access to scissors and glue sticks. | Aiming for 6 students use the Student book to draw flow charts describing what happens when someone drinks a large volume of water, and what happens when someone is dehydrated. They are given some hints to help them. | Aiming for 8 students continue building up their visual summary. They can peer assess their summaries. |
|  | **Kerboodle resource:** B3.3 Checkpoint follow-up: Aiming for 4, B3.3 Checkpoint follow-up: Aiming for 6, B3.3 Checkpoint follow-up: Aiming for 8 | | |
| **Plenary** | **Higher or lower? (5 minutes)** Each student will need two cards of different colours. Read out a series of statements and ask students to hold up a card to show whether the answer is higher or lower. Examples include – the glucose concentration of blood after a chocolate bar? The volume of urine after a large amount to drink? | | |
| **Progression** | The Aiming for 4 activities provide highly structured questions. Teachers may need to give a brief introduction to each question and check students' answers or provide them with answers to check each other's work. | The Aiming for 6 activities are reasonably structured. The questions should not require introduction. Teachers will need to check students' answers or provide them with answers to check each other's work. | The Aiming for 8 activity has very little structure. Students should be able to complete the task without introduction. There are no specific answers to their task but students can check their understanding through peer assessment or by using the Student book. |

# B3 Organism-level systems: Topic summary

**B3.1** Coordination and control – the nervous system
**B3.2** Coordination and control – the endocrine system
**B3.3** Maintaining internal environments

| Spec ref | Statement | Book spreads | |
|---|---|---|---|
| B3.1a | Describe the structure of the nervous system | B3.1.1 | |
| B3.1b | Explain how the components of the nervous system can produce a coordinated response | B3.1.1 | |
| B3.1c | Explain how the structure of a reflex arc is related to its function | B3.1.2 | |
| B3.1d | Explain how the main structures of the eye are related to their functions | B3.1.3 | S |
| B3.1e | Describe common defects of the eye and explain how some of these problems may be overcome | B3.1.3 | S |
| B3.1f | Describe the structure and function of the brain | B3.1.4 | S |
| B3.1g | Explain some of the difficulties of investigating brain function | B3.1.4 | H S |
| B3.1h | Explain some of the limitations in treating damage and disease in the brain and other parts of the nervous system | B3.1.5 | H S |
| B3.2a | Describe the principles of hormonal coordination and control by the human endocrine system | B3.2.1 | |
| B3.2b | Explain the roles of thyroxine and adrenaline in the body as examples of negative feedback systems | B3.2.2 | H |
| B3.2c | Describe the role of hormones in human reproduction including the control of the menstrual cycle | B3.2.1, B3.3.3 | |
| B3.2d | Explain the interactions of FSH, LH, oestrogen and progesterone in the control of the menstrual cycle | B3.3.3 | H |
| B3.2e | explain the use of hormones in contraception and evaluate hormonal and non-hormonal methods of contraception | B3.2.4 | |
| B3.2f | Explain the use of hormones in modern reproductive technologies to treat infertility | B3.2.5 | H |
| B3.2g | Explain how plant hormones are important in the control and coordination of plant growth and development, with reference to the role of auxins in phototropisms and gravitropisms | B3.2.6 | S |
| B3.2h | Describe some of the variety of effects of plant hormones, relating to auxins, gibberellins and ethene | B3.2.7 | S |
| B3.2i | Describe some of the different ways in which people use plant hormones to control plant growth | B3.2.7 | H S |
| B3.3a | Explain the importance of maintaining a constant internal environment in response to internal and external change | B3.3.1 | |
| B3.3b | Describe the function of the skin in the control of body temperature | B3.3.1 | S |
| B3.3c | Explain how insulin controls blood sugar levels in the body | B3.3.2 | |
| B3.3d | Explain how glucagon interacts with insulin to control blood sugar levels in the body | B3.3.2 | |
| B3.3e | Compare type 1 and type 2 diabetes and explain how they can be treated | B3.3.2 | |
| B3.3f | Explain the effect on cells of osmotic changes in body fluids | B3.3.3 | S |
| B3.3g | Describe the function of the kidneys in maintaining the water balance of the body | B3.3.3 | S |
| B3.3h | Describe the gross structure of the kidney and the structure of the kidney tubule | B3.3.4 | |
| B3.3i | Describe the effect of ADH on the permeability of the kidney tubules | B3.3.4 | H S |
| B3.3j | Explain the response of the body to different temperature and osmotic challenges | B3.3.1, B3.3.5 | H S |

## Maths

| Specification | | Book spread | |
|---|---|---|---|
| Spec ref | Statement | Main content | Maths chapter |
| BM3.1i | Extract and interpret data from graphs, charts and tables | | 6, 13, 14 |
| BM3.2i | Extract and interpret data from graphs, charts and tables | B3.2.3 | 6, 13, 14 |
| BM3.2ii | Translate information between numerical and graphical | B3.2.3 | 6, 13, 14 |
| BM3.3iii | Extract and interpret data from graphs, charts and tables | | 6, 13, 14 |

## Working scientifically

| Specification | | Book spread | |
|---|---|---|---|
| Spec ref | Statement | Main content | WS chapter |
| WS1.1b | Use models to solve problems, make predictions, and to develop scientific explanations and understanding of familiar and unfamiliar facts. | B3.1.3, B3.3.2–3 | WS2 |
| WS1.1d | Discuss ethical issues arising from developments in science. | B3.1.4, B3.2.4–5 | WS1 |
| WS1.1e | Explain everyday and technological applications of science. | B3.1.3, B3.1.5, B3.2.4–5, B3.2.7, B3.3.2 | WS1 |
| WS1.1f | Evaluate associated personal, social, economic, and environmental implications. | B3.1.5, B3.2.4–5, B3.2.7 | WS1 |
| WS1.1h | Evaluate risks both in practical science and the wider societal context. | B3.1.5 | WS1, WS4 |
| WS1.1g | Make decisions based on the evaluation of evidence and arguments. | B3.2.5 | |
| WS1.2a | Use scientific theories and explanations to develop hypotheses. | B3.2.6 | WS3 |
| WS1.2b | Plan experiments or devise procedures to make observations, produce or characterise a substance, test hypotheses, check data, or explore phenomena. | B3.1.2 | WS3, WS4 |
| WS1.3c | Carry out and represent mathematical and statistical analysis. | B3.1.1 | WS5 |
| WS1.3e | Interpret observations and other data. | B3.2.3 | WS7 |
| WS1.3f | Present reasoned explanations. | B3.1.1 | WS7 |
| WS1.3h | Identify potential sources of random and systematic error. | B3.1.1 | WS8 |
| WS1.3e | Interpreting observations and other data. | B3.3.2 | WS7 |
| WS1.4a | Use scientific vocabulary, terminology, and definitions. | B3.2.1, B3.3.1, B3.3.4 | WS2 |
| WS2a | Carry out experiments. | B3.1.1–3, B3.2.6–7, B3.3.1–5 | |
| WS2b | Make and record observations and measurements using a range of apparatus and methods. | B3.1.1–2, B3.2.7, B3.3.2–5 | |
| WS2c | Present observations using appropriate methods | B3.1.1–2, B3.2.7, B3.3.2–3, B3.3.5 | |
| WS2d | Communicate the scientific rationale for investigations, methods used, findings, and reasoned conclusions. | B3.1.1–2, B3.2.7, B3.3.2–3, B3.3.5 | |

# B4 Community-level systems
## B4.1 Ecosystems
### B4.1.1 Ecosystems

**Specification links:**

B4.1e Describe different levels of organisation in an ecosystem from individual organisms to the whole ecosystem.

B4.1h Describe the differences between the trophic levels of organisms within an ecosystem. To include the use of the terms producer and consumer. **S**

WS1.4a Use scientific vocabulary, terminology and definitions.

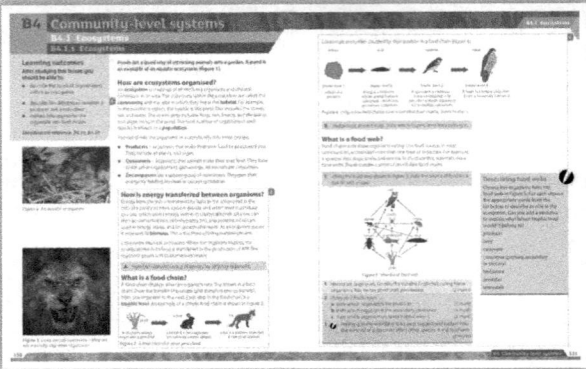

| Target | Outcome | Checkpoint | |
|---|---|---|---|
| | | Question | Activity |
| **Aiming for GRADE 4** ↓ | State the names of the different levels of organisation in an ecosystem. | | Starter 1<br>Main |
| | Describe the differences between a producer and a consumer. | A, 2 | Starter 2<br>Plenary 2 **S** |
| | Use some scientific vocabulary and terminology. | 2, 3 | Starter 1 and 2<br>Main<br>Plenary 1 and 2 |
| **Aiming for GRADE 6** ↓ | Describe the levels of organisation within an ecosystem. | | Starter 1<br>Main |
| | Describe how organisms are organised into food chains and food webs. | A, C, 1, 2, 3 | Starter 2<br>Main<br>Plenary 1 and 2 **S** |
| | Use scientific vocabulary, terminology, and definitions. | 2, 3 | Starter 1 and 2<br>Main<br>Plenary 1 and 2 |
| **Aiming for GRADE 8** ↓ | Explain how the different levels of organisation are related. | | Starter 1<br>Main |
| | Explain how organisms can be categorised into trophic levels. | B, 2 | Main<br>Plenary 1 and 2 **S** |
| | Use a full range of scientific vocabulary, terminology, and definitions appropriately and fluently. | 2, 3 | Main<br>Plenary 1 and 2 |

**Literacy**
During the main activity, students will be required to use appropriate vocabulary and terminology, with correct spelling.

**Key words**
biomass, community, consumer, decomposer, ecosystem, habitat, population, producer, trophic level, omnivore

# B4.1 Ecosystems

| Starter | Support/Extend | Resources |
|---|---|---|
| **Levels of organisation** (10 minutes) Issue groups of students with a sheet of paper with three circles overlapping (like a Venn diagram). At the centre of each circle is one word (habitat, community, or ecosystem). Ask students to write a short definition of each term. In the overlapping sections, they write about how the two terms relate to one another. | **Support:** Introduce the idea of ecosystems, or allow students to use examples rather than definitions. | |
| **Feeding relationships keywords** (5 minutes) Use the interactive, which asks students to link the key words for the lesson to their definitions. | | **Interactive:** Feeding relationships key words |

| Main | Support/Extend | Resources |
|---|---|---|
| **Food chains and webs in a habitat**<br>**1. Species list** (10 minutes) Display an image of a habitat. The students make a list of as many of the organisms as they can identify, or use their knowledge to add organisms that they know might live in the habitat.<br>**2. Food chains** (15 minutes) Ask students to create as many food chains as they can using the organisms from their list. Identify the different trophic levels of the organisms in each food chain.<br>**3. Food webs** (15 minutes) Now use the food chains to construct a food web. | **Support:** Select a habitat that the students will be familiar with, with many examples of organisms. Names of plants will be particularly helpful.<br>**Support:** Remind students about food chains and remind them that they can use organisms more than once.<br>**Extend:** Identify the different trophic levels in the food web and place organisms into the correct tropic level. | |

| Plenary | Support/Extend | Resources |
|---|---|---|
| **Trophic levels** (5 minutes) Write the headings Trophic level 1,2,3, and 4 in a simple four by two table on the board. The teacher calls out the names of several organisms from a given food chain, and students decide the correct column and instruct a scribe to write it on the board. Avoid using omnivores – use producers, herbivores, and carnivores. | **Extend:** Introduce the term omnivores and use examples of omnivores – this should introduce conflict for the students. Ask students to explain why organisms have been placed where they are. | |
| **Riddles** (10 minutes) Ask students to write a riddle, the answer to which would be one of the feeding groups of organisms. Read out some of the best riddles and ask the class to work out the answers. | **Support:** Provide an example of a riddle. | |

| Homework | | |
|---|---|---|
| You are taking part in an RSPB survey based on the birds that visit your garden or local park. List the birds you see and observe what they eat. Create as many food chains as you can for your garden or park. | **Extend:** Build your chains into a food web for your garden or park. | |

**kerboodle**

A Kerboodle highlight for this lesson is **Literacy interactive: Trophic levels**. Refer to the **Content map** on Kerboodle for a full list of resources and assessment.

# B4.1.2 Abiotic and biotic factors

**Specification links:**

B4.1f Explain how abiotic and biotic factors can affect communities. To include temperature, light intensity, moisture level, pH of soil, predators, and food.

WS1.2d Recognise when to apply knowledge of sampling techniques to ensure any samples collected are representative.

WS1.3a Present observations and other data using appropriate methods.

WS1.3b Translate data from one form to another.

WS1.3e Interpret observations and other data.

WS1.3h Identify potential sources of random and systematic error.

WS2a Carry out experiments.

WS2b Make and record observations and measurements using a range of apparatus and methods.

WS2c Present observations using appropriate methods.

WS2d Communicate the scientific rational for investigations, methods used, findings, and reasoned conclusions.

BM4.1iv Plot and draw appropriate graphs, selecting appropriate scales for the axes (M4a, M4c).

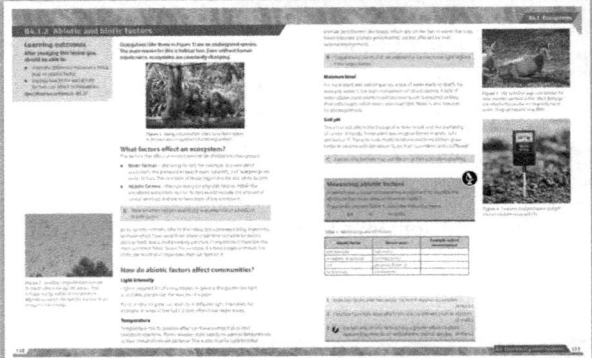

| Target | Outcome | Checkpoint | |
|---|---|---|---|
| | | Question | Activity |
| **Aiming for GRADE 4** ↓ | State the difference between a biotic and an abiotic factor. | A, 1 | Starter 2<br>Plenary 1 |
| | Use a sampling technique to record organisms in their environment. | | Starter 1<br>Main<br>Plenary 2 |
| | Plot data from an experiment onto a graph with given axes. | | Main |
| **Aiming for GRADE 6** ↓ | Describe how a named biotic or abiotic factor might affect a species. | B, 2 | Starter 2<br>Main<br>Plenary 1 |
| | Explain that sampling techniques produce results that are representative of the environment as a whole. | | Starter 1<br>Main<br>Plenary 2 |
| | Plot data from an experiment in an appropriate graph. | | Main |
| **Aiming for GRADE 8** ↓ | Explain how biotic and abiotic factors can affect communities. | C, 3 | Starter 2<br>Main<br>Plenary 1 |
| | Justify the number and frequency of samples collected to produce unbiased and representative data. | | Main<br>Plenary 2 |
| | Plot data from an experiment in an appropriate graph with suitable and correctly labelled axes. | | Main |

**Maths**
During the main activity, students will be expected to calculate means (M2b), and plot and draw appropriate graphs, selecting appropriate scales for the axes (M4a, M4c).

**Literacy**
During the main activity, students will need to produce succinct, coherent statements to explain their findings.

**Key words**
abiotic factors, biotic factors

# B4.1 Ecosystems

| Starter | Support/Extend | Resources |
|---|---|---|
| **Another brick in the wall** (10 minutes) Show students a brick wall. Ask them to estimate how many bricks are in the wall. Ask for suggestions about how to work it out. Then show the students a quadrat. Count the number of bricks in the area of one quadrat as a sample and then scale up for the wall size. | **Support:** Actually move the quadrat to show how many quadrats fit on the wall and multiply by the number of bricks. | |
| **Biotic and abiotic factors** (5 minutes) Give each group a series of cards, each of which contains the name of a factor. Students first separate the factors into a list of biotic and abiotic factors, and establish the difference. Then randomly select one of the factors and ask how it might affect an organism. | **Support:** Avoid obscure factors. | |

| Main | Support/Extend | Resources |
|---|---|---|
| **Fieldwork** (40 minutes) Investigate the effect of an abiotic factor on the distribution of an organism. For example,<br>• the distribution of daisies in the school field related to light levels<br>• distribution of named plants (possibly dogs mercury) in a woodland related to light levels<br>• frond length of seaweed related to exposure value of a beach.<br>Follow the guidance on the worksheet, which provides methods for measuring the named factor and for sampling the distribution of one or more species, by using quadrats and transect lines.<br>Tabulate results and plot a scatter graph.<br>Finally, construct a conclusion using a series of questions that examine the relationship between the factor and the distribution.<br>SAFETY: Follow local guidance on fieldwork activities. | **Support:** Sample a species that is easy to identify and distinguish.<br>**Support:** Provide a table and a graph with axes.<br>**Extend:** Ask evaluative questions in the conclusion that allow students to justify the sampling technique used. | **Practical:**<br>Fieldwork |

| Plenary | Support/Extend | Resources |
|---|---|---|
| **Sorting factors** (5 minutes) Use the interactive in which students sort factors into biotic and abiotic.| | **Interactive:**<br>Sorting factors |
| **How good was my sampling?** (10 minutes) Write a series of criteria on the board, such as<br>• unbiased<br>• repeatable<br>• accurate<br>• sufficient.<br>Then ask students to discuss the extent to which they felt that their method achieved these criteria. | **Support/Extend:** Can be achieved by the words you select. | |

| Homework | | |
|---|---|---|
| Complete the conclusion for the experiment if it has not been completed in the lesson. Alternatively, suggest why it is important for biologists to be able to sample organisms. | **Extend:** Consider the method and provide examples of a species counted using that method. | |

*kerboodle*

A Kerboodle highlight for this lesson is **Calculation sheet: Mean, median, and mode**. Refer to the **Content map** on Kerboodle for a full list of resources and assessment.

# B4.1.3 Competition and interdependence

**Specification links:**

B4.1g Describe the importance of interdependence and competition in a community. To include interdependence relating to predation, mutualism, and parasitism.

WS1.4a Use scientific vocabulary, terminology, and definitions.

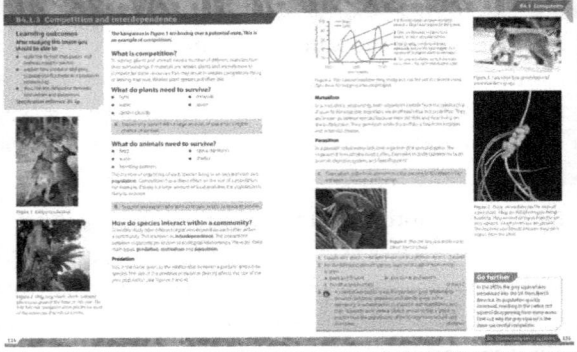

| Target | Outcome | Checkpoint | |
|---|---|---|---|
| | | Question | Activity |
| **Aiming for GRADE 4** ↓ | State the factors plants and animals need to survive. | | Starter 2<br>Main |
| | State different types of interdependent relationships. | C, 2 | Main<br>Plenary 1 |
| | Use some scientific vocabulary and terminology. | C, 2, 3 | Starter 2<br>Main<br>Plenary 1 and 2 |
| **Aiming for GRADE 6** ↓ | Describe how species compete with each other for a factor. | | Starter 2<br>Main |
| | Describe the difference between mutualism and parasitism. | | Main<br>Plenary 1 and 2 |
| | Use scientific vocabulary, terminology, and definitions. | C, 2, 3 | Starter 2<br>Main<br>Plenary 1 and 2 |
| **Aiming for GRADE 8** ↓ | Explain how the availability of a factor affects the population of a species. | A, B, 1 | Starter 2<br>Main |
| | Explain how predator and prey populations fluctuate in a predation relationship. | 3 | Main<br>Plenary 1 and 2 |
| | Use a full range of scientific vocabulary, terminology, and definitions appropriately and fluently. | C, 2, 3 | Starter 2<br>Main<br>Plenary 1 and 2 |

**Maths**
During the second part of the main activity, students will translate information between graphical and numerical form (M4a).

**Literacy**
During the main activity, students will need to produce coherent, well-structured statements to explain the different types of relationships.

**Key words**
competition, interdependence, parasitism, population, predation, mutualism

# B4.1 Ecosystems

| Starter | Support/Extend | Resources |
|---|---|---|
| **Competition and interdependence** (5 minutes)  Use the interactive in which students match the terms to the correct definitions. These include: predation, parasitism, and mutualism.<br>**Factors for survival** (10 minutes)  Divide the class into groups of six. Half of the groups of six will consider the needs of a plant, the other half will consider animals.<br>Sub-divide each group into three pairs. Give the first pair some cards, each with the name of a factor that affects organisms. Some factors affect only plants, some affect only animals, some affect both, some neither. The first pair in each group selects a factor from the cards that they believe is needed. They pass this onto the second pair, who make a statement to explain why it is needed. The second pair then pass the card to the third pair who explain how organisms compete for the factor. Share learning. | **Support/Extend:** Place students into appropriate pairs in the groups. | **Interactive:** Competition and interdependence |

| Main | Support/Extend | Resources |
|---|---|---|
| **Harlequin ladybird – an alien species** (20 minutes)  Students use ICT resources to research the conditions harlequin ladybirds need to survive. They then find out about competition between this species and native ladybirds. What has been the effect on the populations of the two species?<br>**Interdependence** (20 minutes)  Students use the Student Book and ICT resources to find definitions and examples of three types of relationships: predator/prey, mutualism, parasitism. | **Support:** Provide suitable web links. | **Activity:** Competition and interdependence |

| Plenary | Support/Extend | Resources |
|---|---|---|
| **Game of pairs** (10 minutes)  Provide students with cards showing pictures of organisms. Each card shows one of a relationship pair and there should be sufficient pairs of cards to cover three relationships. Students place them face down. They pick up a card and find a second card that has the image of the other organism in the relationship. Name the relationship.<br>**Sliding scale** (5 minutes)  Have four students lined up at the front of the class each with a card that says one of:<br>• competition<br>• predation<br>• mutualism<br>• parasitism.<br>One end of the line represents a negative relationship, causing harm to species, the other end of the line represents a positive relationship that benefits organisms. The class decide where along the line the students with cards should stand. | **Extend:** Describe the nature of the relationship and the impact on the species.<br><br>**Extend:** Justify the decision. | |

| Homework |
|---|
| You will be provided with either data to plot a predator/prey graph or a completed graph. Describe and explain the relationship. |

**kerboodle**

A Kerboodle highlight for this lesson is **Working Scientifically: Predator–prey relationship**. Refer to the **Content map** on Kerboodle for a full list of resources and assessment.

# GCSE BIOLOGY ONLY
## B4.1.4 Pyramids of biomass

**Specification links:**

B4.1h Describe the differences between the trophic levels of organisms within an ecosystem. To include use of the terms producer and consumer.

B4.1i Describe pyramids of biomass and explain, with examples, how biomass is lost between the different trophic levels. To include loss of biomass related to egestion, excretion, respiration.

WS1.3c Carry out and represent mathematical and statistical analysis.

WS1.3e Interpret observations and other data.

BM4.1v Extract and interpret information from charts, graphs and tables.

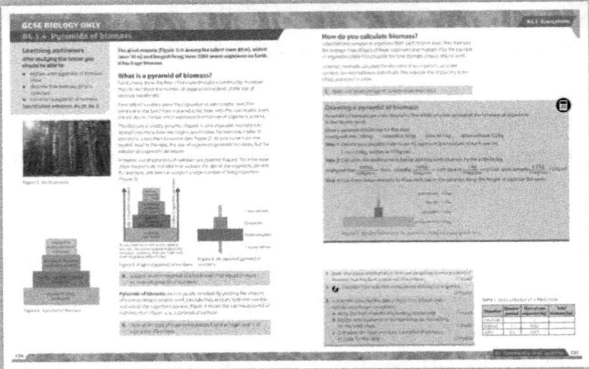

| Target | Outcome | Checkpoint | |
|---|---|---|---|
| | | Question | Activity |
| Aiming for GRADE 4 ↓ | State what a pyramid of numbers shows. | A | Starter 1 and 2<br>Main<br>Plenary 1 |
| | State what is meant by the term biomass. | 2 | Main<br>Plenary 1 |
| | Use data to sketch a pyramid of biomass. | 3 | Main |
| Aiming for GRADE 6 ↓ | Explain what pyramids of biomass show. | 1 | Main<br>Plenary 1 and 2 |
| | Describe how biomass data is collected. | C, 2 | Plenary 1 |
| | Calculate biomass data and sketch a pyramid of biomass to represent the data. | 3 | Main |
| Aiming for GRADE 8 ↓ | Explain the advantage of plotting a pyramid of biomass. | 1 | Plenary 1 |
| | Suggest advantages and disadvantages of collecting biomass data. | C, 3 | Plenary 1 |
| | Calculate biomass data and accurately plot a pyramid of biomass to represent the data. | 3 | Main |

**Maths**
During the main activity, students will be required to translate information between graphical and numeric form, by constructing and interpreting bar charts or histograms (M4a, M2c).

**Literacy**
During the main activity, students will need to produce coherent, well-structured, and purposeful texts.

**Key words**
pyramid of biomass

# B4.1 Ecosystems

| Starter | Support/Extend | Resources |
|---|---|---|
| **Spot the pyramid** (5 minutes)   Use the interactive showing a food chain. Students select which of the images of pyramids is correct for that food chain. | **Extend:** Discuss why each of the other images would be unsuitable. | **Interactive:** Spot the pyramid |
| **Labelling a pyramid** (10 minutes)   Draw a simple large pyramid on the board with four levels. Ask students to write labels (for example, producer, herbivore, primary consumer, etc.) on paper and stick them onto the correct level on the pyramid. Another group creates a food chain, and writes the names of the organisms on paper and sticks them onto the pyramid. | **Support:** Target support groups with the food chain names.<br><br>**Extend:** Draw a second pyramid with an inverted shape and ask a new group of students to do the same task. | |

| Main | Support/Extend | Resources |
|---|---|---|
| **Plot a pyramid of numbers** (10 minutes)   Plot a pyramid of numbers for a given food chain. The pyramid should have an inverted format.<br>**Problems with pyramids of numbers** (5 minutes)   Establish why the pyramid has an unusual shape and discuss how it might be changed.<br>**Plot a pyramid of biomass** (15 minutes)   Students create a table and calculate the biomass. Finally, plot a pyramid of biomass. | **Support:** You may need to start with a conventional pyramid, and simply sketch the shape and label. | **Activity:** Pyramid of numbers or biomass |
| **Questions on pyramids of biomass** (10 minutes)   Students compare the pyramid of numbers with the pyramid of biomass. They should explain how a pyramid shape is produced due to loss of biomass at each link. Finally, they should consider the problems with collecting biomass data. | **Extend:** Ask for other examples of inverted pyramids of numbers, for example, parasites. | |

| Plenary | Support/Extend | Resources |
|---|---|---|
| **For or against?** (10 minutes)   Outline how biomass data can be collected. Then divide the class in half and subdivide each half into small groups. One half discusses reasons why pyramids of biomass are useful and how they are better than pyramids of numbers. The other half discusses their disadvantages, including the challenges of collecting suitable data. After 5 minutes, ask each side to put forward points and discuss in turn. | **Support:** Suggest the issues and get the students to think about explaining them. | |
| **Modelling pyramids** (5 minutes)   Line students in four equal rows. Provide a food chain, and ask them to use individuals in their line to create a row of a pyramid of biomass, to illustrate the food chain. They will need to decide which line represents each trophic level and how many students to use. | **Extend:** Repeat for different food chains with different-shaped pyramids. | |

| Homework | | |
|---|---|---|
| Produce a simple, but attractive page for a magazine that is trying to show people how a named animal has become endangered over time. As part of the article, you will need to sketch several pyramids of biomass to show how your named animal, and possibly its food source, has changed over time. | | |

**kerboodle**

A Kerboodle highlight for this lesson is **Maths skills: Constructing a pyramid of biomass**. Refer to the **Content map** on Kerboodle for a full list of resources and assessment.

# GCSE BIOLOGY ONLY
## B4.1.5 Efficiency of biomass transfer

**Specification links:**

B4.1i Describe pyramids of biomass and explain, with examples, how biomass is lost between the different trophic levels. To include loss of biomass related to egestion, excretion, and respiration.

B4.1j Calculate the efficiency of biomass transfers between tropic levels and explain how this affects the number of trophic levels in a food chain.

WS1.3c Carry out and represent mathematical and statistical analysis.

WS1.3e Interpret observations and other data.

BM4.1ii Calculate the percentage of mass (M1c).

BM4.1iii Use fractions and percentages (M1c).

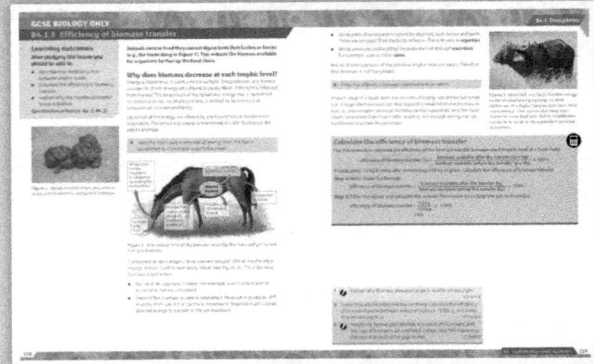

| Target | Outcome | Checkpoint | |
|---|---|---|---|
| | | Question | Activity |
| **Aiming for GRADE 4** | State that biomass is lost between trophic levels. | | Starter 1 and 2<br>Main 2<br>Plenary 1 |
| | Calculate the biomass loss at each link in a food chain. | | Starter 2<br>Main 1<br>Plenary 2 |
| | Compare biomass losses at each link in the food chain. | | Starter 2<br>Main 1<br>Plenary 2 |
| **Aiming for GRADE 6** | Describe how biomass is lost between trophic levels. | B, 1 | Starter 1 and 2<br>Main 2<br>Plenary 1 |
| | Calculate the efficiency of biomass transfer. | 2 | Starter 2<br>Main 1<br>Plenary 2 |
| | Interpret data on the efficiency of biomass transfer. | | Starter 2<br>Main 1 |
| **Aiming for GRADE 8** | Explain why the loss of biomass limits the number of trophic levels. | 1 | Main 2 |
| | Compare the efficiency of biomass transfer for different organisms. | 3 | Main 1<br>Plenary 2 |
| | Interpret data on the efficiency of biomass transfer between different links in the food chains or between different food chains. | | Main 1 |

**Maths**
During the main activity, students will need to use fractions and percentages when calculating percentage efficiency of biomass transfer (M1c).

**Literacy**
During the main activity, students will need to produce coherent, well-structured, and purposeful texts.

**Key words**
egestion, excretion, urine

# B4.1 Ecosystems

| Starter | Support/Extend | Resources |
|---|---|---|
| **Losing pyramids** (5 minutes)   Remind the class about pyramids of biomass from the last lesson. Ask why the pyramid gets smaller towards the top. Establish that each trophic level gets smaller as biomass has been lost. | **Extend:** Ask for ideas about how the biomass is lost. | |
| **Counting the losses** (10 minutes)   Place three sheets of paper on the table in front of you, labelled producer, herbivore, and carnivore. On the producer sheet place a beaker containing a large number of counters, to represent the mass of the plant. Ask students whether or not the herbivore would eat all of the plant. Then remove some counters for all of the areas that the class suggests the herbivore does not eat. Then transfer the beaker with the balance of counters to the herbivore. Repeat for the carnivore. | **Extend:** Could estimate the percentage of mass being transferred. Consider losses due to egestion, excretion, and respiration in the animals. | |

| Main | Support/Extend | Resources |
|---|---|---|
| **Biomass efficiency** (15 minutes)   Show the class a pyramid of biomass and ask them to calculate the percentage of biomass passed between each trophic level. Then, they can calculate the efficiency of transfer for each. Ask students to summarise the reasons why biomass decreases as you go up a food chain. | **Support:** Show students how to calculate the percentage and efficiency from producer to primary consumer, and allow the students to calculate these between primary and secondary consumer. | **Calculations sheet:** Biomass transfers |
| **Modelling biomass transfers** (25 minutes)   Use a model to show biomass loss through trophic levels. One example is an outside activity. Arrange a course with four posts about 10 m apart. Post 1 represents a producer and has two large containers of water next to it. Post 2 represents a primary consumer and has two buckets with holes in the bottom – this is the same for post 3, which represents a secondary consumer. Post 4 represents a tertiary consumer and has an empty container next to it. Pairs of students stand at posts 2 and 3. Students at post 2 collect water from the producer and run to post 3. They pass the water on to students at post 3, who tip the water into the container. The water represents biomass. Discuss how this models what happens in real food chains. | **Extend:** Students can evaluate the model used and discuss its limitations. They should also be able to use ideas about energy transfer to explain why biomass is lost at each trophic level. | **Activity:** Modelling biomass transfers |

| Plenary | Support/Extend | Resources |
|---|---|---|
| **Highlight the loss** (5 minutes)   Use the interactive, which asks students to read the paragraph that describes biomass moving through a food chain. Students highlight the statements about loss of biomass. | | **Interactive:** Highlight the loss |
| **Quick calculations** (10 minutes)   Prepare a food chain diagram that shows the amount of biomass in each link and the amounts lost at each link (the losses can be subdivided, for example, egestion, never eaten, etc.). The diagram is then written on the board, but some of the values are missing. Students calculate the missing values. | **Support:** Prepare all of the answers and show the students the full list of numbers. They then need to select the correct number for each gap.<br><br>**Extend:** Include percentage efficiency of transfers. | |

| Homework | | |
|---|---|---|
| Explain why an intensive farm tends to rear cattle in small barns. They may mow grass to bring to the cows. Use your knowledge of efficiency of biomass transfers to explain this. | **Extend:** Consider humane farming methods – why they are better for the animal, but why they reduce yield and increase costs. | |

**kerboodle**
A Kerboodle highlight for this lesson is **Calculation sheet: Efficiency of energy transfer**. Refer to the **Content map** on Kerboodle for a full list of resources and assessment.

# B4.1.6 Nutrient cycling

**Specification links:**

B4.1a Recall that many different materials cycle through the abiotic and biotic components of an ecosystem. To include examples of cycled materials, for example, nitrogen and carbon.

B4.1b Explain the role of microorganisms in the cycling of materials through an ecosystem. To include the role of microorganisms in decomposition.

B4.1c Explain the importance of the carbon cycle and the water cycle to living organisms. To include maintaining habitats, fresh water, flow of nutrients.

WS1.2b Plan experiments or devise procedures to make observations, produce or characterise a substance, test hypotheses, check data, or explore phenomena.

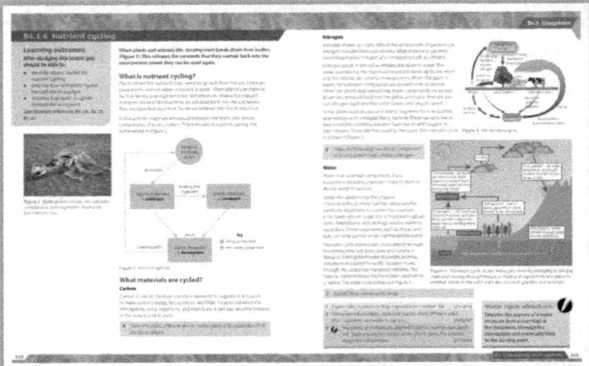

| Target | Outcome | Checkpoint | |
|---|---|---|---|
| | | Question | Activity |
| **Aiming for GRADE 4** | Describe what nutrient cycling means. | | Starter 1 and 2<br>Main |
| | State that carbon, nitrogen, and water are essential for living organisms. | A, B, 1, 2 | Starter 1 and 2<br>Main |
| | Describe an activity that illustrates a process in the nutrient cycle. | | Main |
| **Aiming for GRADE 6** | Describe how nitrogen and water are cycled through the ecosystem. | C, 3 | Starter 1<br>Main<br>Plenary 1 |
| | Describe how living organisms make use of carbon, nitrogen, and water. | A, B, 1, 2, 3 | Starter 1 and 2<br>Main<br>Plenary 1 |
| | Suggest activities or experiments that would provide observations that could be used to show a process in a nutrient cycle. | | Main |
| **Aiming for GRADE 8** | Explain the processes involved in achieving the steps in the cycling of nitrogen and water through an ecosystem. | C, 3 | Main<br>Plenary 1 and 2 |
| | Explain the role of microorganisms in the recycling of materials for living organisms. | 3 | Main<br>Plenary 2 |
| | Suggest activities or experiments that would provide observations to explain processes in a nutrient cycle. | | Main |

**Literacy**
During the main activity, students will need to communicate ideas effectively, using appropriate scientific vocabulary.

## B4.1 Ecosystems

| Starter | Support/Extend | Resources |
|---|---|---|
| **Am I made of a dinosaur?** (10 minutes) Hold a large sponge ball in the air with the word 'atom' written on it. Pass the atom to a volunteer who role-plays the plant. Explain that it has taken up atoms of several elements to join together to form the compounds that build into its body. Then pass the atom from the plant to a second student who represents a herbivore. Discuss the movement of the atom through the food chain, as part of molecules of different compounds, until finally death and decay returns the atom back to you (the abiotic world). Repeat the process with different students. This shows that the atoms now make up a new group of organisms, so you could contain atoms that once made up a dinosaur. | **Extend:** Ask students to suggest elements that are cycled to build up our bodies. | |
| **Coal** (5 minutes) Show a piece of coal or an image. Ask students what it is made of, or how it is formed. Then ask them to name the substances produced when it burns (could show film of burning coal). Ask what happens to the carbon dioxide gas – draw the class to the idea that it is taken up by plants. Stress the idea that the carbon has been recycled. Point out that other elements can also be recycled, such as nitrogen, etc. | | |

| Main | Support/Extend | Resources |
|---|---|---|
| **Nutrient cycling** (20 minutes) Elicit from students that carbon, nitrogen and water are essential for living organisms, and draw on learning from the starter to explain what nutrient cycling means. Students then read about the nitrogen cycle in the Student Book, and study Figure 3. In pairs, they make up questions for each other and peer assess the answers. The questions should cover the following points: how nitrogen is cycled through the ecosystem, how plants make use of nitrogen and its compounds, the role of microorganisms in the recycling of nitrogen compounds. | **Support:** Differentiate the stage in the cycle allocated, or provide suggested activities for stages. | |
| **Hands-on science** (20 minutes) The aim is to produce an exhibit for an interactive museum aimed at students.<br><br>Divide class into groups of about eight students. These groups sub-divide into pairs. Give each group a diagram of the water cycle, for example, from the Student Book. Allocate each pair one of the stages in the water cycle.<br><br>Their task is to design an activity or an experiment (they don't actually need to do the experiment – although, of course, it would be good if they could) to illustrate their stage in the cycle. It must be fun, easy for students to understand, practical, must show the stage clearly, and suggest why it is important for living things.<br><br>Finally, they come back together as a group to complete the exhibit, and show and explain their work to each other. | | **Activity:** Hands-on science |

| Plenary | Support/Extend | Resources |
|---|---|---|
| **The water cycle** (5 minutes) Use the interactive activity in which students label a diagram of the water cycle. | **Extend:** Ask students to explain what each of the processes are. | **Interactive:** The water cycle |
| **How important is decay?** (10 minutes) Pose the question, 'What would happen if we stopped the process of decay?' Ask the class to discuss this in groups. Ask for the consequences, including both the immediate and long-term impact on the cycles. Then hold a short class discussion. | **Support:** Run this as a class discussion and pose questions at each step in the discussion. | |

| Homework | | |
|---|---|---|
| Draw a large picture or make a model to illustrate the water cycle. | | |

**kerboodle**
A Kerboodle highlight for this lesson is **Literacy worksheet: Story of a carbon atom**. Refer to the **Content map** on Kerboodle for a full list of resources and assessment.

# B4.1.7 The carbon cycle

**Specification links:**

B4.1c Explain the importance of the carbon cycle and the water cycle to living organisms. To include maintaining habitats, fresh water, flow of nutrients.

WS1.1b Use models to solve problems, make predictions, and develop scientific explanations and understanding of familiar and unfamiliar facts.

WS1.4a Use scientific vocabulary, terminology, and definitions.

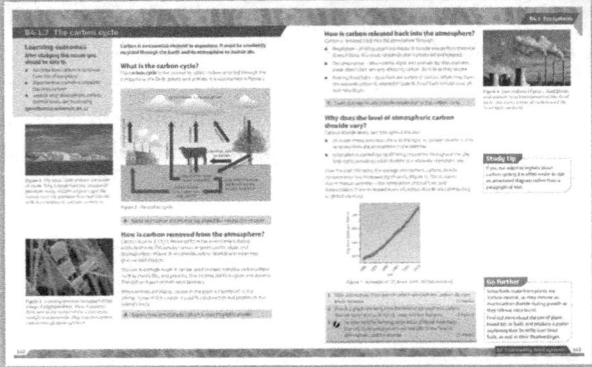

| Target | Outcome | Checkpoint | |
|---|---|---|---|
| | | Question | Activity |
| **Aiming for GRADE 4** ↓ | State that carbon is cycled between the biotic and abiotic world. | | Starter 1 and 2<br>Main<br>Plenary 1 |
| | State that carbon dioxide levels in the atmosphere are increasing. | A, 1, 3 | Main<br>Plenary 2 |
| | Identify connections between statements that help develop an understanding of some stages of the carbon cycle, using some key vocabulary. | | Starter 1<br>Main<br>Plenary 1 and 2 |
| **Aiming for GRADE 6** ↓ | Describe how carbon is added to, or removed from, the atmosphere. | C, 2 | Starter 1 and 2<br>Main<br>Plenary 1 and 2 |
| | Describe the ways in which carbon dioxide is being added to the atmosphere in excess. | 1, 3 | Main<br>Plenary 2 |
| | Identify connections between statements, to describe all the stages in the carbon cycle, using a range of appropriate terminology. | | Main<br>Plenary 1 and 2 |
| **Aiming for GRADE 8** ↓ | Explain the processes that bring about the steps in the carbon cycle. | B | Main |
| | Explain fully why atmospheric carbon dioxide levels are increasing, resulting in a cycle that is no longer in balance. | 1, 3 | Main<br>Plenary 2 |
| | Use a full range of appropriate scientific vocabulary and terminology when explaining the links in the carbon cycle. | 3 | Main<br>Plenary 2 |

**Literacy**
During the main activity, students will need to use vocabulary appropriate to purpose when producing coherent, well-structured, and varied sentences.

**Key words**
carbon cycle

# B4.1 Ecosystems

| Starter | Support/Extend | Resources |
|---|---|---|
| **Where does the carbon dioxide go?** (5 minutes) Have a plant and animal (or pictures) in front of you. Have a card with carbon dioxide and an arrow, and ask the class what happens to carbon dioxide in a plant. Establish that plants take in carbon dioxide that is used in photosynthesis. Repeat for respiration in both the plant and the animal.<br><br>**Testing for carbon dioxide** (10 minutes) Use a few students to demonstrate the test for carbon dioxide in exhaled air using limewater. Ask 'Where does the carbon dioxide come from that we are breathing out?' Link the process to respiration of carbohydrates in the body. | **Extend:** Write carbon dioxide and sugar on the board, and draw arrows between the two for the processes. This creates a simple cycle.<br><br>**Extend:** Use bicarbonate indicator solution as well. | |

| Main | Support/Extend | Resources |
|---|---|---|
| **Processes in the carbon cycle** (25 minutes) Split the class into groups and give each one a process of the carbon cycle to study in more detail (photosynthesis, respiration, combustion, decay and decomposition, feeding). Ask each group to research how it moves carbon from one place to another, name the places, write down any word equations for the process, and draw a picture to represent it. Then ask them to present their findings and use them to compile a class diagram of the carbon cycle. Use an animation of the carbon cycle to check and reinforce their understanding.<br><br>**Question** (15 minutes) Present students with a long answer question that asks for a description of the carbon cycle, and allow 10 minutes to answer the question and 5 minutes to peer-mark.<br><br>Example question:<br>Describe how the carbon in a plant can become available to the next generation of plants.<br><br>Answer:<br>• The plant dies/is eaten by animal.<br>• Animals die or release waste.<br>• The body is decayed by decomposers/bacteria/fungi.<br>• Decomposition releases carbon dioxide (by respiration).<br>• Carbon dioxide returns to the atmosphere.<br>• Carbon dioxide is absorbed by the next generation, via photosynthesis.<br>• Fossilisation and combustion. | **Extend:** Students should write down balanced symbol equations as well.<br><br><br><br>**Support:** Provide some key words in sequence to help frame a response.<br>**Extend:** Expect explanations of the processes and more technical vocabulary. | **Activity:** Processes in the carbon cycle<br>**Animation:** The carbon cycle |

| Plenary | Support/Extend | Resources |
|---|---|---|
| **Carbon cycle sort** (5 minutes) Use the interactive, which asks students to drag and drop into a suitable order a series of statements that describe the events in the carbon cycle.<br><br>**Carbon footprint** (10 minutes) Provide a sheet of paper to each group with an outline of a foot. Ask the students to discuss and list ways in which they are increasing the amount of carbon dioxide in the atmosphere (their carbon footprint). | **Extend:** Suggest ways of reducing their carbon footprints. | **Interactive:** Carbon cycle sort |

| Homework | | |
|---|---|---|
| Describe and explain the cause of global warming. Explain what is happening in the carbon cycle and why it is out of balance. | | |

**kerboodle**

A Kerboodle highlight for this lesson is **Literacy sheet: Pass the carbon**. Refer to the **Content map** on Kerboodle for a full list of resources and assessment.

# B4.1.8 Decomposers

**Specification links:**

B4.1b Explain the role of microorganisms in the cycling of materials through an ecosystem. To include the role of microorganisms in decomposition.

B4.1d Explain the effects of factors such as temperature, water content, and oxygen availability on the rate of decomposition. To include the terms aerobic and anaerobic. **S**

WS1.2b Plan experiments or devise procedures to make observations, produce or characterise a substance, test hypotheses, check data, or explore phenomena.

WS1.2e Evaluate methods and suggest possible improvements and further investigations.

WS1.3a Present observations and other data using appropriate methods.

WS1.3e Interpret observations and other data.

WS1.3f Present reasoned explanations.

WS1.3g Evaluate data in terms of accuracy, precision, repeatability, and reproducibility.

WS2a Carry out experiments.

WS2b Make and record observations and measurements using a range of apparatus and methods.

WS2c Present observations using appropriate methods.

WS2d Communicate the scientific rational for investigations, methods used, findings, and reasoned conclusions.

| Target | Outcome | Checkpoint | |
|---|---|---|---|
| | | Question | Activity |
| **Aiming for GRADE 4** | State some examples of decomposers and detritivores. | A, 1 | Starter 2 Main Plenary 1 |
| | Describe a simple plan, which lacks detail, to test the effect of a factor on decomposition. | | Main  **S** |
| | State from their observations that a factor has affected decomposition. | | Main Plenary 2 |
| **Aiming for GRADE 6** | Describe what is meant by decomposition. | B, 1 | Starter 1 and 2 Main Plenary 1 and 2 |
| | Describe a plan that will test a hypothesis of the effect of a factor on the rate of decomposition. | | Main  **S** |
| | Use their observations to describe the effect of their factor on the rate of decay. | | Main Plenary 2 |
| **Aiming for GRADE 8** | Explain how environmental factors affect the rate of decomposition. | C, 2, 3 | Starter 2 Main Plenary 2 |
| | Suggest a detailed plan, which will test a hypothesis of the effect of a number of factors on the rate of decomposition. | | Main |
| | Interpret their observations to explain the effect of a series of factors on the rate of decomposition. | | Main Plenary 2 |

# B4.1 Ecosystems

**Literacy**
During the main activity, students will need to use a vocabulary appropriate to purpose when producing coherent, well-structured, and varied sentences.

**Key words**
detritivores

| Starter | Support/Extend | Resources |
|---|---|---|
| **Decay or no decay?** (10 minutes) Issue groups with a pack of cards. Students suggest whether or not the factors shown on the cards affect the rate of decay. Words could include: smells, bacteria, temperature, dirt, air, dark, carbon dioxide, animals, light, moisture, movement, and chemicals.<br><br>**Decomposition** (5 minutes) Show a time-lapse video of decay. Students write down what caused the decay and what might affect the rate of decay. | **Support:** Avoid the term rate – simply ask if the factor contributes to decay.<br>**Extend:** Ask students to explain why the factors might have that effect.<br>**Extend:** Good or bad? Consider examples of decay in both contexts. | **Activity:** Decay or no decay? |

| Main | Support/Extend | Resources |
|---|---|---|
| **Practically investigate factor(s) that might affect the rate of decomposition** (40 minutes) Elicit from students some examples of decomposers and detritivores. Then create a list of factors that might affect the rate of decomposition by these organisms. Students investigate the effect of one or more factors that affect the rate of decomposition.<br>• Start by generating a hypothesis.<br>• Plan an investigation by selecting one or more factors. Use pieces of bread or a fruit, such as banana, in a Petri dish taped closed at several points (SAFETY: Do not seal). The conditions will vary. Allow 3–5 days for the results to develop.<br>• Make observations about how each factor affects the decay process.<br>• Interpret the results. Do they support the hypothesis? Suggest a reason for the effect of the factor on the rate of decomposition. | **Support:** Show the students the method of putting bread in a Petri dish, and focus a discussion on what factor to change and how to change it.<br>**Support:** Produce a frame of questions to help with the conclusion.<br>**Extend:** Evaluate the method – are the results repeatable, etc.? | **Practical:** Investigating factors that affect the rate of decomposition |

| Plenary | Support/Extend | Resources |
|---|---|---|
| **What affects the rate of decay?** (10 minutes) Students sort conditions (warm temperature, cold temperature, lots of oxygen, no oxygen, moist conditions, dry conditions, no carbon dioxide, lots of carbon dioxide) into groups of what will speed up, slow down, or have no effect on decay.<br><br>**Tiered knowledge** (10 minutes) Create a series of three concentric shapes. In the innermost shape students write the name of a factor that has affected the decomposition. In the next shape out, students write a description of the effect of that factor. Finally, in the outer-most shape students write an explanation of the effect on rate. | **Extend:** Ask students to explain why each condition has this effect.<br><br>**Support/Extend:** Vary the shape to allow students to consider more factors. Circles suggest one factor; triangles suggest three factors to consider, one each side; or squares suggest four factors. | **Interactive:** What affects the rate of decay? |

| Homework | | |
|---|---|---|
| Describe and explain the conditions that lead to a fence post rotting in the garden. Suggest ways to prevent it. Or describe methods used to prevent food decomposing, explaining how the methods work. | | |

**kerboodle**
A Kerboodle highlight for this lesson is **Calculation sheet: Rate of decomposition**. Refer to the **Content map** on Kerboodle for a full list of resources and assessment.

# Checkpoint
## B4.1 Ecosystems

### Overview of B4.1 Ecosystems

In this chapter, students have studied how ecosystems are organised and should be able to use the terms ecosystem, community, habitat, producer, consumer, and decomposer. They should understand that biomass is transferred through a food chain and is a measure of energy flow. They should be able to use food chains and to define trophic level, herbivore, primary consumer, secondary consumer, and tertiary consumer. They should understand that a food web is many interlinking food chains. They should link this work with B1.4 *Photosynthesis*.

Students should be able to give examples of abiotic and biotic factors that can affect an ecosystem, and explain how they can affect communities. They should be able to define competition, and list some factors plants and animals need and compete over. They should understand the interdependence of organisms in a food web, including predation, mutualism, and parasitism.

Students should be able to compare pyramids of numbers and pyramids of biomass. They should have carried out biomass calculations and know how to draw a pyramid of biomass on graph paper. They should be able to explain why biomass decreases at each trophic level and how to calculate the efficiency of biomass transfer.

Students should be able to give examples of materials that are cycled, including carbon, nitrogen, and water. They should have studied the carbon cycle and the water cycle in more detail, linking with the chemicals that make up cells in B1.1 *Cell structures*, B1.3 *Respiration*, and transpiration in B2.2 *The challenges of size*.

Students should be familiar with different types of decomposer and their roles in material cycling, and should be able to list factors that affect the rate of decomposition, including temperature, moisture level, and aerobic conditions. They should be able to calculate the rate of decay.

You can find additional support for the maths skills covered in this chapter on **MyMaths**, including calculating the mean, working with graphs, and calculating percentage efficiency.

For this chapter, the following assessments are available on Kerboodle:

B4.1 Checkpoint quiz: Ecosystems
B4.1 Progress quiz: Ecosystems 1
B4.1 Progress quiz: Ecosystems 2
B4.1 On your marks: Ecosystems
B4.1 Exam-style questions and mark scheme: Ecosystems

### Checkpoint follow-up lesson

A student's route through this lesson can be determined using the Checkpoint assessment. Percentage pass marks are supplied in the Checkpoint teacher notes.

For each successive route through it is assumed that the student can perform to their current route as well as previous routes. For example, students working at Aiming for 6 are assumed to be secure in Aiming for 4 knowledge and understanding and working towards achieving all the learning objectives for Aiming for 6.

# B4.1 Ecosystems

|  | Aiming for 4 | Aiming for 6 | Aiming for 8 |
|---|---|---|---|
| **Learning outcomes** | State some abiotic and biotic factors. | State some abiotic and biotic factors. | State some abiotic and biotic factors. |
|  | State some things that animals and plant compete for. | Describe some things that animals and plant compete for. | Explain some ways that species interact with each other. |
|  | State how biomass is lost between trophic levels. | Describe how biomass is lost between trophic levels. | Explain how biomass is lost between trophic levels. |
|  | State the factors that affect the rate of decomposition. | Describe the factors that affect the rate of decomposition. | Explain the factors that affect the rate of decomposition. |
| **Starter** | **Food chain (5 minutes)** Draw a food chain on the board. Ask targeted questions, such as – name the producer. Name the secondary consumer. Name a predator. Use this to introduce the idea of interdependence. ||| 
| **Differentiated checkpoint activity** | **Activity 1 Ecosystems (45 minutes)** There are five stations, each with a different activity. Students spend up to 10 minutes at each station, following their differentiated worksheets. The following equipment is needed: <ul><li>station 1 – scissors, glue sticks, and A3 paper (pair work)</li><li>station 2 – scissors, glue sticks, mini whiteboards, and marker pens (pair work)</li><li>station 3 – calculators and rulers</li><li>station 4 – Aiming for 4 students, blank copies of the water and carbon cycles; Aiming for 6 and Aiming for 8 students, the Student book and A3 paper</li><li>station 5 – three samples of bread –A kept in damp warm conditions for a few days, B kept in the freezer, C kept in a sealed bag with as much air removed as possible. These should be sealed in sandwich bags for safety and need to be prepared a few days in advance.</li></ul> **Kerboodle resource:** B4.1 Checkpoint follow-up: Aiming for 4, B4.1 Checkpoint follow-up: Aiming for 6, B4.1 Checkpoint follow-up: Aiming for 8 |||
| **Plenary** | **Review (5 minutes)** Ask all the students to stand up. They may sit when they have answered a question correctly. Ask targeted questions such as: <ol><li>Is this factor abiotic or biotic?</li><li>Name a factor that plants / animals compete for.</li><li>How is biomass lost?</li><li>How does carbon enter / leave the atmosphere?</li><li>What conditions are needed for decomposition?</li></ol> |||
| **Progression** | The Aiming for 4 activities provide highly structured instructions and questions, including cut-and-paste exercises. There are many opportunities in this chapter to research real examples of food chains, food webs, and predator–prey cycles, which can be targeted to different students. | The Aiming for 6 activities are reasonably structured. There are many opportunities in this chapter to research real examples of food chains, food webs, and predator–prey cycles, which can be targeted to different students. | The Aiming for 8 activities have very little structure. Students should be able to complete the activities without introduction. A possible extension to the carbon cycle is to research examples of fuels made from plants that have carbon-neutral advantages. |

# B4 Community-level systems: Topic summary

## B4.1 Ecosystems

| Spec ref | Statement | Book spreads |
|---|---|---|
| B4.1a | Recall that many different materials cycle through the abiotic and biotic components of an ecosystem | B4.1.6 |
| B4.1b | Explain the role of microorganisms in the cycling of materials through an ecosystem | B4.1.6, B4.1.8 |
| B4.1c | Explain the importance of the carbon cycle and the water cycle to living organisms | B4.1.6, B4.1.7 |
| B4.1d | Explain the effect of factors such as temperature, water content, and oxygen availability on rate of decomposition | B4.1.8 [S] |
| B4.1e | Describe different levels of organisation in an ecosystem from individual organisms to the whole ecosystem | B4.1.1 |
| B4.1f | Explain how abiotic and biotic factors can affect communities | B4.1.2 |
| B4.1g | Describe the importance of interdependence and competition in a community | B4.1.3 |
| B4.1h | Describe the differences between the trophic levels of organisms within an ecosystem | B4.1.1, B4.1.4 [S] |
| B4.1i | Describe pyramids of biomass and explain, with examples, how biomass is lost between the different trophic levels | B4.1.4, B4.1.5 [S] |
| B4.1j | Calculate the efficiency of biomass transfers between trophic levels and explain how this affects the number of trophic levels in a food chain | B4.1.5 [S] |

## Maths

| Specification | | Book spread | |
|---|---|---|---|
| Spec ref | Statement | Main content | Maths chapter |
| BM4.1i | Calculate rate changes in the decay of biological material | | 14 [S] |
| BM4.1ii | Calculate the percentage of mass | B4.1.5 | 3 |
| BM4.1iii | Use fractions and percentages | B4.1.5 | 3 |
| BM4.1iv | Plot and draw appropriate graphs selecting appropriate scales for the axes | B4.1.2 | 13, 14 |
| BM4.1v | Extract and interpret information from charts, graphs and tables | B4.1.4 | 6, 13, 14 |

## Working scientifically

| Specification | | Book spread | |
|---|---|---|---|
| Spec ref | Statement | Main content | WS chapter |
| WS1.1b | Use models to solve problems, make predictions, and to develop scientific explanations and understanding of familiar and unfamiliar facts. | B4.1.7 | WS2 |
| WS1.2b | Plan experiments or devise procedures to make observations, produce or characterise a substance, test hypotheses, check data, or explore phenomena. | B4.1.6, B4.1.8 | WS3, WS4 |
| WS1.2d | Recognise when to apply a knowledge of sampling techniques to ensure any samples collected are representative. | B4.1.2 | |
| WS1.2e | Evaluate methods, and suggest possible improvements and further investigations. | B4.1.8 | |
| WS1.3a | Presenting observations and other data using appropriate methods. | B4.1.2, B4.1.8 | WS6 |
| WS1.3b | Translating data from one form to another. | B4.1.2 | WS6 |
| WS1.3c | Carrying out and representing mathematical and statistical analysis. | B4.1.4, B4.1.5 | WS5 |
| WS1.3e | Interpreting observations and other data. | B4.1.2, B4.1.4, B4.1.5, B4.1.8 | WS7 |
| WS1.3f | Presenting reasoned explanations. | B4.1.8 | WS7 |
| WS1.3g | Evaluating data in terms of accuracy, precision, repeatability, and reproducibility. | B4.1.8 | WS5, WS7 |
| WS1.3h | Identify potential sources of random and systematic error. | B4.1.2 | WS8 |
| WS1.4a | Use scientific vocabulary, terminology, and definitions. | B4.1.1, B4.1.3, B4.1.7 | WS2 |
| WS2a | Carry out experiments. | B4.1.2, B4.1.8 | |
| WS2b | Make and record observations and measurements using a range of apparatus and methods. | B4.1.2, B4.1.8 | |
| WS2c | Present observations using appropriate methods. | B4.1.2, B4.1.8 | |
| WS2d | Communicate the scientific rational for investigations, methods used, findings, and reasoned conclusions. | B4.1.2, B4.1.8 | |

# B5 Genes, inheritance, and selection
## B5.1 Inheritance
### B5.1.1 Variation

**Specification links:**

B5.1c Describe that the genome, and its interaction with the environment, influence the development of the phenotype of an organism. To include use of examples of discontinuous and continuous variation, for example, eye colour, weight, and height.

B5.1l Recall that most phenotypic features are the result of multiple genes rather than single gene inheritance.

WS1.3a Present observations and other data using appropriate methods.

WS1.3b Translate data from one form to another.

WS1.3e Interpret observations and other data.

WS2a Carry out experiments.

WS2b Make and record observations and measurements using a range of apparatus and methods.

WS2c Present observations using appropriate methods.

WS2d Communicate the scientific rational for investigations, methods used, findings, and reasoned conclusions.

BM5.1iii Extract and interpret information from charts, graphs, and tables (M2c, M4a).

| Target | Outcome | Checkpoint | |
|---|---|---|---|
| | | Question | Activity |
| **Aiming for GRADE 4** | State what is meant by variation. | | Starter 1 and 2<br>Main |
| | Name some examples of continuous or discontinuous variation. | C, 3 | Starter 1 and 2<br>Main<br>Plenary 2 |
| | Record observations in a basic table. | | Main |
| **Aiming for GRADE 6** | Describe the two causes of variation, genetic and environmental, and give examples. | A, B, 1 | Starter 1 and 2<br>Plenary 2 |
| | Describe the differences between discontinuous and continuous variation. | 3 | Starter 2<br>Main<br>Plenary 2 |
| | Record data from experiments in a clear table with full headings, and plot a simple graph. | | Main<br>Plenary 1 |
| **Aiming for GRADE 8** | Explain the differences between genetic and environmental variation. | 2 | Plenary 2 |
| | Distinguish between the causes of discontinuous and continuous variation. | | Main<br>Plenary 2 |
| | Record data from experiments in a clear table with full headings, and plot appropriate graphs to represent the data. | | Main<br>Plenary 1 |

**Maths**
During the main activity, students will be required to construct and interpret frequency tables and diagrams, bar charts, and histograms (M2c, M4a).

**Literacy**
During the main activity, students will be required to produce succinct, coherent, well-structured text when explaining their findings.

**Key words**
continuous variation, discontinuous variation, environmental variation, genetic variation, phenotype, variation

150

# B5.1 Inheritance

| Starter | Support/Extend | Resources |
|---|---|---|
| **Spot the difference** (10 minutes)  Show images of several examples of different breeds of cat or dog. Give the class one minute to identify as many differences as possible. Discuss the differences in the animals. Ask the question 'What caused the differences?' They should remember the causes from Key Stage 3. | **Extend:** You could discuss the similarities and link to them being the same species. | |
| **Continuous or discontinuous?** (5 minutes)  Use the interactive in which students sort characteristics into whether they show continuous or discontinuous variation. | | **Interactive:** Continuous or discontinuous? |

| Main | Support/Extend | Resources |
|---|---|---|
| **Measuring variation**<br>**1. Measure continuous variation** (20 minutes)  Measure a continuous variant. For example, length of middle finger. Pool data for the class and create a frequency table. Plot the data as a histogram.<br><br>**2. Measure discontinuous variation** (20 minutes)  Measure a discontinuous variant, for example, tongue rolling or free/attached ear lobes. Be aware of student sensitivities. Create a table of class data. Plot a bar graph.<br>Ask students a series of questions about the type of variation and its causes. Questions for each could include:<br>• What type of variation have you measured?<br>• How do you know?<br>• Suggest the cause of this variation.<br>• If the variation is caused by genes, is it caused by one gene or many genes?<br>• What evidence are you using to decide how many genes are involved?<br>• Suggest other types of variation of this type in humans. | **Support:** Give headings for the results tables and axes for the graphs. Or supply details about how to plot a bar graph and histogram.<br>**Extend:** Plan the method as a class. They should take into account the need to maximise the accuracy of the data. | **Practical:** Measuring variation |

| Plenary | Support/Extend | Resources |
|---|---|---|
| **Sample size** (10 minutes)  Discuss the shapes of the graphs from Mains 1 and 2. Are they as expected? The continuous graph may not be a simple normal distribution. Can they account for the unexpected shape of the graph (sample too small)? How could they obtain better data? | **Extend:** Did gender have an effect? Should they have thought of that? | |
| **Explain how** (5 minutes)  Show images of a few animals, such as zebra, that have a pattern on the fur colour. Ask students to:<br>• identify some variations<br>• state what caused the variation<br>• explain how the factor (genes or the environment) caused the variation.<br>For any genetic variations the students identify, ask how many genes are involved (one or many). | **Extend:** Ask if they can identify the variation as being continuous or discontinuous. | |

| Homework | | |
|---|---|---|
| Plan an investigation to find out more about people's liking for Marmite (yeast extract). The manufacturers claim you either love it or hate it – can you produce data and a graph to support this claim? | | |

**kerboodle**

A Kerboodle highlight for this lesson is **Working scientifically: Twin studies**. Refer to the **Content map** on Kerboodle for a full list of resources and assessment.

# B5.1.2 Sexual and asexual reproduction

**Specification links:**

B5.1f Explain some of the advantages and disadvantages of asexual and sexual reproduction in a range of organisms. To include the number of live offspring per birth, how quickly the organisms can reproduce versus the need for the introduction of variation in a population caused by environmental pressures.

WS1.1e Explain everyday and technological applications of science.

WS1.1f Evaluate associated personal, social, economic, and environmental implications.

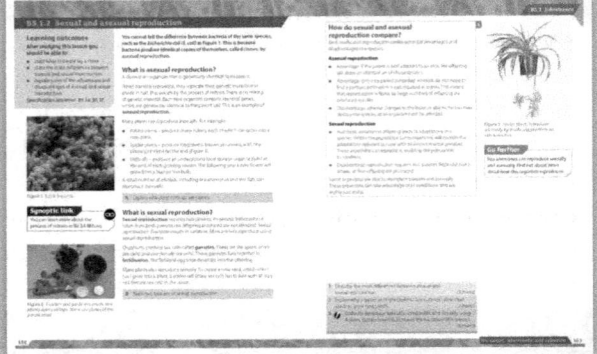

| Target | Outcome | Checkpoint | |
|---|---|---|---|
| | | Question | Activity |
| **Aiming for GRADE 4** | State that there are two types of reproduction. | | Starter 1 and 2<br>Main |
| | State what is meant by a clone. | A | Main<br>Plenary 2 |
| | State some applications of a scientific knowledge of reproduction. | | Starter 1 and 2<br>Main |
| **Aiming for GRADE 6** | Describe the differences between asexual and sexual reproduction. | B, 1 | Starter 1 and 2<br>Main<br>Plenary 1 |
| | Describe the process by which some organisms are able to produce clones. | A | Starter 1<br>Main<br>Plenary 1 and 2 |
| | Describe the application of science to reproductive technologies. | | Main |
| **Aiming for GRADE 8** | Explain some of the advantages and disadvantages of asexual and sexual reproduction. | 2, 3 | Main<br>Plenary 1 and 2 |
| | Explain why clones lack genetic variation. | | Main<br>Plenary 1 and 2 |
| | Explain how an application of science to reproductive technologies has brought about new or improved varieties. | | Main |

**Literacy**

During the main activity, students will be expected to write coherent, well-structured sentences to describe and explain the differences between the types of reproduction.

**Key words**

asexual reproduction, clones, fertilisation, gametes, sexual reproduction

# B5.1 Inheritance

| Starter | Support/Extend | Resources |
|---|---|---|
| **Spider plants** (10 minutes)  Show the class a spider plant or strawberry plant with runners and new plants, or show images. Introduce the idea that the plant is reproducing and give a basic definition of reproduction. Then divide the class into groups, and ask them to discuss and make quick notes about how they think the plant is reproducing – what are the advantages and disadvantages of the process? Take class feedback, and define the terms asexual and sexual reproduction. | **Support:** Do the activity as a class discussion. | |
| **Cuttings and seeds** (5 minutes)  Demonstrate (or use a student to demonstrate) taking a cutting and planting a seed. Show examples of cuttings and seeds that have been sown, set up two weeks previously. Compare the two methods, for example, time to produce new individuals, resources needed for seed production, and so on. Name the two processes. | **Extend:** Discuss the time and resources needed to produce the seed. | |

| Main | Support/Extend | Resources |
|---|---|---|
| **Case study – comparing reproductive technologies** (45 minutes) Compare the production of daffodil bulbs and breeding new varieties of dogs. The students will require an information card about the process and costs involved in both of these types of production.<br><br>Students then answer a series of questions such as:<br>• State what is meant by sexual reproduction.<br>• Explain why the dogs are produced by sexual reproduction.<br>• State and explain the advantages and disadvantages of the process.<br>• State and explain the cost of producing puppies like this.<br><br>Then similar questions for the daffodil, including:<br>• Explain what a clone is.<br>• Explain why clones lack genetic variation. | **Support:** Only deal with one form of reproduction at a time.<br><br>**Extend:** Discuss the potential of artificial cloning in animals, such as cows, to produce high yields of milk. Discuss the advantages and disadvantages. | **Activity:** Comparing reproductive technologies |

| Plenary | Support/Extend | Resources |
|---|---|---|
| **Advantages and disadvantages of sexual and asexual reproduction** (5 minutes)  Use the interactive in which students drag and drop statements about the advantages and disadvantages of sexual and asexual reproduction into one of two columns. | | **Interactive:** Advantages and disadvantages |
| **Dutch elm disease** (10 minutes)  Show some images of elm trees and explain that they were one of the common trees in British woodlands. Show images from the internet of their reproduction via asexual reproduction. Identify the main drawbacks of asexual reproduction. Then introduce the idea of the infecting fungus. Ask them to suggest what would happen. Then reveal the full story of the spread of Dutch elm disease and the consequent near-elimination of elm trees in Britain. | | |

| Homework | | |
|---|---|---|
| Describe the use of artificial cloning to produce animals or plants. Focus on the use of the techniques to produce more animals from an endangered species. Discuss the advantages of the process here. | **Extend:** Produce a balanced discussion of the advantages and disadvantages of the process. | |

# B5.1.3 Meiosis

**Specification links:**

B5.1b Describe the genome as the entire genetic material of an organism.

B5.1g Explain the terms haploid and diploid.

B5.1h Explain the role of meiotic cell division in halving the chromosome number to form gametes. To include that this maintains diploid cells when gametes combine, and is a source of genetic variation.

WS1.4a Use scientific vocabulary, terminology, and definitions.

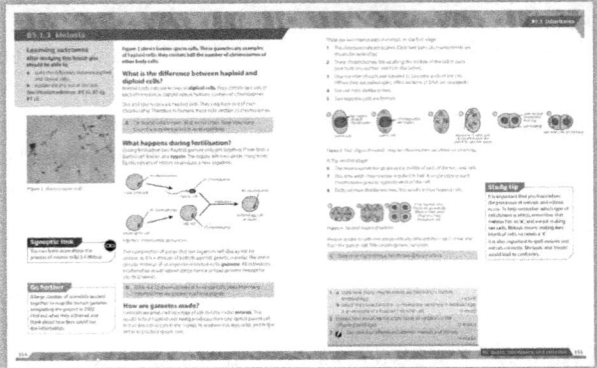

| Target | Outcome | Checkpoint | |
|---|---|---|---|
| | | Question | Activity |
| **Aiming for GRADE 4** ↓ | State that gametes are produced by meiosis. | | Starter 1 and 2<br>Main<br>Plenary 2 |
| | State that the chromosome number halves when an organism makes gametes. | A | Starter 2<br>Main<br>Plenary 2 |
| | Use some scientific vocabulary to communicate simply and clearly. | | Starter 2<br>Main<br>Plenary 2 |
| **Aiming for GRADE 6** ↓ | Explain the process of meiosis. | C, 3 | Main<br>Plenary 1<br>Plenary 2 |
| | Describe the difference between haploid and diploid cells. | A, B, 1 | Starter 2<br>Main<br>Plenary 2 |
| | Use scientific vocabulary and terminology to communicate effectively, sustaining interest. | | Main<br>Plenary 2 |
| **Aiming for GRADE 8** ↓ | Explain the significance of meiosis in genetic variation. | 2 | Main |
| | Explain the role of meiosis in maintaining the chromosome number. | | Starter 2<br>Main |
| | Use scientific vocabulary and terminology to communicate with impact. | | Main |

**Literacy**

During the main activity, students will need to use a range of scientific vocabulary, terminology, and definitions, which they are able to communicate effectively, sustaining the readers' interest.

**Key words**

diploid cell, haploid cell, genome, meiosis, zygote

# B5.1 Inheritance

| Starter | Support/Extend | Resources |
|---|---|---|
| **Inheritance** (5 minutes)  Use the interactive activity in which students answer questions on mitosis, meiosis, and the differences between asexual and sexual reproduction.<br><br>**Chromosome number** (10 minutes)  Show on the board a series of cells that represent zygotes from three or four generations. One student will write the chromosome numbers in these during the activity. Give a few students bank coin bags, each containing eight pipe cleaners. This represents a cell with eight chromosomes. Then record the chromosome number in this, the first cell. Get two students to join their cells to show fertilisation. They combine the chromosomes so that the chromosome number increases – record this number. Continue a few times. Then discuss the problems that would occur if this process actually happened. Ask for suggestions of what might actually happen. Simulate halving the chromosome number and combining. | **Extend:** Discuss why this process cannot be used to produce gametes.<br><br>**Extend:** Introduce the terms haploid and diploid. | **Interactive:** Inheritance |

| Main | Support/Extend | Resources |
|---|---|---|
| **Meiosis film script** (40 minutes)  Recap mitosis. Show a film of meiosis (there are many available on the internet). Do not spend time talking about the process, but do evaluate the film – consider the quality of the images, the information it provides, and the quality of the script.<br><br>Ask students to plan and produce a stop-motion film to illustrate the stages of meiosis, including a film script to explain events in each scene (supply strands of wool or pipe cleaners to act as chromosomes).<br><br>The films should include: the name of the process that makes gametes, the difference between haploid and diploid cells, the significance of meiosis in genetic variation, and reference to chromosome number. | **Support:** Provide a framework for the film, such as scene titles. | **Activity:** Meiosis film script |

| Plenary | Support/Extend | Resources |
|---|---|---|
| **Loop cards** (10 minutes)  Write short steps from the sequence of events in meiosis on cards, with one statement per card. (The more cards the better.) Deal out the cards randomly. Students read out the cards in the correct order.<br>**What word am I?** (5 minutes)  Students work in small groups. All, apart from one student in each group, choose a key word from the lesson and write it on a sticky note. The other student places the note on their head without reading it. This student asks questions to guess what the word is. | **Support:** Tell the students which is the first card. | |

| Homework | | |
|---|---|---|
| Produce a summary table with the similarities and differences between mitosis and meiosis. | | |

**kerboodle**
A Kerboodle highlight for this lesson is **Homework: Reproduction and variation**. Refer to the **Content map** on Kerboodle for a full list of resources and assessment.

# B5.1.4 Dominant and recessive alleles

**Specification links:**

B5.1a Explain the following terms: gamete, chromosome, gene, allele/variant, dominant, recessive, homozygous, heterozygous, genotype, and phenotype.

B5.1c Describe that the genome, and its interaction with the environment, influence the development of the phenotype of an organism. To include use of examples of discontinuous and continuous variation, for example, eye colour, weight, and height.

WS1.4a Use scientific vocabulary, terminology, and definitions.

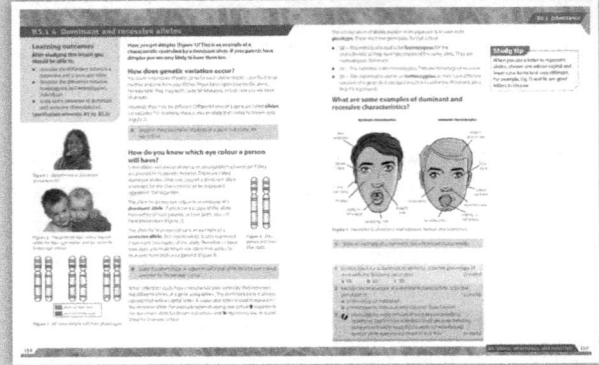

| Target | Outcome | Checkpoint | |
|---|---|---|---|
| | | Question | Activity |
| **Aiming for GRADE 4** ↓ | State some examples of characteristics controlled by dominant or recessive alleles. | C | Starter 1 and 2 |
| | State that individuals have two alleles for a characteristic. | 2 | Starter 1 and 2<br>Main |
| | Use some scientific vocabulary to communicate simply and clearly. | 3 | Starter 1 and 2<br>Main<br>Plenary 1 and 2 |
| **Aiming for GRADE 6** ↓ | Describe the difference between a dominant and recessive allele. | | Starter 1 and 2<br>Main<br>Plenary 1 and 2 |
| | Describe the difference between homozygous and heterozygous. | 3 | Starter 2<br>Main<br>Plenary 1 and 2 |
| | Use scientific vocabulary and terminology to communicate effectively, sustaining interest. | 3 | Main<br>Plenary 1 and 2 |
| **Aiming for GRADE 8** ↓ | Explain how the combination of alleles in the genotype can be expressed in the phenotype. | 1 | Starter 2<br>Main |
| | Explain how sexual reproduction leads to new combinations of alleles in the genotype. | | Starter 2<br>Main |
| | Use scientific vocabulary and terminology to communicate with impact. | 3 | Main<br>Plenary 1 and 2 |

**Literacy**
During the main activity, students will need to use a range of scientific vocabulary, terminology, and definitions, which they are able to communicate effectively, sustaining the reader's interest.

**Key words**
allele, dominant allele, genotype, heterozygous, homozygous, recessive allele

# B5.1 Inheritance

| Starter | Support/Extend | Resources |
|---|---|---|
| **Mendel and his peas** (5 minutes)  Show an image of Mendel. Then show part of his cross of peas, showing tall peas crossed with dwarf peas. Ask the class to predict the outcome. Then reveal the real outcome. Ask how organisms, such as peas, inherit characteristics. This should initiate reference to genes. Introduce the idea of dominant and recessive alleles, and link to the peas. | **Extend:** Include words genes and alleles. | |
| **Human karyotypes** (10 minutes)  Show an image of a human karyotype. Ask a series of questions that build the following ideas: the image shows human chromosomes; the chromosomes are in pairs; the chromosomes contain genes; individuals must have two copies of a gene; we are a mix of characteristics of our two parents; some genes must have more influence than others; the idea of dominant and recessive. | **Extend:** Include the words homozygous and heterozygous. | |

| Main | Support/Extend | Resources |
|---|---|---|
| **Genetics webpage** (40 minutes)  Create a web page for a museum to explain the language associated with genetics. It must have a home page that shows about 10 key words.<br><br>Divide the class into groups of about six, which will subdivide into pairs. Each pair is responsible for creating a hyperlink for about three of the words. The hyperlink page content should:<br>• be as imaginative as possible<br>• define the term<br>• use images to illustrate the word<br>• give examples.<br>Then the pairs reunite into their groups of six, reveal their work, and collate it into one complete page. | **Support:** Show an example and show students how to create a hyperlink. List the key words.<br><br>**Extend:** Explain the impact of some of the key words on the final phenotype. | **Activity:** Genetics webpage |

| Plenary | Support/Extend | Resources |
|---|---|---|
| **Genetics definitions** (5 minutes)  Use the interactive to link the key words from this spread with their correct meanings. | | **Interactive:** Genetics definitions |
| **Spelling bee** (10 minutes)  Organise a spelling bee competition within groups. Provide a list of the key words from this lesson on separate cards. Each student in a group takes their turn to be asked to spell the word and to come up with a sentence that uses the word correctly. | **Support:** Provide anagrams of the words, or words with missing letters to help spelling. | |

| Homework | | |
|---|---|---|
| Create a spider diagram between the words from the spelling bee, with explanations for the links written on the lines. | | |

# B5.1.5 Genetic crosses (1)

**Specification links:**

B5.1i Explain single gene inheritance. To include in the context of homozygous and heterozygous crosses involving dominant and recessive genes.

B5.1j Predict the results of single gene crosses.

WS1.1b Use models to solve problems, make predictions, and to develop scientific explanations and understanding of familiar and unfamiliar facts.

WS1.1e Explain everyday and technological applications of science.

BM5.1i Understand and use direct proportions and simple ratios in genetic crosses (M1c).

BM5.1ii Understand and use the concept of probability in predicting the outcome of genetic crosses (M2e).

BM5.1iii Extract and interpret information from charts, graphs, and tables (M2c, M4a).

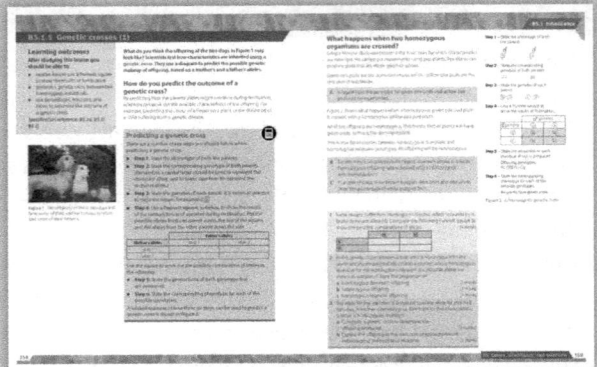

| Target | Outcome | Checkpoint | |
|---|---|---|---|
| | | Question | Activity |
| **Aiming for GRADE 4** | State that alleles are passed from one generation to the next during reproduction. | | Starter 1 and 2 Main Plenary 2 |
| | State that it is possible to predict the outcome of a genetic cross. | | Starter 1 and 2 Main Plenary 2 |
| | Complete models, such as Punnet squares, given the alleles, to show the outcome of a genetic cross. | 1 | Main Plenary 1 and 2 |
| **Aiming for GRADE 6** | Describe the steps in a genetic cross between two homozygous individuals. | A, B, 1, 3 | Main Plenary 2 |
| | Use any one of percentages, fractions, or ratios to represent the outcome of a genetic cross. | C, 2 | Main Plenary 2 |
| | Complete models, such as Punnet squares, to predict the outcome of a genetic cross. | 1, 3 | Main Plenary 1 and 2 |
| **Aiming for GRADE 8** | Explain how to use a Punnet square to show the results of fertilisation. | B, 1 | Main Plenary 1 and 2 |
| | Compare and evaluate the use of percentages, fractions, and ratios to represent the outcome of a genetic cross. | C, 2, 3 | Main |
| | Draw, and confidently use models, such as Punnet squares, to predict the outcome of a genetic cross. | 3 | Main Plenary 1 and 2 |

**Maths**
During the main activity, students will use ratios, fractions, and percentages to express genetic outcomes (M1c).

**Literacy**
During the main activity, students will be required to show understanding of explicit and implicit meanings.
They will also have to make coherent, well-structured statements to describe the condition.

**Key words**
genetic cross, Punnett square

158

# B5.1 Inheritance

| Starter | Support/Extend | Resources |
|---|---|---|
| **Combining alleles** (5 minutes)  Select two students to stand at the front of the class. Provide one with two circular cards, each with a capital letter. The second student has two circular cards each with the lower case letter. New students now act by randomly selecting a card from each of the students to give an offspring. Repeat for the second cards. You have now created new individuals with new genotypes. <br> **Inheritance – is it important?** (10 minutes)  Introduce the fact that we have inherited some characteristics from one of our parents, for example, hair colour. Ask if it is important to know how and from where you inherited your hair colour; answer – probably not. However, sometimes it is important to know. Student groups discuss examples of when it would be important to know how and from where characteristics are inherited. Feedback to class. State that the aim of the lesson is to understand how we can track inheritance. | | |

| Main | Support/Extend | Resources |
|---|---|---|
| **Single gene inheritance** (15 minutes)  Model how to use a Punnet square for a homozygous cross of a single characteristic. Students then carry out 2–3 basic homozygous genetic crosses, so as to gain some confidence in the skills required. <br> **Research a genetic disorder** (15 minutes)  Then introduce an application, for example, a genetic disorder. Students research a named disorder, for example, cystic fibrosis or Huntington's disease. List key features about the disorder and the alleles that control it. <br> **Inheriting the genetic disorder** (10 minutes)  Students carry out a homozygous cross of such a disorder. They write a short explanation of the steps and the outcomes. | **Extend:** Predict outcomes in ratios, fractions, and percentages. Is any type of outcome more useful than the others? <br> **Support:** Provide websites (possibly using QR (Quick Response) codes on the board), and a frame of questions to structure their research and responses. | **Activity:** Single gene inheritance |

| Plenary | Support/Extend | Resources |
|---|---|---|
| **Spot the mistakes** (5 minutes)  Use a multiple-choice interactive with images of several Punnet squares, only one of which is correct. Identify the correct one and explain the mistakes in the others. <br> **Pure lines** (10 minutes)  Show pictures of two cat breeds of different colours, or a red and white flowering geranium, and state that they are pure lines (homozygous). Ask students how they could work out which was the dominant allele (characteristic). Allow them to discuss the problem in groups and present a solution. | **Extend:** Ask how you could breed more of the recessive characteristic. | **Interactive:** Spot the mistakes |

| Homework | | |
|---|---|---|
| Select a genetic cross. Write out a genetic cross for crossing two pure-breed examples. Then draw cells next to key points in the diagrams, for example, parents' genotypes, the gametes, and the zygote. Draw in the alleles and colour the diagrams. | | |

*kerboodle*
A Kerboodle highlight for this lesson is **Animation: The inheritance of cystic fibrosis**. Refer to the **Content map** on Kerboodle for a full list of resources and assessment.

# B5.1.6 Genetic crosses (2)

**Specification links:**

B5.1i Explain single gene inheritance. To include in the context of homozygous and heterozygous crosses involving dominant and recessive genes.

B5.1j Predict the results of single gene crosses.

B5.1k Describe sex determination in humans using a genetic cross.

WS1.1b Use models to solve problems, make predictions, and to develop scientific explanations and understanding of familiar and unfamiliar facts.

WS1.1e Explain everyday and technological applications of science.

BM5.1i Understand and use direct proportions and simple ratios in genetic crosses (M1c).

BM5.1ii Understand and use the concept of probability in predicting the outcome of genetic crosses (M2e).

BM5.1iii Extract and interpret information from charts, graphs, and tables (M2c, M4a).

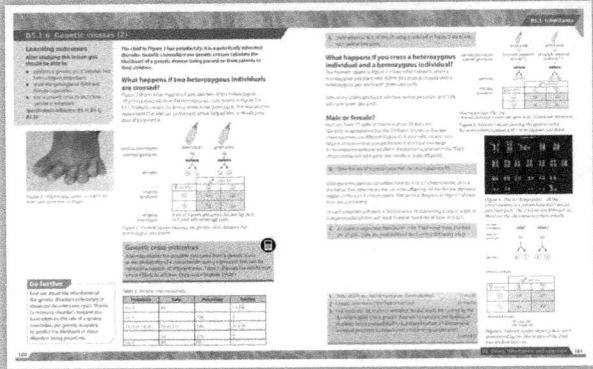

| Target | Outcome | Checkpoint | |
|---|---|---|---|
| | | Question | Activity |
| **Aiming for GRADE 4** | State that a heterozygous genetic cross can result in offspring of a different phenotype to the parents. | | Starter 1, Main |
| | State the genotype of a male and female organism. | B, 1 | Starter 2, Main, Plenary 1 |
| | Complete models, such as Punnet squares, given the alleles, to show the outcome of a heterozygous genetic cross. | | Main |
| **Aiming for GRADE 6** | Describe the steps in a genetic cross between two heterozygous individuals. | | Main, Plenary 2 |
| | Use a genetic cross to show how gender is inherited. | 2 | Main |
| | Complete models, such as Punnet squares, to predict the outcome of a heterozygous genetic cross. | | Main, Plenary 2 |
| **Aiming for GRADE 8** | Use percentages, fractions, and ratios to represent the outcome of a heterozygous genetic cross. | A | Main, Plenary 1 and 2 |
| | Compare and evaluate the use of percentages, fractions, and ratios to represent the probability of having male or female offspring. | C | Main, Plenary 1 |
| | Draw, and confidently use models, such as Punnet squares, to predict the outcome of a heterozygous genetic cross. | | Main, Plenary 1 and 2 |

**Maths**
During the main activity, students will use ratios, fractions, and percentages to express genetic outcomes (M1c).

**Literacy**
During the main activity, students will be required to make valid responses to explicit and implicit meanings. They will also have to make coherent, well-structured statements to describe the condition.

# B5.1 Inheritance

| Starter | Support/Extend | Resources |
|---|---|---|
| **Skipping a generation** (5 minutes) Ask students what they think people mean when they say a characteristic skips a generation. Use words to write out the inheritance of a characteristic, for example flower colour, through two generations. Explain that this is an example of a family tree. Recap that the first part represents what they learnt in the last lesson. So the aim of this lesson is to learn the second part. **Karyotypes** (10 minutes) Show students two karyotypes, one for a male, one for a female. Ask them to spot the difference. Name the sex chromosomes and explain that they contain the alleles that control sex determination. Ask students to work out the genotype for a male and female. | | |

| Main | Support/Extend | Resources |
|---|---|---|
| **Heterozygous crosses** (25 minutes) Return to the genetic disorder and ask students to carry out a heterozygous cross. They can then state the chances of such a couple having a child with the disorder as a ratio, percentage, or fraction. Now try a heterozygote with a sufferer or a non-sufferer and recalculate the chances of having a child with the disorder. If needed, try additional heterozygous crosses for different traits to secure knowledge. **Sex determination** (15 minutes) Prepare sets of sperm and egg cards with either an X or a Y on the back, and egg cards, all with an X on the back. Working in pairs, the students choose pairs of cards at random and turn them over. They record the genotype and phenotype each time, and record in a tally table. They can do this for 5–7 minutes. Discuss what their evidence shows about the ratio and how it would change if they repeated this activity 1000 times. | **Support:** Supply the Punnet square and place alleles into the square **Extend:** Ask students how they could work out an unknown genotype (backcross with the double recessive). | **Activity sheet:** Heterozygous crosses **Activity:** Sex determination |

| Plenary | Support/Extend | Resources |
|---|---|---|
| **Genetic crosses** (10 minutes) Use the interactive in which students match the genetic cross to the offspring genotypes and the ratio it would produce. **Family trees** (10 minutes) Draw a family tree on the board that traces the inheritance of a particular characteristic. The tree should contain some genotypes. Ask students to complete missing genotypes using the knowledge gained. | **Extend:** Students can make up their own sentences to test a partner. **Extend:** Predict ratios for further crosses. | **Interactive:** Genetic crosses |

| Homework |
|---|
| Produce an exam question about genetic crosses using heterozygous crosses, genotypes, phenotypes, etc., and produce the mark scheme for the question. |

**kerboodle**

A Kerboodle highlight for this lesson is **Calculation sheet: Direct proportion and ratio**. Refer to the **Content map** on Kerboodle for a full list of resources and assessment.

# B5.1.7 Mutations

**Specification links:**

B5.1d Recall that all variants arise from mutations, and that most have no effect on the phenotype, some influence phenotype, and a very few determine phenotype.

> B5.1e Describe how genetic variants may influence phenotype:
> - in coding DNA by altering the activity of a protein, to include DNA related to mutations affecting protein structure, including active sites of enzymes
> - in non-coding DNA by altering how genes are expressed, to include DNA related to stopping transcription of mRNA (use of terms promoter, transcription factor not required).

H S

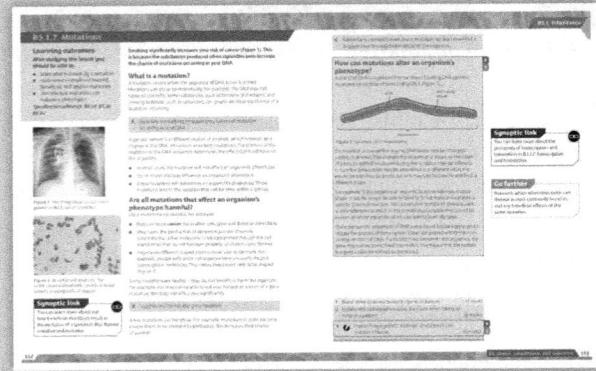

WS1.3f Present reasoned explanations.

BM5.1i Understand and use direct proportions and simple ratios in genetic crosses (M1c).

BM5.1ii Understand and use the concept of probability in predicting the outcome of genetic crosses (M2e).

| Target | Outcome | Checkpoint | |
|---|---|---|---|
| | | Question | Activity |
| **Aiming for GRADE 4** | State what is meant by a mutation. | | Starter 1 and 2<br>Plenary 2 |
| | State some examples of harmful, beneficial, and neutral mutations. | B, 1 | Starter 1 and 2<br>Main<br>Plenary 1 |
| | Use some key facts to present a basic description of a genetic disorder. | | Main |
| **Aiming for GRADE 6** | Describe how a mutation can influence phenotype. | | Starter 2<br>Main<br>Plenary 1 and 2 |
| | Describe the consequences of harmful or beneficial mutations. | C | Main<br>Plenary 2 |
| | Use a range of factual information to present an explanation of the causes and effects of a genetic disorder. | | Main |
| **Aiming for GRADE 8** | Explain how a mutation alters the way in which the gene functions in the cell. | 3 | Starter 2<br>Main<br>Plenary 1 and 2 |
| | Explain the causes of mutations. | A, 2 | Main |
| | Use a wide range of relevant factual information, including data, to present a reasoned explanation of the causes, effects, and inheritance of a genetic disorder. | | Main |

**Maths**
During the main activity, students will use ratios, fractions, and percentages to express genetic outcomes (M1c).

**Literacy**
During the main activity, students will be required to make valid responses to explicit and implicit meanings. They will also have to make coherent, well-structured statements to describe the condition.

**Key words**
cancer, mutation

# B5.1 Inheritance

| Starter | Support/Extend | Resources |
|---|---|---|
| **Types of mutations** (5 minutes) Ask if students know what we mean by mutation. Present a clear definition of a mutation. Then issue a series of cards each with a different mutation. Ask students to sort the mutations in some way, but do not suggest any particular way. Then feedback on the process. Suggest sorting according to harmful, helpful, or neutral. | **Support**: Tell them to sort into harmful, helpful, and neutral from the start. | |
| **Damaging codes** (10 minutes) Present a few statements where changes to one letter can alter the meaning of the sentence. For example, 'You are now learning about mutations' changes to 'You are not learning about mutations'. Discuss how the small changes alter the meaning. Now apply these ideas to DNA. What effect will the change have in a cell? | **Extend**: Recap protein synthesis and ask for more detail about the mutation changing the protein produced. | H S |

| Main | Support/Extend | Resources |
|---|---|---|
| **Inherited disorders**<br>**Research** (20 minutes) Present the class with a small range of genetic mutations (e.g. cystic fibrosis and polydactyly), from which each group can select one. They will need to research the cause and effects of the mutations in the organism. Genetic disorders are well explained on several websites. Students could be directed to these websites or given printouts.<br>**Production of information leaflet** (20 minutes) Students use the facts and figures they have found in their research to produce an information leaflet about the mutation. The leaflet should cover the following areas:<br>State the name of the mutation or disorder.<br>Describe the effect of the disorder, or symptoms.<br>Describe the genetic mutation responsible.<br>State the frequency of the mutation in the population.<br>Explain how the mutation is inherited and the probability of inheriting the condition from different parental genotypes. | **Support:** Select the condition and provide the websites. Produce a frame of questions based on the final product that will structure students' research.<br><br>**Extend:** Students explain what has happened to the DNA, and how the change in the DNA has resulted in a change to the proteins involved in cell function, leading to the condition. H S | **Activity:** Inherited disorders |

| Plenary | Support/Extend | Resources |
|---|---|---|
| **Mutations and protein synthesis** (5 minutes) Use the interactive in which students drag and drop into the correct order statements that explain how mutations alter the gene structure and, in turn, the protein structure. | | **Interactive:** Mutations and protein synthesis H S |
| **White fur** (10 minutes) Many mammals have white fur. Ask students to describe how this would have arisen. Ask them if they think it is harmful, helpful, or neutral, and to justify their decision. | **Extend:** Ask students to suggest a biochemical explanation for the development of the white fur. | |

| Homework | | |
|---|---|---|
| Haemophilia is a mutation that affects the blood. It occurred in the royal families of Europe. Find out what the mutation does, whether or not it is harmful, and trace it through the Royal family from Queen Victoria. | | |

# GCSE BIOLOGY ONLY
## B5.1.8 The history of genetics

**Specification links:**

B5.1m Describe the development of our understanding of genetics. To include the work of Mendel.

WS1.1a Understand how scientific methods and theories develop over time.

WS1.1d Discuss ethical issues arising from developments in science.

WS1.1f Evaluate associated personal, social, economic, and environmental implications.

WS1.1i Recognise the importance of peer review of results and of communicating results to a range of audiences.

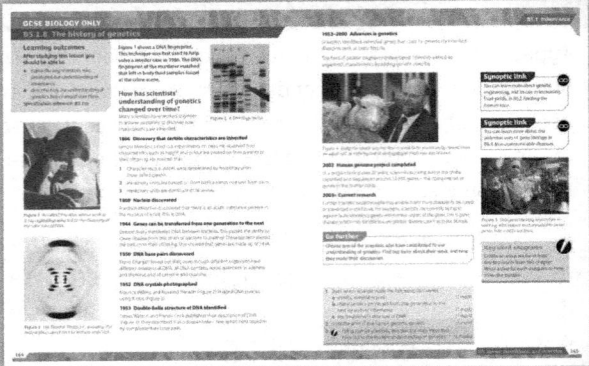

| Target | Outcome | Checkpoint | |
|---|---|---|---|
| | | Question | Activity |
| **Aiming for GRADE 4** ↓ | Name the key scientist who developed our understanding of inheritance. | 1 | Main |
| | State that Mendel's work led to further discoveries. | 3 | Main, Plenary 2 |
| | State that scientists publish their results and ideas for other scientists to read. | | Starter 1, Main, Plenary 1 |
| **Aiming for GRADE 6** ↓ | Describe the conclusions Mendel drew from his experiments. | | Main, Plenary 2 |
| | Describe how our understanding of genetics has changed over time. | 3 | Main, Plenary 1 |
| | Describe how scientists publish their results and how they are checked. | | Starter 1, Main |
| **Aiming for GRADE 8** ↓ | Discuss the importance of Mendel's work on genetics. | | Main, Plenary 1 and 2 |
| | Explain how scientific ideas are built upon prior work of other scientists. | 3 | Main, Plenary 1 and 2 |
| | Explain the importance of peer review of results and of communicating those results. | | Starter 1, Main, Plenary 1 |

**Literacy**
During the main activity, students will need to communicate effectively, sustaining the reader's interest.

**Key words**
DNA

# B5.1 Inheritance

| Starter | Support/Extend | Resources |
|---|---|---|
| **Communicating ideas** (10 minutes) Issue A3 paper and pens to each group. Ask them to jot down any of the ways in which they have found out about new scientific discoveries. Have some short feedback. They will probably mainly suggest media-based sources. Ask them where the journalists have found out about the ideas. Lead to the idea of scientific journals and show some examples. | **Extend:** Suggest why scientific publications are important. Discuss evaluating the quality of reports, for example, internet sites versus scientific journals. | **Interactive:** Genetic discoveries |
| **Genetic discoveries** (5 minutes) Use the interactive in which students drag the scientific advances into the correct order in which they occurred. | **Extend:** Note that the later discoveries have built upon the earlier work. | |

| Main | Support/Extend | Resources |
|---|---|---|
| **Genetics timeline** The students can work in groups with the aim of producing a TV script about major discoveries in genetics from Mendel's work to the modern day, including the life and work of Mendel: | **Support:** Provide headings for the research and writing, thus acting as a writing frame. Good sources might be given to the students. | **Activity:** Genetics timeline |
| **Research** (15 minutes) Allow students to use the internet or a range of textbooks to find out facts, including how and why Mendel did not communicate his results. Students could use the Activity sheet to ensure that they include the main points needed. | **Extend:** Evaluate the contribution of Mendel. Suggest how his work has led to modern developments, and any benefits or ethical issues arising. | |
| **Scriptwriting** (25 minutes) Produce a script that tells of the major discoveries in genetics from Mendel's work to the modern day. The script should include details of Mendel's work in the gardens, the experiments he conducted, and a list of his key findings. | | |

| Plenary | Support/Extend | Resources |
|---|---|---|
| **Mendel today** (5 minutes) If Mendel lived today, discuss how scientists might have reacted to his discoveries, and how modern technology would have helped advance his ideas. What impact would the internet have had? | **Extend:** How might better communication have influenced other scientists? | |
| **Tree of knowledge** (10 minutes) Issue groups with a diagram of a plant with a number of bare branches. Ask the groups to list on the branches the various ideas that Mendel had discovered that they have learnt about in the last few lessons, or that are important to modern genetics. These ideas could include:<br>• Characteristics are controlled by genes.<br>• Genes/alleles occur in pairs in the adult.<br>• There are different versions of genes (alleles).<br>• The ideas of dominant and recessive alleles.<br>• We inherit alleles from our parents.<br>• Ratios can be predicted. | **Support:** Provide the group with a list of statements, some of which were discovered by Mendel, some of which are from other scientists.<br>**Extend:** How important do you think Mendel was?<br>What have some of his discoveries led to? | |

| Homework | | |
|---|---|---|
| Write a series of questions to be used on the TV quiz show about the life and work of Mendel. There should be a minimum number of questions (depending on the class) and all answers must be supplied.<br>Alternatively, write a TV script for a follow-up programme, to describe some of the key developments in genetics since the work of Mendel. | | |

**kerboodle**

A Kerboodle highlight for this lesson is **Homework: Inheritance**. Refer to the **Content map** on Kerboodle for a full list of resources and assessment.

# Checkpoint
## B5.1 Inheritance

### Overview of B5.1 Inheritance

In this chapter, students have studied the causes of variation, including continuous and discontinuous variation. They should be able to outline asexual and sexual reproduction, explain the term clone, and state advantages and disadvantages of each type of reproduction. They should be able to link this work with mitosis in B2.1 *Supplying the cell*. Students have studied the process of meiosis, and in distinguishing this from mitosis should be able to define haploid and diploid numbers of chromosomes. They should be able to apply their knowledge about meiosis to non-human examples including plants.

Students should understand the relative scales involved in genetic concepts, from DNA to genes, chromosomes, the nucleus, and the genome. They should be able to apply genetic concepts such as the allele, including the terms dominant and recessive, assign genotypes, and be able to set out a genetic cross in a Punnett square, using this to predict ratios of different phenotypes. They should be aware of the link between inheritance and the structure of DNA from B1.2 *What happens in cells?* They should have studied several genetic crosses including sex inheritance.

Students should be aware that variants arise from mutations. A higher-tier focus is the various ways a mutation can affect an organism's phenotype. Students should be aware of the link with B5.2 *Natural selection and evolution* and that both processes rely on mutation. They should also link this study with the higher-tier studies of transcription and translation in B1.2 *What happens in cells?*

Finally students have studied the history of genetics. They should be aware of the relevance of this to genetic engineering in B6.2 *Feeding the human race* and gene therapy in B6.3 *Monitoring and maintaining health*.

You can find additional support for the maths skills covered in this chapter on **MyMaths**, including working with frequency tables and diagrams, bar charts, and histograms, and using ratios, fractions, and percentages.

For this chapter, the following assessments are available on Kerboodle:

B5.1 Checkpoint quiz: Inheritance
B5.1 Progress quiz: Inheritance 1
B5.1 Progress quiz: Inheritance 2
B5.1 On your marks: Inheritance
B5.1 Exam-style questions and mark scheme: Inheritance

### Checkpoint follow-up lesson

A student's route through this lesson can be determined using the Checkpoint assessment. Percentage pass marks are supplied in the Checkpoint teacher notes.

For each successive route through it is assumed that the student can perform to their current route as well as previous routes. For example, students working at Aiming for 6 are assumed to be secure in Aiming for 4 knowledge and understanding and working towards achieving all the learning objectives for Aiming for 6.

## B5.1 Inheritance

|  | Aiming for 4 | Aiming for 6 | Aiming for 8 |
|---|---|---|---|
| **Learning outcomes** | State the advantages and disadvantages of asexual and sexual reproduction. | Describe the advantages and disadvantages of asexual and sexual reproduction. | Explain the advantages and disadvantages of asexual and sexual reproduction. |
|  | State what occurs during the process of meiosis. | Describe what occurs during the process of meiosis. | Explain what occurs during the process of meiosis. |
|  | Interpret a genetic cross diagram. | Complete a genetic cross diagram. | Draw a genetic cross diagram. |
|  | State some examples of mutation. | Describe what mutation is. | Explain how cells can be mutated. |
| **Starter** | **Variation (5 minutes)** Each student will ned a mini whiteboard. Read out different characteristics, such as eye colour, blood group, ability to play an instrument, weight. Students write on their whiteboards whether each characteristic is caused by genetic variation, environmental variation, or both. ||||
| **Differentiated checkpoint activity** | **Activity 1 Inheritance (45 minutes)** There are five stations, each with a different activity. Students spend up to 10 minutes at each station, following their differentiated worksheets. The following equipment is needed:<br>• station 1 – Student books, scissors and glue sticks for Aiming for 4 students, coloured pencils for Aiming for 6 students<br>• station 2 – pictures of various stages of meiosis (these will need to be prepared in advance), scissors and glue sticks for Aiming for 4 students<br>• station 3 – no equipment needed<br>• station 4 – Student books and coloured pencils<br>• station 5 – student books and coloured pencils. Timeline templates could be provided for Aiming for 4 students. ||||
|  | Aiming for 4 students cut and paste statements as advantages and disadvantages of sexual and asexual reproduction. They match statements about meiosis with pictures and cut and paste them in order. They answer questions about a family tree, and complete a table giving examples of mutations that are harmful, beneficial, or neutral. They are prompted to draw a timeline of the history of genetics given hints about what to include | Aiming for 6 students list advantages and disadvantages of sexual and asexual reproduction. They write a flow chart of meiosis using prompts. They analyse genetic crosses using a Punnett square template, draw a visual summary of mutation using prompts, and draw a timeline of the history of genetics given hints about what to include. | Aiming for 8 students are asked for detailed explanations. They list and explain advantages and disadvantages of sexual and asexual reproduction. They write a flow chart of meiosis and analyse genetic crosses. They draw a visual summary of mutation and draw a timeline of the history of genetics. ||
|  | **Kerboodle resource:** B5.1 Checkpoint follow-up: Aiming for 4, B5.1 Checkpoint follow-up: Aiming for 6, B5.1 Checkpoint follow-up: Aiming for 8 ||||
| **Plenary** | **Quiz (5 minutes)** Ask a series of questions to check understanding, for example – what type of reproduction do bacteria use? Name a genetic disease. What type of cell does meiosis produce? Students write their answers on paper or in their books, and check each other's answers. ||||
| **Progression** | The Aiming for 4 activities provide highly structured questions including cut and paste exercises. There is a practical investigation in this chapter on how characteristics of the class vary which is suitable for all abilities. | The Aiming for 6 activities are reasonably structured. All students could look up different types of characteristic that are controlled by genes to extend and reinforce their learning that variation is genetic, environmental, or both. | The Aiming for 8 activities have very little structure. As an extension, students could research examples of organisms that use both sexual and asexual and reproduction and go on to explain which method is better in the long term.<br><br>Aiming for 8 students should be able to compare and contrast the processes of mitosis and meiosis. They could research the Human Genome Project including what the information is now used for. ||

# B5.2 Natural selection and evolution
## B5.2.1 Natural selection

**Specification links:**

B5.2a State that there is usually extensive genetic variation within a population of a species.

B5.2c Explain how evolution occurs through the natural selection of variants that have given rise to phenotypes best suited to their environment. To include the concept of mutation.

B5.2d Describe evolution as a change in the inherited characteristics of a population over time, through a process of natural selection, which may result in the formation of new species.

WS1.3f Presenting reasoned explanations.

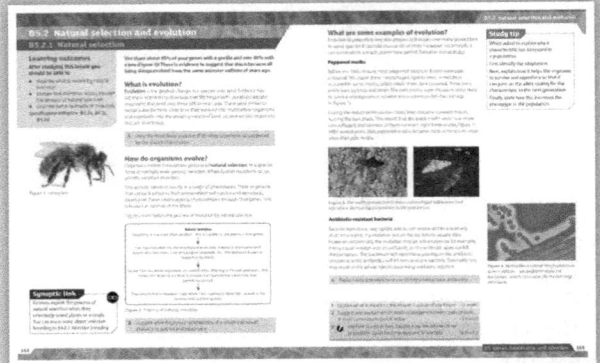

| Target | Outcome | Checkpoint | |
|---|---|---|---|
| | | Question | Activity |
| **Aiming for GRADE 4** ↓ | State that evolution is the gradual change in the characteristics of a population over time. | | Starter 1 and 2 |
| | List some examples of evolution. | A, B | Starter 2, Main |
| | Use observations to present a simple description of the evolution of a characteristic. | | Starter 1, Main |
| **Aiming for GRADE 6** ↓ | Describe what is meant by natural selection. | B, C, 1 | Main, Plenary 1 and 2 |
| | Describe some examples of evolution. | C, 2 | Main |
| | Use some scientific facts to present a simple explanation for the evolution of a characteristic. | | Main |
| **Aiming for GRADE 8** ↓ | Explain how evolution occurs through the process of natural selection. | C, 3 | Main, Plenary 1 and 2 |
| | Explain the role of mutations in bringing about evolution. | C, 3 | Main, Plenary 1 and 2 |
| | Use a range of scientific facts to present a reasoned explanation for the evolution of a characteristic. | | Main |

**Literacy**
During the main activity, students will be expected to use a varied sentence structure, including use of appropriate scientific vocabulary to communicate effectively, sustaining the readers' interest.

**Key words**
evolution, natural selection

## B5.2 Natural selection and evolution

| Starter | Support/Extend | Resources |
|---|---|---|
| **Create an evolutionary family tree** (10 minutes) Present the class with a small selection of related items, for example, types of lab glassware or stationary. Ask them to define evolution and suggest an evolutionary relationship between the items. There would be no wrong answer.<br><br>**Changing channels** (5 minutes) Give groups a small selection of pictures of televisions through the years. Ask them to put them in date order. Use this as a vehicle to define the term evolution. Ask the class if living things change over time. Ask for examples. | **Support:** Reduce the number of items and accept a straight chain.<br><br>**Extend:** Ask them to justify their family tree or suggest the idea of side branches.<br><br>**Extend:** Ask them to justify the order; ask if the complexity has changed. Consider complexity to the living examples. | |

| Main | Support/Extend | Resources |
|---|---|---|
| **Evolution information board** Students work in a museum and have been asked to produce an information board to explain the process of evolution for the natural history section:<br><br>**Create information board** (25 minutes) Present each group with a different example of a characteristic that has evolved. (e.g. giraffes: long neck; elephants: long trunk; wings in bats; thick fur in polar bears, etc.). Ask them to produce an information board that explains in steps how natural selection has brought about the evolution of the characteristic over time. The Student Book can be used to help them build the information board. However, avoid any characteristics that have been directly explained in the Student Book. Allow drawings, time permitting.<br><br>**Peer assessment** (15 minutes) Each group takes a few minutes to explain their presentation to others in the class. Other groups give positive or constructive feedback.<br><br>Finally, a class discussion should draw together the idea that regardless of the examples, the sequence of steps for evolution is the same. | **Support:** Suggest headings for the explanation to act as a frame for the process.<br><br>**Extend:** Students should mention mutations. | **Activity:** Evolution information board |

| Plenary | Support/Extend | Resources |
|---|---|---|
| **Rules of evolution** (10 minutes) Following the main activity, ask groups to construct five or six generic statements that could be used to explain the evolution of any characteristic.<br><br>**Describing natural selection** (5 minutes) Students put statements into the correct order to describe the process of natural selection. | | **Interactive:** Describing natural selection |

| Homework | | |
|---|---|---|
| Draw a mythical creature and suggest how it might have evolved over time, by adding annotations.<br><br>Alternatively, produce a glossary of as many key terms as you can think of in this topic, for example, evolution, natural selection, characteristic, survival of the fittest, gene, variation, population, etc. | | |

**kerboodle**

A Kerboodle highlight for this lesson is **Video: Evolution by natural selection**. Refer to the **Content map** on Kerboodle for a full list of resources and assessment.

# B5.2.2 Evidence for evolution

**Specification links:**

B5.2e Describe the evidence for evolution. To include fossils and antibiotic resistance in bacteria.

WS1.1c Understand the power and limitations of science.

WS1.1d Discuss ethical issues arising from developments in science.

WS1.1g Make decisions based on the evaluation of evidence and arguments.

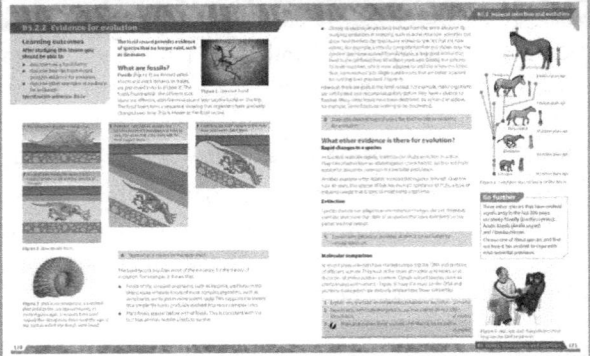

| Target | Outcome | Checkpoint | |
|---|---|---|---|
| | | Question | Activity |
| **Aiming for GRADE 4** ↓ | State what a fossil is. | A | Starter 1 and 2 |
| | Name other types of evidence for evolution. | 3 | Main<br>Plenary 2 |
| | Recognise links between pieces of fossil evidence. | | Main<br>Plenary 1 |
| **Aiming for GRADE 6** ↓ | Describe how a fossil forms. | 2 | Starter 2<br>Plenary 2 |
| | Describe other examples of evidence for evolution. | 3 | Main<br>Plenary 2 |
| | Use fossil evidence to make decisions about the evolution of a characteristic in a species. | | Main<br>Plenary 1 |
| **Aiming for GRADE 8** ↓ | Explain how the fossil record provides evidence for evolution. | B, C, 1 | Starter 1<br>Main<br>Plenary 1 and 2 |
| | Explain how the other types of evidence provide evidence for evolution. | 3 | Main<br>Plenary 2 |
| | Evaluate the quality of fossil evidence when explaining the evolution of a characteristic in a species. | | Main<br>Plenary 1 |

**Maths**
During the main activity, students will be asked to use ratios and fractions when calculating the scale of fossil images (M1c).

**Literacy**
During the main activity, students will need to produce coherent, well-structured text, using vocabulary appropriate to purpose.

**Key words**
fossil, fossil record

# B5.2 Natural selection and evolution

| Starter | Support/Extend | Resources |
|---|---|---|
| **Did dinosaurs exist?** (5 minutes)   Play devil's advocate and suggest that dinosaurs never existed. Students will probably argue that they did – ask them for evidence. They will usually suggest fossils. Elicit a definition of a fossil and show some examples of fossils.<br><br>**How do fossils form?** (10 minutes)   Ask the class to explain what a fossil is and how many fossils are formed. Then demonstrate one common method, explaining each step. Set up a small margarine tub with a layer of fresh plaster of Paris, representing wet mud. Press a bone or animal shell onto the plaster. Then pour over a layer of sand, with a little water, which contains enough sand to cover the specimen. You can reveal the result at the end of the lesson, by dusting off the sand/water and removing the bone, revealing a cast in the plaster of Paris. | | |

| Main | Support/Extend | Resources |
|---|---|---|
| **1. The evolution of the horse**  This is an activity made up of three smaller tasks. You are a palaeontologist working in a natural history museum. You have been asked to sort out samples of fossils that have been sent to the museum.<br>**Part 1 Evolutionary sequence** (15 minutes)   Present each group of students with a set of five skeletal images of different stages of the evolution of the horse (or any other species). The images represent fossils of the horse, and need to clearly show skulls, teeth, and leg digits. They should be enlarged onto A4, but have scale bars. Students calculate the actual size of the fossils. They then place the fossils in date order to show how the horse has evolved over time.<br>**Part 2 Using the evidence** (5 minutes)   Use the fossil evidence to produce a description of the changes in a characteristic over time.<br>**Part 3 Class feedback** (10 minutes)   Students compare a range of different characteristics they have described. Discuss how useful the evidence can be.<br>**2. Is evolution happening today?** (10 minutes)   Discuss the development of antibiotics. Penicillin was first used about 70 years ago and is now becoming less useful, as are many other antibiotics. Discuss how bacteria become resistant to antibiotics. | **Support:** Eliminate the need for calculations. Provide the images at proportional sizes.<br><br><br><br><br><br>**Extend:** Discuss the problems with fossil formation, and any examples of species evolution where evidence is missing or the fossils have been misinterpreted. | **Activity:** The evolution of the horse |

| Plenary | Support/Extend | Resources |
|---|---|---|
| **Incomplete record** (10 minutes)   Show images of two related children (e.g. the Queen and Princess Margaret) and one of the Queen today. Ask the students which of the children becomes the Queen. Then show students images of the two women between the two ages, and they will begin to see connections. Then compare the photographic record to the fossil record. Ask them to identify problems with the fossil record. Why are there gaps in the record?<br>**Fossil formation** (5 minutes)   Use the interactive in which students put the stages of fossil formation into the correct order. | **Extend:** Students should give examples of gaps in a fossil record making it difficult to explain the evolution of a species. | **Interactive:** Fossil formation |

| Homework | | |
|---|---|---|
| Produce a written explanation of how bacteria have become resistant to antibiotics. Use the knowledge of evolution from the last lesson and the discussion of resistance in Main 2. | **Extend:** Explain how modern scientists are working to reduce the problem. | |

**kerboodle**

A Kerboodle highlight for this lesson is **Animation: How fossils are formed**. Refer to the **Content map** on Kerboodle for a full list of resources and assessment.

# GCSE BIOLOGY ONLY
## B5.2.3 The theory of evolution

**Specification links:**

B5.2f Describe the work of Darwin and Wallace in the development of the theory of evolution by natural selection and explain the impact of these ideas on modern biology. To include seed banks being used as a store of biodiversity.

WS1.1a Understand how scientific methods and theories develop over time.

WS1.1d Discuss ethical issues arising from developments in science.

WS1.1g Make decisions based on the evaluation of evidence and arguments.

WS1.1i Recognise the importance of peer review of results and of communicating results to a range of audiences.

WS1.3i Communicating the scientific rationale for investigations, methods used, findings, and reasoned conclusions.

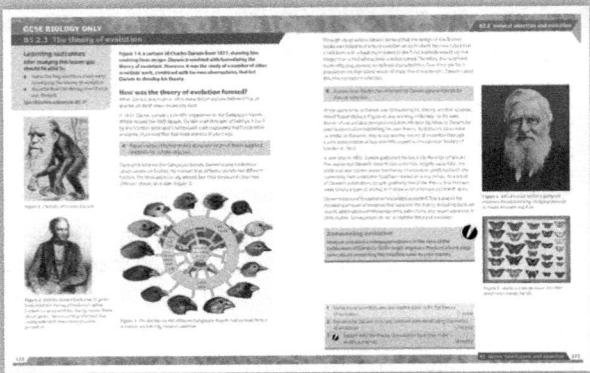

| Target | Outcome | Checkpoint | |
|---|---|---|---|
| | | Question | Activity |
| **Aiming for GRADE 4** | Name the key scientists involved in developing the theory of evolution. | 1 | Main<br>Plenary 1 and 2 |
| | State one reason why many people rejected the theory of evolution. | 3 | Starter 2<br>Main<br>Plenary 1 |
| | State that the theory of evolution was published for others to read. | 3 | Starter 1 and 2<br>Main<br>Plenary 1 |
| **Aiming for GRADE 6** | Describe how these scientists formed their theory of evolution. | | Main<br>Plenary 1 and 2 |
| | Describe the reaction of other scientists and the public to the theory of evolution when it was published. | 3 | Starter 2<br>Main<br>Plenary 1 |
| | Describe the importance of peer review for the acceptance of Darwin and Wallace's work. | 2, 3 | Starter 1 and 2<br>Main |
| **Aiming for GRADE 8** | Explain how the evidence that the scientists collected allowed them to develop their theory. | A, B | Main<br>Plenary 2 |
| | Explain how the theory of evolution has become more accepted and has had an impact on modern biology. | 3 | Starter 2<br>Main<br>Plenary 2 |
| | Explain the importance of the recognition of the work of Darwin and Wallace by scientists to the public acceptance of the ideas. | 2, 3 | Main<br>Plenary 2 |

**Literacy**
During the main activity, the students will need to communicate effectively, sustaining the readers'/listeners' interest.

**Key words**
evolution, natural selection

# B5.2 Natural selection and evolution

| Starter | Support/Extend | Resources |
|---|---|---|
| **Scientific methodology** (10 minutes) Provide groups with a matching exercise about the scientific processes Darwin went through in devising his theory of evolution. Students link each scientific process to what Darwin did. <table><thead><tr><th>Scientific process</th><th>What Darwin did</th></tr></thead><tbody><tr><td>collect evidence by doing a survey or experiment</td><td>observed the beaks and claws on finches on different Galapagos islands, and noted what they ate.</td></tr><tr><td>analyse evidence</td><td>realised that beak shape was linked to food available</td></tr><tr><td>devise a theory</td><td>suggested ideas about natural selection</td></tr><tr><td>publish the theory</td><td>wrote a scientific paper and told other scientists about his idea</td></tr></tbody></table> | **Extend:** Suggest how Darwin would have carried out his work today. | |
| **Public reaction** (5 minutes) Show an image of Darwin as he was vilified looking like a monkey, as published in many newspapers of the time (1871 in the Hornet magazine). Ask the class who is in the picture; what does the image represent? Why was he shown in this way? What does it tell you about public feeling at the time towards the man and his theory? | **Extend:** What caused people to change their opinion? | |

| Main | Support/Extend | Resources |
|---|---|---|
| **Evaluating the work of Darwin and Wallace** (40 minutes) You work for the Royal Botanic Gardens at Kew. They want to open a new building to act as a seed bank, and don't know whether to name it the Darwin building or the Wallace building.<br><br>Students find out about the work of these two scientists and evaluate the contribution they made to our understanding of biology by researching answers to a series of questions. They draw up a comparison table between the two scientists. For example:<br>• What were the full names of the scientists?<br>• What evidence did they collect?<br>• Where did the evidence come from?<br>• What theory did they suggest?<br>• Did they work alone?<br>• Did they publish the work?<br>• Was the work accepted?<br>• What impact has the work had?<br>• Who gained more credit and why?<br><br>Students then decide which name to use for the seed bank. Consider:<br>• What is the purpose of a seed bank?<br>• Why would their name be appropriate to use as the name for a seed bank? | **Support:** Provide the table with the questions written in as a writing frame and name the websites students should use.<br><br>**Extend:** Explain how the evidence allowed them to develop the theory and influence modern biological thought, including the conservation of species to preserve biodiversity and maintaining variation to allow survival of the species. How was the work of Darwin and Wallace regarded by other scientists? | **Activity:** Evaluating the work of Darwin and Wallace |

| Plenary | Support/Extend | Resources |
|---|---|---|
| **Darwin versus Wallace** (5 minutes) Use the drag and drop interactive to sort statements about the work of Darwin and Wallace into one of three columns, titled Darwin, Wallace, or Both. | | **Interactive:** Darwin versus Wallace |
| **£10 for Darwin** (10 minutes) Darwin is on the £10 note; show an example. Explain that the pictures of people on bank notes can change. Draw a list of ten reasons why the work of Darwin is so important that his picture should stay on the £10 note. | | |

| Homework | | |
|---|---|---|
| Imagine that you were actually present at the presentation of Darwin and Wallace's work to the Linnean Society. Create lecture notes that explain how Darwin used any one piece of evidence to help explain his theory of evolution by natural selection. | **Support:** Describe one piece of evidence that you heard in the lecture. | |

**kerboodle**
A Kerboodle highlight for this lesson is **Literacy sheet: The theory of evolution**. Refer to the **Content map** on Kerboodle for a full list of resources and assessment.

# B5.2.4 Classification systems

**Specification links:**

B5.2b Describe the impact of developments in biology on classification systems. To include natural and artificial classification systems, and use of molecular phylogenetics, based on DNA sequencing.

WS1.1a Understand how scientific methods and theories develop over time.

WS1.1b Use models to solve problems, make predictions, and to develop scientific explanations and understanding of familiar and unfamiliar facts.

WS1.1g Make decisions based on the evaluation of evidence and arguments.

WS1.3e Interpret observations and other data.

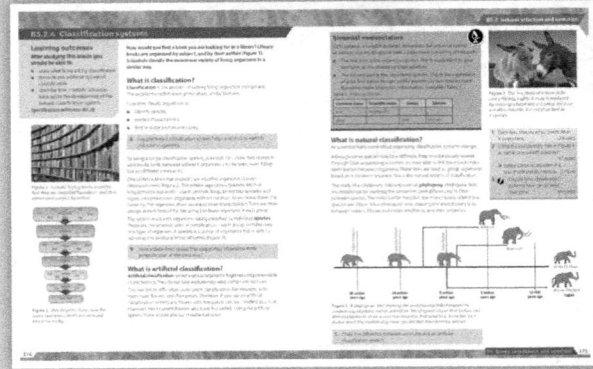

| Target | Outcome | Checkpoint | |
|---|---|---|---|
| | | Question | Activity |
| **Aiming for GRADE 4** | State what is meant by classification. | 1 | Starter 1 and 2 |
| | Record some observations and form basic groups of organisms. | | Starter 1 and 2<br>Main |
| | State that classification systems use a variety of evidence. | | Starter 2<br>Main<br>Plenary 1 |
| **Aiming for GRADE 6** | Describe the artificial system of classification. | B, C | Starter 1 and 2<br>Main<br>Plenary 1 |
| | Record observable differences between species and use this evidence to group species. | | Starter 1 and 2<br>Main |
| | Describe new technologies that are used in classification. | 3 | Main<br>Plenary 2 |
| **Aiming for GRADE 8** | Explain how scientific advances have led to the development of the natural classification system. | C, 2, 3 | Main<br>Plenary 1 and 2 |
| | Evaluate recorded observations and make decisions to group organisms based on that evaluated evidence. | | Main |
| | Discuss how new technologies have influenced the development of scientific classification over time. | 3 | Main<br>Plenary 2 |

**Literacy**
During the main activity, students will need to communicate effectively, using appropriate vocabulary.

**Key words**
artificial classification, classification, phylogeny, species

## B5.2 Natural selection and evolution

| Starter | Support/Extend | Resources |
|---|---|---|
| **Why classify?** (5 minutes) Present a student with a collection of different coins and ask the student to sort them out. The class can contribute ideas. They will probably separate the coins into groups of the same denomination. Ask them why they have done this, and how they were able to do this, for example, used same size/colour. Then ask them why it will help. Then draw comparisons to classification. **How do we classify?** (10 minutes) Ask students what we mean by the term classification. Then show the class a random collection of books and ask for ideas about how to group them. They will probably suggest sorting by size or colour. State that this is an artificial system. Show them a family tree for an animal, for example, the elephant in the Student Book. Ask how this classification was drawn up. Name it as a natural system, and make comparisons between natural and artificial classification systems. Point out that the natural system makes more sense biologically. | | |

| Main | Support/Extend | Resources |
|---|---|---|
| **Classifying animals** This activity is made up of four smaller tasks. **Observing features** (10 minutes) Issue groups with a landscape sheet of paper divided into eight columns, with pictures of eight animals, one at the top of each column. (Animals could include lion, tiger, leopard, cheetah, spotted jaguar, horse, zebra, and donkey.) Students make a list of as many features as they can about each of the animals in the column below each picture. **Grouping organisms** (10 minutes) Ask students to use the evidence they have observed to make decisions about grouping the organisms. They should justify their decisions. **Scientific advances** (10 minutes) Ask students a series of questions. What type of classification have the students produced? What would the study of the animals' DNA or proteins add to our knowledge of classification? Would this improve the classification? Does the use of these pieces of evidence change the type of classification system you have created? **Introduction of another animal** (10 minutes) Provide the image of another animal. Ask the students to collect evidence and justify whether it would belong to either of the major groups they have formed, or if it belongs in a new group altogether. Provide the scientific names for the species and ask if this suggests whether or not some organisms are closely linked and why. | **Support:** Students must distinguish at least two groups. **Extend:** Students should be able to sub-group the cats. **Support:** Introduce an animal like a domestic cat. **Extend:** Introduce an animal like a hippo. | **Activity:** Classifying animals |

| Plenary | Support/Extend | Resources |
|---|---|---|
| **Which system is which?** (5 minutes) Use the interactive to drag and drop statements about classification into the most appropriate of one of three boxes: artificial, natural, and both. **DNA evidence** (10 minutes) Present students with data for the % similarity of DNA between humans and chimpanzees as 99%. Then provide the class with a family tree showing humans, chimpanzees (close branches), lemurs (a short distance from the first two), and lions (further away still). Ask the students to estimate how similar the DNA would be between species (record this as high, medium, low). They should then explain how they worked it out. | **Extend:** Add additional organisms. | **Interactive:** Which system is which? |

| Homework | | |
|---|---|---|
| You have discovered a new species. Describe how you would go about classifying the species and how you would name the new species. | | |

A Kerboodle highlight for this lesson is **Working Scientifically: How to read an evolutionary tree**. Refer to the **Content map** on Kerboodle for a full list of resources and assessment.

# Checkpoint
## B5.2 Natural selection and evolution

### Overview of B5.2 Natural selection and evolution

In this chapter, students have studied natural selection and the theory of evolution. They should be able to give examples of evolution including that of the peppered moth and the emergence of antibiotic-resistant bacteria. They should link this work with mutation and meiosis in B5.1 *Inheritance*, placing mutation and the variation it confers at the start of the process of evolution. Another link is with selective breeding as an example of artificial selection in B6.2 *Feeding the human race*. Students should understand that a population is changed by natural selection over a long period of time, and that it is a population rather than an individual that becomes adapted to a new environmental change over successive generations. They should understand the role of chance rather than design in producing new phenotypes, of which only the best adapted survive and reproduce to pass on their advantageous characteristics.

Students should be able to explain how fossils are made and their role in the fossil record as evidence for evolution. They should be aware of the evidence of the fossil record as well as other sources of evidence including the study of antibiotic-resistant bacteria and the use of molecular studies in analysing similarities between the DNA base sequences of organisms.

Students should be able to describe the theory of evolution and the key scientists involved in its development, focusing on the work of Darwin and the Galapagos finches, and the work of Wallace.

Students should be able to explain the concept of classification and the difference between the artificial hierarchical grouping of taxa and the more modern natural system of phylogenetics. They should link this with the structure of eukaryotic and prokaryotic cells in B1.1 *Cell structures*.

You can find additional support for the maths skills covered in this chapter on **MyMaths**, including using ratios and fractions when calculating the scale of fossil images.

For this chapter, the following assessments are available on Kerboodle:

B5.2 Checkpoint quiz: Natural selection and evolution
B5.2 Progress quiz: Natural selection and evolution 1
B5.2 Progress quiz: Natural selection and evolution 2
B5.2 On your marks: Natural selection and evolution
B5.2 Exam-style questions and mark scheme: Natural selection and evolution

### Checkpoint follow-up lesson

A student's route through this lesson can be determined using the Checkpoint assessment. Percentage pass marks are supplied in the Checkpoint teacher notes.

For each successive route through it is assumed that the student can perform to their current route as well as previous routes. For example, students working at Aiming for 6 are assumed to be secure in Aiming for 4 knowledge and understanding and working towards achieving all the learning objectives for Aiming for 6.

# B5.2 Natural selection and evolution

| | Aiming for 4 | Aiming for 6 | Aiming for 8 |
|---|---|---|---|
| **Learning outcomes** | State what natural selection is. | Describe the process of natural selection. | Explain the process of natural selection. |
| | State that fossils provide evidence for evolution. | Describe how fossils provide evidence for evolution. | Explain how fossils provide evidence for evolution. |
| | Interpret an evolutionary tree. | Interpret an evolutionary tree. | Interpret an evolutionary tree. |
| **Starter** | **Unscrambling (5 minutes)** Scramble the names of Charles Darwin, Alfred Wallace, and Carl Linnaeus and tell students these are the names of famous scientists in evolution. Ask students to unscramble the names. Show a range of images of different organisms and explain that the variety in life is due to evolution. | | |
| **Differentiated checkpoint activity** | **Activity 1 Evolution by natural selection (25 minutes)** Students answer question 1 on the differentiated worksheets. They will require A4 paper and coloured pencils. | | |
| | Introduce the Aiming for 4 activity by reviewing the theories of evolution by natural selection. Students prepare a comic strip using the captions provided. You could give them a template instead of A4 paper. Students will need scissors and glue sticks. They are then prompted to write a letter from a priest about evolution by natural selection. | Aiming for 6 students should be able to start the activity without introduction. They will need access to the Student book to help them draw a comic strip to describe the process of natural selection using peppered moths or antibiotic resistance as an example. They then write a letter from a priest about evolution by natural selection. | Aiming for 8 students should be able to start the activity without introduction. They draw a comic strip to describe the process of natural selection using peppered moths or antibiotic resistance as an example. They then write a letter from a priest about evolution by natural selection. |
| | **Activity 2 Fossils (20 minutes)** The activity requires fossils or shells and plasticine. Show fossils and give a brief description of the process of fossilisation. Organise the class into small groups to make casts of fossils or shells using plasticine. All students should then be able to complete question 2 on the differentiated worksheets with no further introduction. | | |
| | The Aiming for 4 sheet provides structured questions about fossils and the fossil record. | The Aiming for 6 sheet asks for descriptions about fossils and the fossil record. Students will need access to the Student book. | The Aiming for 8 sheet asks for explanations about fossils and the fossil record. |
| | **Activity 3 Evolutionary trees (15 minutes)** Show an example of an evolutionary tree and briefly describe how to interpret this. Images of evolutionary trees are readily available on the Internet – horses and humans are good examples. This explanation could be shown to the whole class or Aiming for 4 students only. All students should then be able to complete question 3 on the differentiated worksheets with no further introduction. | | |
| | The Aiming for 4 sheet provides an evolutionary tree which students interpret by answering structured questions. | The Aiming for 6 sheet provides an evolutionary tree which students interpret by answering structured questions. | The Aiming for 8 sheet provides an evolutionary tree which students interpret by answering an unstructured question. Students could peer assess each other's work, or the teacher could check understanding. |
| | **Kerboodle resource:** B5.2 Checkpoint follow-up: Aiming for 4, B5.2 Checkpoint follow-up: Aiming for 6, B5.2 Checkpoint follow-up: Aiming for 8 | | |
| **Plenary** | **Make a mnemonic (5 minutes)** Ask students to make up their own mnemonic for the seven levels of classification. A prize could be given for the best one. | | |
| **Progression** | Looking at fossils in school or via a recording may help Aiming for 4 students to understand the information fossils give us about evolution. Carrying out a case study about the extinction of the dinosaurs can challenge all abilities. | Carrying out a case study about the extinction of the dinosaurs can challenge all abilities. | Aiming for 8 students could research modern examples of evolution as an extension exercise. In studying classification they could research how some organisms are classified, comparing the artificial system with the natural system. |

# B5 Genes, inheritance and selection: Topic summary

**B5.1** Inheritance
**B5.2** Natural selection and evolution

| Spec ref | Statement | Book spreads |
|---|---|---|
| B5.1a | Explain the following terms: gamete, chromosome, gene, allele/ variant, dominant, recessive, homozygous, heterozygous, genotype and phenotype | B5.1.4 |
| B5.1b | Describe the genome as the entire genetic material of an organism | B5.1.3 |
| B5.1c | Describe that the genome, and its interaction with the environment, influence the development of the phenotype of an organism | B5.1.1, B5.1.4 |
| B5.1d | Recall that all variants arise from mutations, and that most have no effect on the phenotype, some influence phenotype and a very few determine phenotype | B5.1.7 |
| B5.1e | Describe how genetic variants may influence phenotype:<br>• in coding DNA by altering the activity of a protein<br>• in non-coding DNA by altering how genes are expressed | |
| B5.1f | Explain some of the advantages and disadvantages of asexual and sexual reproduction in a range of organisms | B5.1.2 |
| B5.1g | Explain the terms haploid and diploid | B5.1.3 |
| B5.1h | Explain the role of meiotic cell division in halving the chromosome number to form gametes | B5.1.3 |
| B5.1i | Explain single gene inheritance | B5.1.5, B5.1.6 |
| B5.1j | Predict the results of single gene crosses | B5.1.5, B5.1.6 |
| B5.1k | Describe sex determination in humans using a genetic cross | B5.1.6 |
| B5.1l | Recall that most phenotypic features are the result of multiple genes rather than single gene inheritance | B5.1.1 |
| B.1m | Describe the development of our understanding of genetics | B5.1.8 |
| B5.2a | State that there is usually extensive genetic variation within a population of a species | B5.2.1 |
| B5.2b | Describe the impact of developments in biology on classification systems | B5.2.4 |
| B5.2c | Explain how evolution occurs through the natural selection of variants that have given rise to phenotypes best suited to their environment | B5.2.1 |
| B5.2d | Describe evolution as a change in the inherited characteristics of a population over time, through a process of natural selection, which may result in the formation of new species | B5.2.1 |
| B5.2e | Describe the evidence for evolution | B5.2.1 |
| B5.2f | Describe the work of Darwin and Wallace in the development of the theory of evolution by natural selection and explain the impact of these ideas on modern biology | B5.2.3 |

## Maths

| Specification | | Book spread | |
|---|---|---|---|
| Spec ref | Statement | Main content | Maths chapter |
| BM5.1i | Understand and use direct proportions and simple ratios in genetic crosses | B5.1.5, B5.1.6, B5.1.7 | 3 |
| BM5.1ii | Understand and use the concept of probability in predicting the outcome of genetic crosses | B5.1.5, B5.1.6, B5.1.7 | 8 |
| BM5.1iii | Extract and interpret information from charts, graphs and tables | B5.1.1, B5.1.5, B5.1.6 | 13, 14 |

## Working scientifically

| Specification | | Book spread | |
|---|---|---|---|
| Spec ref | Statement | Main content | WS chapter |
| WS1.1a | Understand how scientific methods and theories develop over time. | B5.1.8, B5.2.3, B5.2.4 | WS2 |
| WS1.1b | Use models to solve problems, make predictions, and to develop scientific explanations and understanding of familiar and unfamiliar facts. | B5.1.5, B5.1.6, B5.2.4 | WS2 |
| WS1.1c | Understand the power and limitations of science. | B5.2.2 | WS1 |
| WS1.1d | Discuss ethical issues arising from developments in science. | B5.1.8, B5.2.2, B5.2.3 | WS1 |
| WS1.1e | Explain everyday and technological applications of science. | B5.1.2, B5.1.5, B.1.6 | WS1 |
| WS1.1f | Evaluate associated personal, social, economic, and environmental implications. | B5.1.2, B5.1.8 | WS1 |
| WS1.1g | Make decisions based on the evaluation of evidence and arguments. | B5.2.2, B5.2.3, B5.2.4 | WS1 |
| WS1.1i | Recognise the importance of peer review of results and of communicating results to a range of audiences. | B5.1.8, B5.2.3 | WS2 |
| WS1.3a | Present observations and other data using appropriate methods. | B5.1.1 | WS6 |
| WS1.3b | Translating data from one form to another. | B5.1.1 | WS6 |
| WS1.3e | Interpreting observations and other data. | B5.1.1, B5.2.4 | WS7 |
| WS1.3f | Presenting reasoned explanations. | B5.1.7, B5.2.1 | WS7 |
| WS1.3i | Communicating the scientific rationale for investigations, methods used, findings, and reasoned conclusions. | B5.2.3 | |
| WS1.4a | Use scientific vocabulary, terminology, and definitions. | B5.1.3, B5.1.4 | WS2 |
| WS2a | Carry out experiments. | B5.1.1 | |
| WS2b | Make and record observations and measurements using a range of apparatus and methods. | B.1.1 | |
| WS2c | Present observations using appropriate methods. | B5.1.1 | |
| WS2d | Communicate the scientific rational for investigations, methods used, findings, and reasoned conclusions. | B5.1.1 | |

# B6 Global challenges
## B6.1 Monitoring and maintaining the environment
### B6.1.1 Sampling techniques (1)

**Specification links:**

**B6.1a** Explain how to carry out a field investigation into the distribution and abundance of organisms in a habitat, and how to determine their numbers in a given area. To include sampling techniques (random and transects, capture-recapture), use of quadrats, pooters, nets, keys, and scaling-up methods.

**WS1.2b** Plan experiments or devise procedures to make observations, produce or characterise a substance, test hypotheses, check data, or explore phenomena.

**WS1.2c** Apply a knowledge of a range of techniques, instruments, apparatus, and materials to select those appropriate to the experiment.

**WS1.2d** Recognise when to apply a knowledge of sampling techniques to ensure any samples collected are representative.

**WS1.3h** Identify potential sources of random and systematic error.

**WS2a** Carry out experiments.

**WS2b** Make and record observations and measurements using a range of apparatus and methods.

**WS2c** Present observations using appropriate methods.

**WS2d** Communicate the scientific rational for investigations, methods used, findings, and reasoned conclusions.

**BM6.1i** Construct and interpret frequency tables and diagrams, bar charts, and histograms (M2c).

**BM 6.1ii** Understand the principles of sampling as applied to scientific data (M2d).

| Target | Outcome | Checkpoint | |
|---|---|---|---|
| | | Question | Activity |
| **Aiming for GRADE 4** ↓ | Describe what is meant by a sample. | 3 | Starter 2 |
| | State that there are two types of identification keys that are used to identify organisms. | | Starter 1 |
| | Use quadrats to sample the abundance of organisms. | | Main |
| **Aiming for GRADE 6** ↓ | Describe some techniques for sampling. | B, C, 1, 3 | Main, Plenary 1 |
| | Use an identification key to identify organisms. | D, 2 | Main, Plenary 2 |
| | Use transect lines and quadrats to investigate the distribution or abundance of organisms. | | Main |
| **Aiming for GRADE 8** ↓ | Justify the selection of a particular sampling technique for a given organism. | C | Main, Plenary 1 |
| | Explain how to use an identification key. | D | Main, Plenary 2 |
| | Justify the use of transect lines and quadrats to investigate the distribution or abundance of organisms. | | Main |

## B6.1 Monitoring and maintaining the environment

**Maths**
During the main activity, students will collect data and record them in frequency tables (M2c). They will also understand the principles of sampling as applied to scientific data (M2d).

**Literacy**
During the main activity, students will need to produce coherent explanations, using appropriate scientific vocabulary.

**Key words**
identification key, sample

| Starter | Support/Extend | Resources |
|---|---|---|
| **What's a key?** (5 minutes)  Place a selection of books on the table. Ask a student to pick out a book you want by giving you a series of questions to identify the book.<br>Then draw a comparison between this short demonstration and the use of a key.<br>**Valid samples** (10 minutes)  Have an opaque bag containing different-coloured sweets of the same size. Take one sweet out as a sample. Make the statement that the sweet is of a colour, therefore all sweets of this type are the same colour. Invite argument, in which the students should disagree. Ask them how you could prove that your original statement is wrong. Lead them to take more samples. Ask the students what plants grow on the school field? How can we prove it's not just grass? | **Support:** Turn the activity around. The student selects the book without telling you, and you ask the questions.<br><br>**Extend:** Ask students to consider how many samples would be needed – and to suggest why – to get a reliable representation of the possible colours of sweets, and their frequency. | |

| Main | Support/Extend | Resources |
|---|---|---|
| **Sampling methods** (15 minutes)  Take a variety of sampling equipment out into the school field. Students fill in a worksheet that compares the use of the different pieces of apparatus, what they are used for, and perhaps their limitations.<br>SAFETY: Follow local guidance on fieldwork activities.<br>**Investigating the distribution of a number of named plants on the school field** (25 minutes)  Use a simple key (designed by the teacher) to identify some common flowering plants on the school field. Include about five species, such as daisies, dandelions, grass, speedwells, and so on.<br>Having identified the plants, students will use a transect line and quadrat on the school field to record the distribution of each plant throughout the school field in a tally chart.<br>SAFETY: Follow local guidance on fieldwork activities.<br>Analyse the data as a homework. | **Extend:** Provide students with a few examples of samples you want to record, and ask them to justify which technique they would use.<br><br>**Support:** Restrict the survey to two species. | **Practical:** Investigating distribution |

| Plenary | Support/Extend | Resources |
|---|---|---|
| **Equipment** (5 minutes)  Use the interactive in which students link the names of pieces of apparatus to descriptions of how they are used.<br>**Making keys** (10 minutes)  Provide the class with images of five animal species, for example, different duck species. Ask student groups to create a simple key to identify the ducks. Then groups exchange the keys and try them out. | **Extend:** Explain why each piece of equipment might be selected rather than any of the others. | **Interactive:** Equipment |

| Homework | | |
|---|---|---|
| Analyse the experimental results. Describe the changes in distribution of the species across the field. Suggest a possible explanation for your findings and provide a graphical illustration of your results. | **Support:** Provide axes for a line graph, which will now only contain two lines, one for each species, as only two species will have been sampled in a support group. | |

**kerboodle**
A Kerboodle highlight for this lesson is **Maths skills: Sampling**. Refer to the **Content map** on Kerboodle for a full list of resources and assessment.

# B6.1.2 Sampling techniques (2)

**Specification links:**

B6.1a Explain how to carry out a field investigation into the distribution and abundance of organisms in a habitat, and how to determine their numbers in a given area. To include sampling techniques (random and transects, capture-recapture), use of quadrats, pooters, nets, keys, and scaling-up methods.

WS1.2b Plan experiments or devise procedures to make observations, produce or characterise a substance, test hypotheses, check data, or explore phenomena.

WS1.2c Apply a knowledge of a range of techniques, instruments, apparatus, and materials to select those appropriate to the experiment.

WS1.2d Recognise when to apply knowledge of sampling techniques to ensure any samples collected are representative.

WS1.3h Identify potential sources of random and systematic error.

WS2a Carry out experiments.

WS2b Make and record observations and measurements using a range of apparatus and methods.

WS2c Present observations using appropriate methods.

WS2d Communicate the scientific rational for investigations, methods used, findings, and reasoned conclusions.

BM6.1ii Understand the principles of sampling as applied to scientific data (M2d).

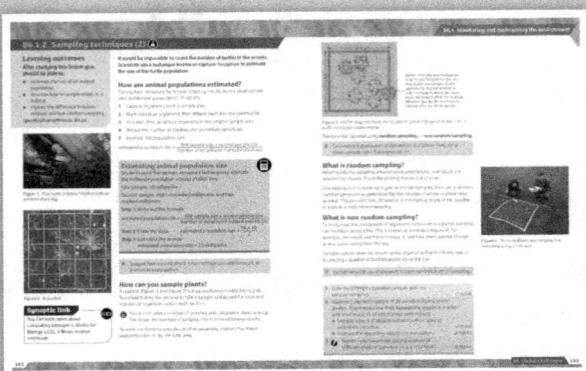

| Target | Outcome | Checkpoint | |
|---|---|---|---|
| | | Question | Activity |
| **Aiming for GRADE 4** | Describe how to sample plants in a habitat. | | Starter 1<br>Main<br>Plenary 2 |
| | Describe how to sample motile animals in a habitat. | 2 | Main<br>Plenary 1 and 2 |
| | State what is meant by bias in sampling techniques. | | Starter 2<br>Plenary 2 |
| **Aiming for GRADE 6** | Explain the difference between random and non-random sampling techniques. | C, 1 | Main<br>Plenary 2 |
| | Explain why the same method of sampling must be used each time when carrying out the capture-recapture technique. | | Main<br>Plenary 1 |
| | Describe methods of avoiding bias in sampling techniques when collecting data to estimate population size. | | Starter 2<br>Main |
| **Aiming for GRADE 8** | Explain how to calculate a plant population for an area using the scaling-up method. | B, 3 | Starter 1 |
| | Estimate the size of an animal population using data from the capture-recapture technique. | 2, 3 | Main<br>Plenary 1 |
| | Explain why we are often only able to calculate an estimate of an animal population in a habitat. | A | Main |

**Maths**
Students will collect and record data from sampling (M2d). They will then substitute values into algebraic equations, and solve simple algebraic equations (M3c, M3d).

**Literacy**
Students will need to use appropriate scientific vocabulary.

**Key words**
capture-recapture, non-random sampling, random sampling

182

# B6.1 Monitoring and maintaining the environment

| Starter | Support/Extend | Resources |
|---|---|---|
| **Estimating the number of tiles** (10 minutes) Find a suitable tiled surface, for example, floor or ceiling, or show an image. Ask the students how many tiles there are. They may guess. Point out that it would be impractical to count them and ask the students to suggest how to estimate the number of tiles more accurately. Lead them to the idea of taking a sample (for example, count the number in one row or a small square) and then multiplying up. Link to the method for sampling plants. | **Support:** Tell them the scaling-up method, and possibly ask someone to count and check. **Extend:** Ask students why this is an estimate only. | |
| **Bias** (5 minutes) Introduce a hypothesis 'There are more boys than girls in the school' (or alternative in single-sex school). Then say that you have decided on an experiment and that you will take a sample to test your hypothesis. Deliberately choose a table with a bias towards boy numbers, count the numbers, and calculate a percentage of boys, which proves your hypothesis. Then invite the class to criticise your method. They should recognise your poor sample technique, but will need to be introduced to the term bias. | | |

| Main | Support/Extend | Resources |
|---|---|---|
| **Estimating the number of screws in a tray** (40 minutes) Use a tray containing sawdust and a fixed number of nails. Student experimenters use a magnet on a string to fish for the nails in a fixed period of time. Discuss how this method is random and fair. They count the number of nails they catch and mark them in some way, such as by adding a piece of cotton. Then someone in the group replaces the nails and buries them. This student should stir up the tray, but ensure that no nails are obvious to the experimenters in the group. Students then fish again for the same period of time, using the same method. They use the data collected to estimate the population size using the formula. They can then count the actual number and compare accuracy. Students should answer questions asking them to compare random and non-random testing to justify why the method used a random technique, and to suggest how to collect data to measure plant populations. | **Support:** Provide a results table where the three numbers can be recorded, and guidance about how to substitute into the equation. **Extend:** Explain why the value is an estimate, and why this method is useful when measuring animal populations, including motile animals. Ask why a non-random technique would not be useful in this case. | **Activity:** Estimating the number of screws in a tray |

| Plenary | Support/Extend | Resources |
|---|---|---|
| **Capture-recapture technique** (5 minutes) Use the interactive to correctly sequence a set of method statements for the capture-recapture procedure. | | **Interactive:** Capture-recapture technique |
| **Random or non-random** (10 minutes) Describe a series of different fieldwork-based sampling methods. After each method, hold up a card to show whether the method is random or non-random. Ask a student to explain why they have voted the way they have. | **Extend:** Introduce the question 'Is the method biased or not?' | |

| Homework | | |
|---|---|---|
| Every year the RSPB run a survey where people count and record the numbers and types of birds that they see in their garden or local park. They use this to report on the populations of our common birds. Evaluate why this approach might be useful. What information might it provide? Write about problems with the method – answers might include problems with identification, bias, erratic sampling, and so on. | | |

**kerboodle**
A Kerboodle highlight for this lesson is **Calculation sheet: Sampling**. Refer to the **Content map** on Kerboodle for a full list of resources and assessment.

The Practical Skills lesson for PAG 3 Sampling techniques could follow this lesson.

# B6.1.3 Loss of biodiversity

**Specification links:**

B6.1b Describe both positive and negative human interactions within ecosystems, and explain their impact on biodiversity. To include the conservation of individual species and selected habitats, and threats from land use and hunting.

WS1.1c Understand the power and limitations of science.

WS1.1f Evaluate associated personal, social, economic, and environmental implications.

WS1.1g Make decisions based on the evaluation of evidence and arguments.

WS2a Carry out experiments.

WS2b Make and record observations and measurements using a range of apparatus and methods.

WS2c Present observations using appropriate methods.

WS2d Communicate the scientific rationale for investigations, methods used, findings, and reasoned conclusions.

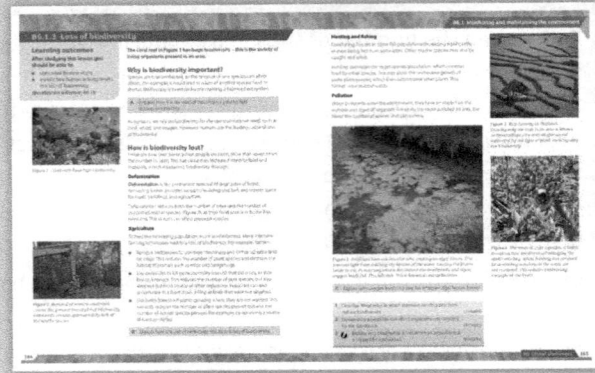

| Target | Outcome | Checkpoint | |
|---|---|---|---|
| | | Question | Activity |
| **Aiming for GRADE 4** | State what biodiversity is. | | Starter 1 and 2 |
| | State that science allows us to understand how we can affect our environment. | 1, 2, 3 | Starter 2<br>Plenary 2 |
| | State that a loss of biodiversity has negative implications. | | Starter 2<br>Plenary 2 |
| **Aiming for GRADE 6** | Describe some processes that result in a loss of biodiversity. | A, B, 1, 2, 3 | Starter 1 and 2<br>Main<br>Plenary 1 |
| | Describe how developments in science have allowed us to understand that we are reducing biodiversity. | 1, 2, 3 | Starter 2<br>Main<br>Plenary 1 |
| | Describe some of the social, economic, and environmental implications of the loss of biodiversity. | C, 2 | Starter 2<br>Main<br>Plenary 2 |
| **Aiming for GRADE 8** | Explain how human activity results in a loss of biodiversity. | B, C, 1, 2, 3 | Starter 2<br>Main<br>Plenary 1 and 2 |
| | Explain how our developing scientific knowledge has increased our understanding of ways to modify our management of the environment. | | Main |
| | Evaluate the social, economic, and environmental implications associated with a loss of biodiversity. | | Main<br>Plenary 2 |

**Literacy**
During the main activity, students should communicate effectively, sustaining interest, and use appropriate scientific vocabulary.

**Key words**
biodiversity, deforestation

## B6.1 Monitoring and maintaining the environment

| Starter | Support/Extend | Resources |
|---|---|---|
| **Deforestation** (5 minutes)   Ask the students what they think biodiversity is. Then show them a series of satellite images of a rainforest, taken over several years as the forest was gradually cut down. Ask the class what they are observing, and about the effects of the changes on biodiversity.<br><br>**Reasons for the loss of biodiversity** (10 minutes)   Ask the students what they think biodiversity is. Then issue them with a large sheet of paper with four concentric circles. In the centre is written 'Loss of biodiversity'. Ask the groups to write between five and ten causes for the loss of biodiversity in the first ring. In the second ring, ask the class to describe or explain how these cause the reduction in biodiversity. Finally, in the third ring ask the class to explain why this is a problem. Between each step, have a short class discussion. | **Extend:** Why is the loss of biodiversity a problem? | |

| Main | Support/Extend | Resources |
|---|---|---|
| **Human impact on the environment**   Operate a market place activity in which students are given information cards about deforestation, pollution, fishing, and agriculture. These cards should explain what the processes are, why we carry them out, and what we gain from them. The cards then discuss the effects of the process on biodiversity, including how it reduces it and how we are trying to reduce the impact.<br><br>**Step 1: Becoming an expert** (15 minutes)   Students work in groups (of 3 or 4) to become experts on one of the processes, by producing a diagram with limited numbers of words.<br><br>**Step 2: Gathering information** (15 minutes)   One student remains in place as the expert, and teaches the other students who visit them. At the same time, the other students move to other groups, and learn from them about the type of activity they are experts in.<br><br>**Step 3: Sharing information** (10 minutes)   Original groups reform. Students use their notes taken from the other groups to teach other students in their group about the impacts of all the process. | **Support:** Increase the number of words to use when becoming experts. Also, provide a set of questions to frame their learning from other groups.<br><br>**Extend:** Students need to evaluate the effects of each process in terms of extent to which they affect the environment, for example, local/global effects, which has the greatest effect, etc. | **Activity:** Human impact on the environment |

| Plenary | Support/Extend | Resources |
|---|---|---|
| **Loss of biodiversity** (5 minutes)   Use the interactive to link the name of a cause of reduction of biodiversity to how it causes a reduction in biodiversity.<br><br>**Environmental protest** (10 minutes)   Provide the class with either an international or local issue that results in the loss of biodiversity, for example, the loss of the rainforest in Brazil for farmland. Divide the class into groups, some of the groups are in favour of the process, whilst other groups are against it. The groups design slogans for use in a protest campaign, representing different points of view. | | **Interactive:** Loss of biodiversity |

| Homework | | |
|---|---|---|
| Plan a scientific investigation to monitor the effect of increasing strengths of acid rain on the germination of seeds. | | |

**kerboodle**

A Kerboodle highlight for this lesson is **Working scientifically: Human population**. Refer to the **Content map** on Kerboodle for a full list of resources and assessment.

# B6.1.4 Increasing biodiversity

## Specification links:

B6.1b Describe both positive and negative human interactions within ecosystems, and explain their impact on biodiversity. To include the conservation of individual species and selected habitats, and threats from land use and hunting.

WS1.1c Understand the power and limitations of science.

WS1.1d Discuss ethical issues arising from developments in science.

WS1.1f Evaluate associated personal, social, economic, and environmental implications.

WS1.1g Make decisions based on the evaluation of evidence and arguments.

WS1.3f Present reasoned explanations.

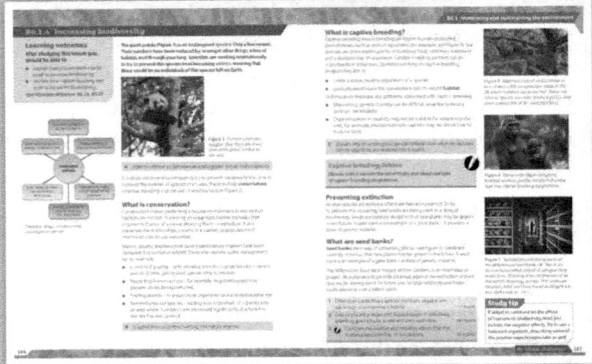

| Target | Outcome | Checkpoint | |
|---|---|---|---|
| | | Question | Activity |
| Aiming for GRADE 4 | State what is meant by conservation. | | Starter 1 and 2, Plenary 1 |
| | List at least two methods of conservation. | 3 | Starter 1 and 2, Main |
| | State one reason for conserving a species. | 1 | Starter 1 and 2, Main, Plenary 1 and 2 |
| Aiming for GRADE 6 | Describe the importance of conservation for endangered species. | A, 1, 2 | Starter 1 and 2, Main, Plenary 1 and 2 |
| | Describe a method of conservation that will maintain biodiversity. | B, C, 2, 3 | Main, Plenary 1 |
| | Describe the ethical issues that might arise from some conservation methods to increase biodiversity. | B, C, 2, 3 | Main, Plenary 2 |
| Aiming for GRADE 8 | Explain how conservation can be used to increase biodiversity. | C, 3 | Main, Plenary 2 |
| | Explain how captive breeding or seed banks can lead to increased biodiversity. | 3 | Main |
| | Discuss the ethical responsibility to increase species and biodiversity. | 2 | Starter 2, Main, Plenary 2 |

### Literacy
During the main activity, students will need to produce coherent, well-structured, and purposeful texts, using varied sentence structures and appropriate scientific vocabulary.

### Key words
conservation, endangered species, extinct, habitat, seed banks

## B6.1 Monitoring and maintaining the environment

| Starter | Support/Extend | Resources |
|---|---|---|
| **World Wildlife Fund** (10 minutes)  Start with the WWF logo. Ask the class if they know what it is. Then show a short advertisement or film about the WWF protecting an endangered species, for example, the snow leopard. Hold a short discussion about the role of the WWF, the idea of conservation, and why it is important. | | |
| **Endangered or extinct** (5 minutes)  Show images of extinct animals, for example, a dinosaur or the dodo, then some examples of endangered species, for example, tigers and pandas. Ask the class the difference between the two terms. Discuss the role of humans in the loss of the dodo. Discuss how we could help to protect the endangered species by using conservation methods. | **Support:** Discuss the extinct species, before moving on to the endangered species.  **Extend:** Ask why we have an ethical responsibility to maintain species. | |

| Main | Support/Extend | Resources |
|---|---|---|
| **WWF campaign**  **Research** (20 minutes)  Students work for the WWF or similar conservation organisation. They are going to lead a campaign to protect or conserve an endangered species. Give them specific examples, for example, tiger, panda, or a local case. They look up information about the particular animal, its problems in terms of numbers, and a specific strategy being used to help the species.  **Campaign** (20 minutes)  Students then produce a leaflet, TV advertisement, or web page to explain the problem with the given species, how we could use the money raised to help save that species, and the importance of this for maintaining and increasing biodiversity. | **Support:** Provide a series of questions to guide the research and act as a writing frame.  **Extend:** Students should consider the ethical issues involved in the methods they might use to conserve the species. They also need to discuss the ethical responsibility of humans to maintain a species. | **Activity:** WWF campaign |

| Plenary | Support/Extend | Resources |
|---|---|---|
| **Conservation methods** (5 minutes)  Use the interactive, which contains a paragraph about conservation methods being used to protect an endangered species. Students fill in the gaps by selecting the most appropriate word from a drop down list. | | **Interactive:** Conservation methods |
| **Pros and cons in conservation** (10 minutes)  Make a series of statements to which students vote by raising a card with 'right' or 'wrong'. Statements could include:  • Keeping animals in zoos.  • Wearing fur coats.  • Nature should take its course, we should not interfere.  • Setting up nature reserves.  • Introducing a natural predator. | **Extend:** Students need to provide a justification, including some ethical justifications for their vote. | |

| Homework | | |
|---|---|---|
| Produce a written justification for the use of the panda as the emblem for the WWF. | **Extend:** Recently some scientists have suggested that we would spend our money more effectively by protecting other species. Include a discussion of this in the homework. | |

**kerboodle**

A Kerboodle highlight for this lesson is **Literacy sheet: What can be done to rebuild and maintain biodiversity?** Refer to the **Content map** on Kerboodle for a full list of resources and assessment.

# B6.1.5 Maintaining biodiversity

**Specification links:**

B6.1c Explain some of the benefits and challenges of maintaining local and global biodiversity. To include the difficulty in gaining agreements for, and the monitoring of, conservation schemes, along with the benefits of ecotourism.

WS1.1c Understand the power and limitations of science.

WS1.1d Discuss ethical issues arising from developments in science.

WS1.1f Evaluate associated personal, social, economic, and environmental implications.

WS1.1g Make decisions based on the evaluation of evidence and arguments.

WS1.3f Present reasoned explanations.

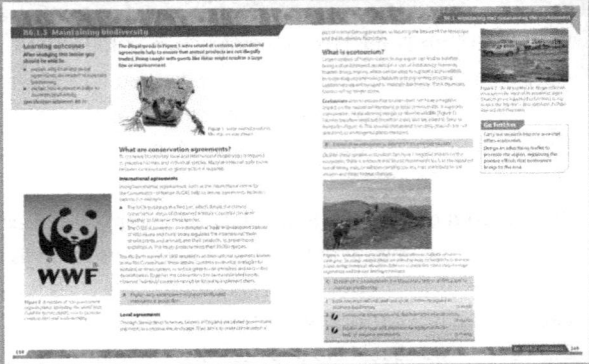

| Target | Outcome | Checkpoint | |
|---|---|---|---|
| | | Question | Activity |
| **Aiming for GRADE 4** ↓ | Name some global agreements used to maintain biodiversity. | 1 | Starter 1, Main |
| | State what is meant by ecotourism. | C | Starter 2 |
| | State that there are advantages and disadvantages to methods used to maintain biodiversity. | 2 | Starter 2, Main, Plenary 2 |
| **Aiming for GRADE 6** ↓ | Describe how global agreements function to maintain biodiversity. | A, 3 | Starter 1, Main |
| | Describe how ecotourism is different from ordinary tourism. | B | Starter 2 |
| | Discuss some of the social, economic, and environmental benefits or challenges of maintaining biodiversity. | A, C, 2, 3 | Main, Plenary 2 |
| **Aiming for GRADE 8** ↓ | Explain why local and global agreements are needed to maintain biodiversity. | A, C, 3 | Main, Plenary 2 |
| | Explain how ecotourism helps to maintain biodiversity. | C, 2 | Main |
| | Evaluate the social, economic, and environmental benefits and challenges of maintaining biodiversity. | 2 | Main, Plenary 2 |

**Maths**
During the main activity, students might be involved in handling data in various forms.

**Literacy**
During the main activity, students will need to communicate effectively, sustaining the readers interest.

**Key words**
ecotourism

# B6.1 Monitoring and maintaining the environment

| Starter | Support/Extend | Resources |
|---|---|---|
| **Antique sales** (5 minutes) Remind students about TV antique shows. Ask them if they know anything about the sale of animal products, such as ivory. State that, since 1947, it has been illegal to trade in ivory products. Ask them why this international law was passed. How has this law helped to maintain biodiversity? | | |
| **Ecotourism** (10 minutes) Show images of a variety of ecotourism holidays, for example, safaris, whale-watching, glass-bottomed boats, etc. Ask why people are interested in this type of holiday. What will the effect of this type of holiday be on the environment? How might it lead to protection of the environment? Compare this type of holiday to a traditional beach holiday, and ask students how this type of holiday might affect the environment. | **Extend:** Consider the advantages and disadvantages of either/both type of holiday. | |

| Main | Support/Extend | Resources |
|---|---|---|
| **UN debate on protecting species** (40 minutes) Organise a UN debate on the future protection of an endangered species. Divide the class into groups. Different groups represent different organisations, for example, the International Union for the Conservation of Nature (IUCN), national governments, local pressure groups, and tourism companies. Each of these organisations has a point of view about whether or not to protect the species. For example:<br>• IUCN – in favour of conservation.<br>• Scientists – might propose a conservation method.<br>• National government – finance might be required from trade/UN, etc. to allow for conservation.<br>• Local pressure groups – protection might not be wanted as it might affect their way of life, use of land, etc.<br>• Tourism companies – might be able to develop ecotourism and improve the economy.<br>Each group needs to research facts and figures to prepare an argument for their side in the debate about protecting a species, for example, the tiger or mountain gorilla.<br>Then have a short debate in which students present facts and figures to support their arguments. Teacher to chair the debate.<br>Class could vote for or against any possible proposals. | **Support:** Provide a series of questions the students can use to find the information. List possible websites they could use, for example, WWF.<br><br>**Extend:** Evaluate the benefits and costs of any protection methods discussed. | **Activity:** UN debate on protecting species |

| Plenary | Support/Extend | Resources |
|---|---|---|
| **Biodiversity** (10 minutes) Use the interactive in which students sort statements into whether they are benefits or potential problems when making international agreements to maintain biodiversity. | | **Interactive:** Biodiversity |
| **Changing attitudes** (10 minutes) Show old images of animal products, for example, fur coats, crocodile shoes and bags, whale oil, etc. Ask the class to comment on the images. What does it say about people's lifestyle? Were the products glamorous? What were people's attitudes? Then discuss what people might think about these today. Why have the attitudes changed? How does this reflect on our ideas about maintaining biodiversity? | **Extend:** What have been the benefits and costs to society of this changing attitude? | |

| Homework |
|---|
| Produce a page for a holiday brochure advertising an ecotourism holiday. The page could be of any type of ecotourism holiday, but needs to describe/explain the environmental benefits of this holiday. |

**kerboodle**

A Kerboodle highlight for this lesson is **Literacy sheet: What can be done to rebuild and maintain biodiversity?** Refer to the **Content map** on Kerboodle for a full list of resources and assessment.

# GCSE BIOLOGY ONLY — HIGHER TIER
## B6.1.6 Monitoring biodiversity

**Specification links:**

B6.1d Evaluate the evidence for the impact of environmental changes on the distribution of organisms, with reference to water and atmospheric gases.

WS1.1f Evaluate associated personal, social, economic, and environmental implications.

WS1.1h Evaluate risks both in practical science and the wider societal context.

WS2a Carry out experiments.

WS2b Make and record observations and measurements using a range of apparatus and methods.

WS2c Present observations using appropriate methods.

WS2d Communicate the scientific rational for investigations, methods used, findings, and reasoned conclusions.

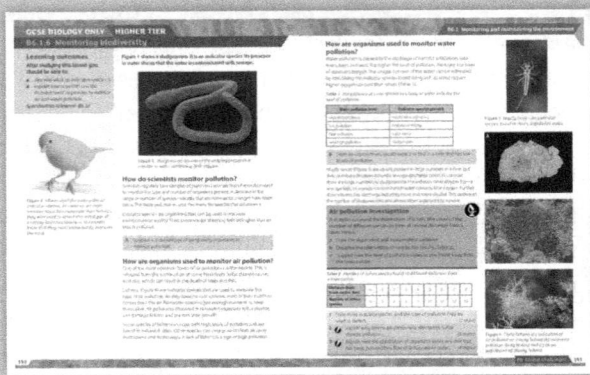

| Target | Outcome | Checkpoint | |
|---|---|---|---|
| | | Question | Activity |
| **Aiming for GRADE 6** ↓ | Describe what an indicator species is. | B, 1, 2 | Starter 1<br>Plenary 1 |
| | Compare indicator species distributions with physical data of environmental pollution. | | Starter 1<br>Main<br>Plenary 1 and 2 |
| | Describe the risks to wildlife of environmental pollution. | 1, 2 | Starter 2<br>Main<br>Plenary 2 |
| **Aiming for GRADE 8** ↓ | Explain how scientists use the distribution of organisms to monitor air and water pollution. | 3 | Main<br>Plenary 1 and 2 |
| | Evaluate indicator species as a measure of environmental pollution. | A | Main<br>Plenary 1 and 2 |
| | Evaluate the risks posed to wildlife and society from environmental pollution. | | Starter 2<br>Main<br>Plenary 2 |

**Maths**
During the main activity, students will plot two variables from experimental or other data (M4c).

**Literacy**
During the main activity, students will need to produce coherent, well-structured responses to questions, using appropriate scientific vocabulary.

**Key words**
indicator species

## B6.1 Monitoring and maintaining the environment

| Starter | Support/Extend | Resources |
|---|---|---|
| **Indicators** (10 minutes)  State that indicators tell us something about a situation. We can test the pH of a water sample by using pH indicator solution. It changes colour to indicate the pH level. (could demonstrate this). Ask them how many students eat lunch in school. What would happen to the number if the quality of the food dropped? This gives an indication of the food quality. The species present in an area can indicate the quality of the environment. Show examples, for example, hydrangea flower colour and soil pH, mayfly larvae in clean water. | | |
| **Oil spills** (5 minutes)  Show a film from a news report, or show a still image of an oil spill affecting wildlife close to the coastline. Ask the class to describe what they can see on the image or in the report. Ask what the effect will be of the oil on the wildlife. How might it kill them? What will happen to the biodiversity in the area? Suggest how scientists would monitor the situation. | **Support:** Name any other types of pollution incidents that might affect species.<br><br>**Extend:** Name other types of pollution, rank their seriousness, or evaluate how dangerous different events are to wildlife. | |

| Main | Support/Extend | Resources |
|---|---|---|
| **Investigating a river pollution incident from a local factory**<br>This activity is made up of three smaller tasks.<br>**Part 1 Measuring river pollution experiment** (20 minutes)  Students measure the pH in simulated river water samples taken from at least ten sites along a local river that passes a factory. (If Starter 1 has been used, students could plan the investigation.)<br>**Part 2 The students plot the data** (10 minutes)  Use Student Book spread B6.1.6 and look at the table of the types of species found in clean and polluted water. Suggest which species would be present in the river samples at each sample site along the river.<br>**Part 3 Conclusion** (10 minutes)  Conclusion should establish that the factory along the river has released a pollutant. It should also evaluate the use of both physical data and indicator species as a measure of the pollution levels. | **Extend:** Students should then be given secondary data of temperature, oxygen, and nitrate levels.<br><br>**Extend:** Evaluate the impact of the factory spill of effluent on local wildlife. | **Practical:**<br>Investigating a river pollution incident from a local factory |

| Plenary | Support/Extend | Resources |
|---|---|---|
| **Monitoring biodiversity** (5 minutes)  Use the interactive to select true or false for a series of statements about indicator species.<br>**Anti-fouling paint scenario** (10 minutes)  Present the class with a situation:<br>A company makes anti-fouling paint, which is used to protect boats and stop barnacles sticking to them. However, the paint contains toxic chemicals. The company sets up production in a small seaside town. The following happens:<br>• Some sailors paint their boats with the paint.<br>• Some people wash their brushes in the sea water.<br>• The company might have a small leakage of the paint.<br>In groups, evaluate the severity of each problem. Decide which might need action. What action could you take? What might be the effect on the wildlife? How will it be monitored? | | **Interactive:**<br>Monitoring biodiversity |

| Homework |
|---|
| Explain the use of other indicator species, for example, lichens for air pollution. Plan an experiment to monitor levels of air pollution as they move away from a local major road, factory, or railway line. |

**kerboodle**
A Kerboodle highlight for this lesson is **Homework: Biodiversity**. Refer to the **Content map** on Kerboodle for a full list of resources and assessment.

# Checkpoint
## B6.1 Monitoring and maintaining the environment

### Overview of B6.1 Monitoring and maintaining the environment

In this chapter students have studied sampling techniques. They should be able to explain why a sample needs to be taken and how it is used to estimate the total population size. They should be familiar with several methods to sample small animals, and with the use of identification keys. Students should be able to use the capture–recapture method to estimate an animal population size, use a quadrat to sample plants, and understand the difference between random sampling and non-random sampling.

Students have studied loss of biodiversity and should understand why biodiversity is important. They should link this with ideas about producers in B1.4 *Photosynthesis*, concepts of interdependence and biotic and abiotic factors in B4.1 *Ecosystems*, and how genetic variation in a population is important for the survival of a species in B5.1 *Inheritance* and B5.2 *Natural selection and evolution*. Students should have studied deforestation, agriculture, hunting, fishing, and pollution as causes of biodiversity reduction.

Students should be able to outline ways in way biodiversity can be increased. They should be able to explain conservation and give examples of conservation practices, including captive breeding programmes and the use of seed banks.

In their studies of maintaining biodiversity, students should be aware of the role of international and local agreements, as well as the advantages and disadvantages of ecotourism as a tool for conservation. They should appreciate that humans undertake many positive as well as negative actions within ecosystems.

Students should understand how scientists monitor biodiversity, specifically the monitoring of water and air pollution. They should be able to describe indicator species that are used to track changes in pollution, including the role of lichens for air pollution and different invertebrate species for water pollution. Higher-tier students should have evaluated evidence for the impact of environmental changes on the distribution of organisms, with reference to water and atmospheric gases. Finally, students should be able to apply their knowledge of the general principles of conservation to unfamiliar examples.

You can find additional support for the maths skills covered in this chapter on **MyMaths**, including collecting and recording data from sampling, substituting values into algebraic equations, solving algebraic equations, and plotting data.

### PAGs

All students are expected to have carried out the PAG *3 Sampling techniques*. A full lesson plan for each PAG is provided in the Practical skills chapter. PAG *3 Sampling techniques* should be completed after lesson B6.1.2 *Sampling techniques*.

# B6.1 Monitoring and maintaining the environment

For this chapter, the following assessments are available on Kerboodle:

B6.1 Checkpoint quiz: Monitoring and maintaining the environment
B6.1 Progress quiz: Monitoring and maintaining the environment 1
B6.1 Progress quiz: Monitoring and maintaining the environment 2
B6.1 On your marks: Monitoring and maintaining the environment
B6.1 Exam-style questions and mark scheme: Monitoring and maintaining the environment

## Checkpoint follow-up lesson

A student's route through this lesson can be determined using the Checkpoint assessment. Percentage pass marks are supplied in the Checkpoint teacher notes.

For each successive route through it is assumed that the student can perform to their current route as well as previous routes. For example, students working at Aiming for 6 are assumed to be secure in Aiming for 4 knowledge and understanding and working towards achieving all the learning objectives for Aiming for 6.

| | Aiming for 4 | Aiming for 6 | Aiming for 8 |
|---|---|---|---|
| **Learning outcomes** | State some techniques to sample plants and animals. | Describe some techniques to sample plants and animals. | Explain some techniques to sample plants and animals. |
| | State ways in which biodiversity is lost. | Describe ways in which biodiversity is lost. | Explain ways in which biodiversity is lost. |
| | State ways in which biodiversity can be maintained or increased. | Describe ways in which biodiversity can be maintained or increased. | Explain ways in which biodiversity can be maintained or increased. |
| **Starter** | **Making a key (10 minutes)** You will need a selection of liquorice allsorts for each pair. Students pairs make a key to classify liquorice allsorts. Aiming for 4 students may need some tips, such as – first sort by shape, then by colour. Aiming for 6 and Aiming for 8 students should be able to complete the key unaided. | | |
| **Differentiated checkpoint activity** | **Activity 1 Capture–recapture (20 minutes)** In pairs or small groups, students answer question 1 on the differentiated worksheets, which simulates a capture–recapture study. They will require sandwich bags containing 2–3 handfuls of paper holes from a hole punch, marker pens, and a calculator. | | |
| | The Aiming for 4 sheet is highly structured, with a step-by-step approach to the calculation to support students in calculating the mean estimated population size. Students may need a brief introduction. Ensure that students are able to carry out the calculations. | Aiming for 6 students should be able to start the activity without introduction. The sheet provides guidance on carrying out the calculation, and asks students to explain the difference between the estimated and actual population size. | Aiming for 8 students should be able to tackle the activity without introduction. The sheet provides the equation to calculate the mean estimated population size. It asks for an explanation of the difference between the estimated and actual population size, and for ideas about improving the accuracy of the process. |
| | **Activity 2 Biodiversity poster (20 minutes)** Students tackle question 2 on the differentiated worksheets which asks them to make a biodiversity poster. They will need A3 paper, coloured pencils, and access to the Student book. Each section has been given a rough time so that students can work through the task independently. The best posters can be kept for display. | | |
| | Aiming for 4 students may need a brief introduction to the activity. The sheet lists information for students to include. Remind students to move on to the next area of their poster at designated times. | Aiming for 6 students should be able to complete their poster independently. The sheet asks students for descriptions of aspects of biodiversity. | Aiming for 8 students should be able to complete their poster independently. |
| | **Kerboodle resource:** B6.1 Checkpoint follow-up: Aiming for 4, B6.1 Checkpoint follow-up: Aiming for 6, B6.1 Checkpoint follow-up: Aiming for 8 | | |
| **Plenary** | **Sampling review (5 minutes)** Hold a thought shower about different sampling techniques, collating ideas on the board. Then ask students to work in groups. Give each group a different scenario and an organism to monitor. Ask the groups to quickly plan which sampling technique they would use. Their decisions can be presented to the class. Scenarios can be targeted to different groups – suggestions include zonation, estimating the number of daisies in a field, estimating the number of invertebrates in a stream. | | |
| **Progression** | Any practical work with sampling techniques will help consolidate Aiming for 4 students' understanding of these techniques. | There are plenty of opportunities for research and debate in this chapter which would challenge all abilities. | Aiming for 8 students could research specific examples of ecotourism and how it has helped or hindered a conservation project. |

# GCSE BIOLOGY ONLY
## B6.2 Feeding the human race
### B6.2.1 Food security

**Specification links:**

B6.2a Describe some of the biological factors affecting levels of food security. To include increasing human population, changing diets in wealthier populations, new pests and pathogens, environmental change, sustainability, and cost of agricultural inputs.

WS1.1d Discuss ethical issues arising from developments in science.

WS1.1e Explain everyday and technological applications of science.

WS1.1f Evaluate associated personal, social, economic, and environmental implications.

WS1.1g Make decisions based on the evaluation of evidence and arguments.

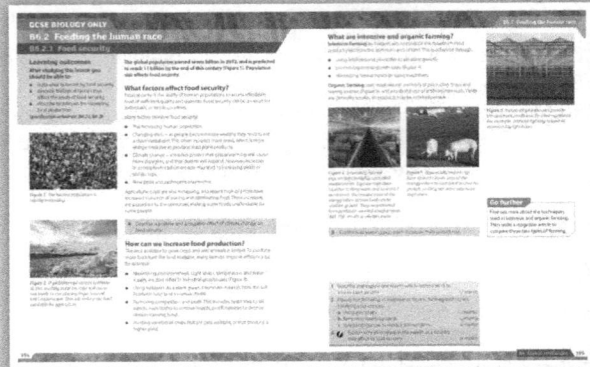

| Target | Outcome | Checkpoint | |
|---|---|---|---|
| | | Question | Activity |
| **Aiming for GRADE 4** | State what is meant by food security. | | Starter 1 and 2 |
| | List techniques used for increasing food security. | 1, 2 | Starter 1 and 2<br>Main<br>Plenary 1 |
| | State some arguments for and against methods to give greater food security. | | Main<br>Plenary 2 |
| **Aiming for GRADE 6** | Describe biological factors that affect the levels of food security. | A, B | Starter 2<br>Main<br>Plenary 1 |
| | Describe techniques for increasing food production. | B, 1, 2 | Starter 2<br>Main<br>Plenary 1 |
| | Compare arguments and evidence for and against methods used to give greater food security. | | Main |
| **Aiming for GRADE 8** | Explain why food security is important for the human population. | 1, 3 | Starter 2<br>Main |
| | Evaluate the effectiveness of the different methods for increasing food production. | | Starter 2<br>Main |
| | Evaluate the arguments and evidence used to make decisions about the use of methods to give greater food security. | | Main |

**Literacy**
During the main activity, students will need to summarise and evaluate texts with accuracy, showing a clear understanding. They will also make links and comparisons between texts.

**Key words**
food security, intensive farming, organic farming

# B6.2 Feeding the human race

| Starter | Support/Extend | Resources |
|---|---|---|
| **Food security** (5 minutes)  Show a graph of human population growth. Ask students what the implications are arising from the graph. Home in on a need for greater food production. State what is meant by the term food security. Ask students to suggest what farmers are doing to increase food security. | | |
| **Factors affecting food security** (10 minutes)  Define food security. Ask students to suggest why it is an issue. Then present a series of factors, written on a card or a PowerPoint presentation. Students should state whether the factor would improve or harm food security. (This could be done as a quiz between two teams.) Explain how the factor works. | **Extend:** Ask students to rank the factors from greatest harm to greatest improvement to food security, with a justification. | |

| Main | Support/Extend | Resources |
|---|---|---|
| **Read all about it!** (40 minutes)  Supply students with newspaper articles discussing some advantages and disadvantages of intensive farming. Students read the articles, and note the advantages and disadvantages.<br><br>Students then feedback to the class describing and explaining the advantages and disadvantages. Advantages will include: food security – providing plenty of food for the population; cost of production; protection from predators. Disadvantages will include: spread of disease; inhumane; pollution from fertilisers; lower quality of food. Then discuss possible organic alternatives.<br><br>Students produce a balanced article to explain how we can feed the expanding population of the world. It should describe the methods that are used, and discuss the advantages and disadvantages. They could also describe the organic alternatives. | **Support:** Ask students to list four or five advantages and then to use the evidence from the newspaper articles to describe them. Repeat for the disadvantages.<br><br>**Extend:** Students evaluate the evidence by distinguishing between arguments that are based on scientific evidence or that are just personal opinion.<br><br>Evaluate the use of intensive farming techniques. Students should decide whether or not the technique is worth using. | **Activity:** Read all about it! |

| Plenary | Support/Extend | Resources |
|---|---|---|
| **Organic versus intensive farms** (5 minutes)  Ask students to classify a series of statements about farming methods to increase food security as either organic or intensive farming techniques. | | |
| **Intensive farming** (5 minutes)  Use the interactive in which students decide which statements are true and false about intensive farming. | | **Interactive:** Intensive farming |

| Homework | | |
|---|---|---|
| You are a UN adviser for food production, and you have been sent to an economically less well developed country prone to famines. What advice would you give the government's agriculture department about how best to feed their population? | | |

# GCSE BIOLOGY ONLY
## B6.2.2 Feeding the world

**Specification links:**

B6.2b Describe and explain some possible agricultural solutions to the demands of the growing human population. To include increased use of hydroponics, biological control, gene technology, fertilisers, and pesticides.

WS1.1c Understand the power and limitations of science.

WS1.1d Discuss ethical issues arising from developments in science.

WS1.1e Explain everyday and technological applications of science.

WS1.1f Evaluate associated personal, social, economic, and environmental implications.

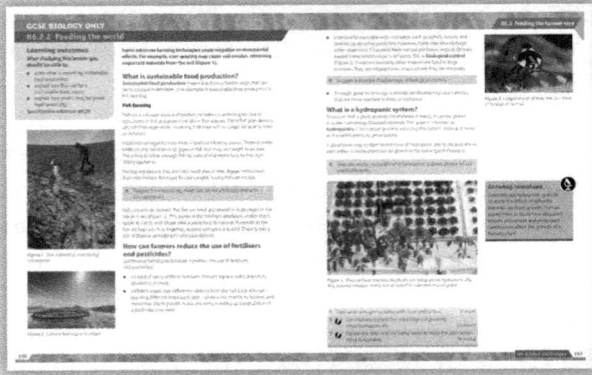

| Target | Outcome | Checkpoint | |
|---|---|---|---|
| | | Question | Activity |
| **Aiming for GRADE 4** ↓ | State what is meant by sustainable food production. | 1 | Main |
| | Name two modern methods for increasing food production. | | Starter 1<br>Main<br>Plenary 1 and 2 |
| | State that our understanding of science has led to the development of new farming techniques. | | Starter 1 and 2<br>Main<br>Plenary 2 |
| **Aiming for GRADE 6** ↓ | Describe how fertilisers, pesticides, and biological control improve food production. | B | Starter 2<br>Main |
| | Describe how modern methods, such as fish farming and hydroponics, can be used to produce food. | A, C, 2 | Starter 1<br>Main<br>Plenary 2 |
| | Describe how newly developed farming techniques have led to an improved quality of life. | 2 | Starter 1 and 2<br>Main<br>Plenary 2 |
| **Aiming for GRADE 8** ↓ | Evaluate the advantages and disadvantages of the use of fertilisers, pesticides, and biological control in improving food production. | B | Main |
| | Explain how modern methods of farming, such as hydroponics and fish farming, provide a sustainable food source. | C, 3 | Starter 1<br>Main |
| | Discuss how scientific developments in farming have led to an improved quality of life, whilst limitations in the scientific process still pose problems. | | Starter 1<br>Main<br>Plenary 2 |

**Literacy**
During the main activity, students will need to communicate effectively to sustain the interest of others. They will also need to use appropriate technical vocabulary.

**Key words**
biological control, hydroponics, sustainable food production

## B6.2 Feeding the human race

| Starter | Support/Extend | Resources |
|---|---|---|
| **Hydroponics** (10 minutes)  In advance of the lesson, set up a plant (for example, a bean seedling) in a glass jar of colourless solution as an example of a hydroponics system, or show a short film on hydroponics. Discuss how the plant is able to grow in the system, and how it obtains the substances it requires. Can students suggest how the system might produce a commercial crop? | **Extend:** Suggest some limitations with this method. | |
| **Feed the world** (5 minutes)  Play a short clip from the Band Aid single 'Feed the world'. Ask the class about the purpose of this song. Why are famines common? Can science prevent them? Ask students to suggest techniques they have learnt about that increase food production. | | |

| Main | Support/Extend | Resources |
|---|---|---|
| **Farming in Futureland** (40 minutes)  You are working for a science-based theme park resort called Futureland. You have been asked to design displays for an area of land that is to be dedicated to the practices of agriculture, and how modern approaches ensure that there is plenty of food for the world population.<br><br>Allocate one farming practice to each student group, who must come up with an idea for a display to explain this practice. Practices could include: use of fertilisers, use of pesticides, hydroponics, biological control, and fish farming. Give groups around 15 minutes to research their idea.<br><br>Groups create a display to explain the practice they have researched. They should cover the following areas:<br>• name of method<br>• how the method is carried out<br>• how it improves food production<br>• the extent to which it is sustainable<br>• advantages and disadvantages of the method.<br><br>Allow around 15 minutes for creating the displays.<br><br>Student groups present their displays to the rest of the their class and explain how their practice has contributed to increasing food production. | **Support:** Provide the group with the questions listed in the display section to structure their research.<br><br>**Extend:** Students could also discuss the limitations of the technique and how science needs to provide solutions to expand the method. | **Activity:** Farming in Futureland |

| Plenary | Support/Extend | Resources |
|---|---|---|
| **Feeding the world** (5 minutes)  Use the interactive in which students answer a multiple choice question about how fishing can be made more sustainable. | **Extend:** Discuss the extent of the scientific involvement in the method. | **Interactive:** Feeding the world |
| **Most interesting display** (10 minutes)  Hold a class discussion that evaluates the display boards. Ask students to identify features of the display boards that helped them to understand the farming practices. Can they decide which was the most interesting technique, and explain their choice? | | |

| Homework |
|---|
| Design and draw a hydroponic plant-growing facility. Label the drawing to explain how the plants obtain the nutrients they require, how food production is increased using this method, how plants are harvested, etc. |

**kerboodle**

A Kerboodle highlight for this lesson is **Literacy sheet: Maximising growth**. Refer to the **Content map** on Kerboodle for a full list of resources and assessment.

# B6.2.3 Selective breeding

**Specification links:**

B6.2c Explain the impact of the selective breeding of food plants and domestic animals.

WS1.1c Understand power and limitations of science.

WS1.1e Explain everyday and technological applications of science.

WS1.1f Evaluate associated personal, social, economic, and environmental implications.

BM6.2iii Use ratios, fractions, and percentages (M1c).

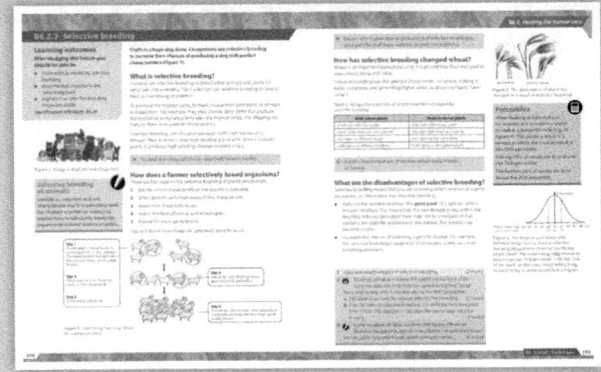

| Target | Outcome | Checkpoint | |
|---|---|---|---|
| | | Question | Activity |
| **Aiming for GRADE 4** | State what is meant by selective breeding. | | Starter 1 and 2 |
| | State some advantages of selectively bred organisms. | C | Starter 1 and 2, Main |
| | State that an understanding of science has enhanced the process of selective breeding. | | Starter 2, Main, Plenary 2 |
| **Aiming for GRADE 6** | Describe how organisms are selectively bred. | B, 3 | Starter 2, Main, Plenary 1 |
| | Describe the advantages and disadvantages of selective breeding. | B | Starter 2, Main |
| | Describe how the understanding of science has given us the power to plan a selective breeding programme. | | Main, Plenary 2 |
| **Aiming for GRADE 8** | Explain how selective breeding increases yields. | C, 3 | Main, Plenary 2 |
| | Evaluate the advantages and disadvantages of selective breeding. | B | Main, Plenary 2 |
| | Discuss how the limitations of the science of selective breeding have driven scientists to seek other methods to increase yields. | | Main, Plenary 2 |

**Maths**
During the main activity, students may use and interpret percentages (M1c).

**Literacy**
During the main activity, students will need to communicate effectively to sustain the reader's interest.

**Key words**
gene pool, selective breeding

## B6.2 Feeding the human race

| Starter | Support/Extend | Resources |
|---|---|---|
| **Variation in tools** (5 minutes) Show the class a range of different screwdrivers. Ask if they are the same tool. Ask them why humans have made so many types of screwdrivers. Are we still developing new types? Then draw a comparison with selective breeding in plants and animals. **Selective breeding in domestic animals** (10 minutes) Ask if any of the class have a dog; if so, what type? Show an image of a range of different dog breeds (or any other domestic or farm animal). Ask the class why there are so many types. What do they do? Ask if they have always been around, or if humans bred them. Some might be able to describe how the animals were bred. | **Extend:** Ask the class if they know of any disadvantages of the process of selective breeding. | |

| Main | Support/Extend | Resources |
|---|---|---|
| **Victorian farming** (40 minutes) Students should imagine that they are working for a TV station that is producing a show where it sends modern farmers back 150 years to a Victorian farm. They will need to discuss examples of differences, such as how the cattle on the farm produced so much less milk than they produce today. Divide the students into groups and give each group a different example of a farm animal that has been selectively bred. Their job is to write the voiceover script for the show, to explain, for example, how the cattle have been selectively bred over the years. They should research facts, figures and details of the process. Allow around 20 minutes for research. They should produce a script that explains the process. There could be some evaluation of the process, including its advantages and disadvantages, and an overall assessment of its worth. Allow around 25 minutes for writing the script. | **Support:** Choose one example for the class, and suggest books or websites. Create a frame with specific questions to structure their research/writing. Students could create a storyboard instead of a long written answer. **Extend:** Students could evaluate the advantages and limitations of the process. They could suggest how scientists have looked at alternative methods to increase yields. | **Activity:** Victorian farming |

| Plenary | Support/Extend | Resources |
|---|---|---|
| **Wolf to greyhound** (5 minutes) Use the interactive in which students order a set of sentences so that they describe how people developed greyhounds from wolves by selective breeding. **Selective-breeding scientist** (10 minutes) On a sheet of paper ask groups to generate a spider diagram that indicates all the biological, mathematical, and scientific knowledge needed by a selective-breeding scientist. Extend out to a second layer where the class explains why these skills are useful. | **Extend:** Evaluate which skills or knowledge will have been most useful to the scientist. Suggest how science can only take this process so far. | **Interactive:** Wolf to greyhound |

| Homework | | |
|---|---|---|
| Write a synopsis of the TV programme from the Main lesson activity for a TV listings magazine. It should include details of how the animals have been changed by scientists. Alternatively, select a feature that you feel would be useful in an animal. Identify a suitable animal to breed, list the advantageous characteristics you might start with and explain how you would selectively breed the animal. | | |

**kerboodle**
A Kerboodle highlight for this lesson is **Bump up your grade: Selective breeding techniques**. Refer to the **Content map** on Kerboodle for a full list of resources and assessment.

# B6.2.4 Genetic engineering

**Specification links:**

B6.2d Describe genetic engineering as a process that involves modifying the genome of an organism to introduce desirable characteristics.

B6.2f Explain some of the possible benefits and risks of using gene technology in modern agriculture. To include practical and ethical considerations. **S**

WS1.1c Understand the power and limitations of science.

WS1.1d Discuss ethical issues arising from developments in science.

WS1.1e Explain everyday and technological applications of science.

WS1.1f Evaluate associated personal, social, economic, and environmental implications.

WS1.1g Make decisions based on the evaluation of evidence and arguments.

WS1.1h Evaluate risks both in practical science and the wider societal context.

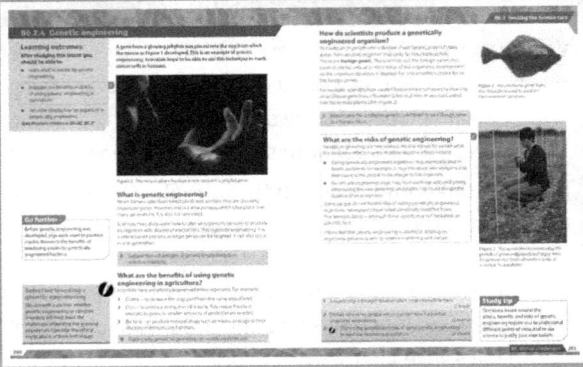

| Target | Outcome | Checkpoint | |
|---|---|---|---|
| | | Question | Activity |
| Aiming for GRADE 4 | State what is meant by genetic engineering. | | Starter 1 and 2<br>Main |
| | State that an understanding of science has led to genetic engineering. | | Starter 1 and 2<br>Main<br>Plenary 2 |
| | State an ethical objection to genetic engineering. | 2 | Starter 2<br>Main<br>Plenary 1 |
| Aiming for GRADE 6 | Describe simply how an organism is genetically engineered. | B, C | Starter 2<br>Main |
| | Describe how the understanding of science has allowed us to develop the process of genetic engineering. | | Starter 2<br>Main<br>Plenary 2 |
| | Discuss a range of ethical concerns arising from genetic engineering. | C, 2 | Main<br>Plenary 1 |
| Aiming for GRADE 8 | Evaluate the benefits and risks of using genetic engineering in agriculture. | A, B, 1, 2, 3 | Main<br>Plenary 1 |
| | Discuss the scientific achievement and limitations of the process of genetic engineering. | | Main<br>Plenary 2 |
| | Evaluate the ethical issues raised by governments, scientists, and the wider public about genetic engineering. | 2 | Main<br>Plenary 1 |

**Literacy**

During the main activity, students will need to write coherent, well-structured, and purposeful text, which uses vocabulary appropriate to purpose.

**Key words**

foreign genes, genetic engineering

## B6.2 Feeding the human race

| Starter | Support/Extend | Resources |
|---|---|---|
| **Creating a smart phone** (5 minutes) Ask what the mobile phone was originally made for. Ask if the students' modern phones have had anything added. They will probably talk about cameras, music, etc. Compare the addition of the technology to perform a new additional function to the process of adding a gene for a useful characteristic. | | |
| **Frankenstein's tomatoes** (10 minutes) Remind the class about selectively breeding crops or animals. Ask for the disadvantages of the process – answers include the time it takes, and the fact that progress is limited. Wouldn't it be great if we could choose characteristics from one species and put them into another? Ask what characteristics they would add to tomatoes to get an even better crop. State that we can do this. Finally, show an image or short film of the Frankenstein story. Explain that Dr Frankenstein combined different characteristics in one person. Explain that this has long been an idea, but early scientists lacked the power to do so, but now – to some extent – scientists are able to. | **Extend:** Ask what additional knowledge scientists now have to allow us to be more successful at genetic engineering. Are there still problems? | |

| Main | Support/Extend | Resources |
|---|---|---|
| **Reporting to the Department of Agriculture** (40 minutes) Currently there is not much GM food grown in the UK, and Wales has banned its production entirely. The government needs a balanced report about the advantages and disadvantages of the process of genetic engineering in order to inform policy development, both in the UK and as part of its international aid programme. The class should form groups, and research and write the report. Students review a number of websites to find out:<br>• supermarket policies on GM food<br>• government views, including that of the Welsh government<br>• about GM research companies for example, Monsanto.<br>Allow around 20 minutes for research and 25 minutes for writing the report. | **Support:** Divide the research up, by giving each group one website only to research. Ask them to list and describe the advantages and disadvantages.<br><br>**Extend:** Compare the views in a more economically developed country (MEDC), such as Wales in the UK, with a less economically developed country (LEDC). | **Activity:** Reporting to the Department of Agriculture |
| It should describe the advantages and disadvantages of genetic engineering, ethical issues, and the views of the scientific community. | | |

| Plenary | Support/Extend | Resources |
|---|---|---|
| **Advantages and disadvantages** (5 minutes) Use the interactive where students sort a series of statements, which are either advantages or disadvantages of genetic engineering, by dragging and dropping the statements into one of two boxes. | **Extend:** Ask students to evaluate the disadvantages and justify their answers. | **Interactive:** Advantages and disadvantages |
| **Contributions of scientists** (10 minutes) Divide the class into groups. Half of the groups discuss achievements scientists have made to food production; the other half discuss the problems scientists might have created, or the limitations of science. They discuss their views, and the class decides, on balance, whether or not scientists have had a positive effect. | **Support:** Provide a list of achievements and problems mixed together, and ask the class to sort them into the two categories, before holding a short discussion. | |

| Homework |
|---|
| You work for a scientific research company that plans to conduct genetic engineering experiments to develop crops that can be grown in harsh conditions. Write a policy statement for your company that would outline the advantages of the process and counter some possible objections. |

**kerboodle**
A Kerboodle highlight for this lesson is **Literacy sheet: GM crops**. Refer to the **Content map** on Kerboodle for a full list of resources and assessment.

# HIGHER TIER
## B6.2.5 Producing a genetically engineered organism

**Specification links:**

B6.2e Describe the main steps in the process of genetic engineering. To include restriction enzymes, sticky ends, vectors (e.g. plasmids), ligase, host bacteria, and selection using antibiotic resistance markers.

WS1.1b Use models to solve problems, make predictions, and to develop scientific explanations and understanding of familiar and unfamiliar facts.

WS1.1c Understand the power and limitations of science.

WS1.1e Explain everyday and technological applications of science.

WS1.1f Evaluate associated personal, social, economic, and environmental implications.

WS1.1h Evaluate risks both in practical science and the wider societal context.

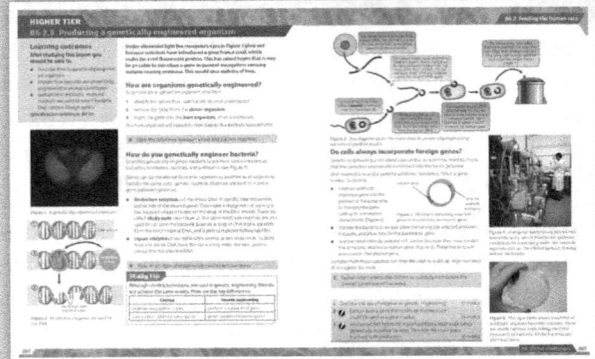

| Target | Outcome | Checkpoint | |
|---|---|---|---|
| | | Question | Activity |
| **Aiming for GRADE 6** | Describe how to genetically engineer an organism. | A, 3 | Starter 1 and 2<br>Main<br>Plenary 1 and 2 |
| | Describe the role of the various enzymes used in the process of genetic engineering. | B, 1 | Starter 1 and 2<br>Main<br>Plenary 1 and 2 |
| | Describe some technological processes involved in genetic engineering. | | Starter 2<br>Main<br>Plenary 2 |
| **Aiming for GRADE 8** | Explain how bacteria are genetically engineered to produce hormones. | 3 | Main<br>Plenary 2 |
| | Explain how antibiotic-resistance markers are used to select bacteria that contain foreign genes. | C | Main<br>Plenary 1 and 2 |
| | Explain in detail the technological applications of science in genetic engineering. | | Main |

**Literacy**
During the main activity, students will need to communicate effectively and maintain the reader's interest. They will also need to use appropriate scientific vocabulary.

**Key words**
donor organism, host organism, ligase, restriction enzymes, sticky ends

# B6.2 Feeding the human race

| Starter | Support/Extend | Resources |
|---|---|---|
| **Copy and paste** (5 minutes)   Project a passage of a word processing document and ask how to insert a section of text into the middle of the passage. Then perform the action. Draw comparisons between this process and cutting and inserting a gene into the genome. | **Extend:** Ask the class what the copied text represents, what performs the 'cut' process in the cell, etc. | |
| **Cutting DNA** (10 minutes)   Divide the class into pairs. The aim is to cut a gene from one drawing of DNA and insert it into a second drawing of DNA. Give one of the pair an A3 sheet with a length of host DNA drawn on it, with one potential point to cut (restriction site). The other student is given a drawing of donor DNA with two potential restriction sites. They use scissors and listen to the teacher as they describe the sequence of cuts. They should be able to insert the small gene into the host DNA. | **Extend:** Draw a comparison between the scissors, glue, and the different enzymes. | |

| Main | Support/Extend | Resources |
|---|---|---|
| **Genetically modified play** (40 minutes)   Students will write and perform a short play. Divide the class into groups of about four.<br><br>Each group writes a short play to explain the process of genetic engineering. They will each play a part in the play. Students can narrate or they could act as a cell, enzyme, piece of DNA, and so on. Allow around 20 minutes for writing the script. Once the script is written, each group will perform the play for neighbouring groups.<br><br>Students critique each other's plays. Allow 25 minutes for the performances and feedback on the plays. | **Extend:** Students could comment in the script about the scientific innovations that have been developed in the process. | **Activity:** Genetically modified play |

| Plenary | Support/Extend | Resources |
|---|---|---|
| **Making a genetically modified organism** (5 minutes)   Use the interactive, which asks students to drag and drop a series of statements describing the process of making a genetically modified organism into the correct order. | | **Interactive:** Making a genetically modified organism |
| **Memory aid** (10 minutes)   Place a list of the following terms on the board: host, donor, restriction enzyme, sticky ends, ligase, plasmid, and so on. Students produce a memory aid to remember the definition of each term and its role in the process. It could take the form of a rhyme, spider diagram, humorous story, and so on. | **Support:** Produce a mnemonic for the sequence of steps in genetic engineering. | |

| Homework |
|---|
| Write a newspaper article set in the 1980s when the process of genetic modification was developed. The story should take the standpoint that there is a miraculous new way to produce the hormone insulin for diabetics. Include details of the processes and advantages. |

**kerboodle**

A Kerboodle highlight for this lesson is **Animation: Genetic modification**. Refer to the **Content map** on Kerboodle for a full list of resources and assessment.

# B6.2.6 Use of biotechnology in farming

**Specification links:**

B6.2g Describe and explain some possible biotechnological solutions to the demands of the growing human population. To include genetic modification.

WS1.1c Understand the power and limitations of science.

WS1.1d Discuss ethical issues arising from developments in science.

WS1.1f Evaluate associated personal, social, economic, and environmental implications.

WS1.1g Make decisions based on the evaluation of evidence and arguments.

WS1.1h Evaluate risks both in practical science and the wider societal context.

BM6.2i Use percentiles and calculate percentage gain and loss of mass.

BM6.2iv Extract and interpret information from charts, graphs and tables (M2c, M4a).

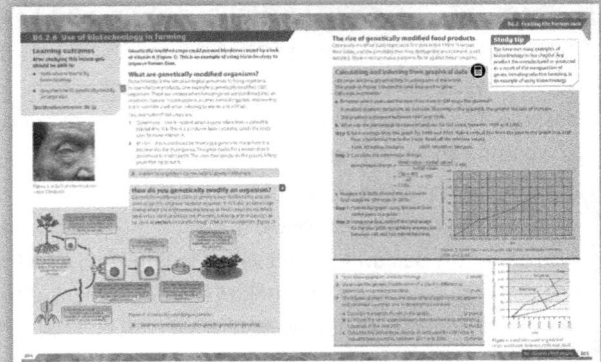

| Target | Outcome | Checkpoint | |
|---|---|---|---|
| | | Question | Activity |
| **Aiming for GRADE 4** ↓ | State what is meant by biotechnology. | 1 | Starter 1<br>Plenary 1 |
| | State that the global use of GM crops is increasing. | 3 | Starter 2<br>Main |
| | Use a piece of evidence to support a viewpoint on the use of GM crops. | | Main<br>Plenary 2 |
| **Aiming for GRADE 6** ↓ | Describe some examples of biotechnology. | 1 | Starter 1<br>Main<br>Plenary 1 |
| | Compare the use of GM crops between industrial and developing countries. | 3 | Starter 2<br>Main |
| | Use evidence to make a decision about the use of GM crops. | | Main<br>Plenary 2 |
| **Aiming for GRADE 8** ↓ | Explain how biotechnology provides possible solutions to the demands of the growing human population. | A | Starter 2<br>Main<br>Plenary 1 |
| | Explain how the use of GM crops contributes to food security in different economically developed countries. | 3 | Starter 2<br>Main |
| | Evaluate the evidence and arguments when making a decision about the use of GM crops. | | Main<br>Plenary 2 |

**Maths**
During the main activity, students might need to use and interpret data, including fractions and percentages (M1c), and frequency tables and diagrams, bar charts, and histograms (M2c). They may also translate information between graphical and numerical forms (M4a).

**Literacy**
During the main activity, students will need to communicate effectively to sustain interest.

**Key words**
biotechnology, vector

## B6.2 Feeding the human race

| Starter | Support/Extend | Resources |
|---|---|---|
| **What is biotechnology?** (10 minutes) Ask what is meant by the term biotechnology. Arrive at a definition. Ask the class to think of as many examples of biotechnology as they can (e.g., making alcohol, cheese, drugs, disease-resistant crops, antibodies, enzymes for washing powder). Identify what organism or process is used for each example. Explain why this has improved the quality of life. | **Support:** Provide the definition. | |
| **GM tomatoes** (5 minutes) Inform the class that a high percentage of tomatoes used in ketchup in the USA are from GM crops. Ask what advantages there may be from using GM crops, and what disadvantages there may be. | **Extend:** Discuss why GM crops might be viewed in a more favourable light in a less economically developed country than they would be in the UK. | |

| Main | Support/Extend | Resources |
|---|---|---|
| **GM debate** (40 minutes) The class will debate the statement, 'The world should ban genetically modified crops'.<br><br>Divide the class into groups. Each group will represent an interest group, for example, farmers from LEDC and well developed communities; politicians from the same two countries; scientists; environmentalists. Students can use all that they have learnt from the previously taught lessons in this chapter, as well as data from reliable sources on the internet, to prepare for the debate. Allow around 25 minutes for research.<br><br>Then hold the debate. Use the evidence presented in the debate to make a decision as a class by voting on the motion. Allow 20 minutes for the debate and voting. | **Support:** Reduce the number of groups in the debate. Provide websites and a series of questions for them to find answers to.<br><br>**Extend:** Introduce time to question each speaker. Evaluate the evidence before coming to the decision. | **Activity:** GM debate |

| Plenary | Support/Extend | Resources |
|---|---|---|
| **Golden rice** (5 minutes) Use the interactive, which contains a paragraph about the development of golden rice as an example of biotechnology. Within the paragraph there are blanks into which students must drag and drop words. | **Extend:** Evaluate the process. | **Interactive:** Golden rice |
| **Quality evidence** (10 minutes) There are arguments for and against the use of GM crops. Ask students to suggest what evidence scientists should be collecting to help the world community make decisions about their use. How would this evidence be reliable, accurate, and unbiased? What piece of evidence might be the most convincing? | | |

| Homework | | |
|---|---|---|
| Design a questionnaire to find the views of the public on biotechnology in farming and the use of GM crops. | | |

**kerboodle**

A Kerboodle highlight for this lesson is **Literacy sheet: Genetically modified crops**. Refer to the **Content map** on Kerboodle for a full list of resources and assessment.

# Checkpoint
## B6.2 Feeding the human race

### Overview of B6.2 Feeding the human race

In this chapter, students have studied food security and the factors that affect it. They should be able to describe ways to increase food production including the roles of intensive farming and organic farming. They should be familiar with sustainable food production, fish farming, and the use of hydroponics. They should link this work with the conditions needed by plants for photosynthesis in B1.4 *Photosynthesis* and with interactions between species in a food web in B4.1 *Ecosystems*.

Students should be familiar with selective breeding as an example of artificial selection, be able to give examples, and explain the disadvantages of this process. They should link this with the idea of variability between species in B5.1 *Inheritance* and the natural selection of characteristics in B5.2 *Natural selection and evolution*. They should understand that although selective breeding is much faster than natural selection, it still takes many generations to achieve the end result.

Students should be able to give examples of applications of the use of genetic engineering in bacteria, plants, and animals, and outline some of the potential risks of the technology. Higher-tier students should be able to describe the steps in the process of genetic engineering, linking with the organisation of DNA and enzyme action in B1.2 *What happens in cells?* and with human insulin for the treatment of diabetes in B3.3 *Maintaining internal environments*.

Finally students should be familiar with the use of biotechnology in farming, including the example of Golden rice. They should be able to outline the stages involved in the process of genetically modifying an organism.

You can find additional support for the maths skills covered in this chapter on **MyMaths**, which might include using and interpreting data, fractions and percentages, frequency tables and diagrams, bar charts, and histograms. Students may translate information between graphical and numerical forms.

For this chapter, the following assessments are available on Kerboodle:

B6.2 Checkpoint quiz: Feeding the human race
B6.2 Progress quiz: Feeding the human race 1
B6.2 Progress quiz: Feeding the human race 2
B6.2 On your marks: Feeding the human race
B6.2 Exam-style questions and mark scheme: Feeding the human race

### Checkpoint follow-up lesson

A student's route through this lesson can be determined using the Checkpoint assessment. Percentage pass marks are supplied in the Checkpoint teacher notes.

For each successive route through it is assumed that the student can perform to their current route as well as previous routes. For example, students working at Aiming for 6 are assumed to be secure in Aiming for 4 knowledge and understanding and working towards achieving all the learning objectives for Aiming for 6.

# B6.2 Feeding the human race

|  | Aiming for 4 | Aiming for 6 | Aiming for 8 |
|---|---|---|---|
| **Learning outcomes** | State the factors affecting food security. | Describe the factors affecting food security. | Explain the factors affecting food security. |
|  | State methods of sustainable food production. | Describe methods of sustainable food production. | Explain methods of sustainable food production. |
|  | State the process of selective breeding. | Describe the process of selective breeding. | Explain the process of selective breeding. |
|  | State what is meant by genetic engineering. | Describe the process of genetically engineering an organism. | Explain the process of genetically engineering an organism. |
| **Starter** | **Organic or intensive? (5 minutes)** Students will each need a mini whiteboard. Give a quick reminder of the difference between organic and intensive farming. Read out features of farming for students to classify as organic or intensive on mini whiteboards. | | |
| **Differentiated checkpoint activity** | **Activity 1 Food security and sustainability (10 minutes)** Students answer question 1 on the differentiated worksheets, which asks them to produce a visual summary of this topic. | | |
|  | Aiming for 4 students will need access to the Student book and may require a brief introduction from the teacher. They complete an outline visual summary. | Aiming for 6 students should be able to complete this task independently using the Student book. They are given factors to describe on their summary. | Aiming for 8 students should be able to complete this task independently using the Student book They are given factors to discuss on their summary. |
|  | **Activity 2 Selective breeding (15 minutes)** Students use question 2 on the differentiated worksheets to produce a comic strip on selective breeding. They will require access to A4 paper and coloured pencils. The best comic strips could be kept for display. | | |
|  | Aiming for 4 students are provided with captions for their comic strip. They could be given a template to use, which will need to be photocopied in advance of the lesson. | Aiming for 6 students describe how they would selectively breed for a chosen feature in an animal in their comic strip. They are given a brief description of the process of selective breeding. | Aiming for 8 students describe how they would selectively breed for a chosen feature in an animal in their comic strip, with no prompts. |
|  | **Activity 3 Genetic engineering (15 minutes)** Students complete question 3 about genetic engineering on the differentiated worksheets. They work in pairs to discuss part (b). | | |
|  | The Aiming for 4 sheet provides structured questions and a cut and paste exercise. These students will need access to scissors and glue sticks. Briefly introduce the activity and review students' answers. | Aiming for 6 students will require access to the Student book. They draw a flow chart including the labels provided to describe the production of genetically engineered insulin. They should be able to complete this task independently. Students can peer assess each other's work if time allows. | Aiming for 8 students may require access to the Student book. They draw a flow chart to describe the production of genetically engineered insulin. They should be able to complete this task independently. Students can peer assess each other's work if time allows. |
|  | **Kerboodle resource:** B6.2 Checkpoint follow-up: Aiming for 4, B6.2 Checkpoint follow-up: Aiming for 6, B6.2 Checkpoint follow-up: Aiming for 8 | | |
| **Plenary** | **Genetic engineering opinions (10 minutes)** Student pairs write down as many advantages and risks of genetic engineering as they can think of. Briefly review these on the board. Then give a range of uses of genetic engineering, for example – developing drought-resistant plants, producing insulin to treat people with diabetes, the possibility of developing crops that provide vaccines. Students raise their hands if they agree with each use. | | |
| **Progression** | The Aiming for 4 activities provide highly structured questions. When studying selective breeding, all students could find out different examples of pedigree breeding in terms of the health problems they cause. | The Aiming for 6 activities are reasonably structured. There are plenty of opportunities for research and debate in this chapter which would challenge all abilities. | Genetic engineering is challenging has some parts in the higher tier. Diagrams showing the steps of the process may aid understanding. Aiming for 8 students could research the history of diabetes treatment, which now uses GM human insulin. |

# B6.3–Part 1 Monitoring and maintaining health
## B6.3.1 Health and disease

**Specification links:**

B6.3a Describe the relationship between health and disease.

B6.3b Describe different types of diseases. To include communicable and non-communicable diseases.

B6.3c Describe the interactions between different types of disease. To include HIV and tuberculosis; and HPV and cervical cancer.

B6.3d Explain how communicable diseases (caused by viruses, bacteria, protists, and fungi) are spread in animals and plants. To include scientific quantities, number of pathogens, number of infected cases, estimating number of cases.

WS1.1f Evaluate associated personal, social, economic, and environmental implications.

WS1.1g Make decisions based on the evaluation of evidence and arguments.

WS1.1h Evaluate risks both in practical science and the wider societal context.

WS1.4b Recognise the importance of scientific quantities and understand how they are determined.

BM6.3i Translate information between graphical and numerical forms (M4a).

BM6.3ii Construct and interpret frequency tables and diagrams, bar charts, and histograms (M2c).

BM6.3iv Use a scatter diagram to identify a correlation between two variables (M2g).

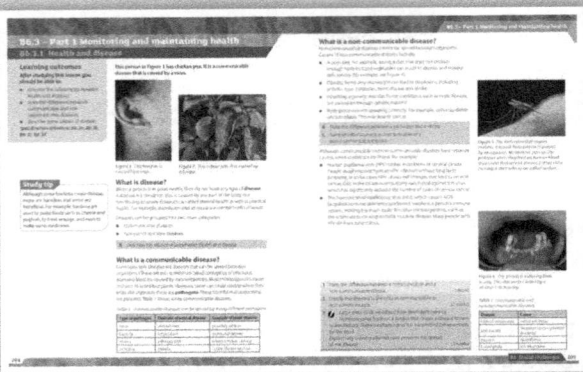

| Target | Outcome | Checkpoint | |
|---|---|---|---|
| | | Question | Activity |
| **Aiming for GRADE 4** ↓ | Describe the relationship between health and disease. | A | Starter 1<br>Main<br>Plenary 1 |
| | State the difference between communicable and non-communicable diseases. | C, 1, 2 | Starter 1<br>Main<br>Plenary 1 |
| | Recognise trends in epidemiological data. | | Starter 2<br>Main<br>Plenary 2 |
| **Aiming for GRADE 6** ↓ | Describe some causes of disease. | B | Main |
| | Describe how scientists track the progress of a disease in the study of epidemiology. | 3 | Starter 2<br>Main<br>Plenary 2 |
| | Plot two variables from an epidemiological study in a suitable graph and recognise a trend. | | Main |
| **Aiming for GRADE 8** ↓ | Explain the interaction between some different types of disease. | | Main |
| | Explain the importance of epidemiological studies in the control of communicable diseases. | 3 | Main<br>Plenary 2 |
| | Plot two variables from an epidemiological study in a suitable graph and interpret the significance of the graph. | | Main |

# B6.3–Part 1 Monitoring and maintaining health

**Maths**
During the main activity, students will need to plot two variables from data (M4c). They will need to use the scatter diagrams produced to identify correlations (M2g). They will also need to interpret frequency tables (M2c), and translate information between graphical and numerical forms (M4a).

**Literacy**
During the main activity, students will need to produce coherent, well-structured responses to questions.

**Key words**
communicable disease, disease, pathogens

| Starter | Support/Extend | Resources |
|---|---|---|
| **What sort of disease?** (5 minutes)  Ask the class to suggest as many different diseases as possible, and record these on the board. Student groups then sort the diseases into groups, and justify their classification systems. Each group reports to the class. Then identify the importance of dividing into communicable and non-communicable, and explain the difference. | **Extend:** Ask students to suggest why dividing into communicable and non-communicable diseases is important. | |
| **Tracking sales** (10 minutes)  Show the class sales figures for mobile phones. Ask the class to suggest uses of the data. How could it help the company? If the company had sales data for different countries how might it help their planning? Now draw a comparison with the study of epidemiology, and ask students to suggest why it is useful. Focus on controlling the spread of disease, education, and medical resource management. | **Extend:** Ask the class what shape the sales graph might be over time. When would financing research for that product no longer be viable? Look at the idea of control of the disease and scaling back investment. | |

| Main | Support/Extend | Resources |
|---|---|---|
| **Epidemiology study of tuberculosis** (40 minutes)  Present the class with a worksheet containing data for the numbers of cases of, or deaths from, a disease such as tuberculosis (TB). Compare data for the UK and sub-Saharan Africa since 1900. Students plot the data as two line graphs. Students then answer questions to establish the following points: 1. Definitions and causes of disease, and of communicable and non-communicable diseases. 2. Why studying data like this is important (for example, planning healthcare, education, public awareness, travel). 3. Reasons for there being different trends in different regions. Then discuss possible links between the prevalence of TB and HIV/AIDS by stating when HIV became a problem and looking for correlations on the graphs. | **Support:** Provide axes for the graphs. Amend data to whole numbers. **Extend:** Students could evaluate the importance of the data. Students should make decisions based on the data. | **Activity:** Epidemiology study of tuberculosis |

| Plenary | Support/Extend | Resources |
|---|---|---|
| **Health and disease definitions** (5 minutes)  Use the interactive where students link key words (including disease, health, communicable, non-communicable, pathogen, etc.) to their meanings. | | **Interactive:** Health and disease definitions |
| **The problem with epidemiology** (10 minutes)  Ask students to suggest problems with epidemiology, such as difficulties in collecting data and maintaining high quality record systems, challenges in diagnosing diseases correctly, and so on. Evaluate whether or not epidemiology is still a valid exercise. The World Health Organisation (WHO) have been tracking diseases such as polio for many years. Discuss the importance of this, and ask why the WHO insists on a number of years without cases in order to class a disease as eradicated. | | |

| Homework |
|---|
| Scientists have developed a vaccine for HPV, a virus that may cause cervical cancer in some women. Explain how scientists would collect and present epidemiological data to track the effectiveness of the vaccine. Sketch a graph to predict its effect. |

# B6.3.2 Spread of communicable diseases

**Specification links:**

B6.3d Explain how communicable diseases (caused by viruses, bacteria, protists, and fungi) are spread in animals and plants. To include scientific quantities, number of pathogens, number of infected cases, estimating number of cases.

WS1.1f Evaluate associated personal, social, economic, and environmental implications.

WS1.1g Make decisions based on the evaluation of evidence and arguments.

WS1.1h Evaluate risks both in practical science and the wider societal context.

WS1.4b Recognise the importance of scientific quantities and understand how they are determined.

BM6.3i Translate information between graphical and numerical forms (M4a).

BM6.3ii Construct and interpret frequency tables and diagrams, bar charts, and histograms (M2c).

BM6.3iv Use a scatter diagram to identify a correlation between two variables (M2g).

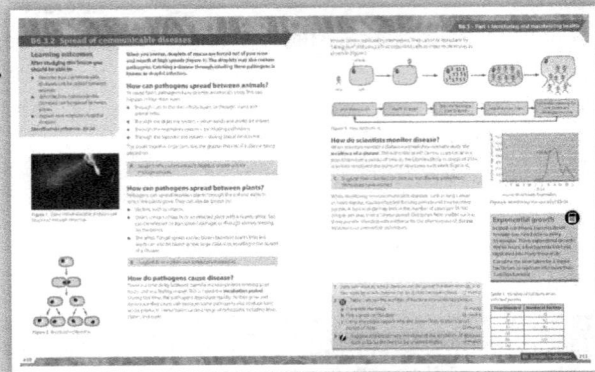

| Target | Outcome | Checkpoint | |
|---|---|---|---|
| | | Question | Activity |
| **Aiming for GRADE 4** | State what is meant by a communicable disease. | | Starter 1 and 2<br>Main<br>Plenary 1 and 2 |
| | State that an infection by a pathogen produces a range of symptoms. | | Starter 1<br>Main<br>Plenary 2 |
| | State that communicable diseases present a risk to society. | | Starter 1 and 2<br>Main<br>Plenary 1 and 2 |
| **Aiming for GRADE 6** | Describe how communicable diseases can be spread between animals or plants. | A, B, 1 | Starter 1 and 2<br>Main<br>Plenary 1 and 2 |
| | Describe how pathogens cause illness. | 2 | Main<br>Plenary 2 |
| | Describe how scientists attempt to reduce the risk to society of a communicable disease. | C, 3 | Starter 1 and 2<br>Main<br>Plenary 2 |
| **Aiming for GRADE 8** | Explain how scientists monitor disease. | C, 3 | Starter 1 and 2<br>Main<br>Plenary 1 and 2 |
| | Examine how the lifecycle of a pathogen contributes to its ability to cause illness and to spread. | 2 | Main |
| | Evaluate the control methods used to reduce the risk to society of spread of a communicable disease. | C, 3 | Main<br>Plenary 2 |

## B6.3–Part 1 Monitoring and maintaining health

**Maths**
Students will need to use the scatter diagrams produced to identify correlations (M2g). They will also need to interpret frequency tables (M2c), and translate information between graphical and numerical forms (M4a).

**Literacy**
During the main activity, students will need to communicate effectively and sustain interest.

**Key words**
droplet infection, incubation period, incidence of disease

| Starter | Support/Extend | Resources |
|---|---|---|
| **Outbreak** (10 minutes) Show a short news item about a recent epidemic. Use the film as a stimulus to extract definitions of these terms: communicable diseases, epidemic, control measures. Ask students to suggest possible roles of scientists in the epidemic. | | |
| **Red card disease** (5 minutes) At the start of the lesson, give one student a number of small red cards (fewer than the total number in the class). Ask the student to move around the room, and quickly and quietly give the red cards to other students. When the class has settled, ask who has a red card. State that they have all been infected with a disease. Ask how they became infected – contact; why it was easy to infect people in the room – closeness; how others in the room could avoid infection – stay away. | **Extend:** How would the scientists monitor the condition? | |

| Main | Support/Extend | Resources |
|---|---|---|
| **News report on an epidemic** (40 minutes) Divide the class into groups. Assign each group a particular disease outbreak or epidemic. Select anything topical, but examples could include Ebola, ash dieback, or influenza. The groups should write the script for a news report about the outbreak.<br><br>The report must discuss the following:<br>• what causes the disease, and how the pathogen causes illness<br>• the range of symptoms caused by the pathogen<br>• how the disease is spread, and why it is classified as a communicable disease<br>• numbers involved in the outbreaks<br>• conditions in the affected area<br>• how scientists are monitoring the spread of the disease<br>• control methods<br>• treatment.<br><br>The groups can produce the TV news item on tablets or similar, and play it for others to peer assess. | **Support:** Suggest suitable websites. Provide the students with the research headings suggested. Provide each student with a role for the TV broadcast.<br><br>**Extend:** The groups could also evaluate the control methods used. | **Activity:** News report on an epidemic |

| Plenary | Support/Extend | Resources |
|---|---|---|
| **Disease outbreak** (5 minutes) Use the interactive, which contains a paragraph explaining the outbreak and spread of Ebola. The paragraph has missing words, which students fill in. | | **Interactive:** Disease outbreak |
| **Typhoid Mary** (10 minutes) Tell the story of 'typhoid Mary' who worked in New York, or ask students to find the story on the internet. Then ask what caused the disease, how it spread, what the symptoms were, and how scientists treated her. | **Extend:** Students could evaluate the treatment methods the scientists used then and find out how the case would be treated today. | |

| Homework |
|---|
| Look at the list of methods by which pathogens can spread between plants or animals, such as touch, droplets, vectors, blood, sexual intercourse. Explain how the method works and provide an example for each method. |

A Kerboodle highlight for this lesson is **Webquest: The world's worst pathogen?** Refer to the **Content map** on Kerboodle for a full list of resources and assessment.

# B6.3.3 Preventing the spread of communicable diseases

**Specification links:**

B6.3e Explain how the spread of communicable diseases may be reduced or prevented in animals and plants. To include detection of the antigen, DNA testing, visual identification of the disease by a plant pathologist.

WS1.1e Explain everyday and technological applications of science.

WS1.1f Evaluate associated personal, social, economic, and environmental implications.

WS1.1g Make decisions based on the evaluation of evidence and arguments.

WS1.1h Evaluate risks both in practical science and the wider societal context.

WS1.4b Recognise the importance of scientific quantities and understand how they are determined.

BM6.3ii Construct and interpret frequency tables and diagrams, bar charts, and histograms (M2c).

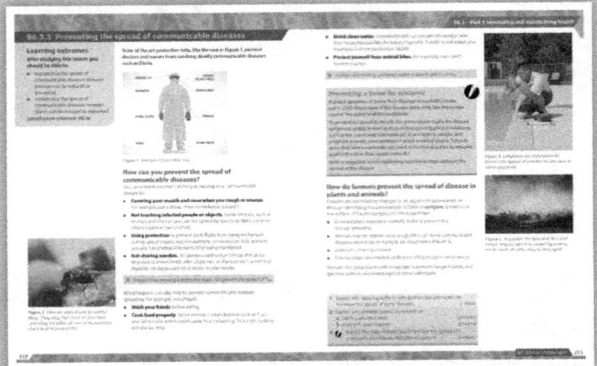

| Target | Outcome | Checkpoint | |
|---|---|---|---|
| | | Question | Activity |
| Aiming for GRADE 4 | Lists some methods of preventing the spread of a communicable disease. | 3 | Starter 1<br>Main<br>Plenary 1 and 2 |
| | Name a method of detecting whether or not an organism has been infected with a communicable disease. | | Starter 2<br>Main |
| | State that science has helped to reduce the spread of communicable diseases. | | Starter 1<br>Main<br>Plenary 2 |
| Aiming for GRADE 6 | Describe some methods of preventing the spread of communicable diseases in plants or animals. | A, B | Starter 1<br>Main<br>Plenary 1 and 2 |
| | Describe how scientists might test an organism to check for infection. | | Starter 2<br>Main |
| | Explain how the application of science has helped to reduce the spread of communicable diseases. | A, B, 1 | Starter 1<br>Main<br>Plenary 2 |
| Aiming for GRADE 8 | Explain how the spread of communicable diseases can be reduced or prevented in plants or animals. | A, B, 1, 2, 3 | Main<br>Plenary 2 |
| | Explain the importance of identifying infected organisms when trying to prevent the spread of a communicable disease. | | Main |
| | Evaluate the application of science in helping to reduce the spread of communicable diseases. | | Main |

**Maths**

Students will need to interpret frequency tables (M2c), containing data on the spread of disease.

**Literacy**

During the main activity, students will need to communicate effectively and sustain interest.

**Key words**

antigens

# B6.3—Part 1 Monitoring and maintaining health

| Starter | Support/Extend | Resources |
|---|---|---|
| **Coughs and sneezes** (10 minutes)  Show the class a public health poster, such as 'coughs and sneezes spread diseases'. Ask why governments produce posters like this. What was their aim? How informative are they? Do students think they work? Ask students to think of more recent examples, such as hand-washing campaigns during flu outbreaks. | **Extend:** Explain the science behind the poster. | |
| **Doctor, doctor!** (5 minutes)  If you were a doctor, how could you tell if your patient had a communicable disease? Allow the class to discuss this for a minute in groups, and then collect their answers. They will probably suggest asking about symptoms, and doing blood tests. Establish that, in blood tests, the blood is tested for pathogens and/or antigens. | **Extend:** Students could test for the presence of the pathogen's DNA. | |

| Main | Support/Extend | Resources |
|---|---|---|
| **Public health campaign** (40 minutes)  Students produce a detailed public health poster about the methods by which a communicable disease spreads. Divide the class into groups and give details about recent epidemics, for example, Swine flu in the UK, Ebola in Africa, MERS in South Korea, Cholera in Haiti, and so on. Groups research the disease and how it is spread. They then create a campaign to educate people about how to keep healthy and reduce the spread.<br><br>Each poster should include:<br>• An explanation of methods for preventing the spread of the diseases.<br>• A description of how to test to identify infected organisms.<br><br>Students use the Student Book or the internet to research the required information. | **Support:** Show a range of posters to give the students ideas. Possibly suggest headings, and focus on one or two diseases.<br><br>**Extend:** Explain how the application of scientific knowledge, and technological developments have improved this process. | **Activity:** Public health campaign |

| Plenary | Support/Extend | Resources |
|---|---|---|
| **Preventing the spread** (5 minutes)  Use the interactive in which students link the name of a method with a statement that explains how it prevents the spread of a communicable disease. | | **Interactive:** Preventing the spread |
| **Dr Semmelweis/Florence Nightingale** (10 minutes)  Tell the story, or show a film clip, to explain how Ignaz Semmelweis and/or Florence Nightingale introduced the idea of hygiene, including washing hands, to the medical profession. Ask the class to discuss this contribution in preventing the spread of disease. How important do they think it was? Explain how science has now provided an explanation for the success of the processes they introduced. | **Extend:** Suggest why Semmelweis found it difficult to convince other doctors at the time. | |

| Homework | | |
|---|---|---|
| Explain as many methods as possible taken in modern operating theatres by medical staff to prevent the spread of a communicable infection during an operation. | | |

**kerboodle**

A Kerboodle highlight for this lesson is **Literacy sheet: Preventing the spread of communicable diseases**. Refer to the **Content map** on Kerboodle for a full list of resources and assessment.

# B6.3.4 Human infections

**Specification links:**

B6.3f Describe a minimum of one common human infection, one plant disease, and sexually transmitted infections in humans including HIV/AIDS.

WS1.1e Explain everyday and technological applications of science.

WS1.1f Evaluate associated personal, social, economic, and environmental implications.

WS1.1h Evaluate risks both in practical science and the wider societal context.

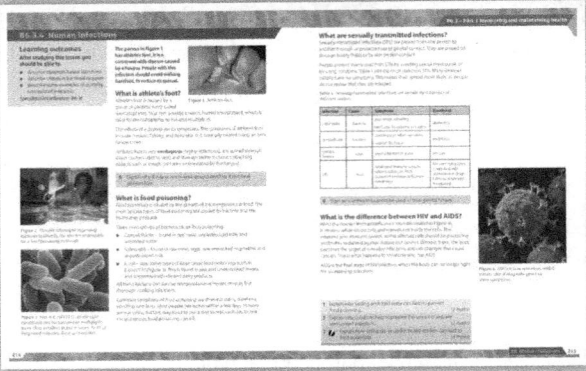

| Target | Outcome | Checkpoint | |
|---|---|---|---|
| | | Question | Activity |
| **Aiming for GRADE 4** ↓ | Name a fungal, a bacterial, and a sexually transmitted infection in humans. | | Starter 1 and 2<br>Main<br>Plenary 1 and 2 |
| | State a method of preventing the spread of each of a named fungal, bacterial, and sexually transmitted infection in humans. | | Starter 2<br>Main<br>Plenary 2 |
| | State that human diseases have some personal, social, and economic implications. | | Starter 2<br>Main<br>Plenary 2 |
| **Aiming for GRADE 6** ↓ | Describe the symptoms of at least one fungal, one bacterial, and one sexually transmitted infection in humans. | | Starter 1 and 2<br>Main<br>Plenary 2 |
| | Describe methods of preventing the spread of each of a named fungal, bacterial, and sexually transmitted infection in humans. | A, 1, 2, 3 | Starter 2<br>Main<br>Plenary 2 |
| | Describe some personal, social, and economic implications of a human disease. | | Starter 2<br>Main<br>Plenary 2 |
| **Aiming for GRADE 8** ↓ | Discuss the causes of and transmission of at least one fungal, one bacterial, and one sexually transmitted infection in humans. | A, 1, 2, 3 | Starter 2<br>Main<br>Plenary 2 |
| | Explain the treatment of each of a named fungal, bacterial and sexually transmitted infection in humans. | B | Main |
| | Evaluate the personal, social, and economic implications of a range of human diseases. | | Main<br>Plenary 2 |

**Maths**
During the main activity, students will need to interpret frequency tables (M2c), containing data on the case numbers.

**Literacy**
During the main activity, students will need communicate effectively and sustain interest.

**Key words**
contagious

# B6.3–Part 1 Monitoring and maintaining health

| Starter | Support/Extend | Resources |
|---|---|---|
| **What sort of disease?** (10 minutes) Write the names of diseases on sets of cards, one set per group (including athletes foot, ringworm, food poisoning, common cold, gonorrhoea, HIV/AIDS). Ask a series of questions and, for each question, give the groups a few seconds to choose and hold up the correct answer card. Questions could include: caused by a virus; a sexually transmitted disease; symptoms include a runny nose; caused by a bacteria; can be treated by antibiotics.<br><br>**Doctors' notes** (5 minutes) Present each group with an A3 sheet of paper, with three outlines of the human body, as well as a few sticky notes. Above each outline write the name of a viral, bacterial, and fungal disease. Read out a few statements, which cover the following areas:<br><br>Causes of the disease; its symptoms; methods of preventing the spread; an indication of personal risk.<br><br>Groups write each statement on a sticky note and stick it onto the most appropriate outline. | **Extend:** Discuss the treatment for the diseases, and the economic impact the disease might have. | |

| Main | Support/Extend | Resources |
|---|---|---|
| **Human infections** (40 minutes) Divide the class into six or more groups. Each group is to become an expert on one type of disease. They spend 20 minutes researching the disease to find answers to the following questions:<br><br>1. What causes the disease?<br>2. How is the disease transmitted?<br>3. What are the symptoms of the disease?<br>4. What are the global or national numbers of people with the disease?<br>5. In which parts of the world are people particularly at risk?<br>6. Does the disease interact with other diseases?<br>7. Is there any treatment for the disease? If so, what is it?<br><br>The groups teach other students about the disease they have learnt about. This could be done through short presentations, or members of each group could circulate to collect the information.<br><br>During the presentations, or as they circulate, students complete a table to note the answers to each question for each disease. | **Support:** Produce a writing frame, with each question listed, to structure the research. Also provide the Student Book and names of websites.<br><br>**Extend:** Students could evaluate the personal, social, and economic implications of the infections. | **Activity:** Human infections |

| Plenary | Support/Extend | Resources |
|---|---|---|
| **Human infections** (5 minutes) Use the interactive in which students sort diseases into whether they are caused by a bacteria, virus, or fungus.<br><br>**Diagnosis dilemma** (10 minutes) Write the names of several diseases on the board. Divide the class into teams. Team members take turns to act as the player. Read out a statement about a disease, and the players from each team come to the board and place their hand over the correct disease. The first to do so scores a point. Statements should cover causes, symptoms, prevention, treatment, and personal impact. | **Extend:** Statements could also cover economic impact. | **Interactive:** Human infections |

| Homework | | |
|---|---|---|
| Produce a leaflet for a doctors' surgery that describes the details of a named communicable disease. | | |

**kerboodle**

A Kerboodle highlight for this lesson is **Go further: HIV**. Refer to the **Content map** on Kerboodle for a full list of resources and assessment.

# B6.3.5 Plant diseases

**Specification links:**

B6.3f Describe a minimum of one common human infection, one plant disease, and sexually transmitted infections in humans including HIV/AIDS. To include plant diseases: virus tobacco mosaic virus (TMV), fungal *Erysiphe graminis* barley powdery mildew, bacterial *Agrobacterium tumafaciens* crown gall disease.

WS1.1e Explain everyday and technological applications of science.

WS1.1f Evaluate associated personal, social, economic, and environmental implications.

WS1.1g Make decisions based on the evaluation of evidence and arguments.

WS1.1h Evaluate risks both in practical science and the wider societal context.

WS1.4b Recognise the importance of scientific quantities and understand how they are determined.

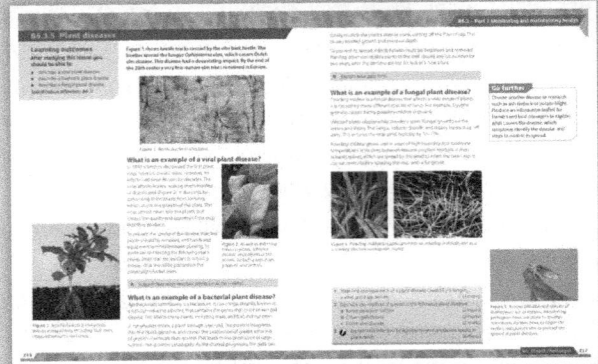

| Target | Outcome | Checkpoint | |
|---|---|---|---|
| | | Question | Activity |
| **Aiming for GRADE 4** | Name a viral, bacterial, and fungal plant disease. | 1 | Starter 2<br>Main<br>Plenary 1 and 2 |
| | State a method of preventing the spread of each of a named viral, bacterial, and fungal plant disease. | | Starter 1 and 2<br>Main |
| | State that plant diseases have some social and economic implications. | | Starter 1 and 2<br>Main<br>Plenary 2 |
| **Aiming for GRADE 6** | Describe each of a viral, bacterial, and fungal plant disease. | B, 2, 3 | Starter 2<br>Main<br>Plenary 1 and 2 |
| | Describe methods of preventing the spread of each of a named viral, bacterial, and fungal plant infection. | A | Starter 2<br>Main |
| | Describe some social and economic implications of a plant disease. | | Starter 2<br>Main<br>Plenary 2 |
| **Aiming for GRADE 8** | Discuss the causes and transmission of a viral, a bacterial, and a fungal plant disease. | 2, 3 | Main<br>Plenary 1 |
| | Explain how methods of preventing the spread of each of a named viral, bacterial, and fungal plant infection work. | | Main |
| | Evaluate the social and economic implications of a range of plant diseases. | | Main<br>Plenary 2 |

**Literacy**
During the main activity, students will need to communicate effectively and sustain interest.

## B6.3–Part 1 Monitoring and maintaining health

| Starter | Support/Extend | Resources |
|---|---|---|
| **True or false** (5 minutes)  Issue voting cards (green and red for true or false). Then ask a series of questions to introduce the idea that plants suffer from communicable diseases. Students vote true or false to each question. Questions could include: Do plants get diseases? Do they get communicable diseases? Can plants become infected by a virus? Do plants show symptoms? | **Extend:** Ask students to justify the vote. | |
| **Ash dieback** (10 minutes)  Show the class a short TV news item or newspaper article about a topical plant disease, such as ash dieback. Ask questions about the content of the film or newspaper article: What causes the disease? How does it spread? Can the spread be prevented and, if so, how? What are the economic implications of the disease? | **Support:** Make questions directly linked to a statement made in the film or article.<br>**Extend:** Ask students to discuss how the methods of prevention of spread actually work. | |

| Main | Support/Extend | Resources |
|---|---|---|
| **Country garden TV** (20 minutes)  Students imagine they work for the Department For Environment, Food and Rural Affairs (DEFRA). They have been asked to be the science advisor for a small item on a TV programme called Country garden. They will explain to the public about the causes and implications of plant diseases.<br>Students need to decide what information they need to supply to the public about the causes of plant diseases, how they are spread, and what methods are used to prevent their spread.<br>They could use the Student Book to discuss specific diseases. | **Support:** Suggest the areas that need to be discussed in the item.<br>**Extend:** Students could also justify why they have included the information and consider the economic implications of plant diseases. | |
| **Preventing the spread of plant diseases** (20 minutes)  Still working for DEFRA, students now plan an experiment that could be carried out to test the effectiveness of a given method of preventing the spread of a plant disease. Students should consider variables, fair testing, sample size, bias, and how to analyse data. | **Support:** List the areas that must be considered in the plan.<br>**Extend:** Students could also include the time scales needed, how to include a control, and consider the ethics of risking the spread of a disease from the sample area to other crops. | **Activity:** Preventing the spread of plant diseases |

| Plenary | Support/Extend | Resources |
|---|---|---|
| **What is the disease?** (5 minutes)  Use the interactive in which students see a series of images of plant diseases and match them to the names of the diseases. | | **Interactive:** What is the disease? |
| **The cost of plant diseases** (10 minutes)  Read a poem about the Irish potato famine, for example, 'At a potato digging' by Seamus Heaney. Ask the class to consider the economic and social impact of a potato disease. Consider modern implications of a plant disease. This could include reference to food prices, ability to feed people, tourism, etc. | | |

| Homework | | |
|---|---|---|
| Imagine you are a horticulturalist. You need to produce a self-help questionnaire that a gardener can follow to establish if plants in their garden have a disease, and then suggests what to do about it. | | |

B6 Global challenges

# GCSE BIOLOGY ONLY
## B6.3.6 Plant defences

**Specification links:**

B6.3g Describe physical plant defence responses to disease. To include leaf cuticle, cell wall.

B6.3h Describe chemical plant defence responses. To include antimicrobial substances.

WS1.1h Evaluate risks both in practical science and the wider societal context.

WS2a Carry out experiments.

WS2b Make and record observations and measurements using a range of apparatus and methods.

WS2c Present observations using appropriate methods.

WS2d Communicate the scientific rational for investigations, methods used, findings, and reasoned conclusions.

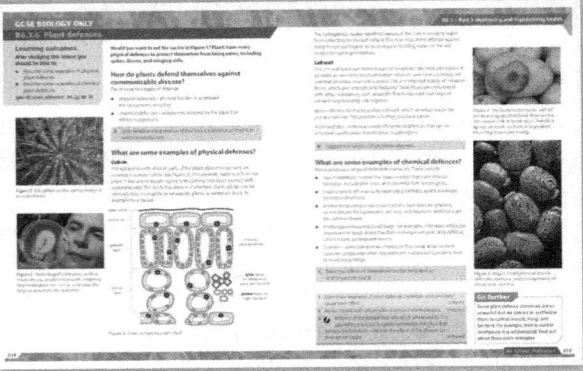

| Target | Outcome | Checkpoint | |
|---|---|---|---|
| | | Question | Activity |
| **Aiming for GRADE 4** | Name a physical plant defence. | A | Starter 1 and 2, Plenary 1 |
| | Name a chemical plant defence. | C, 1 | Starter 1 and 2, Main, Plenary 1 and 2 |
| | Identify some major risks in a practical scientific procedure. | | Main |
| **Aiming for GRADE 6** | Describe some examples of physical plant defences. | A | Starter 1 and 2, Plenary 1 |
| | Describe some examples of chemical plant defences. | B, C, 1 | Starter 1 and 2, Main, Plenary 1 and 2 |
| | Describe most of the risks in a practical scientific procedure. | | Main |
| **Aiming for GRADE 8** | Explain how physical plant defences protect the plant from plant diseases. | 2 | Starter 2, Plenary 1 |
| | Explain how chemical plant defences protect the plant from plant diseases. | | Starter 2, Main, Plenary 1 and 2 |
| | Evaluate all major risks in a practical scientific procedure. | | Main |

**Maths**
During the main activity, students will need to record results to an appropriate number of significant figures (M2a) and calculate arithmetic means (M2b).

**Literacy**
During the main activity, students will need to produce coherent, well-structured responses to questions.

## B6.3–Part 1 Monitoring and maintaining health

| Starter | Support/Extend | Resources |
|---|---|---|
| **Plant protection** (5 minutes)    Ask the question, 'How do animals prevent themselves becoming infected by a pathogen?' Briefly discuss students' ideas. Then ask, 'Does a plant have a way of preventing infection?' They will probably know little here, so tell them about the thick cell walls and so on. Now ask, What do human bodies do when they are infected? They will probably mention white blood cells. Then ask, 'Does the plant have any internal protection against disease?' In answer to this question, mention one or two chemical defence methods. | | |
| **Physical and chemical defences** (10 minutes)    Define physical defence mechanisms and chemical defences in plants. Then present the class with a list of defence mechanisms and ask groups to classify them as physical methods or chemical methods. Then provide an image of a section through a leaf blade. Ask them to annotate the drawings in the appropriate place with the physical methods and then the chemical methods. | **Extend:** Explain how each mechanism might work. Discuss which of the mechanisms prevent entry of the pathogen (primary responses) and which deal with the pathogen when it has entered (secondary responses). Identify which are passive and which are active responses by the plant. | |

| Main | Support/Extend | Resources |
|---|---|---|
| **Investigating chemical defences in plants** (40 minutes)    Tell students that they will be carrying out an experiment looking at the effect of extracts of mint and garlic on the growth of bacteria. Students begin by reading the method and completing a risk assessment sheet.<br><br>Students will need to plate bacteria (either *E. coli* or live yoghurt). They will also need to make extracts of mint and garlic by grinding the mint leaves or garlic cloves in a pestle and mortar with a little distilled water. Soak filter paper discs in the extract and place these in the centre of the Petri dish, or create a well with a sterile cork borer and fill the well with the extract. Set up repeats. Fix the lid with four short lengths of tape. Do not seal all the way round. Incubate for 24–48 hours, at 25 °C.<br><br>In the next lesson, seal all the way round to prevent accidental opening, and measure the zone of inhibition in four directions (north, south, east, and west). Record the results in a table. Calculate the mean size of the zone of inhibition for both garlic and mint.<br><br>Ask the students questions about the relative effect of the two extracts. Do the plants produce natural antibacterial chemicals as a chemical defence against plant diseases? | **Support:** You could use plates with a mix of agar and bacterial suspension already plated out.<br><br>**Support:** Aid might be required in the calculating of a mean.<br><br>**Extend:** Questions should ask students to explain how the antibacterial substances work. | **Practical:** Investigating chemical defences in plants |

| Plenary | Support/Extend | Resources |
|---|---|---|
| **Physical and chemical plant defences** (5 minutes)    Use the interactive in which students select the correct physical defences from a range of plant defences.<br><br>**Toothpaste** (10 minutes)    Ask students to think about the experiment in the main activity, and suggest why mint is often in toothpaste, but garlic is not. Then consider other examples of plant defences given in the Student Book. | | **Interactive:** Physical and chemical plant defences |

| Homework |
|---|
| Design a clinical trial to measure how effective mint extracts in toothpaste actually are. Consider the method, sample size, and controlling the subjects' lifestyles for the experiment period. |

**kerboodle**

A Kerboodle highlight for this lesson is **Working Scientifically: Plant antibiotics**. Refer to the **Content map** on Kerboodle for a full list of resources and assessment.

# GCSE BIOLOGY ONLY — HIGHER TIER
## B6.3.7 Identification of plant disease

**Specification links:**

B6.3i Describe different ways plant diseases can be detected and identified, in the lab and in the field. To include the laboratory detection of the DNA or antigen from the disease-causing organism. The field diagnosis by observation and microscopy.

WS1.1e Explain everyday and technological applications of science.

WS2a Carry out experiments.

WS2b Make and record observations and measurements using a range of apparatus and methods.

WS2c Present observations using appropriate methods.

WS2d Communicate the scientific rational for investigations, methods used, findings, and reasoned conclusions.

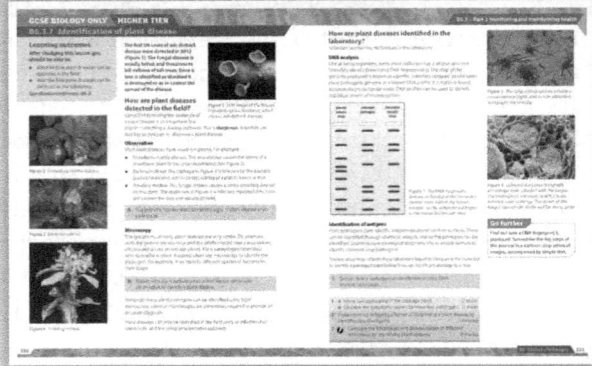

| Target | Outcome | Checkpoint | |
|---|---|---|---|
| | | Question | Activity |
| **Aiming for GRADE 6** ↓ | Describe how plant diseases can be detected in the field. | 1 | Starter 1 and 2<br>Plenary 1 |
| | Describe how plant diseases can be detected in the laboratory. | C | Starter 2<br>Main<br>Plenary 1 and 2 |
| | Discuss how everyday observation techniques have been used to diagnose plant diseases. | 3 | Starter 1 and 2<br>Plenary 1 |
| **Aiming for GRADE 8** ↓ | Evaluate the limitations of field testing to identify a plant disease. | A, B, 3 | Starter 1 and 2<br>Plenary 1 |
| | Explain how DNA analysis and ELISA tests are used in the laboratory to identify a plant disease. | C, 3 | Starter 2<br>Main<br>Plenary 1 and 2 |
| | Explain how technology has improved the identification of plant pathogens. | B, 2, 3 | Main<br>Plenary 1 and 2 |

**Literacy**
During the main activity, students will need to produce coherent, well-structured sentences with appropriate scientific vocabulary to explain their findings.

**Key words**
diagnosis

# B6.3—Part 1 Monitoring and maintaining health

| Starter | Support/Extend | Resources |
|---|---|---|
| **Field testing** (5 minutes)  Show images of plant diseases, for example, barley powdery mildew on leaves, crown gall disease, and tobacco mosaic virus. Ask students what they observe. How would microscopy help in their observations? If possible, show microscope images of these diseases. Could a plant pathologist identify the disease? If so, how?<br><br>**Detecting plant infections** (10 minutes)  Provide a list of four different techniques for diagnosing plant infections: field observation, microscopy, DNA analysis, and antigen identification. Ask students to outline how these methods might work. Which is the simplest, and which the most difficult? Which provides the most information? What are the cost implications? | **Extend:** Ask students to answer the following question. How could more detailed identification be attempted? | |

| Main | Support/Extend | Resources |
|---|---|---|
| **ELISA tests for antigens** (35 minutes)  Use a commercial kit to carry out an ELISA test for antigens. The different kits available have slightly different methods so follow the methods provided by the manufacturer. However, all kits will produce a colour change, indicating the presence of an antigen in the sample (which would have been extracted from an infected plant). As the students perform the procedure, discuss with them how the process identifies antigens from a plant pathogen. This antigen is first attached to the wall of the vessel by a receptor attached to the wall. It then remains on the wall throughout the test. By attaching a labelled antibody to the antigen, a colour change is produced, identifying the antigen.<br>SAFETY: Follow CLEAPSS safety guidance.<br><br>**DNA analysis** (5 minutes)  Present a series of five statements in a random order. Students put the statements in the correct order to describe the main steps in the process of the analysis of pathogen DNA. | **Extend:** Discuss how this technique has advanced our ability to detect a plant pathogen. | ELISA test for antigens |

| Plenary | Support/Extend | Resources |
|---|---|---|
| **Reviewing analysis techniques** (5 minutes)  Use the interactive to complete a paragraph about the advances in techniques to identify plant diseases. The paragraph contains gaps, which the students fill using a dropdown menu.<br><br>**Diagnosis DNA** (10 minutes)  Provide the students with an image of the DNA banding pattern produced in DNA analysis. Students should be able to identify which pathogen's DNA is present in the sample taken from the infected plant. Ask them how these new techniques have improved our ability to diagnose disease, and to identify any disadvantages of these new techniques. | | **Interactive:** Reviewing analysis techniques |

| Homework |
|---|
| Find an animation online that explains how the ELISA test works. Then write a short account of how this technique is used by plant pathologists to identify a plant disease. |

# B6.3.8 Blood and body defence mechanisms

**Specification links:**

B6.3j Explain how white blood cells and platelets are adapted to their defence functions in the blood.

B6.3k Describe the non-specific defence systems of the human body against pathogens.

B6.3l Explain the role of the immune system of the human body in defence against disease.

WS1.1b Use models to solve problems, make predictions, and to develop scientific explanations and understanding of familiar and unfamiliar facts.

WS1.4a Use scientific vocabulary, terminology, and definitions.

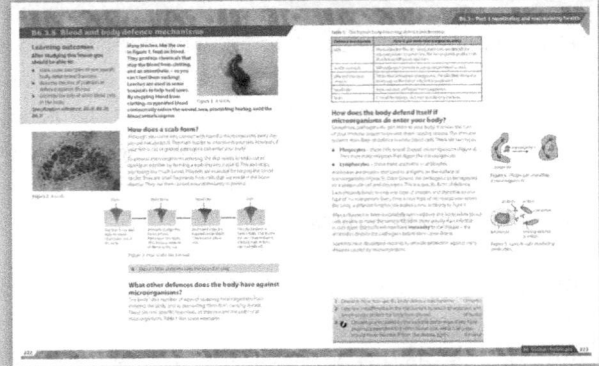

| Target | Outcome | Checkpoint | |
|---|---|---|---|
| | | Question | Activity |
| **Aiming for GRADE 4** | State some examples of the primary body defence mechanisms (nonspecific). | 1 | Starter 1<br>Main<br>Plenary 2 |
| | Name the two main types of white blood cells. | | Starter 2<br>Main<br>Plenary 1 and 2 |
| ↓ | Recognise that models can be used to illustrate a body process. | | Main |
| **Aiming for GRADE 6** | Describe the role of platelets in defence against disease. | A, 1 | Starter 1<br>Main<br>Plenary 2 |
| | Describe the role of white blood cells in the body. | 2 | Starter 2<br>Main<br>Plenary 1 and 2 |
| ↓ | Illustrate a body defence mechanism using models. | | Main |
| **Aiming for GRADE 8** | Explain the sequence of events that results in scab formation. | A | Main<br>Plenary 2 |
| | Explain the process of antibody formation by lymphocytes. | B, 3 | Main<br>Plenary 1 and 2 |
| ↓ | Use a model to develop a scientific explanation and understanding of a body defence mechanism. | | Main |

**Literacy**
During the main activity, students will need to communicate effectively and sustain the listener's interest. They will also use vocabulary fit for purpose.

**Key words**
immunity, lymphocytes, phagocytes

## B6.3–Part 1 Monitoring and maintaining health

| Starter | Support/Extend | Resources |
|---|---|---|
| **Blood and body defence mechanisms** (10 minutes) Interactive activity in which students match the diagram of the cell to the correct name. They then sort descriptions into the correct categories to decide which blood cell they are describing.<br><br>**White blood cells** (5 minutes) Either show an image of a blood smear, or use microscopes and prepared slides. Ask students to describe what they see. They should recognise different cell types. Assist them to identify the red blood cells and two distinct types of white blood cells. | **Extend:** If students do not mentions cuts and scab formation, prompt them to discuss it.<br><br>**Extend:** Discuss the function of the blood cells. | **Interactive:** Blood and body defence mechanisms |

| Main | Support/Extend | Resources |
|---|---|---|
| **Blood-curdling movies** (40 minutes) Divide students into three groups and allocate each group one of the following topics:<br>• blood clotting and platelets<br>• phagocytes and phagocytosis (nonspecific immune response)<br>• lymphocytes and antibody production (specific immune response).<br>Allow students 30 minutes to produce an animated film using tablets to illustrate and explain the process they have been allocated. The films could involve models, drawings, or construction paper.<br>Finally, the students show their films to other groups for peer assessment. | **Support:** Provide a storyboard with scene titles. Students then find the information for each scene.<br><br>**Extend:** Their films must contain explanations of the processes. | **Activity:** Human defense systems |

| Plenary | Support/Extend | Resources |
|---|---|---|
| **Blood cell types** (5 minutes) Use the interactive, which contains images of a red blood cell, a phagocyte, and a lymphocyte. Students sort a series of statements about the structure and function of the cells, and drag them into the correct column.<br><br>**Immune system quiz** (10 minutes) One student sits at the centre of the class. The teacher selects another student to ask a question of the student in the centre about the topic of the lesson. If the student gets the answer correct, select another student to ask another question. If the student in the centre gets the question wrong, they give up the seat for the person who asks the question. The student left on the seat at the end is the winner. | | |

| Homework | | |
|---|---|---|
| Write a section for a first aid manual to explain why it is important to cover cuts with dressings. | | |

**kerboodle**

A Kerboodle highlight for this lesson is **Bump up your grade: Defense mechanisms of the human body**. Refer to the **Content map** on Kerboodle for a full list of resources and assessment.

# GCSE BIOLOGY ONLY — HIGHER TIER
## B6.3.9 Monoclonal antibodies

**Specification links:**

B6.3m Describe how monoclonal antibodies are produced.

B6.3n Describe some of the ways in which monoclonal antibodies can be used. To include their role in detecting antigens in pregnancy testing, detection of diseases (prostate cancer), and potentially treating disease (targeting cancer cells).

WS1.1c Understand the power and limitations of science.

WS1.1d Discuss ethical issues arising from developments in science.

WS1.1e Explain everyday and technological applications of science.

WS1.4a Use scientific vocabulary, terminology, and definitions.

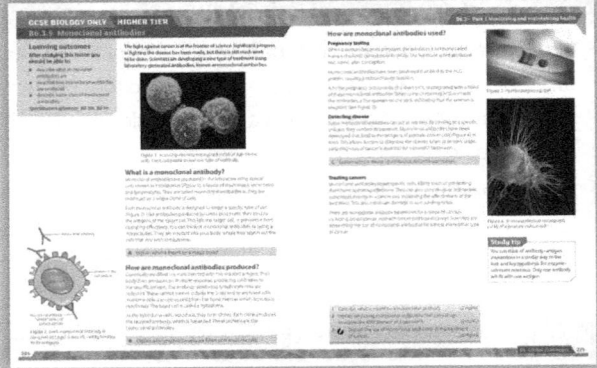

| Target | Outcome | Checkpoint | |
|---|---|---|---|
| | | Question | Activity |
| **Aiming for GRADE 6** | Describe what monoclonal antibodies are. | 1 | Starter 1 and 2<br>Main<br>Plenary 1 |
| | Describe some uses of monoclonal antibodies. | A, 3 | Starter 1 and 2<br>Main<br>Plenary 2 |
| | Describe how advances in science have improved the quality of life. | 2, 3 | Starter 1 and 2<br>Main<br>Plenary 2 |
| **Aiming for GRADE 8** | Explain how monoclonal antibodies are produced. | B | Main<br>Plenary 1 |
| | Explain why a monoclonal antibody's specificity to a target antigen makes it useful. | A, C, 2, 3 | Starter 1 and 2<br>Main<br>Plenary 2 |
| | Evaluate the limitations in the advances in monoclonal antibody science. | 2, 3 | Starter 2<br>Main<br>Plenary 2 |

**Literacy**
During the main activity, students will need to communicate effectively, using appropriate scientific vocabulary.

**Key words**
monoclonal antibodies

## B6.3–Part 1 Monitoring and maintaining health

| Starter | Support/Extend | Resources |
|---|---|---|
| **Blood grouping** (10 minutes)   Ask students about blood groups and how we test for them. Discuss the antigens and antibodies involved. Explain that we are able to mass-produce the antibodies as monoclonal antibodies to produce blood grouping tests. Demonstrate the blood grouping test using a school testing kit. | **Extend:** Discuss specificity. Discuss the use of monoclonal antibodies in the ELISA testing kit. | |
| **Magic bullets** (5 minutes)   Give each group two jigsaw pieces that fit together. One jigsaw piece is coloured and labelled a cancer cell. The second jigsaw piece represents an antibody. Define the term monoclonal antibodies and then ask students to fit the antibody to the cell. Then ask them to explain in cellular terms how the cells can connect (antigen/antibody interactions). Next add a coloured marker to the antibody and tell students that it represents an anti-cancer drug. Ask them to explain how this might destroy the cancer cell. | **Extend:** Discuss why 'magic bullets' are not a universal cure. | |

| Main | Support/Extend | Resources |
|---|---|---|
| **Monoclonal antibodies** (40 minutes)   Discuss with the class what monoclonal antibodies are and explain how they are made. Ask them to use the information in the Student Book to summarise this in writing. Then explain to students how pregnancy tests use monoclonal antibodies.<br><br>Students create a leaflet found in a pregnancy test explaining how it works using simple diagrams.<br><br>Students could use the Internet to further research the use of monoclonal antibodies for their leaflets. | **Extend:** Students could consider the ethical issues of producing monoclonal antibodies.<br><br>**Support:** Supply important key words or steps for them to include. | **Activity:** Monoclonal antibodies |

| Plenary | Support/Extend | Resources |
|---|---|---|
| **Order the stages** (5 minutes)   Use the interactive to drag and drop a series of statements about the production of monoclonal antibodies into the correct sequence. | | **Interactive:** Order the stages |
| **How useful are monoclonal antibodies?** (10 minutes)   Draw a line on the board (or on the floor), which represents a scale of 1 to 10, where 1 represents no improvement in the quality of life and 10 represents a major improvement in the quality of life. Then read out a series of applications of monoclonal antibodies, and ask the students to position each application on the scale and to justify their choice of position. | | |

| Homework | | |
|---|---|---|
| Produce a leaflet for a pregnancy testing kit to explain how it works. It should include some description of how the monoclonal antibodies are made. | | |

**kerboodle**

A Kerboodle highlight for this lesson is **Go further: Monoclonal antibodies: magic bullets?** Refer to the **Content map** on Kerboodle for a full list of resources and assessment.

# B6.3.10 Vaccinations

**Specification links:**

B6.3o Explain the use of vaccines and medicines in the prevention and treatment of disease. To include antibiotics, antivirals, and antiseptics.

WS1.1c Understand the power and limitations of science.

WS1.1e Explain everyday and technological applications of science.

WS1.1f Evaluate associated personal, social, economic, and environmental implications.

WS1.1g Make decisions based on the evaluation of evidence and arguments.

WS1.1h Evaluate risks both in practical science and the wider societal context.

BM6.1i Translate information between graphical and numerical forms (M4a).

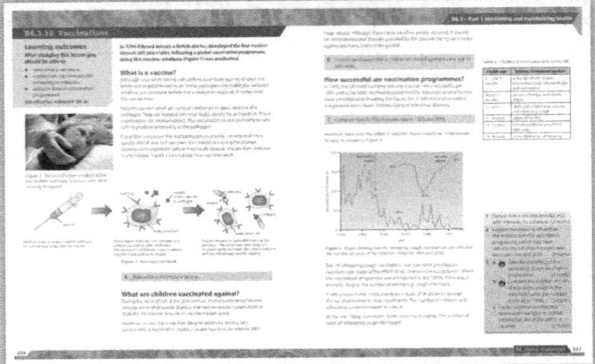

| Target | Outcome | Checkpoint | |
|---|---|---|---|
| | | Question | Activity |
| Aiming for GRADE 4 | State what a vaccine is. | A | Starter 1<br>Main<br>Plenary 1 |
| | List some diseases against which we can be vaccinated. | B | Starter 1 and 2<br>Main |
| | State the personal benefit of a vaccination. | 3 | Starter 2<br>Main<br>Plenary 2 |
| Aiming for GRADE 6 | Describe the development of vaccines. | | Starter 1<br>Main |
| | Describe the impact of vaccination programmes on case numbers. | C, 3 | Starter 2<br>Main<br>Plenary 2 |
| | Describe the implications of a vaccination programme on society. | C, 3 | Starter 2<br>Main<br>Plenary 2 |
| Aiming for GRADE 8 | Explain how vaccines provide immunity to a disease. | 1 | Main<br>Plenary 1 |
| | Evaluate data on vaccination programmes. | C, 2, 3 | Homework |
| | Evaluate the personal, social, and economic implications of a vaccination programme. | C, 3 | Main<br>Plenary 2 |

**Maths**
During the main activity, students will need to translate information between graphical and numeric forms (M4a).

**Literacy**
During the main activity, students will need to communicate effectively and sustain the reader's interest.

**Key words**
vaccine

## B6.3—Part 1 Monitoring and maintaining health

| Starter | Support/Extend | Resources |
|---|---|---|
| **Discovering vaccines** (10 minutes) Show a short film on the life and work of Edward Jenner, or tell the story of Jenner's work. Then hold a discussion about the methods he used, the importance of his discovery, and the effect of his discovery on the population.<br><br>**Vaccination data** (5 minutes) Ask students if they have been vaccinated and why, or discuss a local outbreak that might have triggered a vaccination programme, for example, the measles outbreak in Swansea in 2013. List vaccinations students have had and ask about the impacts of vaccination programmes. Discuss case numbers (specific numbers will be used in the homework). | **Extend:** Introduce the idea of eradicated diseases, for example, smallpox and the extent of polio eradication.<br><br>**Extend:** Discuss how effective a vaccination programme is, for example, the annual flu vaccination programme. | |

| Main | Support/Extend | Resources |
|---|---|---|
| **Jenner Museum** (40 minutes) Students must imagine they work for the Jenner Museum in Berkeley, Gloucestershire. They plan to develop a new wing to explain to the public how vaccinations work. Students split into groups to develop five information boards to answer the following questions:<br><br>1. What are vaccines, and how are they made?<br>2. How do we administer the vaccine?<br>3. How does the immune system respond?<br>4. How does this give us immunity?<br>5. What is the impact of a vaccination programme?<br><br>Each group produces one of the boards and together these boards will tell the whole story. | **Support:** Some questions (questions 1 and 2) are more accessible than others and so might better suit some groups. You could provide prompting questions to help students to research and plan. | **Activity:** Jenner museum |

| Plenary | Support/Extend | Resources |
|---|---|---|
| **Vaccination** (5 minutes) Use the interactive in which students put statements into the correct order for how vaccination works.<br><br>**Vaccines on balance** (10 minutes) Draw a see-saw on the board. Groups have sticky notes and stick them on either end of the see-saw to suggest advantages or disadvantages of the use of vaccination. Then discuss each point made and ask students to justify the statements. Add any major omissions. Finally, evaluate the importance of each statement. | **Support:** Do this as a class activity rather than groups. | **Interactive:** Vaccination |

| Homework | | |
|---|---|---|
| Look at data about the 2013 measles outbreak in Swansea (available on the NHS Wales website). Describe and explain the impact of the vaccinations on the outbreak. Evaluate the effectiveness of the programme. Should children be vaccinated against measles? | **Extend:** Discuss why people in the area stopped having the MMR vaccine. | |

**kerboodle**

A Kerboodle highlight for this lesson is **Extension: Impact of vaccination**. Refer to the **Content map** on Kerboodle for a full list of resources and assessment.

# B6.3.11 Prevention and treatment of disease

**Specification links:**

B6.3o Explain the use of vaccines and medicines in the prevention and treatment of disease. To include antibiotics, antivirals, and antiseptics.

B6.3p Explain the aseptic techniques used in culturing organisms. To include use of alcohol, flaming, autoclaving of glassware and growth media, and measures used to stop contaminants falling onto/into the growth media (for example, working around a Bunsen burner). **S**

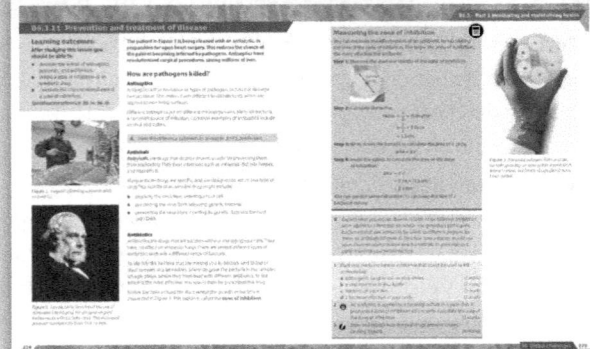

WS1.1g Make decisions based on the evaluation of evidence and arguments.

WS1.1h Evaluate risks both in practical science and the wider societal context.

WS1.2c Apply a knowledge of a range of techniques, instruments, apparatus, and materials to select those appropriate to the experiment.

WS1.3c Carrying out and representing mathematical and statistical analysis.

WS2a Carry out experiments.

WS2b Make and record observations and measurements using a range of apparatus and methods.

WS2c Presenting observations using appropriate methods.

WS2d Communicating the scientific rational for investigations, methods used, findings, and reasoned conclusions.

M2b Find arithmetic means.

M3d Solve simple algebraic equations.

| Target | Outcome | Checkpoint | |
|---|---|---|---|
| | | Question | Activity |
| **Aiming for GRADE 4** | State what antiseptics, antivirals, and antibiotics are used to destroy. | A, 1, 3 | Starter 1 and 2<br>Main<br>Plenary 1 and 2 |
| | Describe what a zone of inhibition is. | | Main<br>Plenary 2 |
| | Use some practical observations to decide on a use of an antiseptic. | | Main<br>Plenary 2 |
| **Aiming for GRADE 6** | Describe the action of antiseptics, antivirals, and antibiotics. | 3 | Starter 1 and 2<br>Main<br>Plenary 1 |
| | Describe how to measure the size of the zone of inhibition. | 2 | Main<br>Plenary 2 |
| | Use practical evidence to describe that different antiseptics have different levels of effectiveness. | | Main<br>Plenary 2 |
| **Aiming for GRADE 8** | Explain why antibiotics have no effect on viruses. | | Starter 1 and 2<br>Main<br>Plenary 1 |
| | Explain why different antiseptics or antibiotics produce different-sized zones of inhibition. | B | Main<br>Plenary 2 |
| | Evaluate practical evidence to make decisions about the most appropriate use for an antiseptic. | | Main<br>Plenary 2 |

## B6.3—Part 1 Monitoring and maintaining health

**Maths**
Students will need to either calculate a mean (M2b), or calculate an area by solving simple algebraic equations (M3d).

**Literacy**
During the main activity, students will use scientific vocabulary appropriate to purpose.

**Key words**
antiseptic, antivirals, zone of inhibition

| Starter | Support/Extend | Resources |
|---|---|---|
| **Antivirals, antiseptics, and antibiotics** (5 minutes)   Write the three names on the board or on cards and ask students the following questions: Where might you have used any of these substances? What do they do? Do you need a prescription to obtain them? | **Extend:** Ask students where might these substances be of no use? Will antibiotics treat a viral infection? | |
| **Antiseptics** (10 minutes)   Show a short film on the work of Joseph Lister (or tell the story). Discuss his contributions to the prevention of disease. What are the limitations of his discovery? Where are antiseptics less useful? If time, repeat for Alexander Fleming and penicillin. | | |

| Main | Support/Extend | Resources |
|---|---|---|
| **Investigating the effect of antiseptics on bacterial growth** (40 minutes)   Technicians prepare five agar plates per group using nutrient agar supplemented with glucose. Students use sterile technique to plate out live yoghurt bacteria, using a glass spreader sterilised by dipping in alcohol and passing through a flame. Set up about five plates per group. Allow this to settle for a few minutes. Students cut small discs of filter paper and soak them in five different types of liquid antiseptic. To the centre of each plate they add a disc containing one of the antiseptics. Then they fix the lid with four short lengths of tape, taking care not to seal all the way round. Incubate the plates at 25 °C for 24–48 hours. Next lesson, students draw a ring around the bacterial growth indicating the zone of inhibition, on the outside of the plate. They should measure the size of the zone of inhibition by measuring the radius in four directions from the disc to the edge of the zone and calculating a mean. Alternatively, they can calculate area if the zone is a circle. Ask students to write a conclusion about the relative strength of the different antiseptics, based on their results. SAFETY: Alcohol is highly flammable. | **Support:** Provide a results table to record the results. Only measure the four directions and calculate a mean. **Extend:** Questions should evaluate the potential uses of the different antiseptics, based on the results. | **Practical:** Investigating the effect of antiseptics on bacterial growth |

| Plenary | Support/Extend | Resources |
|---|---|---|
| **The three 'antis'!** (5 minutes)   Use the interactive in which students drag and drop statements into one of three categories: antiseptics, antibiotics, and antivirals. The statements refer to the action and uses of the three substances. | | **Interactive:** The three 'antis'! |
| **Incubating bacteria** (10 minutes)   Set the scenario: on a maternity ward, staff want to wash possibly infected incubators with antiseptic, but how concentrated should the solutions be? Ask the class to talk through an experiment designed to assess what concentration to use. How will they explain the effect of different concentrations? How could they measure this? Why can they not use a highly concentrated bleach in the incubator? What bacteria will they use in the tests? | **Extend:** Explain how the antiseptics cause the zone of inhibition. | |

| Homework | | | |
|---|---|---|---|
| Write a description of how you could modify this experiment to test the effects of a variety of different antibiotics (or concentrations of antibiotic) on bacteria. | | | |

**kerboodle**
A Kerboodle highlight for this lesson is **Literacy interactive: Prevention and treatment of disease**. Refer to the **Content map** on Kerboodle for a full list of resources and assessment.

**B6 Global challenges** 229

# GCSE BIOLOGY ONLY
## B6.3.12 Aseptic technique

**Specification links:**

B6.3p Explain the aseptic techniques used in culturing organisms. To include use of alcohol, flaming, autoclaving of glassware and growth media, and measures used to stop contaminants falling onto/into the growth media (for example, working around a Bunsen burner).

WS1.1e Explain everyday and technological applications of science.

WS1.1g Make decisions based on the evaluation of evidence and arguments.

WS1.1h Evaluate risks both in practical science and the wider societal context.

WS1.2c Apply a knowledge of a range of techniques, instruments, apparatus, and materials to select those appropriate to the experiment.

WS2a Carry out experiments.

WS2b Make and record observations and measurements using a range of apparatus and methods.

WS2c Present observations using appropriate methods.

WS2d Communicate the scientific rational for investigations, methods used, findings, and reasoned conclusions.

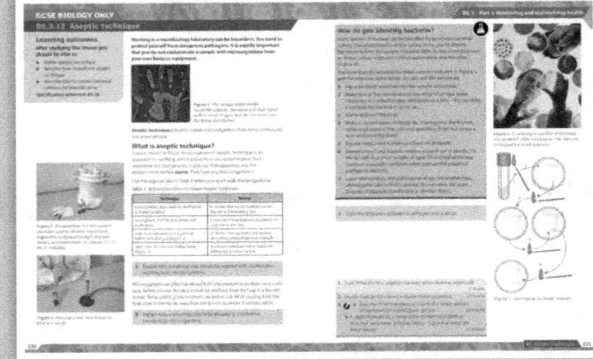

| Target | Outcome | Checkpoint | |
|---|---|---|---|
| | | Question | Activity |
| **Aiming for GRADE 4** | State what is meant by aseptic technique. | | Starter 2, Main, Plenary 1 |
| | Describe briefly how to transfer bacteria from one medium to another. | B | Starter 1, Main |
| | Identify hazards in a practical procedure. | A | Main, Plenary 2 |
| **Aiming for GRADE 6** | Describe how to perform aseptic technique. | A, 1 | Starter 2, Main, Plenary 1 |
| | Describe how to streak for single colonies. | B, 3 | Starter 1, Main |
| | Assess the risks caused by hazards in a practical procedure. | A, C | Main, Plenary 2 |
| **Aiming for GRADE 8** | Explain how methods used in aseptic technique work. | A, 1, 2 | Starter 2, Main, Plenary 1 |
| | Describe how to isolate bacterial colonies for identification. | 3 | Starter 1, Main |
| | Evaluate all the major risks in a practical procedure and suggest control measures for those risks. | A, C | Main, Plenary 2 |

**Literacy**
During the main activity, students will need to use vocabulary appropriate to purpose.

**Key words**
aseptic technique, sterile

## B6.3–Part 1 Monitoring and maintaining health

| Starter | Support/Extend | Resources |
|---|---|---|
| **Single colonies** (10 minutes) In groups, have students pour a small beaker of sand into a deep tray. Using a paint brush they mimic the streaking process by running the brush through the sand lightly, dragging some of it to one side. Then they repeat this at right angles, and then repeat for a third time. This should thin the sand out, such that individual grains can be seen. Explain the comparison to streaking for single colonies. | | |
| **Contamination from the air** (5 minutes) Ask students if the air in the room is clean, or sterile. Then have an open Petri dish with agar on the desk in front of you. Coat a powder puff with talc and create a small talc cloud above the desk. Whilst the cloud settles, compare the talc to bacteria in the air. Then lift the Petri dish to show the dust particles that have stuck to the plate. Discuss various ways of preventing contamination. | **Extend:** Discuss the more complicated methods, such as convection currents. | |

| Main | Support/Extend | Resources |
|---|---|---|
| **Streaking for single colonies** (40 minutes) Use the method on the activity sheet and in the Student Book. Prepare agar plates using nutrient agar supplemented with glucose. | **Extend:** Try to identify the shapes and colours of the bacteria colonies, and any contaminants. Some bacteria colonies can be identified online. | **Practical:** Streaking for single colonies |
| Students carry out a risk assessment. They have carried out plating activities before, so should have a reasonable idea of the risks. | | |
| Use aseptic technique to plate out bacteria using the streaking method. Fix the lid with four short lengths of tape. Do not seal all the way round. Incubate them at 25 °C for 24–48 hours. | | |
| Next lesson, observe the plates to see if single colonies have formed and note the levels of contamination. | | |
| Students write conclusions giving reasons for each step. | | |

| Plenary | Support/Extend | Resources |
|---|---|---|
| **How to grow bacteria** (5 minutes) Use the interactive activity in which students put the steps of the method used to prepare a culture of bacteria in the correct order. | | **Interactive:** How to grow bacteria |
| **Evaluating your risk assessment** (10 minutes) Have a short class discussion about how students completed their risk assessment. Were all of the major hazards identified? Did they evaluate the potential level of risk correctly? Have they considered what will happen to the plates after the practical activity is complete? Are there any additional control measures that could be added? | **Extend:** Explain the process of using an autoclave. | |

| Homework |
|---|
| Select from working in a hospital, veterinary surgery, dentist, or food preparation area. Discuss why working in an aseptic manner is important and what steps they would take to maintain aseptic technique in such workplaces. |

 The Practical Skills lesson for PAG 7 Microbiological techniques could follow this lesson.

# B6.3.13 New medicines

**Specification links:**

B6.3q Describe the process of discovery and development of potential new medicines. To include preclinical and clinical testing.

WS1.1d Discuss ethical issues arising from developments in science.

WS1.1e Explain everyday and technological applications of science.

WS1.1f Evaluate associated personal, social, economic, and environmental implications.

WS1.1h Evaluate risks both in practical science and the wider societal context.

WS1.2b Plan experiments or devise procedures to make observations, produce or characterise a substance, test a hypothesis, check data, or explore phenomena.

WS1.2d Recognise when to apply a knowledge of sampling techniques to ensure any samples collected are representative.

BM6.3ii Construct and interpret frequency tables and diagrams, bar charts, and histograms (M2c).

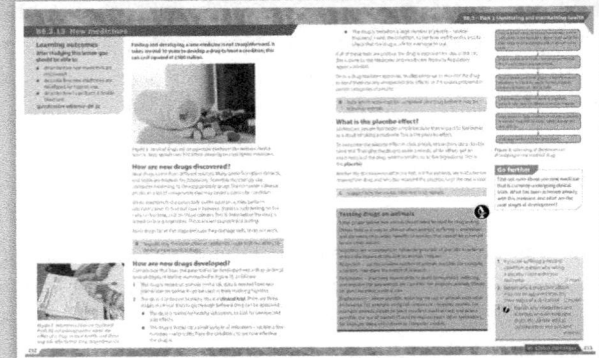

| Target | Outcome | Checkpoint | |
|---|---|---|---|
| | | Question | Activity |
| **Aiming for GRADE 4** | State that scientists are constantly developing new drugs. | A | Starter 2 |
| | State that new drugs must be tested before clinical use. | B | Starter 1, Main |
| | Describe a simple plan to test one stage in the development of a new drug. | | Main |
| **Aiming for GRADE 6** | Describe how new medicines are discovered. | A | Starter 2, Main, Plenary 1 |
| | Describe how to perform a double-blind test. | C | Main, Plenary 2 |
| | Describe a detailed plan that would produce valid results to aid in the development of a new drug. | | Main |
| **Aiming for GRADE 8** | Explain how new medicines are developed for human use. | B, 2, 3 | Starter 1 and 2, Main, Plenary 2 |
| | Distinguish between clinical and laboratory testing of a new drug. | B, 1, 2, 3 | Main, Plenary 2 |
| | Justify the stages in a plan that will produce valid data supporting the development of a new drug. | 3 | Main |

**Maths**
During the main activity, students might suggest how to construct and interpret frequency tables and diagrams, bar charts, and histograms (M2c).

**Literacy**
During the main activity, students will need to produce coherent, well-structured, and purposeful texts, using vocabulary appropriate to purpose.

**Key words**
clinical trial, placebo

232

## B6.3–Part 1 Monitoring and maintaining health

| Starter | Support/Extend | Resources |
|---|---|---|
| **Untested drugs** (10 minutes) Look at images from many years ago advertising drugs, such as cocaine in toothpastes, or heroin in painkillers or cough medicines, or thalidomide as a morning sickness treatment. Ask the class what surprises them. Tell students that these drugs were not fully tested then. With hindsight what do they think should have been done at the time? Discuss the consequences of not testing fully. | | |
| **Old and new drugs** (5 minutes) Ask students where drugs came from in the past. Discuss drugs made from plant extracts. Ask how we discover drugs today. This might require an explanation from you. Finally, discuss why we need to keep looking for new drugs. | **Extend:** You could talk about penicillin and bacterial resistance here. | |

| Main | Support/Extend | Resources |
|---|---|---|
| **Drug-testing protocol** (40 minutes) The aim of this activity is for the class to work in groups to plan methods to test a drug that would help further the development of the drug or introduce it into clinical use.<br><br>Provide the sequence for testing and developing new drugs, see the Student Book. Then split the class into groups. Each group is given one of the major steps.<br><br>• Laboratory tests on cells to test for serious side effects (for example, cell death).<br>• Laboratory tests on tissues or animals to test if the drug works.<br>• Clinical tests on small numbers of volunteers to look for side effects.<br>• Clinical tests on a large sample of population, checking for significant benefits.<br><br>Students develop experiments or surveys that could be carried out to test each step. Allow about 25 minutes for them to complete their plans. They should suggest how the data they collect might be recorded and analysed.<br><br>The groups then teach each other about their plans. Allow about 20 minutes for this part of the task. | **Support:** Provide a framework of key points that should be considered in the design, for example, sample size, time, age/gender/lifestyle of subjects, number of repeats in lab tests, etc.<br><br>**Extend:** Students should be able to suggest all of the above and justify each statement. They could also consider ethical issues and costs. | **Activity:** Drug-testing protocol |

| Plenary | Support/Extend | Resources |
|---|---|---|
| **Drug development** (5 minutes) Use the interactive activity in which students put the stages of developing a new medicine into the correct order. | | **Interactive:** Drug development |
| **Double-blind test** (10 minutes) Have two cans of cola, one branded and one a supermarket's own brand. Pour the branded cola into about five polystyrene cups labelled A and the supermarket version into five cups labelled B. None of the students must know which is which. Then present a student (the researcher) with a tray with the two sets of cups. The student then selects five students who taste both and decide which is the branded version. They vote to say which is branded or supermarket. Draw an analogy with the double-blind technique. | **Extend:** Discuss why using a double-blind test is so important. You could link it to TV taste-testing methods and ask students to criticise the method (for example, sample size, etc.). | |

| Homework | | |
|---|---|---|
| You work for the World Health Organisation (WHO). You have been asked to put together some information about how drugs are tested. This should be a simple series of short statements, which could be used in leaflets or a website. Try to make the information as memorable as possible, for example, the first letter of each step could form a memorable word/phrase, or illustrations or photos could be included. | | |

**kerboodle**

A Kerboodle highlight for this lesson is **Bump up your grade: Past, present, and future development of drugs**. Refer to the **Content map** on Kerboodle for a full list of resources and assessment.

# Checkpoint
## B6.3–Part 1 Monitoring and maintaining health

### Overview of B6.3 Monitoring and maintaining health

In this chapter, students have studied disease and health. They should be able to give some common examples of communicable and non-communicable diseases, and describe the spread of communicable diseases between animals and between plants, how different types of pathogen cause disease, and how scientists monitor the spread of disease by studying disease incidence.

Students should be able to list methods of practising good hygiene to prevent disease and the types of infection they help to minimise, and know how farmers prevent the spread of disease in their animals and plants.

Students should be able to give examples of human fungal infections, bacterial diseases, viral infections, and sexually transmitted diseases, and understand the difference between HIV and AIDS. In plants they should be able to give examples of fungal infections, bacterial infections, and viral infections, and to discuss plant defences, both the physical defences of the cuticle and cell wall and chemical defences. Higher-tier students should have studied the identification of plant disease, including skills of observation, microscopy, DNA analysis, and identification of antigens.

In studying the blood students should be able to describe the role of platelets in the formation of a scab, as well as the non-specific body defences. They should be able to describe white blood cells including phagocytes and lymphocytes, and to outline the production of antibodies and antitoxins in developing immunity. They should link this with work on blood in B2.2 *The challenges of size*.

Higher-tier students should understand what monoclonal antibodies are, how they are produced, and examples of their use. They should link this with the lock and key hypothesis of enzyme action in B1.2 *What happens in cells?*

Students should be able to explain how vaccines work and discuss their use. In considering the prevention and treatment of disease, they should also understand how antiseptics, antivirals, and antibiotics work, and be aware of the aseptic technique and use of sterile conditions. They should be familiar with culturing bacteria as a way to identify bacteria.

Finally students should understand the process of the development of new medicines and be able to outline the placebo effect.

You can find additional support for the maths skills covered in this chapter on **MyMaths**, including calculating means and working with frequency tables and diagrams, bar charts, and histograms.

### PAGs

All students are expected to have carried out the PAG 7 *Microbiological techniques*. A full lesson plan for each PAG is provided in the Practical skills chapter. PAG 7 *Microbiological techniques* should be completed after lesson B6.3.12 *Aseptic technique*.

## B6.3–Part 1 Monitoring and maintaining health

For this chapter, the following assessments are available on Kerboodle:

B6.3 Checkpoint quiz: Monitoring and maintaining health
B6.3 Progress quiz: Monitoring and maintaining health 1
B6.3 Progress quiz: Monitoring and maintaining health 2
B6.3 On your marks: Monitoring and maintaining health
B6.3 Exam-style questions and mark scheme: Monitoring and maintaining health

## Checkpoint follow-up lesson

A student's route through this lesson can be determined using the Checkpoint assessment. Percentage pass marks are supplied in the Checkpoint teacher notes.

For each successive route through it is assumed that the student can perform to their current route as well as previous routes. For example, students working at Aiming for 6 are assumed to be secure in Aiming for 4 knowledge and understanding and working towards achieving all the learning objectives for Aiming for 6.

| | Aiming for 4 | Aiming for 6 | Aiming for 8 |
|---|---|---|---|
| **Learning outcomes** | State some examples of communicable disease in plants and animals. | Describe some examples of communicable disease in plants and animals. | Explain some examples of communicable disease in plants and animals. |
| | State how communicable diseases can be spread and ways that spread can be prevented. | Describe how communicable diseases can be spread and ways that spread can be prevented. | Explain how communicable diseases can be spread and ways that spread can be prevented. |
| | State the ways that animals and plants defend themselves against disease. | Describe the ways that animals and plants defend themselves against disease. | Explain the ways that animals and plants defend themselves against disease. |
| | State some artificial methods of preventing disease. | Describe some artificial methods of preventing disease. | Explain some artificial methods of preventing disease. |
| **Starter** | **Communicable and non-communicable diseases (5 minutes)** In small groups, students list as many communicable and non-communicable diseases as they can in 2 minutes. Collate these on the board. ||||
| **Differentiated checkpoint activity** | **Activity 1 Revision summary (45 minutes)** Students tackle task question 1 on the differentiated worksheets, making a revision visual summary about monitoring and maintaining health. This should include examples of different communicable diseases in plants and animals, how they can be spread, and natural and artificial mechanisms we have to prevent disease. Students will need A3 paper, coloured pencils, and access to the Student book. Each section has been given a rough time so that students can work through the task independently. The best summaries can be kept for display. |||
| | Aiming for 4 students will require a brief introduction, and will need reminding to move on to the next area of their summary at designated times. | Aiming for 6 students will require a brief introduction, and may need reminding to move on to the next area of their summary at designated times. | Aiming for 8 students should be able to start their visual summary independently. |
| | **Kerboodle resource:** B6.3 Checkpoint follow-up: Aiming for 4, B6.3 Checkpoint follow-up: Aiming for 6, B6.3 Checkpoint follow-up: Aiming for 8 |||
| **Plenary** | **Review (5 minutes)** In differentiated pairs or small groups, students can peer assess each other's summaries using question 2 on the differentiated worksheets as a framework. |||
| **Progression** | The Aiming for 4 activity is a highly structured guide to enable students to produce a revision visual summary for this topic. There is opportunity for research at all levels into examples of diseases from the different types of pathogen, including diseases infecting either animals or plants. | The Aiming for 6 activity is a reasonably structured guide to enable students to produce a revision visual summary. An extension activity might be to research the UK vaccination programme, and go onto discuss the advantages and disadvantages of such programmes. | The Aiming for 8 activity has very little structure. and the aim is for students to produce a revision visual summary independently. The higher-tier topics of detecting plant diseases and monoclonal antibodies are suitable for Aiming for 8 students, who could research more uses of monoclonal antibodies. |

# B6.3–Part 2 Non-communicable diseases
## B6.3.14 Non-communicable diseases (1)

**Specification links:**

B6.3r Recall that many non-communicable human diseases are caused by the interaction of a number of factors. To include cardiovascular diseases, many forms of cancer, some lung (bronchitis) and liver (cirrhosis) diseases, and diseases influenced by nutrition, including type 2 diabetes.

B6.3t Analyse the effect of lifestyle factors on the incidence of non-communicable diseases at local, national, and global levels. To include lifestyle factors, such as exercise, diet, alcohol, and smoking.

B6.3u Describe cancer as the result of changes in cells that lead to uncontrolled growth and division.

WS1.1f Evaluate associated personal, social, economic, and environmental implications.

WS1.1g Make decisions based on the evaluation of evidence and arguments.

WS1.1h Evaluate risks both in practical science and the wider societal contexts.

BM6.3i Translate information between graphical and numerical forms (M4a).

BM6.3ii Construct and interpret frequency tables and diagrams, bar charts, and histograms (M2c).

BM6.3iii Understand the principles of sampling as applied to scientific data (M2d).

| Target | Outcome | Checkpoint | |
|---|---|---|---|
| | | Question | Activity |
| **Aiming for GRADE 4** ↓ | State some examples of non-communicable diseases. | A, 3 | Starter 1<br>Main<br>Plenary 1 |
| | Name some lifestyle choices that have a harmful effect on health. | | Starter 1 and 2<br>Main<br>Plenary 1 and 2 |
| | Use a piece of evidence to make a recommendation about a lifestyle choice. | | Main<br>Plenary 1 and 2 |
| **Aiming for GRADE 6** ↓ | Describe the symptoms of some non-communicable diseases. | 2 | Main |
| | Describe how a lifestyle choice might lead to a non-communicable disease. | | Starter 1 and 2<br>Main<br>Plenary 1 and 2 |
| | Use the evidence and arguments to make recommendations about lifestyle choices. | B | Main<br>Plenary 1 and 2 |
| **Aiming for GRADE 8** ↓ | Explain the effects of some non-communicable diseases on the body. | 2, 3 | Main |
| | Explain the link between lifestyle choices and some forms of non-communicable disease. | 3 | Main<br>Plenary 1 and 2 |
| | Evaluate the evidence and arguments to make recommendations about lifestyle choices. | B, 1 | Main<br>Plenary 1 and 2 |

# B6.3–Part 2 Non-communicable diseases

**Maths**
During the main activity, students will need to construct and interpret frequency tables and diagrams, bar charts, and histograms (M2c). They will also need to understand the principles of sampling as applied to scientific data (M2d). Students may also translate information between graphical and numeric forms (M4a).

**Literacy**
During the main activity, students will need to produce coherent, well-structured, and purposeful texts.

**Key words**
cancer, ethanol

| Starter | Support/Extend | Resources |
|---|---|---|
| **Non-communicable diseases Venn diagram** (10 minutes) Draw a three circle Venn diagram. In each circle write one of the words 'smoking', 'alcohol', or 'diet'. Students write in the circles a health problem caused by the factor named in the circle. Where a health problem might be caused by two of the factors, it should be placed in the shared overlap. Ensure that cancers and diabetes are mentioned. | **Support:** Highlight those health problems that crop up in more than one circle. | |
| **Lifestyle and disease** (5 minutes) Use the interactive in which students sort lifestyle choices into categories for which non-communicable diseases they can increase the risk of. | | **Interactive:** Lifestyle and disease |

| Main | Support/Extend | Resources |
|---|---|---|
| **Preventative health** (40 minutes) This lesson on preventative health is divided into three sections, each of which should take 10–15 minutes.<br>1. Provide the class with data on numbers of deaths due to smoking. (This data can be found on many websites.) Students may plot or read the data and then interpret it. They use the data to construct an argument supporting the statement that smoking damages your health. They should also suggest how the risks associated with this lifestyle choice can be reduced.<br>2. Students plan an experiment that demonstrates that alcohol reduces reaction times, and therefore increases the risk of road traffic accidents. Ask students to comment on other problems caused by alcohol, such as long-term use leading to cirrhosis. They should also suggest how the risks associated with this lifestyle choice can be reduced.<br>3. Research possible causes of cancer. Link numbers to smoking and alcohol, so some factors interact. | **Support:** Provide students with only one set of data.<br>**Support:** Provide a structure for the plan. For example, name the variables, range, etc.<br>**Extend:** Comment on the reliability of the data, sample size, and selection of the sample. | **Activity:** Preventative health |

| Plenary | Support/Extend | Resources |
|---|---|---|
| **Attitudes in adverts** (10 minutes) Show students some poster adverts for cigarettes from the 1930s through to the 1970s and discuss how they have changed and why. Look at some adverts (either images or films) for alcoholic drinks and ask if the same pattern has been followed here. Why not? Should it? | | |
| **Healthy living** (5 minutes) Produce a slogan and/or short script for a 30 second TV campaign for the Department of Health. The campaign is designed to promote healthy lifestyle choices. | | |

| Homework | | |
|---|---|---|
| Type 2 diabetes is on the increase in the UK. Produce a TV news article reporting on the causes and how lifestyle choices could reduce this problem. | | |

**kerboodle**
A Kerboodle highlight for this lesson is **Go further: Alcohol: a depressing story**. Refer to the **Content map** on Kerboodle for a full list of resources and assessment.

# B6.3.15 Non-communicable diseases (2)

**Specification links:**

B6.3r Recall that many non-communicable human diseases are caused by the interaction of a number of factors. To include cardiovascular diseases, many forms of cancer, some lung (bronchitis) and liver (cirrhosis) diseases, and diseases influenced by nutrition, including type 2 diabetes.

B6.3t Analyse the effect of lifestyle factors on the incidence of non-communicable diseases at local, national, and global levels. To include lifestyle factors, such as exercise, diet, alcohol, and smoking.

WS1.1f Evaluate associated personal, social, economic, and environmental implications.

WS1.1g Make decisions based on the evaluation of evidence and arguments.

WS1.1h Evaluate risks both in practical science and the wider societal contexts.

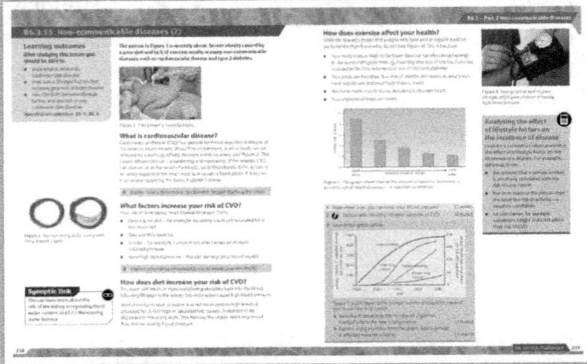

| Target | Outcome | Checkpoint | |
|---|---|---|---|
| | | Question | Activity |
| **Aiming for GRADE 4** | State what is meant by cardiovascular disease. | | Starter 1 and 2<br>Main |
| | State some lifestyle factors that would increase your risk of heart disease. | | Starter 1 and 2<br>Main<br>Plenary 2 |
| ↓ | Use a piece of evidence to recommend a change in a lifestyle choice to reduce the risk of developing heart disease. | | Main<br>Plenary 2 |
| **Aiming for GRADE 6** | Describe the effects of cardiovascular disease on the circulatory system. | A | Starter 1<br>Main |
| | Describe the links between lifestyle factors and the risk of cardiovascular disease. | B, 1, 2 | Starter 1 and 2<br>Main<br>Plenary 2 |
| ↓ | Use evidence to make recommendations about changes in lifestyle choices to reduce the risk of developing cardiovascular disease. | | Main<br>Plenary 2 |
| **Aiming for GRADE 8** | Explain how the effects of cardiovascular disease may lead to a heart attack. | | Starter 1<br>Main<br>Plenary 2 |
| | Explain how lifestyle factors could both increase or decrease the risk of cardiovascular disease. | B, 2 | Starter 1<br>Main<br>Plenary 2 |
| ↓ | Evaluate evidence to make recommendations about changes in lifestyle choices that might influence the risk of developing cardiovascular disease. | | Main<br>Plenary 2 |

**Literacy**
During the main activity, students will need to produce coherent, well-structured, and purposeful texts, using appropriate scientific vocabulary and terminology.

# B6.3–Part 2 Non-communicable diseases

| Starter | Support/Extend | Resources |
|---|---|---|
| **Demonstrating atherosclerosis** (10 minutes)   Cut a half metre length of rubber tubing. This represents a blood vessel, which might be in the heart. Place in a small tank of water and siphon the water into a beaker to demonstrate the flow of blood through the vessel. Time how long it takes to obtain a volume of water in the beaker. Then, using a narrow spatula smear a thick layer of petroleum jelly on one side of the wall at one end of the tubing. Repeat the siphoning process and show a decreased flow. Compare this with atherosclerosis. | **Extend:** Discuss the possible causes of the build-up of cholesterol. | |
| **Causes of heart disease** (5 minutes)   Do not discuss the title of the lesson, but show a series of images, such as a person smoking, a packet of salt, a cream cake, genes, and so on. Ask what health problem these cause. There might be a little discussion before they notice that they all contribute to cardiovascular disease or heart disease. Then discuss the idea of risk – simply eating a cream cake does not mean that you develop heart disease. | **Extend:** Discuss the relative effect of each factor and how the combination of the factors might increase the risk. | |

| Main | Support/Extend | Resources |
|---|---|---|
| **Healthy heart** (40 minutes)   Students produce a leaflet about the causes of heart disease, what heart disease is, and how to reduce the risk of heart disease.<br><br>Provide the students with an A3 sheet with a picture of the heart at the centre. Students then add labels that:<br><br>• discuss the causes of heart disease; to include smoking, cholesterol, exercise, and diet<br>• state what happens in cardiovascular disease and heart attacks<br>• explain how to reduce the risk posed by the factors.<br><br>Students will need to use the Student Book and the internet to find the information for the labels. | **Support:** Divide the lesson into three sections: 1. Causes, 2. Effects and 3. Prevention. In each section, guide the students to the correct source, for example, Student Book section.<br><br>**Extend:** Evaluate the relative risk posed by the factors. | **Activity:** Healthy heart |

| Plenary | Support/Extend | Resources |
|---|---|---|
| **Cardiovascular disease** (5 minutes)   Use the simple interactive in which students match risk factors to how they can cause cardiovascular disease. | | **Interactive:** Cardiovascular disease |
| **Couch potato** (10 minutes)   Show an image of a popular cartoon character who lives an inactive life slouched in an armchair. Ask the class to identify factors that make this an unhealthy lifestyle choice. Ask them to assign each risk factor to a scale they create. Then suggest changes to the character's lifestyle and assess how it might affect the risk factors. | **Extend:** Explain the link between the factor and the cause of cardiovascular disease. | |

| Homework | | |
|---|---|---|
| Design a health warning label for a food or drink to convey the risks that the product might have in contributing to cardiovascular disease. | | |

**kerboodle**
A Kerboodle highlight for this lesson is **Webquest: Judging the risk of disease**. Refer to the **Content map** on Kerboodle for a full list of resources and assessment.

# B6.3.16 Treating cardiovascular disease

**Specification links:**

B6.3s Evaluate some different treatments for cardiovascular disease. To include lifestyle, medical, and surgical.

B6.3t Analyse the effect of lifestyle factors on the incidence of non-communicable diseases at local, national, and global levels. Lifestyle factors to include exercise, diet, alcohol, and smoking.

WS1.1e Explain everyday and technological applications of science.

WS1.1f Evaluate associated personal, social, economic, and environmental implications.

WS1.1g Make decisions based on the evaluation of evidence and arguments.

WS1.1h Evaluate risks both in practical science and the wider societal contexts.

BM6.3i Translate information between graphical and numerical forms (M4a).

BM6.3ii Construct and interpret frequency tables and diagrams, bar charts, and histograms (M2c).

BM6.3iv Use a scatter diagram to identify a correlation between two variables (M2g).

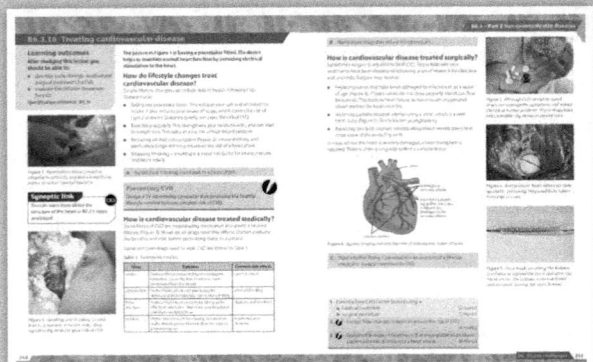

| Target | Outcome | Checkpoint | |
|---|---|---|---|
| | | Question | Activity |
| **Aiming for GRADE 4** ↓ | Name some treatments for cardiovascular disease. | B, 1 | Starter 1 and 2<br>Main<br>Plenary 1 |
| | State that the application of science has improved treatments for cardiovascular disease. | | Starter 1<br>Main<br>Plenary 2 |
| | Use a piece of evidence to make a recommendation about a treatment for cardiovascular disease. | | Main |
| **Aiming for GRADE 6** ↓ | Describe some lifestyle, medical, and surgical treatments for cardiovascular disease. | B, 1, 2 | Starter 1 and 2<br>Main<br>Plenary 1 |
| | Discuss how science has been applied to solve a specific medical problem. | | Starter 1<br>Main<br>Plenary 2 |
| | Use evidence to make recommendations about suitable treatments for cardiovascular disease. | | Main |
| **Aiming for GRADE 8** ↓ | Evaluate different treatments for cardiovascular disease. | 3 | Main |
| | Explain how a range of technological applications of science have solved many cardiovascular problems. | | Starter 1<br>Main<br>Plenary 2 |
| | Evaluate evidence to make recommendations about selecting the most appropriate treatment for cardiovascular disease. | | Main |

**Maths**

During the main activity, students will need to construct and interpret frequency tables and diagrams, bar charts, and histograms (M2c). Students may also translate information between graphical and numeric forms (M4a). They may also look for correlation between two variables (M2g).

**Literacy**

During the main activity, students will need to produce coherent, well-structured, and purposeful texts.

## B6.3–Part 2 Non-communicable diseases

| Starter | Support/Extend | Resources |
|---|---|---|
| **Demonstration of a stent** (10 minutes) Remind students that many cardiovascular problems are caused by narrowed arteries. Use a length of plastic net, such as that used to pack onions in a supermarket. Place a long thin deflated balloon inside this net. Explain how this models a stent. Then inflate the balloon gently to show how the stent is enlarged to allow improved blood flow in the heart.<br><br>**Types of treatment** (5 minutes) Write the names of about ten different treatments for cardiovascular disease onto separate cards. Students sort the treatments into different types. Establish the three categories: lifestyle, medical, and surgical. Explain why the treatments are in each category. | **Extend:** Discuss how this technique is introduced using keyhole surgery, making it less invasive. | |

| Main | Support/Extend | Resources |
|---|---|---|
| **Treatment chart** (40 minutes) Provide a table with five columns, headed lifestyle, medical (drugs), stents, valves, and transplants. Include four rows below each with the following headings:<br>1. Describe the treatment.<br>2. Explain how the treatment works.<br>3. Evaluate the risks and benefits of the treatment.<br>4. Indicate when the treatment is used.<br>Students use the Student Book to complete the sheet, supplemented with research from the internet.<br>Allow time at the end to discuss the findings as a class. | **Support:** Reduce the number of columns to three: lifestyle, medical, and surgical. Ask students to list an example of each before they complete the rest of the table.<br><br>**Extend:** Students could use data in their evaluation of the treatments. | **Activity:** Treatment chart |

| Plenary | Support/Extend | Resources |
|---|---|---|
| **How does it work?** (5 minutes) Use the interactive, which lists many different treatments for cardiovascular disease. Students link each treatment to the explanation of how it works.<br><br>**What type of scientist?** (10 minutes) Having looked at a range of treatments, have students identify the specialisms of the scientists who might have been involved in developing the treatments. Explain the role that the scientist might have played. | **Support:** Have a few suggestions of scientists to start the class off, for example, engineers, dieticians, surgeons, material scientists, etc. | **Interactive:** How does it work? |

| Homework | | |
|---|---|---|
| You are a fundraiser for the local cardiac unit in a hospital. Produce a leaflet or poster to inform the public about what the money raised will be used to buy for the hospital to treat heart disease. | | |

**kerboodle**
A Kerboodle highlight for this lesson is **Working Scientifically: Which one should I have?** Refer to the **Content map** on Kerboodle for a full list of resources and assessment.

# B6.3.17 Modern advances in medicine (1)

**Specification links:**

B6.3v Discuss potential benefits and risks associated with the use of stem cells in medicine. To include tissue transplantation and rejection.

WS1.1c Understand the power and limitations of science.

WS1.1d Discuss ethical issues arising from developments in science.

WS1.1e Explain everyday and technological applications of science.

WS1.1f Evaluate associated personal, social, economic, and environmental implications.

WS1.1g Make decisions based on the evaluation of evidence and arguments.

WS1.1h Evaluate risks both in practical science and the wider societal contexts.

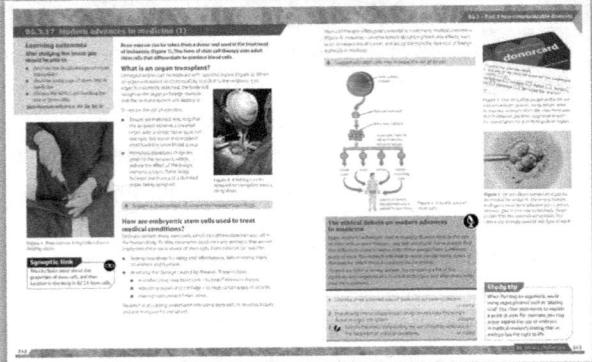

| Target | Outcome | Checkpoint | |
|---|---|---|---|
| | | Question | Activity |
| **Aiming for GRADE 4** | State what a stem cell is. | | Starter 1 and 2<br>Main<br>Plenary 1 and 2 |
| | List some examples of tissue and organ transplant. | | Starter 1<br>Main<br>Plenary 1 |
| | Use a piece of evidence to make a recommendation about the use of replacement cells, tissues, or organs. | | Main |
| **Aiming for GRADE 6** | Describe some uses of stem cells in medicine. | 1 | Starter 1 and 2<br>Main<br>Plenary 1 |
| | Describe some disadvantages of tissue and organ transplantation. | A | Starter 1<br>Main<br>Plenary 1 and 2 |
| | Use evidence and arguments to make recommendations about the use of replacement cells, tissues, or organs. | B | Main |
| **Aiming for GRADE 8** | Discuss the ethics surrounding the use of stem cells. | B, 3 | Main<br>Plenary 1 and 2 |
| | Evaluate the process of tissue and organ transplantation. | 2 | Main<br>Plenary 1 |
| | Evaluate the evidence and arguments to make recommendations about the use of replacement cells, tissues, or organs. | 3 | Main |

**Literacy**
During the main activity, students will either need to produce coherent, well-structured, and purposeful texts, or they will need to communicate effectively, sustaining the listeners' interest.

# B6.3–Part 2 Non-communicable diseases

| Starter | Support/Extend | Resources |
|---|---|---|
| **Spare parts** (10 minutes) Show an image of the human body and ask the class to indicate which organs can be replaced. Discuss why organ replacement is considered such a great advance. Then show an image of a piece of windpipe that has been cultured from stem cells. Explain this development. Ask students to discuss the ways in which this technique is a major advance. | **Extend:** Ask students to suggest any concerns that could exist with the development of stem cell technology. | |
| **New cells for old** (5 minutes) Show students a short film about the formation of stem cells or a news article about the use of stem cells. Discuss the process as it is probably unfamiliar to most students. Suggest possible future uses of the cells. | | |

| Main | Support/Extend | Resources |
|---|---|---|
| Either: **Stem cell presentations and discussion** (40 minutes) The overall question for the presentations and discussion is: 'Have modern medical techniques improved our quality of life or created further problems?' Divide the class into four groups. Allow groups time to research and plan a short presentation on one of the topics listed below. Specify that the presentation should refer to ethical considerations. 1. Benefits of stem cell technology. 2. Problems of stem cell technology. 3. Benefits of transplant surgery. 4. Problems of transplant surgery. Students then give their presentations; there may be time for one or two questions. Then discuss the issues as a class. If you wish, ask students to vote on whether or not these processes should continue. Or: | **Extend:** Students could evaluate the sources of evidence they have used or discuss when a particular technology might be more appropriate than the others. | |
| **Is stem cell research worth it?** (40 minutes) Produce an information sheet (or use the sheet provided) with a series of statements giving benefits and problems of stem cell treatments in no particular order, and a second sheet for transplants. Students sort out the benefits and problems. They decide if, on balance, the technology is a worthwhile advance or if it is of questionable value. | **Support:** This activity is more suitable than the other main activity to students who need more support. | **Activity:** Is stem cell research worth it? |

| Plenary | Support/Extend | Resources |
|---|---|---|
| **Pros and cons of stem cells** (5 minutes) Use the interactive to drag and drop a series of statements into one of two columns – one for advantages of stem cell treatments and one for disadvantages. | | **Interactive:** Pros and cons of stem cells |
| **Transplantation timeline** (10 minutes) Draw a simple timeline on the board. Divide the class into groups and ask each group to use the internet or the Student Book to find out the year of the first routine blood transfusion, first kidney transplant, first heart transplant, and first use of stem cell therapy. Then place these treatments in the correct position on the time line. Discuss how scientific developments have led to new and more successful treatments over time. | **Extend:** Discuss the advantages and disadvantages of the processes at the time they were pioneered. | |

| Homework |
|---|
| Write a pretend letter to the General Medical Council reporting the views of your class debate and decision on stem cell technology or transplants. |

**kerboodle**

A Kerboodle highlight for this lesson is **Literacy interactive: Stem cell dilemmas**. Refer to the **Content map** on Kerboodle for a full list of resources and assessment.

# B6.3.18 Modern advances in medicine (2)

**Specification links:**

B6.3w Explain some of the possible benefits and risks of using gene technology in medicine. To include practical and ethical considerations.

B6.3x Discuss the potential importance for medicine of our increasing understanding of the human genome. To include the ideas of predicting the likelihood of diseases occurring and their treatment by drugs that are targeted to genomes.

WS1.1c Understand the power and limitations of science.

WS1.1d Discuss ethical issues arising from developments in science.

WS1.1e Explain everyday and technological applications of science.

WS1.1f Evaluate associated personal, social, economic, and environmental implications.

WS1.1g Make decisions based on the evaluation of evidence and arguments.

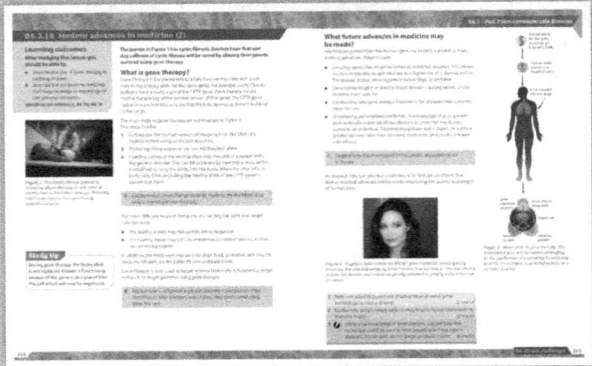

| Target | Outcome | Checkpoint | |
|---|---|---|---|
| | | Question | Activity |
| **Aiming for GRADE 4** | State what is meant by gene therapy. | | Starter 2<br>Main<br>Plenary 1 and 2 |
| | State what is meant by genetic screening. | C | Starter 1 and 2<br>Main<br>Plenary 2 |
| | List some scientific advances involved in gene-related medicine. | | Starter 1 and 2<br>Main<br>Plenary 2 |
| **Aiming for GRADE 6** | Describe the use of gene therapy in treating disease. | A, 2, 3 | Starter 2<br>Main<br>Plenary 1 and 2 |
| | Describe the advances in medicine that may be made as knowledge of the genome increases. | | Starter 1 and 2<br>Main<br>Plenary 2 |
| | Describe the scientific advances used in the development of gene therapies. | A, 3 | Starter 2<br>Main<br>Plenary 2 |
| **Aiming for GRADE 8** | Suggest ways in which gene therapy may be improved and developed in the future. | 2, 3 | Main<br>Plenary 2 |
| | Explain how a greater knowledge of the human genome could lead to the development of personalised medicines. | | Main<br>Plenary 2 |
| | Consider the power and limitations of scientific technologies in developing gene therapies. | B, C, 1, 3 | Main<br>Plenary 2 |

**Literacy**

During the main activity, students will need to produce coherent and well-structured texts, which use appropriate scientific vocabulary and terminology.

**Key words**

gene therapy

# B6.3–Part 2 Non-communicable diseases

| Starter | Support/Extend | Resources |
|---|---|---|
| **Angelina Jolie** (5 minutes)   Show an image of Angelina Jolie, and ask the class if they know of her recent medical procedures. Explain how she underwent genetic screening for a gene mutation responsible for some cancers and outline the surgery she had. Ask students for their opinions on genetic screening – what are the advantages and disadvantages? **Gene therapy** (10 minutes)   Remind the class that we can transplant organs, we can replace tissues, and we can even replace cells. Ask them whether or not they think we have the technology to replace genes. State that we do. Remind them about genetic disorders, and point out that the potential to replace defective genes might offer great hope. Show an image of genetic engineering and ask students to suggest a method by which we might be able to get genes into our cells. | **Extend:** Ask the class: Should everyone be screened for genes? Should we replace all defective genes? What ethical problems could this cause? | |

| Main | Support/Extend | Resources |
|---|---|---|
| **Gene therapy exam questions** (40 minutes)   Students work in small groups to write at least two or three exam-style questions on the topic of gene therapy. They use the Student Book for information and the internet for additional images or facts. The total number of marks for the questions should be around 20. The questions should cover: <br>• gene therapy <br>• genetic screening <br>• ethical considerations <br>• possible future developments. <br>Remind students to include different question styles, such as multiple choice, short answer, and long answer. Students should also write comprehensive mark schemes. Allow 25 minutes for question-writing and research. Allow 15 minutes for students to swap questions between groups, and to answer and mark each others' questions. | **Support:** Remind students of question styles. You could present them with a short paragraph that they could use as a stem to write questions from. **Extend:** Should include more extended writing questions. The questions should look for answers that consider how the techniques work and what the limitations of the techniques are. | **Activity:** Gene therapy exam questions |

| Plenary | Support/Extend | Resources |
|---|---|---|
| **Gene therapy sequence** (5 minutes)   Use the interactive in which students drag and drop a series of statements into the correct order for the technique of gene therapy. **Medical horizons?** (10 minutes)   Ask the class if gene therapy is the ultimate cure. Students then write one possible future use of the technique on a sticky note. Look at some of the statements, and discuss the following: Could it be done? Should it be done? | **Extend:** Students justify their decisions. | **Interactive:** Gene therapy sequence |

| Homework | | |
|---|---|---|
| Explain how gene therapy could be used to treat disorders like haemophilia. | | |

*kerboodle*
A Kerboodle highlight for this lesson is **Working Scientifically: Genetic engineering and inherited disorders**. Refer to the **Content map** on Kerboodle for a full list of resources and assessment.

# Checkpoint
## B6.3–Part 2 Non-communicable diseases

### Overview of B6.3 Non-communicable diseases

In this chapter, students have studied non-communicable diseases, exemplified by the effects on health of smoking and drinking alcohol. They should be able to outline the types of damage caused by smoking and alcohol abuse, and be aware of the effects of nicotine, carbon monoxide, and tar in cigarette smoke, and how each specifically affects health. They should link this work with the heart and its blood vessels and the gaseous exchange system of the lungs in B2.2 *The challenges of size*, and also studies of the brain in B3.1 *The nervous system*.

Students should understand what is meant by cardiovascular disease (CVD), its risk factors, and how each risk factor affects health. They should be aware that a high salt diet results in too much water being reabsorbed into the blood, and should link this with work on the kidney in B3.3 *Maintaining internal environments*. In studying the treatment of CVD, students should be able to describe lifestyle changes, treatment with drugs, and surgery options.

Students should be aware of some modern advances in medicine. They should be able to describe organ transplantation including the problem of finding donors and tissue matching, and to discuss the problem of organ rejection and the use of immunosuppressant drugs. They should know how stem cells can be used to treat medical conditions, linking with studies on stem cells and their functions in B2.1 *Supplying the cell*. They should be aware of the ethical debate on the use of stem cells.

Finally students should be able to outline the main steps involved in gene therapy, and the problems encountered with this technology. They should be able to list some areas in medicine where future advances are being made using the data collected from the Human Genome Project.

You can find additional support for the maths skills covered in this chapter on **MyMaths**, including working with frequency tables and diagrams, bar charts, and histograms, the principles of sampling as applied to scientific data, and translating information between graphical and numeric forms.

For this chapter, the following assessments are available on Kerboodle:

B6.4 Checkpoint quiz: Non-communicable diseases
B6.4 Progress quiz: Non-communicable diseases 1
B6.4 Progress quiz: Non-communicable diseases 2
B6.4 On your marks: Non-communicable diseases
B6.4 Exam-style questions and mark scheme: Non-communicable diseases

# B6.3–Part 2 Non-communicable diseases

## Checkpoint follow-up lesson

A student's route through this lesson can be determined using the Checkpoint assessment. Percentage pass marks are supplied in the Checkpoint teacher notes.

For each successive route through it is assumed that the student can perform to their current route as well as previous routes. For example, students working at Aiming for 6 are assumed to be secure in Aiming for 4 knowledge and understanding and working towards achieving all the learning objectives for Aiming for 6.

| | Aiming for 4 | Aiming for 6 | Aiming for 8 |
|---|---|---|---|
| **Learning outcomes** | State some examples of non-communicable disease. | Describe some examples of non-communicable disease and their effects. | Explain some examples of non-communicable disease and their effects. |
| | State some of the risk factors for some non-communicable diseases. | Describe some of the risk factors for some non-communicable diseases. | Explain some of the risk factors for some non-communicable diseases. |
| | State some methods of prevention or treatment of some non-communicable diseases. | Describe some methods of prevention or treatment of some non-communicable diseases | Explain some methods of prevention or treatment of some non-communicable diseases. |
| **Starter** | **Which diseases? (5 minutes)**   Have a prepared list of non-communicable diseases covered up on the board. Remind the class of the difference between a communicable and a non-communicable disease. In pairs, ask students to write down as many non-communicable diseases as they can in 2 minutes. Show your list om the board. Did they miss any? | | |
| **Differentiated checkpoint activity** | **Activity 1 Non-communicable diseases (45 minutes)**   There are six stations, each with a profile of a different person. In pairs or small groups, students spend up to eight minutes at each station, following their differentiated worksheets to write advice for each person from a GP. It may be useful to provide a few Student books at each station. | | |
| | The Aiming for 4 sheet is highly structured. Students can have a copy each or one per pair or small group, and write their answers directly on the sheet. | The Aiming for 6 sheet is fairly structured. Students can have a copy each or one per pair or small group, and write their answers directly on the sheet. | The Aiming for 8 sheet has little structure. Students can work in pairs or small groups, writing their answers on paper or in their books. |
| | **Kerboodle resource:** B6.4 Checkpoint follow-up: Aiming for 4, B6.4 Checkpoint follow-up: Aiming for 6, B6.4 Checkpoint follow-up: Aiming for 8 | | |
| **Plenary** | **Future treatments (5 minutes)**   Ask questions about future treatments – how might we be able to treat disease in the future? Show a video of stem cell research. A suitable example from Life Noggin is available on YouTube. | | |
| **Progression** | Researching the effects of illegal drugs on health and the non-communicable diseases they cause is a task that could be suitable as extension for all students. | The topic of cardiovascular disease lends itself to further research into risk factors, and an ethical discussion about who should be given which treatments, taking into account the cost to the health service of treatments for CVD. | This chapter offers many opportunities for practising data interpretation and finding correlations in data, which might be suitable tasks for Aiming for 8 students. |

# B6 Global challenges: Topic summary

**B6.1** Monitoring and maintaining the environment
**B6.2** Feeding the human race
**B6.3** Monitoring and maintaining health

| Spec ref | Statement | Book spreads | | |
|---|---|---|---|---|
| B6.1a | Explain how to carry out a field investigation into the distribution and abundance of organisms in a habitat and how to determine their numbers in a given area | B6.1.1, B6.1.2 | | |
| B6.1b | Describe both positive and negative human interactions within ecosystems and explain their impact on biodiversity | B6.1.3, B6.1.4 | | |
| B6.1c | Explain some of the benefits and challenges of maintaining local and global biodiversity | B6.1.5 | | |
| B6.1d | Evaluate the evidence for the impact of environmental changes on the distribution of organisms, with reference to water and atmospheric gases | B6.1.6 | H | S |
| B6.2a | Describe some of the biological factors affecting levels of food security | B6.2.1 | | S |
| B6.2b | Describe and explain some possible agricultural solutions to the demands of the growing human population | B6.2.2 | | S |
| B6.2c | Explain the impact of the selective breeding of food plants and domesticated animals | B6.2.3 | | |
| B6.2d | Describe genetic engineering as a process which involves modifying the genome of an organism to introduce desirable characteristics | B6.2.4 | | |
| B6.2e | Describe the main steps in the process of genetic engineering | B6.2.5 | H | |
| B6.2f | Explain some of the possible benefits and risks of using gene technology in modern agriculture | B6.2.4 | | S |
| B6.2g | Describe and explain some possible biotechnological solutions to the demands of the growing human population | B6.2.6 | | |
| B6.3a | Describe the relationship between health and disease | B6.3.1 | | |
| B6.3b | Describe different types of diseases | B6.3.1 | | |
| B6.3c | Describe the interactions between different types of disease | B6.3.1 | | |
| B6.3d | Explain how communicable diseases (caused by viruses, bacteria, protists and fungi) are spread in animals and plants | B6.3.1, B6.3.2 | | |
| B6.3e | Explain how the spread of communicable diseases may be reduced or prevented in animals and plants | B6.3.3 | | |
| B6.3f | Describe a minimum of one common human infection, one plant disease and sexually transmitted infections in humans including HIV/AIDS | B6.3.4, B6.3.5 | | |
| B6.3g | Describe physical plant defence responses to disease | B6.3.6 | | |
| B6.3h | Describe chemical plant defence responses | B6.3.6 | | |
| B6.3i | Describe different ways plant diseases can be detected and identified, in the lab and in the field | B6.3.7 | | |
| B6.3j | Explain how white blood cells and platelets are adapted to their defence functions in the blood | B6.3.8 | | |
| B6.3k | Describe the non-specific defence systems of the human body against pathogens | B6.3.8 | | |
| B6.3l | Explain the role of the immune system of the human body in defence against disease | B6.3.8 | | |
| B6.3m | Describe how monoclonal antibodies are produced | B6.3.9 | | |
| B6.3n | Describe some of the ways in which monoclonal antibodies can be used | B6.3.9 | | |
| B6.3o | Explain the use of vaccines and medicines in the prevention and treatment of disease | B6.3.10, B6.3.11 | | |
| B6.3p | Explain the aseptic techniques used in culturing organisms | B6.3.11, B6.3.12 | | |
| B6.3q | Describe the processes of discovery and development of potential new medicines | B6.3.13 | | |
| B6.3r | Recall that many non-communicable human diseases are caused by the interaction of a number of factors | B6.3.14, B6.3.15 | | |
| B6.3s | Evaluate some different treatments for cardiovascular disease | B6.3.16 | | |
| B6.3t | Analyse the effect of lifestyle factors on the incidence of non-communicable diseases at local, national and global levels | B6.3.14, B6.3.15, B6.3.16 | | |
| B6.3u | Describe cancer as the result of changes in cells that lead to uncontrolled growth and division | B6.3.14 | | |
| B6.3v | Discuss potential benefits and risks associated with the use of stem cells in medicine | B6.3.17 | | |
| B6.3w | Explain some of the possible benefits and risks of using gene technology in medicine | B6.3.18 | | |
| B6.3x | Discuss the potential importance for medicine of our increasing understanding of the human genome | B6.3.18 | | |

## Maths

| Specification | | Book spread | |
|---|---|---|---|
| Spec ref | Statement | Main content | Maths chapter |
| BM6.1i | Construct and interpret frequency tables and diagrams, bar charts and histograms | B6.1.1, B6.3.10 | |
| BM6.1ii | Understand the principles of sampling as applied to scientific data | B6.1.1, B6.1.2 | |
| BM6.2i | Use percentiles and calculate percentage gain and loss of mass | B6.2.6 | |
| BM6.2ii | Calculate arithmetic means | | |
| BM6.2iii | Use ratios, fractions and percentages | B6.2.3 | |
| BM6.2iv | Extract and interpret information from charts, graphs and tables | B6.2.6 | |
| BM6.3i | Translate information between graphical and numerical forms | B6.3.1, B6.3.2, B6.3.14, B6.3.16 | |
| BM6.3ii | Construct and interpret frequency tables and diagrams, bar charts and histograms | B6.3.1, B6.3.2, B6.3.3, B6.3.13, B6.3.14, B6.3.16 | |
| BM6.3iii | Understand the principles of sampling as applied to scientific data | B6.3.14 | |
| BM6.3iv | Use a scatter diagram to identify a correlation between two variables | B6.3.1, B6.3.2, B6.3.16 | |
| BM6.3v | calculate cross-sectional areas of bacterial cultures and clear agar jelly using $\pi r^2$ | | S |

## Working scientifically

| Specification | | Book spread | |
|---|---|---|---|
| Spec ref | Statement | Main content | WS chapter |
| WS1.1b | Use models to solve problems, make predictions, and to develop scientific explanations and understanding of familiar and unfamiliar facts. | B6.2.5, B6.3.8 | WS2 |
| WS1.1c | Understand the power and limitations of science. | B6.1.3–5, B6.2.2–6, B6.3.9, B6.3.10, B6.3.17, B6,3,18 | WS1 |
| WS1.1d | Discuss ethical issues arising from developments in science. | B6.1.4, B6.1.5, B6.2.1, B6.2.2, B6.2.4, B6.2.6, B6.3.9, B6.3.13, B6.3.17, B6,3,18 | WS1 |
| WS1.1e | Explain everyday and technological applications of science. | B6.2.1–5, B6.3.3–5, B6.3.7, B6.3.9, B6.3.10, B6.3.12, B6.3.13, B6.3.16–18 | WS1 |
| WS1.1f | Evaluate associated personal, social, economic, and environmental implications. | B6.1.3–6, B6.2.1–6, B6.3.1–5, B6.3.10, B6.3.13–18 | WS1 |
| WS1.1g | Make decisions based on the evaluation of evidence and arguments. | B6.1.3–5, B6.2.1, B6.2.4, B6.2.6, B6.3.1–3, B6.3.5, B6.3.10–13 | WS1 |
| WS1.1h | Evaluate risks both in practical science and the wider societal context. | B6.1.6, B6.2.4–6, B6.3.1–6, B6.3.10–17 | WS1, WS4 |
| WS1.2b | Plan experiments or devise procedures to make observations, produce or characterise a substance, test hypotheses, check data, or explore phenomena. | B6.1.1, B6.1.2, B6.3.13 | WS3, WS4 |
| WS1.2c | Apply a knowledge of a range of techniques, instruments, apparatus, and materials to select those appropriate to the experiment. | B6.1.1, B6.1.2, B6.3.11, B6.3.12 | WS4 |
| WS1.2d | Recognise when to apply a knowledge of sampling techniques to ensure any samples collected are representative. | B6.1.1, B6.1.2, B6.3.13 | |
| WS1.3c | Carrying out and representing mathematical and statistical analysis. | B6.3.11 | WS5 |
| WS1.3f | Present reasoned explanations. | B6.1.4, B6.1.5 | WS7 |
| WS1.3h | Identify potential sources of random and systematic error. | B6.1.1, B6.1.2 | WS8 |
| WS1.4a | Use scientific vocabulary, terminology, and definitions. | B6.3.8, B6.3.9 | WS2 |
| WS1.4b | Recognise the importance of scientific quantities and understand how they are determined. | B6.3.1–3, B6.3.5 | |
| WS2a | Carry out experiments. | B6.1.1–3, B6.1.6, B6.3.6, B6.3.7, B6.3.11, B6.3.12 | |
| WS2b | Make and record observations and measurements using a range of apparatus and methods. | B6.1.1–3, B6.1.6, B6.3.6, B6.3.7, B6.3.11, B6.3.12 | |
| WS2c | Present observations using appropriate methods. | B6.1.1–3, B6.1.6, B6.3.6, B6.3.7, B6.3.11, B6.3.12 | |
| WS2d | Communicate the scientific rational for investigations, methods used, findings, and reasoned conclusions. | B6.1.1–3, B6.1.6, B6.3.6, B6.3.7, B6.3.11, B6.3.12 | |

# B7 Practical skills
## Practical activity groups
### B1 Microscopy

**Specification links:**

PAG B1 Use of appropriate apparatus, techniques and magnification, including microscopes, to make observations of biological specimens and produce labelled scientific drawings.

WS2a Carry out experiments.

WS2b Make and record observations and measurements using a range of apparatus and methods.

WS2c Present observations using appropriate methods.

WS2d Communicate the scientific rational for investigations, methods used, findings, and reasoned conclusions.

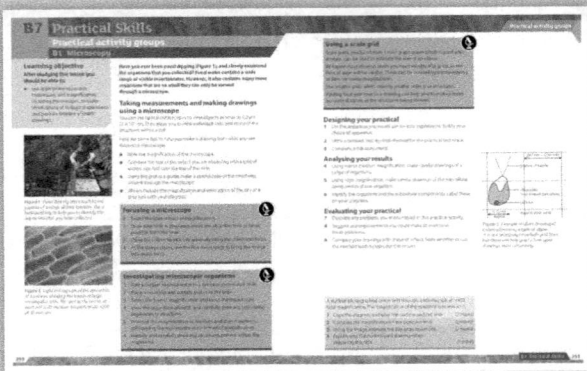

| Target | Outcome | Checkpoint | |
|---|---|---|---|
| | | Question | Activity |
| Aiming for GRADE 4 | Use apparatus to make a temporary microscope slide and view it using a microscope that has been focused. | 4 | Main / Plenary 2 |
| | State that there is a low, medium, and high level of magnification when using a microscope. | | Starter 1 and 2 / Main |
| | Draw a simple sketch of the specimen. | | Main / Plenary 1 |
| Aiming for GRADE 6 | Use a full range of apparatus to make a temporary microscope slide and view it using a microscope at low magnification. | 4 | Main / Plenary 2 |
| | State the magnification of the objective lens. | | Stater 2 / Main |
| | Draw a clear representation of the specimen, including labels of the major structures. | 1 | Main / Plenary 1 |
| Aiming for GRADE 8 | Use a full range of apparatus independently to make a temporary microscope slide and view it using a microscope at appropriate magnifications. | 4 | Main |
| | Calculate the magnification of each lens combination. | 2, 3 | Starter 2 / Main |
| | Draw an accurate, proportioned representation of the specimen, including labels of all the main structures. | 1 | Main / Plenary 2 |

**Maths**
During the practical task students will be asked to use arithmetic and numerical computation, involving the use of percentages (M1c).

**Literacy**
Students will be asked to produce coherent, well-structured, and purposeful texts as they write their experimental methods.

**Key words**
focus, image, magnification, microscope, specimen

250

# Practical activity groups

| Starter | Support/Extend | Resources |
|---|---|---|
| **What is magnification?** (10 minutes) Provide each group with a small coin (e.g., 5 p), and a printed image of the coin that has been magnified to about 10 times the actual size. Ask the students to work out how many times it has been magnified. Then discuss the advantages of magnification, which allows small things to be seen.<br><br>**Calculating magnification** (5 minutes) Issue a microscope to each group. You may need to remind students about the parts of the microscope. Ask students to state how many times the eyepiece magnifies and how many times the low-power lens magnifies. Then ask how to work out the total magnification. Ask students to work out the magnification for all the lens combinations on the microscopes you plan to use. | **Support:** Suggest to students that they work out the magnification by seeing how many times they can place a coin across the image.<br><br>**Extend:** Distinguish between magnification and resolution. | |

| Main | Support/Extend | Resources |
|---|---|---|
| **B1 Microscopy** (40 minutes) Follow the Microscopy activity from the Student Book. Students will investigate different magnification techniques to draw scientific diagrams from a number of biological specimens.<br><br>In a first lesson carry out the practical activity as described, and consider the issues of planning and risk assessment.<br><br>A second lesson could be used to write the final report of the practical activity. | **Support:** Help may be needed with focusing the microscope and calculating the magnification. Provide a formula for calculating the magnification on the board.<br><br>**Extend:** Could look at more than one organism, using different magnifications. | **Practical:** PAG B1 Microscopy |

| Plenary | Support/Extend | Resources |
|---|---|---|
| **Drawing rules** (10 minutes) In groups devise 10 standard rules biologists would use to make a biological drawing. Then look at their own drawing and see if they have followed each rule.<br><br>**Problems with microscopy** (5 minutes) Use the interactive to link lines between a number of problems associated with using a microscope, and their solutions. | **Support:** Mark in pairs to provide more input. | |

| Homework | | |
|---|---|---|
| Create a table with three columns. In the first column list the ways we could observe a biological specimen (naked eye, hand lens, microscope), in the second column, list a few examples of biological specimens that could be appropriately observed using this method, and in the final column explain why you have chosen this method. Finally, produce a labelled biological drawing of a structure observed by eye (e.g., a leaf). | | |

# B2 Testing for Biological molecules

**Specification links:**

PAG B2 Safe use of appropriate heating devices and techniques including use of a Bunsen burner and a water bath or electric heater.

PAG B2 Use of appropriate techniques and qualitative reagents to identify biological molecules (to include: reducing sugars, non-reducing sugars, protein and fats/lipids).

WS2a Carry out experiments.

WS2b Make and record observations and measurements using a range of apparatus and methods.

WS2c Present observations using appropriate methods.

WS2d Communicate the scientific rationale for investigations, methods used, findings, and reasoned conclusions.

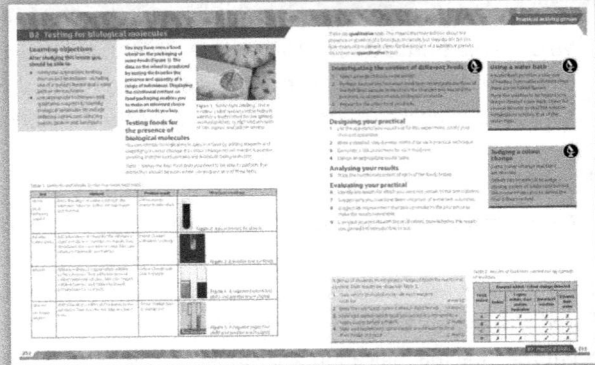

| Target | Outcome | Checkpoint | |
|---|---|---|---|
| | | Question | Activity |
| **Aiming for GRADE 4** ↓ | Name the qualitative reagents used to identify reducing sugars and non-reducing sugars, proteins, and fats/lipids. | 1 | Starter 2<br>Main<br>Plenary 1 |
| | Use the given method to safely test for the presence of a biological molecule, including the safe use of appropriate heating devices. | | Main |
| | State that foods can be tested for the presence of biological molecules. | | Starter 1<br>Main |
| **Aiming for GRADE 6** ↓ | Describe the colour change produced by the presence of reducing sugars and non-reducing sugars, proteins, and fats/lipids. | | Starter 2<br>Main<br>Plenary 1 |
| | Use the range of appropriate methods to safely test for the presence of biological molecules, including the safe use of appropriate heating devices. | | Main<br>Plenary 2 |
| | Interpret the results of tests for biological molecules in a food to determine the nutritional value of that food. | 2 | Starter 1<br>Main<br>Plenary 2 |
| **Aiming for GRADE 8** ↓ | Record the colour change and use it to identify the presence or absence of reducing sugars and non-reducing sugars, proteins, and fats/lipids. | | Main |
| | Justify the method chosen to test for the presence of a specific group of biological molecules. | | Main<br>Plenary 2 |
| | Interpret the results of tests for biological molecules in foods to compare the nutritional value of different foods. | 3, 4 | Main<br>Plenary 2 |

**Literacy**
Students will be asked to produce coherent, well-structured, and purposeful texts as they write their experimental methods.

**Key words**
Benedict's solution, ethanol, fats, glucose, iodine, proteins, qualitative, starch

# Practical activity groups

| Starter | Support/Extend | Resources |
|---|---|---|
| **Nutritional information** (5 minutes) Show students images of nutritional information from food packets or circulate a few food packets. Ask the class what type of information this supplies, why this information is of interest, and how they think scientists find out what nutrients are in the food.<br>**Food colouring** (10 minutes) Ask how we test for substances in food. Ask students if they know what a reagent is. Demonstrate a simple test for vitamin C using DCPIP. Name DCPIP as a reagent. Ask them how we could tell the vitamin was there – they should note the colour change. State that we can test for several biochemical molecules using a reagent and recording a colour change. | **Extend:** Discuss the difference between the types of carbohydrates and fats that might be mentioned.<br><br>**Support:** They may make a summary table listing the biochemical, the reagent, and the colour change.<br>**Extend:** Discuss the difference between a qualitative and a quantitative test. | |

| Main | Support/Extend | Resources |
|---|---|---|
| **B2 Testing for biological molecules** (40 minutes) Follow the Testing for biological molecules activity from the Student Book. Students will investigate foods by testing for the presence of biological molecules.<br>In a first lesson carry out the practical activity as described, and consider the issues of planning and risk assessment.<br>A second lesson could be used to write the final report of the practical activity. | **Support:** Test all foods for reducing sugars and record the results. Then move to the second test, etc.<br>**Extend:** Students should be able to work independently to test a range of foods for each of the chemicals. | **Practical:** PAG B2 Testing for biological molecules |

| Plenary | Support/Extend | Resources |
|---|---|---|
| **Reagent links** (5 minutes) Use the interactive that links the reagent to the biochemical molecule it tests for and the colour change produced.<br>**Limitations of the tests** (10 minutes) In groups give all the students a few minutes to identify the problems and limitations of the experiments. These could include difficulties in judging the colour change, cannot test some liquid foods for fats using this method, dark coloured foods are difficult to test, lack of quantitative evidence, and so on. Then hold a class discussion about the limitations. | | |

| Homework | | |
|---|---|---|
| Keep a diet diary for a day. For each meal try to compile the nutritional information. Discuss how important the identification of the nutritional information might be for some people. | **Support:** Discuss how helpful the students think the traffic-light labelling system is.<br>**Extend:** Discuss the benefits of the added quantitative information. | |

# B3 Sampling

**Specification links:**

PAG B3 Application of appropriate sampling techniques to investigate the distribution and abundance of organisms in an ecosystem via direct use in the field (to include biotic and abiotic factors)

WS2a Carry out experiments.

WS2b Make and record observations and measurements using a range of apparatus and methods.

WS2c Present observations using appropriate methods.

WS2d Communicate the scientific rational for investigations, methods used, findings and reasoned conclusions.

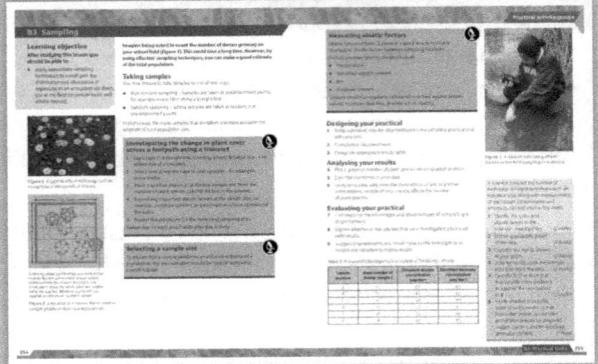

| Target | Outcome | Checkpoint | |
|---|---|---|---|
| | | Question | Activity |
| Aiming for GRADE 4 | Name a biotic or abiotic factor that might affect the distribution of an organism. | 1 | Starter 1, Main |
| | Describe how you would use a quadrat to count the number of organisms in that sample site. | | Starter 2, Main, Plenary 1 |
| | Record data in a frequency table or plot a bar chart to show the distribution of organisms. | | Main, Plenary 2 |
| Aiming for GRADE 6 | Describe a method to measure the identified biotic or abiotic factor. | 5 | Main, Plenary 1 |
| | Explain how quadrats can be used to sample the distribution of the organisms through an ecosystem. | | Starter 2, Main, Plenary 1 |
| | Plot two variables (frequency of organism and level of named factor) from experimental data. | 2 | Main, Plenary 2 |
| Aiming for GRADE 8 | Explain in the method how the measurement of the factor would be accurate, repeatable, and reproducible. | 5 | Main |
| | Explain how the use of sampling techniques, such as transects and quadrats, obtain unbiased data. | | Starter 2, Main |
| | Use a scatter diagram to identify correlation between the distribution of an organism and a named biotic or abiotic factor. | 3, 4, 6 | Main, Plenary 2 |

**Maths**
During the Main task, students will need to understand the principles of sampling as applied to scientific data (M2d). They will construct and interpret frequency tables and diagrams, bar charts, and histograms (M2c). They may record the abiotic factor to an appropriate number of significant figures (M2a) and find arithmetic means (M2b).

**Literacy**
During the main activity, students will need to produce coherent, well-structured, and purposeful texts.

**Key words**
abiotic, biotic, non-random sampling, quadrat, random sampling

# Practical activity groups

| Starter | Support/Extend | Resources |
|---|---|---|
| **Abiotic factors** (5 minutes)  Identify the habitat to be investigated, possibly showing a photograph if it is unfamiliar to the students. In groups, discuss the possible factors that might affect the distribution of plant species in this habitat. Class feedback.<br><br>**Using quadrats** (10 minutes)  Use a quadrat and tape measure (or a scaled-down version) and ask a group of students to demonstrate to the class how to use the equipment to obtain data on species richness or distribution. Have a class discussion about the method they used and address any misconceptions about their use. Show an image of the habitat that the class will be studying, and ask the class to decide how to use the apparatus to record data in this habitat. | **Support:** Put a list of factors on the board, and ask the class to select factors that might be relevant to this habitat.<br><br>**Extend:** Ask for ideas about why the factor might affect the distribution.<br><br>**Extend:** Discuss the ideas of non-random sampling, avoiding bias, and sample size. | |

| Main | Support/Extend | Resources |
|---|---|---|
| **B3 Sampling** (40 minutes)  Follow the Sampling activity from the Student Book. Students will investigate differences in habitats using ecological sampling techniques. This will involve measuring species richness and at least one named abiotic factor.<br><br>In a first lesson carry out the practical activity as described, and consider the issues of planning and risk assessment.<br><br>A second lesson could be used to write the final report of the practical activity. | **Support:** Select the most appropriate abiotic factor to record and demonstrate the method to be used.<br><br>**Extend:** Students could select more than one abiotic factor and research the method to measure this factor.<br><br>**Support:** Students should be able to create a tally chart, but may require support in generating a frequency table. They will require help to plot a histogram of the results. Axes may need to be provided.<br><br>**Extend:** Plot a graph of the species richness against the abiotic factor, looking for a relationship. | **Practical:** PAG B3 Sampling |

| Plenary | Support/Extend | Resources |
|---|---|---|
| **Sampling definitions** (5 minutes)  Use the interactive to link a range of words relevant to the sampling methods to their meanings.<br><br>**Which graph?** (10 minutes)  Sketch about four graphs on the board, a bar graph, histogram, line graph, and a scatter diagram. Suggest a series of experimental data sets (including the ones collected in the investigation). Students decide the most suitable type of graph to use for the data set, and explain why. | | |

| Homework | | |
|---|---|---|
| Link to any current wildlife series on TV (or suggest the distribution of tigers in the jungle). Ask students to suggest as many reasons as possible why it is important for biologists to collect data on the distribution of species. Select one or two reasons and explain how the data help biologists to understand the distributions or changes in the distribution. Explain how the biologists might display the data to an audience of the general public. | | |

# B4 Enzymes

**Specification links:**

PAG B4 Safe use of appropriate heating devices and techniques including use of a Bunsen burner and a water bath or electric heater.

PAG B4 Use of appropriate apparatus and techniques for the observation and measurement of biological changes and/or processes.

PAG B4 Measurement of rates of reaction by a variety of methods including production of gas, uptake of water and colour change of indicator.

WS2a Carry out experiments.

WS2b Make and record observations and measurements using a range of apparatus and methods.

WS2c Present observations using appropriate methods.

WS2d Communicate the scientific rationale for investigations, methods used, findings and reasoned conclusions.

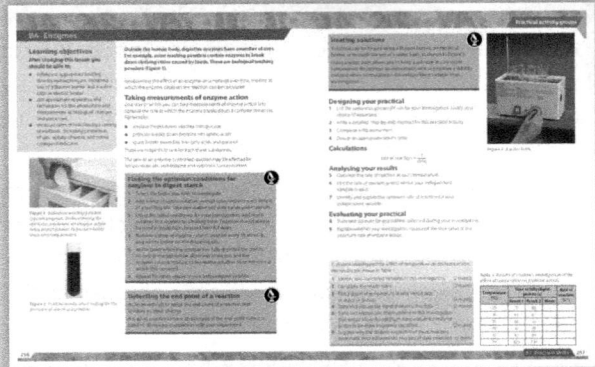

| Target | Outcome | Checkpoint | |
|---|---|---|---|
| | | Question | Activity |
| **Aiming for GRADE 4** | State that temperature is one of the variables that can affect the rate of an enzyme-controlled reaction. | 1 | Starter 1<br>Main |
| | State the colour change of the indicator selected to record the end point of an enzyme-controlled reaction. | | Starter 2<br>Main |
| | Record the time (in suitable units) it takes for an enzyme-controlled reaction to occur. | | Main |
| **Aiming for GRADE 6** | Describe how a water bath can be used to maintain a constant temperature when testing the effect of a factor on an enzyme-controlled reaction. | | Main |
| | Describe a method that would investigate the effect of a factor on the rate of an enzyme-controlled reaction by measuring the end point. | | Starter 2<br>Main<br>Plenary 2 |
| | Calculate the rate of the reaction at each experimental condition as 1/time. | 2 | Main<br>Plenary 1 |
| **Aiming for GRADE 8** | Explain how water baths could be used to either control the temperature or investigate the effect of different temperatures on the rates of enzyme controlled reactions. | 5 | Main |
| | Explain how all variables except the independent variable are controlled when measuring the end point in an enzyme-controlled reaction. | 1 | Main |
| | Plot a rate graph for the effect of a named factor on the rate of an enzyme-controlled reaction. | 3 | Main<br>Plenary 1 |

**Maths**
During the main activity students will solve simple algebraic equations (M3d) and use appropriate number of significant figures (M2a). Whilst handling the data they may calculate an arithmetic mean (M2b). Students will be required to plot two variables from experimental data (M4c).

**Literacy**
During the main activity students will need to produce coherent, well-structured, and purposeful texts.

**Key words**
denature, enzyme, optimum, product, rates of reaction, substrate

# Practical activity groups

| Starter | Support/Extend | Resources |
|---|---|---|
| **The factors: enzymes** (5 minutes) Use the interactive, which asks students to link the name of a factor that affects enzyme-controlled reactions with an explanation of the effects. | | |
| **End points** (10 minutes) Ask the class how they tell when something is finished. Start with a few everyday examples, like how do you tell when a kettle has boiled? How do you tell when a CD has finished? They should be able to describe or state a clear indication. State that we could call this an end point. Then demonstrate the reaction of iodine with starch solution, and iodine with sugar solution. There is a difference, and this could be used as an end point in the digestion of starch. | **Extend:** Ask if all the end points are easy to spot. For example, how do you tell when a cake is cooked? Discuss what might be difficult in recognising the endpoint in this reaction. | |

| Main | Support/Extend | Resources |
|---|---|---|
| **B4 Enzymes** (40 minutes) Follow the Enzymes activity in the Student Book, in which students investigate a factor that could affect the rate of enzyme activity. This will involve selecting a factor and designing an experiment to investigate the factor whilst keeping all the other factors controlled. Students will collect data, calculate the rate of reaction at a given condition, and finally plot rate graphs.<br><br>In a first lesson carry out the practical activity as described, and consider the issues of planning and risk assessment.<br><br>A second lesson could be used to write the final report of the pactical activity.<br><br>SAFETY: Aviod breathing enzyme dust. | **Support:** Provide a prompt sheet that asks students to select a factor, identify how they will change this variable, state what the dependent variable will be, what variables will be controlled, etc., to help them plan their method. Students could complete one condition per group and pool the class data.<br><br>**Support:** Help may be needed in calculating the rate. To help with plotting the rate graph you could multiply the rate by 1000 to obtain easier numbers to plot the graph. Supply the axes. | **Practical:** PAG B4 Enzymes |

| Plenary | Support/Extend | Resources |
|---|---|---|
| **Flipping graphs** (5 minutes) Ask the class why they were asked to calculate rates of reaction and to plot a rate graph rather than just using time. Establish that the rate graph reflects an increase in the factor that causes an increase in rate (e.g., concentration), as the line plotted goes up; whereas a time graph shows an increase in the factor (e.g., concentration) that causes a decrease in time (the line goes down). The line seems to be going the wrong way. You could use a variety of graph shapes to illustrate the point. | **Support:** Look at the numbers only; one set shows an increase, whereas the time data show a decrease.<br><br>**Support:** You do not need to have changes in condition. | |
| **Alternative end points** (10 minutes) Demonstrate the addition of potato (or liver) to hydrogen peroxide. You could show a couple of tests using different conditions, for example, change the temperature or the surface area. State that an enzyme-controlled reaction is occurring. Ask the class how you could measure the rate, what will you measure, and whether or not there is an end point. | | |

| Homework |
|---|
| State why it is important to know the effect of temperature on the action of enzymes in biological washing powders. Design an experiment to show the optimum temperature at which to use biological washing powders. |

# B5 Photosynthesis

**Specification links:**

PAG B5 Use of appropriate apparatus and techniques for the observation and measurement of biological changes and/or processes.

PAG B5 Safe and ethical use of living organisms (plants or animals) to measure physiological functions and responses to the environment.

PAG B5 Measurement of rates of reaction by a variety of methods including production of gas, uptake of water and colour change of indicator.

WS2a Carry out experiments.

WS2b Make and record observations and measurements using a range of apparatus and methods.

WS2c Present observations using appropriate methods.

WS2d Communicate the scientific rationale for investigations, methods used, findings and reasoned conclusions.

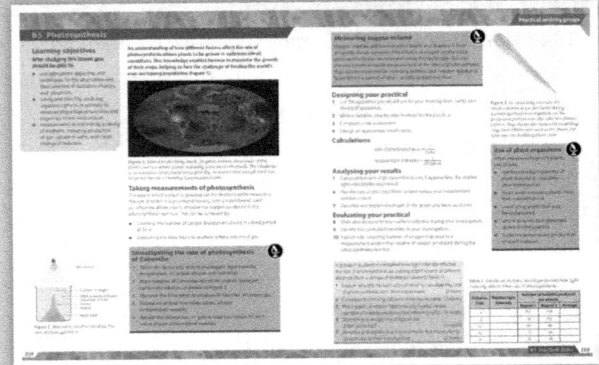

| Target | Outcome | Checkpoint | |
|---|---|---|---|
| | | Question | Activity |
| **Aiming for GRADE 4** ↓ | State one variable that can affect the rate of photosynthesis. | | Starter 2, Main |
| | State that water plants can be used to measure the rate of photosynthesis. | | Starter 1, Main |
| | Record the rate of photosynthesis as either the number of bubbles per unit of time or the time taken to produce a fixed number of bubbles. | | Main |
| **Aiming for GRADE 6** ↓ | Describe a method you could use to investigate how a factor affects the rate of photosynthesis. | 5 | Starter 1, Main |
| | Describe how to safely use water plants when measuring the rate of photosynthesis. | | Starter 1, Main, Plenary 1 |
| | Calculate the rate of the reaction at each experimental condition as 1/time, or explain why the number of bubbles produced provides a rate. | 1 | Main |
| **Aiming for GRADE 8** ↓ | Explain how all variables except the independent and dependent variables are controlled when measuring the rate of photosynthesis. | | Main, Plenary 2 |
| | Discuss the ethical considerations when using any living organism (like water plants) in an experiment. | | Main, Plenary 1 |
| | Plot a rate graph for the effect of a named factor on the rate of photosynthesis. | 3 | Main |

**Maths**
During the main activity students may solve simple algebraic equations (M3d) and use appropriate number of significant figures (M2a). Whilst handling the data they may calculate an arithmetic mean (M2b). Students will be required to plot two variables from experimental data (M4c).

**Literacy**
During the main activity students will need to produce coherent, well-structured, and purposeful texts.

**Key words**
photosynthesis, rate

# Practical activity groups

| Starter | Support/Extend | Resources |
|---|---|---|
| **How can we measure the rate of photosynthesis?** (10 minutes) Ask the class how you could measure the rate of photosynthesis. The more common answers tend to suggest measuring how much starch the leaf contains or measure how quickly the plant grows. Discuss the limitations of these ideas, and then ask for further ideas. They may suggest oxygen production. Then mention the bubbles produced on the top of a pond on a sunny day, and state that these are oxygen released from photosynthesising plants. If possible show a video of the production of oxygen in pondweed experiments.<br><br>**The factors: photosynthesis** (5 minutes) Use the interactive, which asks students to link the name of a factor that affects the rate of photosynthesis with an explanation of the effects. | **Extend:** Discuss how to measure the rate of photosynthesis. | |

| Main | Support/Extend | Resources |
|---|---|---|
| **B5 Photosynthesis** (40 minutes) Follow the Photosynthesis activity from the Student Book. Students will do this by investigating the factors that can affect the rate of photosynthesis on *Cabomba*. This will involve selecting a factor and designing an experiment (using a given test) that will investigate the factor whilst keeping all other factors controlled. Students will collect data, they may calculate a rate of photosynthesis, at a given condition, and finally plot rate graphs<br><br>In a first lesson carry out the practical activity as described, and consider the issues of planning and risk assessment.<br><br>A second lesson could be used to write the final report of the practical activity.<br><br>SAFETY: *Cabomba* might be considered an invasive species: do not dispose of waste plant material into ponds or rivers. | **Support:** Provide a prompt sheet that asks the students to select a factor, identify how they will change this variable, state what the dependent variable will be and what variables will be controlled, etc., to help them plan their method.<br><br>**Support:** Ask students to plot a graph of number of bubbles against distance/temperature/carbon dioxide concentration. Supply the axes. | **Practical:** PAG B5 Photosynthesis |

| Plenary | Support/Extend | Resources |
|---|---|---|
| **Ethical debate** (10 minutes) Ask the class to list the pros and cons of using living things in experiments. Then hold a short debate. What kinds of controls might the class decide on when using living things?<br><br>**Limitations** (5 minutes) List as many limitations with the experiment as the class can recall from the activity. Evaluate how serious the limitation might be and how each might affect the results. | **Support:** List several pros and cons and ask the class to discuss how important each is.<br><br>**Extend:** Justify the opinions raised. | |

| Homework | | |
|---|---|---|
| Design a label for plants to be used in a garden centre. The label will be attached to plants to tell the public when they can expect their plants to grow the most and explains why. | | |

# B6 Physiology

**Specification links:**

PAG B6 Safe and ethical use of living organisms (plants or animals) to measure physiological functions and responses to the environment.

WS2a Carry out experiments.

WS2b Make and record observations and measurements using a range of apparatus and methods.

WS2c Present observations using appropriate methods.

WS2d Communicate the scientific rationale for investigations, methods used, findings, and reasoned conclusions.

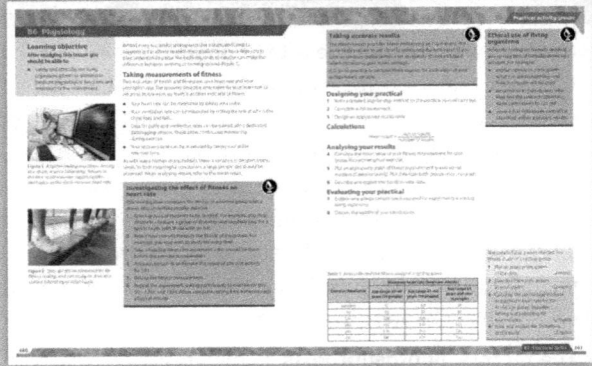

| Target | Outcome | Checkpoint | |
|---|---|---|---|
| | | Question | Activity |
| **Aiming for GRADE 4** ↓ | State that recording pulse and ventilation rate can be used as a measure of fitness. | | Starter 1 and 2<br>Main<br>Plenary 1 |
| | Record data on pulse rate and ventilation rate. | | Main |
| | State that human subjects can be used to monitor physiological responses. | | Starter 1 and 2<br>Main<br>Plenary 2 |
| **Aiming for GRADE 6** ↓ | Describe a method that will investigate the effect of different amounts of exercise on pulse rate and ventilation rate. | | Starter 2<br>Main |
| | Calculate mean values from recorded data of pulse rate and ventilation rate after different amounts of exercise. | | Main |
| | Suggest some safety considerations when using human subjects to monitor physiological responses. | | Main<br>Plenary 2 |
| **Aiming for GRADE 8** ↓ | Explain why the change in pulse rate and ventilation rate following exercise can be used to interpret fitness levels. | 2, 3 | Starter 2<br>Main<br>Plenary 1 |
| | Plot an appropriate graph of the changes in pulse rate and ventilation rate after different amounts of exercise. | 1 | Main |
| | Assess the safety and ethical use of human subjects when monitoring physiological responses. | 4 | Main<br>Plenary 2 |

**Maths**
During the main students will need to calculate the arithmetic means of their data (M2b), and record them to the appropriate number of significant figures (M2a). They will also need to plot two variables from experimental data (M4c).

**Literacy**
During the main activity students will need to produce coherent, well-structured, and purposeful texts.

**Key words**
breathing rate, exercise, fitness, heart rate, recovery

# Practical activity groups

| Starter | Support/Extend | Resources |
|---|---|---|
| **100 m race** (5 minutes) Show a film of a 100 m race. Ask the students to identify as many physiological changes in the athletes as they can. Can they suggest a reason for the changes?<br>**Sports physiology** (10 minutes) Show an image of an athlete on a running machine or bike, with a face mask, chest straps, and so on. Ask the class what they think the physiologist is recording. Ask them if they know what baseline measurement is, and to predict what will happen to each measurement as the athlete exercises. How would a sports physiologist be able to use these measurements to assess levels of fitness, and the effects of training? | **Support:** Use a volunteer, and observe the physiological changes. These will then be more evident.<br>**Extend:** Students could suggest any futher measures of fitness that they know, and discuss any limitations of the measures (e.g., BMI gives poor values for muscular sports people, such as rugby players). | |

| Main | Support/Extend | Resources |
|---|---|---|
| **B6 Physiology** (40 minutes) Follow the Physiology activity from the Student Book. Students will do this by investigating the effect of exercise on pulse rate/ventilation rate and recovery. This will involve designing an experiment (using a given test) that will investigate the effect of different amounts of exercise on the pulse rate and ventilation rate. Students will collect data, they will calculate mean values of pulse and ventilation rates after each period of exercise, and finally plot line graphs.<br>In a first lesson carry out the practical activity as described, and consider the issues of planning and risk assessment.<br>A second lesson could be used to write the final report of the practical activity.<br>SAFETY: Check student suitability and willingness to participate. | **Support:** Record either pulse or ventilation rate. Students often find it difficult to take the pulse manually, so you could use a student confident in recording the pulse to do the recording, or use a digital pulse meter.<br>**Support:** Provide axes for the graph.<br>**Extend:** Calculate percentage increases in the rates. Students could design an experiment to look at recovery rates. | **Practical:** PAG B6 Physiology |

| Plenary | Support/Extend | Resources |
|---|---|---|
| **The effects of exercise** (5 minutes) Use the interactive that contains a paragraph describing the physiological changes that occur during exercise. There are gaps in the paragraph into which students drop the most appropriate answer.<br>**Ethical surveys** (10 minutes) Assuming that sports physiologists want to produce a report on this kind of experiment, they would need to use a large number of human subjects. In groups decide how you would select your survey group. The students should consider issues like sample size, subject age, gender, lifestyle issues, and the safety of subjects. Then they give feedback to the class. | **Support:** Provide prompt questions, such as 'How big would your sample be?' and 'What age would they be and why?' | |

| Homework | | |
|---|---|---|
| You are a sports physiologist. Design a fitness programme for someone, for example, who wants to become a good athlete. Describe the training schedule, giving reasons. Explain how the sports physiologist would monitor the progress of the person. | | |

# B7 Microbiology

**Specification links:**

PAG B7 Use of appropriate apparatus and techniques for the observation and measurement of biological changes and/or processes.

PAG B7 Safe use of appropriate heating devices and techniques including use of a Bunsen burner and a water bath or electric heater.

WS2a Carry out experiments.

WS2b Make and record observations and measurements using a range of apparatus and methods.

WS2c Present observations using appropriate methods.

WS2d Communicate the scientific rationale for investigations, methods used, findings, and reasoned conclusions.

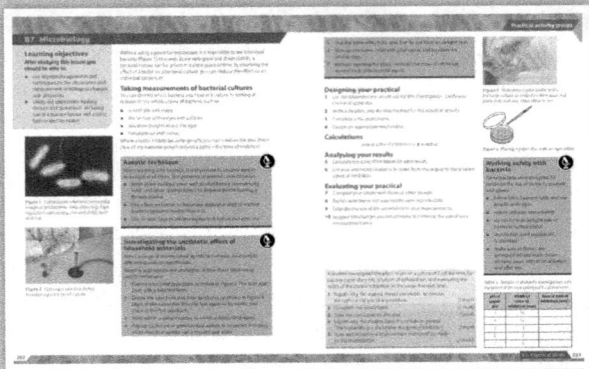

| Target | Outcome | Checkpoint | |
|---|---|---|---|
| | | Question | Activity |
| Aiming for GRADE 4 | State what is meant by aseptic technique. | 1 | Starter 1<br>Main<br>Plenary 1 and 2 |
| | Describe what a zone of inhibition is. | | Main |
| | Identify hazards in this practical procedure. | | Starter 1 and 2<br>Main |
| Aiming for GRADE 6 | Describe several procedures you could use to perform an aseptic technique. | | Starter 1<br>Main<br>Plenary 1 and 2 |
| | Describe how to measure the size of the zone of inhibition. | 2 | Main |
| | Assess the risks caused by hazards in the practical procedure for growing microorganisms. | | Starter 1 and 2<br>Main |
| Aiming for GRADE 8 | Explain how methods used in an aseptic technique work. | 1 | Starter 1<br>Main<br>Plenary 1 and 2 |
| | Explain why different antimicrobial agents produce zones of inhibition of different sizes. | 3, 4 | Main |
| | Evaluate all the major risks in this practical procedure and suggest control measures for those risks. | | Main |

**Maths**
During the main activity students will need to either calculate a mean (M2b) or calculate an area by solving simple algebraic equations (M3d).

**Literacy**
During the main activity students will need to produce coherent, well-structured, and purposeful texts.

**Key words**
antimicrobial agent, aseptic technique, bacterium, colony, culture, zone of inhibition

262

# Practical activity groups

| Starter | Support/Extend | Resources |
|---|---|---|
| **I've got it wrong again** (10 minutes)   Demonstrate how to make a pour plate and place an antimicrobial agent into it. Make as many mistakes as possible (non-aseptic mistakes, NOT dangerous mistakes). Ask the class to pick out all of your mistakes, and explain why this is no longer aseptic.<br><br>**Safety first.** (5 minutes)   Use the interactive, which links a safety method with a description of how that method works, and why it is needed. | **Extend:** Evaluate how serious the mistake might be to the quality of your results. | |

| Main | Support/Extend | Resources |
|---|---|---|
| **B7 Microbiology** (40 minutes)   Follow the Microbiology activity from the Student Book. Students will do this by investigating the effectiveness of antimicrobial agents on the growth of a bacterial lawn. This will involve following an experimental method that will investigate the effect of different antimicrobial agents on the size of the zone of inhibition. Students will collect data, and they may calculate the area of the zone of inhibition for each given antimicrobial agent.<br><br>In a first lesson carry out the practical activity as described, and consider the issues of planning and risk assessment.<br><br>A second lesson could be used to write the final report of the practical activity. | **Support:** Provide a results table to record the results. Only measure the four directions and calculate a mean. | **Practical:** PAG B7 Microbiology |

| Plenary | Support/Extend | Resources |
|---|---|---|
| **How aseptic was your technique?** (5 minutes)   Looking at the plates at the end of the experiment, ask the class if there was any contamination in any of their plates. Ask for ideas about how and when the contaminants got into the plates. How could they improve on this result?<br><br>**Applications of aseptic techniques** (10 minutes)   Ask the class to discuss in groups where they think scientists or other workers need to use aseptic techniques. They should make a list of as many examples of its use in society. They should then explain why aseptic techniques are important. | **Support:** Suggest a few areas of industry for example, food, health, make-up, pharmaceuticals, and so on.<br><br>**Extend:** The students could also suggest how the technique is achieved, especially if their example is a non-scientific area. | |

| Homework | | |
|---|---|---|
| Write a TV script for an advert that will feature scientists explaining how they have tested either a cleaning product or a mouthwash (or any product related to your experiment). They need to provide a scientific reason for the quality of the product. | | |

# B8 Osmosis

**Specification link:**

PAG B8 Use of appropriate apparatus and techniques for the observation and measurement of biological changes and/or processes.

WS2a Carry out experiments.

WS2b Make and record observations and measurements using a range of apparatus and methods.

WS2c Present observations using appropriate methods.

WS2d Communicate the scientific rationale for investigations, methods used, findings, and reasoned conclusions.

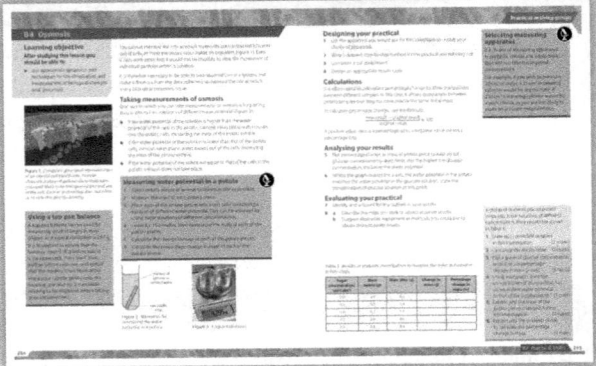

| Target | Outcome | Checkpoint | |
|---|---|---|---|
| | | Question | Activity |
| **Aiming for GRADE 4** ↓ | Use suitable equipment for the technique. | | Starter 2<br>Main<br>Plenary 2 |
| | Use measuring equipment to obtain a reading. | | Starter 2<br>Main<br>Plenary 2 |
| | Record data of the mass of potatoes before and after the experiment. | | Starter 1<br>Main<br>Plenary 1 and 2 |
| **Aiming for GRADE 6** ↓ | Use the most appropriate equipment for the technique. | | Starter 2<br>Main<br>Plenary 2 |
| | Use measuring equipment to obtain an accurate reading. | | Starter 2<br>Main<br>Plenary 2 |
| | Calculate the percentage change in mass of the potatoes at each sugar concentration. | 2 | Starter 1<br>Main |
| **Aiming for GRADE 8** ↓ | Use the most appropriate equipment for the technique and justify the choice. | | Starter 2<br>Main<br>Plenary 2 |
| | Use measuring equipment to obtain an accurate reading. | | Starter 2<br>Main<br>Plenary 2 |
| | Plot a line graph to illustrate the percentage change in mass of the potatoes at different sugar concentrations. | 3 | Main |

**Maths**
During the main activity students will need to calculate the percentage change in mass by solving simple algebraic equations (M3d), and use the percentage (M1b). Then they will need to plot two variables from experimental data (M4c), they will also need to determine the intercept of a linear graph (M4d).

**Literacy**
During the main activity students will need to produce coherent, well-structured, and purposeful texts.

**Key words**
concentration, osmosis, water potential

264

| Starter | Support/Extend | Resources |
|---|---|---|
| **What is osmosis?** (5 minutes) Place a sweet (e.g. a jelly baby) into a beaker of water. It should slowly increase in size. Ask the class to describe and explain what they observe.<br><br>**Accuracy** (10 minutes) Create a carousel of different measuring activities. Include a variety of measuring cylinders and beakers with a volume of water in them; centimetre/millimetre rulers to measure the length of an object; and any different forms of balance you have to record the mass of an object. You should have the accurate values. The class rotates around the instruments, recording the values. Discuss and compare results. Discuss the concept of accuracy in reading. | **Extend:** Record the mass before and after a period of a lesson (or have a pre-soaked jelly baby).<br><br>**Support:** Provide each group with only two pieces of equipment to measure the same variable.<br><br>**Extend:** Students could explain which piece of equipment is the most suitable for a given situation (e.g., measuring 10 $cm^3$ of a solution). | |

| Main | Support/Extend | Resources |
|---|---|---|
| **B8 Osmosis** (40 minutes) Follow the Osmosis practical in the Student Book, which involves investigating the effect of different water potentials on the length and mass of potato chips. This will involve the accurate measurement of volumes of sugar solutions of different concentrations, and the accurate recording of the mass of potatoes. Students will need to calculate the percentage change in mass and plot a graph of the data.<br><br>In a first lesson carry out the practical activity as described, and consider the issues of planning and risk assessment.<br><br>A second lesson could be used to write the final report of the practical activity. | **Support:** Handle each concentration separately by each group carrying out only one or two dilutions and sharing the data.<br><br>**Support:** Students may need help in calculating percentages – carry out a demonstration on the board for them. Provide axes for graph, and illustrate that the graph will cross the *x*-axis. | **Practical:** PAG B8 Osmosis |

| Plenary | Support/Extend | Resources |
|---|---|---|
| **Explaining osmosis** (5 minutes) Use the interactive that contains two short paragraphs explaining the events occurring when potatoes are put in water and in a strong sugar solution. Certain key words are missing and the students need to select the correct word from a dropdown.<br><br>**Sources of error** (10 minutes) In groups the students make a list of sources of error in an experiment. They then pass the list to the next group. This group needs to categorise the cause of the error as the result of equipment, human action, or a flaw in the method. They then pass the list to a third group, who have to suggest a way of improving or removing the error. | **Support:** Provide a list of possible errors, and the class completes the second and third step. | |

| Homework | | |
|---|---|---|
| Search 'osmotic power' online and find an image of the use of osmosis to generate an electric current. Distribute an image and the students will need to produce an explanation of how the process works. | | |

# Answers for Student Book questions

## B1.1 Cell structures

### B1.1.1 In-text questions
A  Eukaryotic cells have a nucleus, prokaryotic cells do not
B  To provide a significant quantity of energy for the muscle cells to enable movement
C  Plant cells have a tough cellulose cell wall, and a sap-filled vacuole

### B1.1.1 Spread questions
1  Similarities: both contain nucleus, cell membrane, cytoplasm and mitochondria *(1 mark)*
   Differences: plant cells contain a vacuole, cell wall and chloroplasts; animal cells do not *(1 mark)*
2  a  Plants perform photosynthesis, animals do not *(1 mark)*
   b  The root cells receive no light so cannot photosynthesise, therefore require no chloroplasts. Leaf cells do receive light, so require chloroplasts to enable photosynthesis *(1 mark)*
3  Any six from:
   Cell membrane – to allow selected substances into or out of the cell *(1 mark)*
   Cell wall – to provide structure *(1 mark)*
   Chloroplasts – to allow the algal cell to produce its own food via photosynthesis *(1 mark)*
   Cytoplasm – where the cell reactions take place *(1 mark)*
   Mitochondria – to release energy for the algal cells *(1 mark)*
   Nucleus – to control the activities of the algal cells *(1 mark)*
   Vacuole – to keep the cells rigid *(1 mark)*

### B1.1.2 In-text questions
A  e.g. *Salmonella, Campylobacter*
B  The genetic information is found in the cytoplasm. It is arranged as a circular chromosome.
C  e.g. Flagella – tail-like structure made of protein strands, which enables the cell to move through liquids / pili – tiny hair-like structure which enables the bacterial cell to attach to a structure / slime capsule – a layer outside the cell wall which helps the bacteria to stick to smooth surfaces / protects the bacteria from environmental dangers e.g. chemicals / drying out.

### B1.1.2 Spread questions
1  Similarities – both cell types have: (2 from) cell wall / cytoplasm / cell membrane *(1 mark)*
   Differences – plant cells have: (2 from) permanent vacuole / nucleus / chloroplasts *(1 mark)*
2  Any two from:
   Flagella – to enable the bacterial cells to move *(1 mark)*
   Pili – to enable the bacterial cells to attach to another structure *(1 mark)*
   Slime capsule – to help the bacterial cells to stick to another structure *(1 mark)*

3  a  $2\,\mu m = 2 \times 10^{-6}\,m$ *(1 mark)*
      Number of bacteria $= \dfrac{\text{size}}{\text{bacterial size}}$
      $= \dfrac{1 \times 10^{-3}}{2 \times 10^{-6}}$ *(1 mark)*
      $= 500$ *(1 mark)*
      OR
      $1\,mm = 1000\,\mu m$ *(1 mark)*
      Number of bacteria $= \dfrac{\text{size}}{\text{bacterial size}}$
      $= \dfrac{1000}{2}$ *(1 mark)*
      $= 500$ *(1 mark)*
   b  Width $= 2 \times 20\,000 = 40\,000\,\mu m$ *(1 mark)*
      $1\,mm = 1000\,\mu m$
      Size $= \dfrac{40\,000}{1000}$
      $= 40\,mm$ *(1 mark)*

### B1.1.3 In-text questions
A  On the stage
B  Coarse focus – to rapidly locate the approximate focus for an object
   Fine focus – to bring the object clearly into focus
C  Iodine because it is a plant cell and iodine stains plant cell nuclei

### B1.1.3 Spread questions
1  Sample → objective lens → eyepiece lens *(1 mark)*
2  Any four from:
   Place tape on a slide, add a drop of stain *(1 mark)*
   Methylene blue *(1 mark)*
   Add a cover slip / tap to remove air bubbles / place on stage *(1 mark)*
   Select lowest magnification *(1 mark)*
   Use coarse focus to roughly view cell / use fine focus to view image clearly *(1 mark)*
   Increase magnification of objective lens to view structures in more detail *(1 mark)*
3  Magnification = objective lens magnification × eyepiece lens magnification *(1 mark)*
   Magnification $= 20 \times 10$ *(1 mark)*
   $= 200X$

### B1.1.4 In-text questions
A  Advantage: produces an image of the highest resolution.
   Disadvantage: does not produce a 3D image of an object.
B  Advantages – cheap to buy/use/ portable/ sample easy to prepare/ natural colours seen/ sample can be alive.
C  Viruses are too small to be seen by light microscopes.

### B1.1.4 Spread questions
1  They do not have a high enough resolution *(1 mark)*
2  A beam of electrons is transmitted through the sample *(1 mark)*
   electrons are then focused to produce an image *(1 mark)*

# Answers

3 Light microscope *(1 mark)*
the organism needs to be alive to see its heartbeating *(1 mark)*

4 $\dfrac{2 \times 10^{-7}\,m}{1 \times 10^{-10}\,m}$ *(1 mark)*
$= 2 \times 10^3$ or 2000X *(1 mark)*

## B1.2 What happens in cells?

### B1.2.1 In-text questions
A They share some characteristics as they inherit half their DNA from one parent and half from the other. They would have to inherit all of their DNA from one parent to be identical.
B Chromosome
C It is a molecule made up of smaller units.

### B1.2.1 Spread questions
1 Nucleotide, gene, chromosome, nucleus, cell *(1 mark)*
2 T A A C G T (1 mark for A bonding to T; 1 mark for C bonding to G)
3 Any six from:
It is formed from two strands *(1 mark)*
The two strands are twisted into a double helix *(1 mark)*
DNA is a polymer *(1 mark)*
made of nucleotides *(1 mark)*
A nucleotide consists of a sugar / deoxyribose, phosphate group and DNA base *(1 mark)*
The two strands are bonded together by complementary base pairs *(1 mark)*
The base pairs are A, C, G, T *(1 mark)*
A bonds to T, C bonds to G *(1 mark)*

### B1.2.2 In-text questions
A ACGU
B Every 3 nucleotides / bases code for an amino acid

### B1.2.2 Spread questions
1 DNA has two strands; mRNA has only one
mRNA has uracil; DNA has thymine
mRNA is small enough to leave the nucleus;
DNA is not
2 Transcription – production of a strand of mRNA *(1 mark)*
Translation – production of a chain of amino acids (protein) *(1 mark)*
3 Any six from:
DNA 'unzips' *(1 mark)*
A copy of the DNA strand is made – mRNA *(1 mark)*
mRNA travels out of the nucleus *(1 mark)*
to the cytoplasm / ribosome *(1 mark)*
Each triplet / three bases / nucleotides code for an amino acid *(1 mark)*
A chain of amino acids is formed *(1 mark)*
These fold to make a protein *(1 mark)*
The amino acids and their order defines the protein made *(1 mark)*

### B1.2.3 In-text questions
A It speeds up reactions, is not used up, only catalyses a specific reaction.
B An enzyme speeds a reaction up but is not changed. The substrate is the molecule an enzyme binds to – it is changed as a result of the reaction.
C Glucose and glycogen are differently shaped molecules. Glucose will not fit into the active site of an enzyme which binds to glucose.

### B1.2.3 Spread questions
1 a Suitable substrate molecule drawn *(1 mark)*
b Active site labelled where the two molecules bind *(1 mark)*
2 Any four from:
Enzymes are specific *(1 mark)*
meaning they only bind to one substrate *(1 mark)*
The active site of the enzyme *(1 mark)*
must fit the shape of the substrate *(1 mark)*
lock and key hypothesis *(1 mark)*
Carbohydrate molecules have different shape to lipid molecules *(1 mark)*
so cannot bind to lipase *(1 mark)*
3 Any four from:
The base sequence on the mRNA code is incorrect *(1 mark)*
so incorrect sequence of amino acids are coded for. *(1 mark)*
Amino acid chain folds incorrectly / differently *(1 mark)*
so shape of enzyme / protein is different *(1 mark)*
active site will not fit substrate. *(1 mark)*

### B1.2.4 In-text questions
A Three from: temperature, pH, concentration of enzyme, concentration of substrate
B It changes shape / unfolds
C pH 2

### B1.2.4 Spread questions
1 Increasing temperature increases rate of reaction *(1 mark)*
until the enzyme becomes denatured *(1 mark)*
2 a 37 °C
b Gradient $= \dfrac{\text{rise}}{\text{run}}$ *(1 mark)*
$= \dfrac{0.03}{20}$ *(1 mark)*
$= 0.0015$ (units: 1 / °C) *(1 mark)*
3 Many body reactions are controlled by enzymes. *(1 mark)*
At increased temperatures, enzymes denature. *(1 mark)*
Reactions are no longer catalysed. *(1 mark)*
Body reactions occur too slowly to sustain life. *(1 mark)*

## B1.3 Respiration

### B1.3.1 In-text questions
A The rate at which the body uses energy.
B Glucose
C Synthesis – creating; breakdown – splitting (into monomers).

### Practical feature: Investigating enzymes
1 The iodine will not change colour as there is no starch left (all converted to glucose).
2 The iodine will always turn black as starch is present, enzyme unable to bind to the starch and convert it to glucose.
3 Initially as temperature increases, the faster the end point of the reaction. Over 37–40 °C reaction no longer occurs as the enzyme is denatured.

**Literacy feature: Word endings**
  Sugars – galactose, fructose
  Enzymes – maltase, catalase

### B1.3.1 Spread questions
1. a  Lipids – fatty acids and glycerol. *(1 mark)*
   b  Carboydrates – glucose. *(1 mark)*
   c  Proteins – amino acids. *(1 mark)*
2. No – they would be different. *(1 mark)*
   Different enzymes operate at different pH values. *(1 mark)*
   Altering a pH can cause enzymes to denature. *(1 mark)*
3. Glucose molecules are joined together. *(1 mark)*
   Many glucose molecules form glycogen. *(1 mark)*
   To breakdown glycogen back into glucose
   an enzyme is required. *(1 mark)*
   This would be a carbohydrase enzyme. *(1 mark)*

### B1.3.2 In-text questions
A  glucose + oxygen → carbon dioxide + water (+ energy)
B  To synthesise new molecules; to produce movement; to keep an organism warm.
C  (Thermal) energy is released during the reaction.

### B1.3.2 Spread questions
1. Carbon dioxide ($CO_2$); water ($H_2O$)
2. Muscle cells require energy to produce movement. *(1 mark)*
   Energy is produced in the mitochondria of cells. *(1 mark)*
   The more mitochondria a cell contains, the more
   energy can be produced in the cells. *(1 mark)*
3. Any six from:
   Eating food supplies the body with glucose. *(1 mark)*
   Glucose is one of the reactants in the respiration
   reaction. *(1 mark)*
   If little food is eaten, the body will lack glucose. *(1 mark)*
   Little respiration will then occur. *(1 mark)*
   Little ATP will be produced. *(1 mark)*
   Processes which require energy – movement / keeping
   warm / synthesis of new molecules – will slow down. *(1 mark)*
   The person will therefore move less / feel cold / stop growing.
   *(1 mark)*

### B1.3.3 In-text questions
A  Reactant – glucose; product – lactic acid.
B  Extra oxygen is required to break down lactic acid in the muscles.
C  It anaerobically respires/undergoes fermentation converting it into ethanol

### B1.3.3 Spread questions
1. Similarity – both require glucose / both produce energy *(1 mark)*
   Difference – animals produce lactic acid as waste product;
   plants produce ethanol and carbon dioxide *(1 mark)*
2. Any 4 from:
   Aerobic – provides more energy / ATP per glucose molecule
   *(1 mark)* accept converse
   Aerobic – requires oxygen *(1 mark)* accept converse
   Aerobic – completely breaks down glucose molecules *(1 mark)*
   accept converse
   Anaerobic – leads to build-up of lactic acid *(1 mark)*
   accept converse
   Anaerobic – can only be performed for short periods of time
   *(1 mark)* accept converse
3. Any six from:
   Aerobic respiration takes place. *(1 mark)*
   Correct statement of aerobic respiration word or chemical
   equation. *(1 mark)*
   Glucose molecules react with oxygen to produce energy.
   *(1 mark)*
   Energy released is used to form ATP. *(1 mark)*
   ATP supplies energy to cells. *(1 mark)*
   Not enough energy id provided by aerobic respiration
   alone. *(1 mark)*
   Anaerobic respiration also occurs. *(1 mark)*
   Glucose is broken down to produce energy
   and lactic acid. *(1 mark)*
   Lactic acid is toxic *(1 mark)*
   and can cause cramp. *(1 mark)*
   Lactic acid is broken down by oxygen /
   oxygen debt needs to be repaid. *(1 mark)*
   Correct statement of anaerobic respiration
   word or chemical equation. *(1 mark)*
   Aerobic respiration produces more ATP per glucose

## B1.4 Photosynthesis

### B1.4.1 In-text questions
A  Carbon dioxide and water.
B  Root hair cells have no chloroplasts.
C  Any three from: the plant converts glucose to starch and / or sucrose; glucose is used in the manufacture of proteins and / or cellulose and / or fats; used in respiration to provide energy.

**Literacy feature: Biological terms**
  Phototropism – Growing towards the light
  Photometer – Instrument for measuring light intensity
  Photoconductive – Material which becomes more electrically conductive when it absorbs light

### B1.4.1 Spread questions
1. Water – obtained through osmosis into the roots / transport
   through the plant *(1 mark)*
   Carbon dioxide – obtained through diffusion through
   the stomata *(1 mark)*
2. Any three from:
   Plants are producers *(1 mark)*
   so pass energy into the food chain; *(1 mark)*
   as you eat plants (or organisms which eat plants) you are
   gaining (a proportion of the) energy in the plant. *(1 mark)*
   Plants produce oxygen *(1 mark)*
   which is required for respiration. *(1 mark)*
3. Any four from (paired sentences required for the mark):
   Reactants of photosynthesis are carbon dioxide and water,
   respiration is oxygen and glucose. *(1 mark)*
   Products of photosynthesis are oxygen and glucose,
   respiration is carbon dioxide and water. *(1 mark)*
   Light is needed for photosynthesis but not for respiration.
   *(1 mark)*
   Photosynthesis only occurs in plants, respiration occurs in
   both plants and animals. *(1 mark)*
   Photosynthesis takes place in chloroplasts, respiration in
   mitochondria. *(1 mark)*

### B1.4.2 In-text questions
A  To allow you to see the iodine colour change more clearly.
B  These parts, which contain chlorophyll, enable the process of photosynthesis to occur, therefore starch was present and the iodine turned blue-black.

C   No light was received in these areas, preventing the process of photosynthesis from occurring, therefore the iodine remained yellow-brown, indicating there was no starch.
D   No carbon dioxide was present, preventing the process of photosynthesis from occurring therefore the iodine remained yellow-brown, indicating there was no starch.

### B1.4.2 Spread questions
1   Glucose – would be tested for by detecting presence of starch. *(1 mark)*
    Iodine used for starch test. *(1 mark)*
    If change is yellow-brown to blue-black, starch is present therefore glucose had been produced. *(1 mark)*
    Oxygen – collected, and tested for presence with a glowing splint which would relight. *(1 mark)*
2   If starch was present from earlier photosynthesis it would appear photosynthesis had occurred during the test, *(1 mark)* which may lead to a false result from the experiment. *(1 mark)*
3   Any six from the following within each experimental design:
    De-starch two plants / place two plants in dark for 24 hours. *(1 mark)*
    Expose one plant to sunlight for several hours; *(1 mark)*
    keep the other plant in the dark. *(1 mark)*
    Test leaves of plant exposed to sunlight and plant kept in the dark for presence of starch *(1 mark)*
    by boiling in ethanol then washing the leaves afterwards. *(1 mark)*
    Add iodine to leaves; *(1 mark)*
    iodine in leaves exposed to sunlight will turn blue-black; *(1 mark)*
    iodine in leaves kept in dark will not change colour. *(1 mark)*
    OR
    De-starch plant / place plant in dark for 24 hours. *(1 mark)*
    Cover individual leaves / parts of individual leaves in black paper. *(1 mark)*
    Expose plant to sunlight for several hours. *(1 mark)*
    Test covered and uncovered leaves for presence of starch *(1 mark)*
    by boiling in ethanol then washing the leaves afterwards. *(1 mark)*
    Add iodine to leaves; *(1 mark)*
    iodine in leaves exposed to sunlight will turn blue-black; *(1 mark)*
    iodine in leaves kept in dark will not change colour. *(1 mark)*

### B1.4.3 In-text questions
A   Carbon dioxide concentration.
B   It would decrease as light intensity decreases.
C   It would decrease.

### B1.4.3 Spread questions
1   Temperature *(1 mark)*
    and light intensity *(1 mark)*
    are higher in summer than winter.
2   The higher the temperature, the higher the rate of photosynthesis *(1 mark)*
    as enzyme-controlled reactions occur faster. *(1 mark)*
    Increasing temperature above an optimal point decreases rate of photosynthesis to zero / stops photosynthesis *(1 mark)*
    because enzymes are denatured. *(1 mark)*
3   a   0.05 *(1 mark)*
        0.13 *(1 mark)*
    b   Correct axes – relative light intensity on x-axis, rate on y-axis *(1 mark)*
        appropriate choice of scales *(1 mark)*
        correct plotting (tolerance ±1mm) *(1 mark)*
        appropriate line of best fit. *(1 mark)*
    c   The higher the light intensity, the greater the rate of photosynthesis. *(1 mark)*
        Light intensity is directly proportional to rate of photosynthesis. *(1 mark)*
        Increasing light intensity increases energy supplied for the photosynthesis reaction. *(1 mark)*

### B1.4.4 In-text questions
A   E.g. measuring volume of oxygen given off per minute, using a gas syringe.
B   16
C   The carbon dioxide concentration has limited the rate of photosynthesis.

### B1.4.4 Spread questions
A   Temperature *(1 mark)*
B   Any three from:
    Greenhouse is warm / light / warm and light *(1 mark)*
    which is / are not limiting factors. *(1 mark)*
    $CO_2$ concentration is the limiting factor *(1 mark)*
    therefore increasing $CO_2$ concentration increases rate of photosynthesis. *(1 mark)*
3   a   2.50, 1.67, 1.25, 0.63 (2 marks for all correct, 1 mark for 2 or more correct)
    b   Correct axes – relative light intensity on x-axis, rate on y-axis *(1 mark)*
        appropriate choice of scales *(1 mark)*
        correct plotting (tolerance ±1mm) *(1 mark)*
        appropriate line of best fit. *(1 mark)*
    c   Any four from:
        Initially, the greater the light intensity, the greater the rate of photosynthesis. *(1 mark)*
        As light intensity increases further, other factors limit the rate of photosynthesis. *(1 mark)*
        Above distances of 0.8 m, light intensity is the limiting factor. *(1 mark)*
        Above distances of 0.8 m, light intensity is proportional to the rate of photosynthesis. *(1 mark)*
        Below distances of 0.8 m temperature / carbon dioxide concentration limits the rate of photosynthesis. *(1 mark)*

## B2.1 Supplying the cell

### B2.1.1 In-text questions
A   The kitchen
B   Because oxygen is at a higher concentration in the air than in your blood.
C   Increase the diffusion distance, decrease the concentration gradient, decrease the surface area

### B2.1.1 Spread questions
1   A difference in concentration between two regions. *(1 mark)*
2   Oxygen is at a higher concentration in the blood. *(1 mark)*
    It diffuses through the cell membrane. *(1 mark)*
    Down a concentration gradient / from a region of high concentration to one of low concentration. *(1 mark)*
3   Any six from:
    Photosynthesis only occurs during the daytime. *(1 mark)*

This process uses carbon dioxide *(1 mark)*
lowering the concentration of $CO_2$ in the plant cells. *(1 mark)*
This increases the $CO_2$ concentration gradient between the air and the plant cells *(1 mark)*
increasing the rate of diffusion into the plant cells. *(1 mark)*
Respiration occurs all the time / still occurs at night time. *(1 mark)*

This process produces carbon dioxide *(1 mark)*
increasing the concentration of $CO_2$ in the plant cells. *(1 mark)*
This increases the $CO_2$ concentration gradient between the plant cells and the air *(1 mark)*
increasing the rate of diffusion out of the plant cells. *(1 mark)*

### B2.1.2 In-text questions
A  Some substances are prevented from passing through the membrane.
B  All of the water molecules are free to move.
C  The water potential around the cell is higher than inside the cell. Water moves into the cell, the vacuole swells, increasing pressure on the cell wall.

### B2.1.2 Spread questions
1  The glucose molecules are too large *(1 mark)*
   to pass through the pores in the selectively permeable membrane. *(1 mark)*
2  Drinking salty water decreases the water potential around cells. *(1 mark)*
   Osmosis occurs moving water molecules out of cells. *(1 mark)*
   This leaves the person requiring more water / dehydrated. *(1 mark)*
3  a  Equal to the concentration / water potential in the blood. *(1 mark)*
   b  If the water potential was too high, water would move into the blood cells *(1 mark)*
      causing lysis. *(1 mark)*
      If the water potential was too low, water would move out of the blood cells *(1 mark)*
      causing the cells to crinkle / become crenated. *(1 mark)*

### B2.1.3 In-text questions
A  Particles are being moved against their concentration gradient.
B  They move molecules across a cell membrane.
C  Mineral ions are being moved against the concentration gradient.

### Literacy feature: Describing cell transport
osmosis; concentration gradient; diffusion; active transport. Definitions as in glossary.

### B2.1.3 Spread questions
1  Across a cell membrane. *(1 mark)*
2  Any two from:
   Diffusion is passive, active transport is active. *(1 mark)*
   Diffusion occurs down a concentration gradient, active transport occurs up a concentration gradient. *(1 mark)*
   Diffusion does not require energy, active transport does. *(1 mark)*
3  Any four from:
   Phosphate ions are dissolved in water. *(1 mark)*
   Phosphate ions are at a lower concentration in the soil than in the plant. *(1 mark)*
   The ions are taken in by active transport *(1 mark)*
   which requires energy to move the ions against their concentration gradient. *(1 mark)*
   The phosphate binds to / is transported by a carrier protein *(1 mark)*
   to move it across the cell membrane. *(1 mark)*
4  Any four from:
   When ingesting large quantities of salt water *(1 mark)*
   the crocodile will build up excess salt *(1 mark)*
   which can be lethal / lead to dehydration. *(1 mark)*
   The concentration of salt in water is higher than inside the crocodile *(1 mark)*
   so active transport must be used to remove it *(1 mark)*
   against the concentration gradient. *(1 mark)*

### B2.1.4 In-text questions
a  Each cell divides to produce two clone cells.
b  TAACGT
c  18 000 million (18 billion) cells

### B2.1.4 Spread questions
1  DNA replication, movement of chromosomes, cell growth. *(1 mark)*
2  To repair damaged tissue e.g. a cut in the skin, *(1 mark)*
   to replace dead cells e.g. blood cells, *(1 mark)*
   for growth e.g. muscle cells. *(1 mark)*
3  Any six from:
   Cells replaced by mitosis. *(1 mark)*
   Sub-cellular structures inside a skin cell are replicated / chromosomes are replicated. *(1 mark)*
   Duplicated chromosome moves to the centre of the cell. *(1 mark)*
   Duplicated chromosome splits into two identical copies. *(1 mark)*
   Each copy of the chromosome is pulled to opposite ends of the cell. *(1 mark)*
   Two nuclei form/ cell increases in size. *(1 mark)*
   Cell membrane breaks and re-fuses to form two new skin cells. *(1 mark)*
   This is occurring in many skin cells at the same time, quickly increasing the number of skin cells present. *(1 mark)*

### B2.1.5 In-text questions
a  E.g. plant – a palisade cell, animal – a red blood cell.
b  The nucleus occupies space. Removing the nucleus allows more space for haemoglobin molecules, which carry oxygen around the body.
c  To enable the cells to perform (lots of) photosynthesis.

### B2.1.5 Spread questions
1  It becomes specialised to perform a particular function. *(1 mark)*
2  E.g. sperm cells *(1 mark)*
   are packed with mitochondria *(1 mark)*
   to produce ATP for movement. *(1 mark)*
3  a  No *(1 mark)*
      as animal cells do not perform photosynthesis. *(1 mark)*
   b  Yes *(1 mark)*
      to provide energy for the rapidly dividing cell. *(1 mark)*
   c  No *(1 mark)*
      but there would be a nucleus containing 23 chromosomes, as sex cells carry half the genetic code for the offspring. *(1 mark)*

# Answers

### B2.1.6 In-text questions
a Stem cells are undifferentiated; specialised cells are differentiated.
b $50 \times 10^9$
c In buds / shoot tips, (rings around) stem, root tips.

### B2.1.6 Spread questions
1 Embryonic – can differentiate to become any cell in the body; adult – can only differentiate to become one of a few cell types. *(1 mark)*
2 This is the growing region of the plant *(1 mark)* where additional plant cells are created. *(1 mark)*
3 Embryonic – advantage – can become any cell in the body. *(1 mark)*
Embryonic – disadvantage – embryo must be destroyed / loss of potential human life. *(1 mark)*
Adult – advantage – taken from a living organism / no loss of life / greater supply. *(1 mark)*
Adult – disadvantage – cannot differentiate into any cell / may not produce required cells to treat condition. *(1 mark)*

## B2.2 The challenges of size

### B2.2.1 In-text questions
A 30:6 or 5:1
B They increase the surface area. The volume is not increased so the surface area to volume ratio increases.

### B2.2.1 Spread questions
1 Substances can diffuse fast enough into the organism. *(1 mark)*

2 
|  | 3 cm side length cube: | 5 cm side length cube: |  |
|---|---|---|---|
| Surface area: | 54 cm² | 150 cm² | *(1 mark)* |
| Volume: | 27 cm³ | 125 cm³ | *(1 mark)* |
| SA / V ratio: | 2 : 1 (or 2) | 1.2 : 1 (or 1.2) | *(1 mark)* |

3 Any six from:
The lung has many alveoli *(1 mark)*
which increase the surface area / surface area : volume ratio of the lungs. *(1 mark)*
The alveoli walls are very thin *(1 mark)*
decreasing the diffusion distance. *(1 mark)*
The lungs have a good blood supply *(1 mark)*
maintaining a high concentration gradient for diffusion. *(1 mark)*
Ventilation replaces the air in the lungs regularly *(1 mark)*
maintaining a high concentration gradient for diffusion. *(1 mark)*

### B2.2.2 In-text questions
A To transport substances around the body.
B Oxygenated – contains a lot of oxygen; deoxygenated – contains little oxygen.
C It has a wall which is only one cell thick (to allow a short diffusion distance).

### B2.2.2 Spread questions
1 Arteries
Structure – thick muscular wall and large lumen. *(1 mark)*
Function – can withstand high pressure *or* carry blood away from the heart. *(1 mark)*
Veins
Structure – thin wall and contain valves. *(1 mark)*
Function – keep blood flowing in only one direction *or* carry blood to the heart. *(1 mark)*
2 Double – as blood flows through the heart twice during each movement around the body. *(1 mark)*
Closed – blood stays within the vessels. *(1 mark)*
3 a The heart only has two chambers *(1 mark)* compared to four in a human. *(1 mark)*
b The blood passes once through the heart for each circulation of the body *(1 mark)* compared to twice for a human. *(1 mark)*

### B2.2.3 In-text questions
a Cardiac muscle contracts without the need for a nervous impulse.
b A lower pressure is required to pump blood to the lungs than the rest of the body.
c Red blood cells.

### B2.2.3 Spread questions
1 Any three from: digested food / amino acids / glucose / waste / carbon dioxide / urea / hormones / antibodies.
2 Assign 1 mark for each paired step correct, max. 3:
(Right atrium →) right ventricle → lungs → left atrium → left ventricle → body → right atrium
3 Any six from:
Muscle cells need extra oxygen/glucose to respire *(1 mark)*
to produce energy for muscle contraction. *(1 mark)*
Ventilation/breathing rate increases *(1 mark)*
body takes in more oxygen. *(1 mark)*
Heart rate increases/beats faster. *(1 mark)*
More oxygen transported by red blood cells *(1 mark)*
more glucose transported by plasma *(1 mark)*
passes into cells through capillaries. *(1 mark)*
More carbon dioxide produced is carried by plasma *(1 mark)*
transported to lungs to be exhaled. *(1 mark)*

### B2.2.4 In-text questions
A Phloem tissue
B Phloem tissue
C Root tissue

### B2.2.4 Spread questions
1 Glucose required for respiration, *(1 mark)*
water required for photosynthesis. *(1 mark)*
2 Any four from:
Found as a network within a leaf *(1 mark)*
to provide structure / support to the soft leaf tissue. *(1 mark)*
Found on the outside of the stem *(1 mark)*
to provide strength / support for the plant stem. *(1 mark)*
Found in the centre of a root *(1 mark)*
to allow the root to bend as the plant moves in the wind. *(1 mark)*
3 Any four from:
xylem – non-living, phloem – living. *(1 mark)*
xylem – transports water for photosynthesis, *(1 mark)*
phloem – transports dissolved sugar for respiration. *(1 mark)*

271

xylem – has no end cell wall, phloem – has end cell wall with
holes / sieve plate. *(1 mark)*
xylem – cell wall thickened for strength *(1 mark)*
phloem – cell wall of normal thickness. *(1 mark)*

### B2.2.5 In-text questions
a  From soil into root hair cell; from the root cells into the xylem of the root; xylem transports water to stem.
b  As it is at a higher concentration inside the leaf, compared to the air surrounding the leaf.
c  To reduce water loss by evaporation from the leaf.

### B2.2.5 Spread questions
1  1 mark for each correct pair of steps, max. 2 marks:
   Water enters plant at roots → water transferred to xylem → water moved up xylem through plant to leaves → water vapour exits the plant from the leaves (transpiration).
2  Transpiration reduces water potential / concentration of water in leaves. *(1 mark)*
   Water moves to replace lost water / flows down concentration gradient. *(1 mark)*
   Increases concentration gradient between soil and root cells. *(1 mark)*
3  Any six from:
   Plants require carbon dioxide for photosynthesis. *(1 mark)*
   Guard cells swell / open *(1 mark)*
   due to becoming turgid *(1 mark)*
   to allow $CO_2$ into the leaf air spaces. *(1 mark)*
   Water evaporates from leaf cells into leaf air spaces. *(1 mark)*
   Concentration gradient now exists between air inside leaf and air outside leaf. *(1 mark)*
   Water vapour moves out of leaf by diffusion. *(1 mark)*
   The more $CO_2$ is required by the plant, the longer the guard cells will be open for *(1 mark)*
   so the greater the rate of transpiration. *(1 mark)*

### B2.2.6 In-text questions
A  It would decrease.
B  It would decrease.

### B2.2.6 Spread questions
1  The greater the rate of photosynthesis, the more $CO_2$ is required. *(1 mark)*
   Stomata open to allow $CO_2$ into the leaves, increasing the rate of water loss. *(1 mark)*
2  Transpiration will be faster on the windowsill. *(1 mark)*
   Because it will be warmer and the light intensity would be higher. *(1 mark)*
3  a  0.33, 2 *(2 marks)*
   b  Bar chart *(1 mark)*
   c  Any three from:
      The highest rate of transpiration was from warm, moving air. *(1 mark)*
      Moving air caused a greater rate of transpiration than still air / warm air caused a greater rate of transpiration than cool air. *(1 mark)*
      Increasing the temperature doubled the transpiration rate. *(1 mark)*
      Moving the air doubled the transpiration rate. *(1 mark)*

## B3.1 The nervous system

### B3.1.1 In-text questions
A  The sensory receptors
B  As the taste receptors in the nose will not detect the stimulus (as efficiently).
C  A neurone is a single cell; a nerve is a bundle of many neurones.

### B3.1.1 Spread questions
1  To detect a stimulus *(1 mark)*
   and produce an electrical impulse. *(1 mark)*
2  Any three from: Sensory receptors *(1 mark)*
   detect pressure *(1 mark)*
   and produce an electrical impulse. *(1 mark)*
   This travels along a sensory neurone to the brain. *(1 mark)*
3  Any six from:
   Light from tennis ball enters eye *(1 mark)*
   detected by light receptors / rods and cones *(1 mark)*
   electrical impulse produced *(1 mark)*
   which travels down the sensory neurone / optic nerve *(1 mark)*
   to the brain *(1 mark)*
   electrical impulse travels along motor neurone *(1 mark)*
   to arm muscle / named muscle *(1 mark)*
   muscle contracts to produce movement. *(1 mark)*

### B3.1.2 In-text questions
A  Reflex reaction does not involve the brain.
B  Reflex
C  E.g. swallowing, controlling blood pressure.

### B3.1.2 Spread questions
1  The impulse has less distance to travel *(1 mark)*
   therefore takes less time to reach the effector *(1 mark)*
2  (a) and (c) reflex actions; *(1 mark)*
   (b) voluntary action. *(1 mark)*
3  Any six in this order from:
   Sharp stone is stimulus. *(1 mark)*
   Pressure detected in skin *(1 mark)*
   by sensory receptors. *(1 mark)*
   Electrical impulse transmitted through sensory neurone *(1 mark)*
   to spinal cord. *(1 mark)*
   Electrical impulse transmitted along motor neurone *(1 mark)*
   to leg / named muscle. *(1 mark)*
   Muscle contracts and moves leg away from object. *(1 mark)*

### B3.1.3 In-text questions
A  Back of the eye.
B  Concave lenses.

### B3.1.3 Spread questions
1  The iris changes the size of the pupil, which is where light enters the eye. *(1 mark)*
2  Any three from:
   The lens is more curved / fatter when viewing the book / nearby object. *(1 mark)*
   The ciliary muscles are contracted. *(1 mark)*
   The front of the classroom is (relatively) distant. *(1 mark)*
   To view this clearly, the ciliary muscles relax, *(1 mark)*
   causing the lens to become thinner. *(1 mark)*

# Answers

3

| Colour | Observed colour | Explanation |
|---|---|---|
| Green | Green *(1 mark)* | Eye responds normally to green light *(1 mark)* |
| Red | Black *(1 mark)* | No response to red light *(1 mark)* |
| Magenta | Blue *(1 mark)* | Eye responds normally to blue light, red light causes no response *(1 mark)* |

### B3.1.4 In-text questions
A   It ensures impulses do not need to travel long distances.
B   Cerebrum
C   It increases the risk of cancer.

### B3.1.4 Spread questions
1   To coordinate the actions of the body. *(1 mark)*
2   The cerebellum *(1 mark)*
    as this part controls movement and balance. *(1 mark)*
3   Techniques (up to 2): e.g. inserting electrodes into animal brains, CT scan.
    Advantages (up to 2): electrodes – allows scientists to make clear links between the region of a brain and the part of the body it controls; CT scan – produces 3D image of the inside of the brain. Disadvantages (up to 2): electrodes – some people disagree with animal testing, as the animal has no choice over taking part; CT scan – X-rays increase risk of cancer.

### B3.1.5 In-text questions
1   E.g. deep cut to a limb, severing the nerve tissue.
2   It is usually not possible to repair damage to the CNS.
3   It is extremely difficult to access the interior of the brain without damaging surrounding tissue.

### B3.1.5 Spread questions
1   This could block the transmission of an impulse from receptor cells e.g. temperature. *(1 mark)*
2   Any three from:
    Damage to the PNS can (sometimes) self-heal. *(1 mark)*
    Some PNS damage can be operated upon *(1 mark)*
    e.g. by grafting healthy nerve tissue to the damaged area. *(1 mark)*
    The CNS cannot regenerate itself. *(1 mark)*
    Surgical procedures on the CNS are extremely difficult *(1 mark)*
    as access is difficult without damaging surrounding healthy tissue. *(1 mark)*
3   The CNS cannot regenerate itself *(1 mark)*
    therefore any damage can only be repaired surgically. *(1 mark)*
    Surgical procedures are extremely challenging *(1 mark)*
    as access to damaged material is within the interior of the brain *(1 mark)*
    or the damaged nerve fibres in the spinal cord are surrounded by (fragile) healthy tissue. *(1 mark)*
    Damaging the healthy tissue can lead to further irreversible nerve damage. *(1 mark)*

## B3.2 The endocrine system

### B3.2.1 In-text questions
A   Nervous
B   Oestrogen, progesterone, testosterone
C   They travel in the blood throughout the body so can reach all areas.

### B3.2.1 Spread questions
1   Helps to control and coordinate body processes. *(1 mark)*
2   To produce and secrete hormones into the bloodstream *(1 mark)*
    e.g. the testes to release testosterone. *(1 mark)*
3   Any six from:
    It is produced in the ovary *(1 mark)*
    and secreted into the bloodstream; *(1 mark)*
    it is carried in plasma *(1 mark)*
    throughout the body; *(1 mark)*
    it has an effect on a target organ / target cells *(1 mark)*
    in the uterus *(1 mark)*
    where it prepares the uterus for implantation of an embryo. *(1 mark)*

### B3.2.2 In-text questions
A   E.g. prior to an exam, walking close to a cliff edge.
B   Hypothalamus / brain
C   To pump oxygen-rich blood around the body so cells can respire to release ATP.

### B3.2 Spread questions
1   Thyroid gland.
2   Brain detects body is under stress / signals adrenal glands. *(1 mark)*
    Adrenal glands release adrenaline. *(1 mark)*
    Any two from:
    Breathing rate / heart rate increases *(1 mark)*
    to allow an increased rate of respiration / to deliver more oxygen to cells *(1 mark)*
    / diverts blood away from digestive system / towards muscles *(1 mark)*
    to allow more energy for muscles. *(1 mark)*
3   Any four from:
    Temperature change detected by receptor cells. *(1 mark)*
    Information sent to control centre / brain. *(1 mark)*
    Brain signals effector cells. *(1 mark)*
    Action taken to decrease body temperature *(1 mark)*
    e.g. sweating. *(1 mark)*
    Body temperature returns to normal level. *(1 mark)*

### B3.2.3 In-text questions
A   The uterus lining has not thickened, so it is not ready to receive the fertilised egg.
B   The pituitary gland; the ovaries.
C   The lining would remain thick.
D   a   Between 12 and 16 days
    b   5 days
    c   7 or 8 days
    d   Any three from:
        • It rises during a period
        • then falls again (to around day 8 of the cycle)
        • there is a small peak around the point of ovulation
        • then rises gradually again until the next period starts

### B3.2.3 Spread questions
1   The lining is shed during a period, so becomes less thick. *(1 mark)*
    It gradually thickens through to the day of ovulation. *(1 mark)*
    It then remains at a constant thickness through to day 28 of the cycle. *(1 mark)*

2  Day 11 *(1 mark)*
   to 16. *(1 mark)*
3  Any six from:
   FSH stimulates the production of oestrogen *(1 mark)*
   and causes egg to mature. *(1 mark)*
   Oestrogen inhibits release of FSH *(1 mark)*
   but stimulates production of LH. *(1 mark)*
   Oestrogen causes the uterus wall to thicken. *(1 mark)*
   LH causes ovulation. *(1 mark)*
   Progesterone inhibits production of LH *(1 mark)*
   and maintains uterus lining thickness. *(1 mark)*

### B3.2.4 In-text questions
A  Prevents the transfer of STIs
B  Once the diaphragm is removed, sperm may remain in the vagina. These must be killed or they may cause pregnancy.

### B3.2.4 Spread questions
1  As they prevent sperm from reaching the egg. *(1 mark)*
2  Hormonal contraceptives are more effective than non-hormonal contraceptives *(1 mark)*
   except the IUD, which is equally as effective. *(1 mark)*
3  a  As bodily fluids are transferred between the male and female. *(1 mark)*
   b  8% per year / 8 females out of 100, per year. *(1 mark)*
   c  Any two from:
      The couple may see the diaphragm as a more natural technique. *(1 mark)*
      Does not involve the use of hormones. *(1 mark)*
      The female may have health problems linked to the use of hormones. *(1 mark)*
      Does not interrupt the act of sexual intercourse as inserted before sex. *(1 mark)*
      The couple may not be concerned about the relatively higher risk of pregnancy. *(1 mark)*

### B3.2.5 In-text questions
a  It could prevent a mature egg travelling to the uterus / it could prevent sperm travelling to fertilise the egg.
b  Blocked sperm ducts.
c  E.g. financial / health (of mother or babies).

### Using maths: IVF success rates
a  Data presented on a histogram
b  The older a woman is, the less likely she is to conceive through IVF.
c  There is approximately twice the chance of success for the 35–37 age group in comparison to the 40–42 age group.
d  The sooner a woman starts IVF, the greater the chance of success. The success rate falls dramatically from the age of 37 onwards.

### B3.2.5 Spread questions
1  Male – blocked sperm duct / low sperm count. *(1 mark)*
   Female – lack of mature eggs / blocked fallopian tubes / failure to release egg. *(1 mark)*
2  Any four from:
   FSH *(1 mark)*
   causes the mother to mature more eggs. *(1 mark)*
   LH *(1 mark)*
   ensures all mature eggs are released. *(1 mark)*
   Progesterone *(1 mark)*
   to ensure the uterus lining thickens to receive a fertilised egg. *(1 mark)*
3  Any three advantages from:
   Allows an infertile / named fertility issue couple to have a baby. *(1 mark)*
   Enables couples to have children later in life. *(1 mark)*
   Once the fertilised egg is implanted, the pregnancy proceeds naturally. *(1 mark)*
   It can result in multiple births which may be welcome. *(1 mark)*
   It allows women to focus on their careers and have a family later in life. *(1 mark)*
   Any three disadvantages from:
   It is expensive *(1 mark)*
   so some people may not be able to afford it. *(1 mark)*
   It can increase the risk of health complications to the mother *(1 mark)*
   and / or baby. *(1 mark)*
   It can result in multiple births which could cause health / emotional / financial concerns. *(1 mark)*
   It only has a low success rate. *(1 mark)*
   Older parents may not be able to cope well with the demands of being a parent. *(1 mark)*

### B3.2.6 In-text questions
A  Positive tropism.
B  Increases rate of photosynthesis which increases plant's survival chances.
C  In shoot cells, more auxin results in more cell elongation. In root cells, more auxin results in less cell elongation.

### B3.2.6 Spread questions
1  As it loses its source of auxins / growth hormones. *(1 mark)*
2  a  E.g. gravity, light. *(1 mark)*
   b  Gravity. *(1 mark)*
3  Any four from:
   The plants will grow towards the light *(1 mark)* phototropism *(1 mark)*
   to maximise the rate of photosynthesis *(1 mark)*
   by auxins moving away from the light *(1 mark)*
   stimulating growth/ cell elongation on the shaded side. *(1 mark)*
   The plant shoots will also grow upwards *(1 mark)*
   and the roots downwards. *(1 mark)*

### B3.2.7 In-text questions
A  Advantage – kills the intended weeds / easier than hand-weeding.
   Disadvantage – may also kill other plants / may enter food chain.
B  Auxin
C  It would cause the unripe fruits to remain unripe for longer.

### B3.2.7 Spread questions
1  Cut a growing shoot *(1 mark)*
   then dip in rooting powder / auxin and plant. *(1 mark)*
2  Bananas release ethene gas *(1 mark)*
   which is a plant hormone for fruit ripening *(1 mark)*
   therefore fruits will ripen more slowly if bananas / ethene is not present. *(1 mark)*

3   Any three named examples, with relevant explanation:
    As weedkillers – auxins  (1 mark)
    because broad-leaved plants are killed whereas narrow-leaved plants are not.  (1 mark)
    To produce clones of desired plants – auxins  (1 mark)
    by taking cuttings of targeted plants.  (1 mark)
    To speed up fruit ripening – ethene to allow fruit crops to be ready earlier in the growing season.  (1 mark)
    To delay fruit ripening – auxins  (1 mark)
    to ensure all of a crop is ripe at the same time.  (1 mark)
    To produce seedless fruit – auxins  (1 mark)
    as seedless crops will be preferred and therefore worth more money.  (1 mark)
    To trigger seeds to germinate – gibberellins or auxins  (1 mark)
    so that crops can germinate at any time of year.

## B3.3 Maintaining internal environments

### B3.3.1 In-text questions
A   Enzyme-based reactions slow down at lower temperatures
B   Nervous system
C   Vasodilation – widening of blood vessels; vasoconstriction – narrowing of blood vessels

### B3.3.1 Spread questions
1   Vasodilation; sweating; hairs on skin lie flat.  (1 mark)
2   Exercise will increase rate of respiration, raising body temperature.  (1 mark)
    This causes the body to sweat;  (1 mark)
    sweat contains salt.  (1 mark)
3   Any six from, for one mark each:
    receptor cells detect body temperature
    impulse is sent to brain / thermoregulatory centre
    impulse is sent to effector cells
    hairs raised on skin
    which traps air around body / insulates the body
    vasoconstriction / narrowing of blood vessels
    which reduces blood flow to capillaries near skin surface
    which minimises heat loss (by radiation).

### B3.3.2 In-text questions
A   Eat less, exercise more.
B   As a chemical store in glycogen.
C   Any two from:
    Type 1 cannot produce insulin, type 2 cannot use insulin effectively.
    Type 1 starts in childhood, type 2 usually starts in adults.
    Type 1 must be controlled through insulin injections, type 2 can usually be controlled through diet.

### Using maths
a   8.30am / immediately after breakfast.
b   Blood glucose levels do not increase as no food is consumed, therefore no stimulus to increase insulin levels.
c   Dinner. The glucose concentration / insulin concentration in the bloodstream during and after the meal remains higher for longer than following the other meals.

### B3.3.2 Spread questions
1   Either:
    if blood sugar levels rise too high  (1 mark)
    it can lead to damage to body systems / nerves / blood vessels;  (1 mark)
    or
    if blood sugar levels fall too low  (1 mark)
    cells can be prevented from respiring effectively.  (1 mark)
2   Insulin is required to decrease blood sugar levels.  (1 mark)
    The footballer would use more glucose / the blood glucose concentration of the footballer would decrease as their rate of respiration would be higher than the office worker.  (1 mark)
3   If the blood sugar level rises above normal levels:
    insulin is released  (1 mark)
    from the pancreas;  (1 mark)
    this causes glucose to be converted to glycogen which is stored in the liver.  (1 mark)
    If the blood sugar level falls below normal levels:
    glucagon is released  (1 mark)
    by the pancreas;  (1 mark)
    this causes the liver to convert glycogen back into glucose.  (1 mark)

### B3.3.3 In-text questions
A   Enters – food / drink; leaves – exhaling / urinating / sweating.
B   Passed through to the bladder; urinated out of the body.
C   Urine would be yellow coloured.

### B3.3.3 Spread questions
1   Blood cells are too large to pass through into the kidney tubes.  (1 mark)
2   Several substances are filtered out of the blood.  (1 mark)
    Useful substances are then reabsorbed into the bloodstream.  (1 mark)
3   Exercise increases the internal temperature of the body;  (1 mark)
    which causes the body to sweat / lose more water;  (1 mark)
    the concentration of water in the bloodstream decreases;  (1 mark)
    urine therefore contains less water.  (1 mark)

### B3.3.4 In-text questions
A   Enters through renal artery and leaves via renal vein.
B   In a nephron.
C   If water potential is high, ADH production is low / vice versa to return water potential to normal levels.

### B3.3.4 Spread questions
1   Blood pressure increases in a glomerulus;  (1 mark)
    this forces smaller molecules through the capillary wall.  (1 mark)
2   Any four from (for one mark each):
    bloodstream carries urea into a glomerulus;
    passes through capillary walls;
    into Bowman's capsule;
    travels through tubule / Loop of Henlé into collecting duct;
    transported to bladder;
    passed out of the body in urine.
3   Any six from (for one mark each):
    sweating causes water to be lost from the body;
    water potential in blood decreases;
    detected in hypothalamus;
    more ADH released;
    permeability of kidney tubules increases;
    more water reabsorbed (into bloodstream);
    less water is lost as urine.

### B3.3.5 In-text questions
**A** The construction worker carries out more physical exertion and / or is exposed to high temperatures. These will cause sweating, so more water is lost from the body.
**B** Salt concentration is lower in blood plasma than in blood cells so water moves into the blood cells by osmosis and they could burst.
**C** Hypotonic (to maximise water intake).

### Working scientifically: Investigating sports drinks
**a** Independent – type of drink; dependent – number of press-ups completed (per unit time); control – e.g. volume of drink, time when drink consumed before exercise.
**b** For example:
 1 Select test group e.g. 25 volunteers
 2 Split volunteers into five groups, one group per sports drink
 3 Volunteers complete as many press-ups as possible in 1 minute
 4 Calculate mean number of press-ups completed per minute
 5 Allow suitable rest period
 6 Volunteers consume 250 cm³ of sports drink 5 minutes prior to exercise
 7 Volunteers re-complete exercise
 8 Calculate mean number of press-ups completed per minute after consuming drink

### B3.3.5 Spread questions
1 Sports drinks also contain salts and glucose *(1 mark)* which may be lost during exercise / dehydration OR sweat contains salt. *(1 mark)*
2 More salt lowers the water potential of blood plasma. *(1 mark)* An impulse is sent to the brain *(1 mark)* which causes the (thirst) response.
3 Any six from (for one mark each):
 - increased ADH production causes kidney tubules to become more permeable;
 - more water is reabsorbed into the blood plasma than required;
 - water potential of blood plasma increases above normal level;
 - taking in additional water / over-hydration causes blood plasma water potential to increase further;
 - concentration of sodium in blood decreases / hyponatremia;
 - cells in the body / named organ will swell / burst;
 - which can lead to (unconsciousness and) death.

## B4.1 Ecosystems
### B4.1.1 In-text questions
**A** The Sun
**B** Level 3
**C** Beetle – green plant
 Owl – shrew, beetle, spider, wood mouse

### B4.1.1 Spread questions
1 Pondweed → pond snail → fish → heron *(1 mark)*
2 a Pondweed *(1 mark)*
 b Heron *(1 mark)*
 c Fish *(1 mark)*
3 Any six from (for *1 mark* each):
 The number of grasshoppers may decrease;
 as shrews / woodmice will have no snails to eat.
 The number of beetles may decrease;
 as grasshoppers have no snails to eat.
 The number of woodmice / shrews may decrease;
 as they have a smaller (range of) food sources.
 The number of green plants may increase;
 as there are no snails to consume them.
 The number of beetles / grasshoppers may increase;
 as there is more food available to support them.
 The number of spiders may decrease.
 As owls may consume more of them, there could be fewer shrews and woodmice.

### B4.1.2 In-text questions
**A** Abiotic.
**B** To absorb more sunlight for photosynthesis.
**C** To determine which crops (plants) will grow well.

### Working scientifically: Measuring abiotic factors

| Abiotic factor | Sensor used | Example unit of measurement |
|---|---|---|
| Light intensity | Light meter | lux |
| Availability of moisture | Humidity sensor | % |
| pH | pH probe | no units |
| Temperature | Thermometer | °C |

### B4.1.2 Spread questions
1 Biotic – e.g. the presence of (named) organisms; competition between (named) organisms (2).
 Abiotic – e.g. temperature, light availability (2).
2 More light allows more plants to grow / plants to grow more quickly *(1 mark)* which increases the availability of food in the ecosystem. *(1 mark)*
3 Animals can move to find new / different resources *(1 mark)* plants can only bend / grow towards a resource. *(1 mark)* Warm-blooded animals are less affected by temperature than plants *(1 mark)* as their metabolism is not slowed down by the external temperature. *(1 mark)*

### B4.1.3 In-text questions
**A** More likely to have good access to light, water and minerals.
**B** To allow access to an adequate food / water supply / mates.
**C** Mosquito – parasite, human – host.

### B4.1.3 Spread questions
1 Plants need to photosynthesise, animals do not *(1 mark)*
2 a Mutualism. *(1 mark)*
 b Predation (predator-prey). *(1 mark)*
 c Parasitism. *(1 mark)*
3 Graph drawn with axes labelled population size / number of organisms (*y*-axis) and time (*x*-axis). *(1 mark)*
 Prey population curves drawn showing cyclical rise and fall. *(1 mark)*
 Predator curve mirroring the prey curve after a short (approximately consistent) time delay. *(1 mark)*
 Up to three marks for correct annotations:
 aphid population grows as plenty of food available / few prey organisms *(1 mark)*

ladybird population rises as large food source / many aphids available *(1 mark)*
aphid population falls as many ladybirds consume many aphids *(1 mark)*
ladybird population falls as aphid / food supply becomes scarce. *(1 mark)*

### B4.1.4 In-text questions
A  E.g. apple tree → aphid → ladybird → swallow
B  Producer / plant.
C  Organisms must be killed to measure the biomass.

### B4.1.4 Spread questions
1  Total mass of organisms / size of organisms at each trophic level.
2  Organisms are killed; *(1 mark)*
   organisms are dried (in a kiln); *(1 mark)*
   mass of dry sample is taken. *(1 mark)*
3  a  Rose bush → aphids → ladybirds *(1 mark)*
   b  An inverted pyramid of numbers would be produced. *(1 mark)*
   c  Biomass: Rose bush – 4 kg; Ladybirds – 0.01 kg; Aphids – 0.2 kg. *(1 mark)*
      Appropriate choice of scale e.g. 1 cm = 0.5 kg. *(1 mark)*
      Accurate drawing of pyramid. *(1 mark)*

### B4.1.5 In-text questions
A  Most light is reflected from the leaves
B  Egestion – removing indigestible substances from the body
   Excretion – removing waste products from the body

### B4.1.5 Spread questions
1  Any four from (for *1 mark* each):
   not all organisms in an area are eaten;
   not all parts of an organism are eaten;
   some parts of an organism are indigestible / are egested;
   respiration requires some biomass;
   some biomass is excreted.
2  Efficiency of biomass transfer
   $= \dfrac{\text{biomass available after the transfer}}{\text{biomass available before the transfer}} \times 100$ *(1 mark)*
   $= \dfrac{90}{15\,000}$ *(1 mark)*
   $= 0.6\%$ *(1 mark)*
3  Warming the environment reduces the need for pigs to generate their body temperature *(1 mark)*
   and restricting movement means less ATP is required *(1 mark)*
   therefore less respiration is required *(1 mark)*
   therefore less biomass is used; *(1 mark)*
   this means the body mass of the pigs increases at a greater rate. *(1 mark)*

### B4.1.6 In-text questions
A  Biotic – animal or plant; abiotic – rock / atmosphere / ocean.
B  Biotic – animal or plant; abiotic – soil / atmosphere.
C  Sun heats the surface of the water causing it turn into water vapour. As this gas rises it cools, and condenses back into water molecules (forming clouds).

### B4.1.6 Spread questions
1  Organisms within a habitat would use up the nutrient resources in an area *(1 mark)*
   so without nutrient cycling the habitat would not sustain (those forms of) life. *(1 mark)*

2  Any three appropriate examples e.g.: named plant – uses water for photosynthesis / combines water with carbon dioxide to produce glucose and oxygen; *(1 mark)*
   named amphibian – uses water for reproduction / place to lay eggs; *(1 mark)*
   named aquatic animal – requires water for habitat. *(1 mark)*
3  Pea plant has roots / nodules containing (nitrogen-fixing) bacteria; *(1 mark)*
   which convert nitrogen gas into nitrates; *(1 mark)*
   nitrates are absorbed by pea plants in water; *(1 mark)*
   and used to synthesise proteins for growth. *(1 mark)*
   Wheat plants gain relatively fewer nitrates from the soil; *(1 mark)*
   which means their gain in biomass will be at a lower rate. *(1 mark)*

### B4.1.7 In-text questions
A  E.g. burning fossil fuels.
B  It is used to make simple sugars, which can then be used to make complex carbohydrates. These enable the plants to grow and develop.
C  Bacteria respire / some bacteria are decomposers / some bacteria can photosynthesise.

### B4.1.7 Spread questions
1  Respiration – all living things respire, releasing carbon dioxide; *(1 mark)*
   decomposition – carbon dioxide released as decomposers respire; *(1 mark)*
   burning fossil fuels – release carbon dioxide through combustion. *(1 mark)*
2  $x$-axis – time (hours), $y$-axis – $CO_2$ concentration / level (ppm) (do not penalise no / incorrect units); *(1 mark)*
   graph with higher atmospheric $CO_2$ level at night time; *(1 mark)*
   drop in $CO_2$ level at position labelled 'sunrise'; rise in $CO_2$ level at position labelled 'sunset'; minimum $CO_2$ level at position labelled 'midday' / 'sun at highest point'. *(1 mark)*
3  Deforestation leads to increase in $CO_2$ level; *(1 mark)*
   because removing trees decreases the number of organisms photosynthesising; *(1 mark)*
   photosynthesis removes atmospheric $CO_2$; *(1 mark)*
   burning trees adds to atmospheric $CO_2$; *(1 mark)*
   as combustion releases $CO_2$. *(1 mark)*

### B4.1.8 In-text questions
A  Decomposer – breaks down materials at a microscopic level;
   detritivore – shreds large pieces of material into smaller pieces.
B  Enzymes are released to chemically break down the material.
C  Three from: heat the material / cool the material / remove moisture / remove oxygen.

### B4.1.8 Spread questions
1  Earthworms break down organic matter into smaller pieces *(1 mark)*
   which speeds up the rate of decomposition / increases the surface area for decomposition. *(1 mark)*
2  Either: limited oxygen supply *(1 mark)*
   prevents large numbers of microorganisms reaching the food / limits microorganism respiration; *(1 mark)*
   or

cool (1 mark)
limits the rate of enzyme-controlled reactions. (1 mark)

3   Rate = $\frac{\text{Change of mass}}{\text{time}}$

10 → 15 days

Rate = $\frac{(25 - 20)}{5}$ (1 mark)

= $\frac{5}{5}$

= 1 g/day (1 mark)

15 → 20 days rate = 2 g/day (no mark, from maths box)
Rate of decay is doubled from 15 → 20 days in comparison to that from 10 → 15 days. (1 mark)
Reasons for the results: little decay at start as only a few microorganisms present, (1 mark)
then rapid decay as microorganisms rapidly reduce, (1 mark)
decay will slow as all food source is used up. (1 mark)

## B5.1 Inheritance

### B5.1.1 In-text questions
A   E.g. language spoken (environmental), eye colour (genetic)
B   E.g. body mass
C   Genetic and environmental

### B5.1.1 Spread questions
1   stem mass – both; number of fruit produced – both; blood group – genetic; skin colour – both; eye colour – genetic; leaf size – both; presence of a scar – environmental
2   Identical twins are genetically identical (1 mark)
    therefore any variation is caused by environmental factors. (1 mark)
3   Any six from (for 1 mark each):
    continuous – named example e.g. arm length;
    can take any value between maximum and minimum values;
    caused by many genes;
    caused by both genetic and environmental causes;
    discontinuous – named example e.g. presence of dimples;
    only has one of a number of specified values (e.g. dimples or no dimples);
    caused by one / only a few genes.

### B5.1.2 In-text questions
A   All the genetic material comes from one parent.
B   Two from: requires two parents; results in variation; genetic material is mixed.

### B5.1.2 Spread questions
1   Sexual – two parents; asexual – one parent. (1 mark)
    Sexual – results in variation; asexual – clones. (1 mark)
    Sexual – mixing of genetic material;
    asexual – no mixing of genetic material. (1 mark)
2   All offspring produced will be identical. (1 mark)
    If parent plant contains advantageous characteristics (e.g. large flowers), all offspring will share the same characteristics. (1 mark)
    Accept converse answer for seeds.
3   Any six from (for one mark each):
    Daffodils gain from being able to use the advantages of both methods.
    Advantages of asexual reproduction:
        Success of reproduction guaranteed
        Does not require pollination
        All advantageous characteristics of parent plant replicated in offspring.
    Advantages of sexual reproduction:
        Variation introduced into species
        Allows colonisation of new areas if advantageous characteristics produced.
    Seeds spread to new areas.
    Combination of reproduction methods lead to increased probability of successful reproduction.
    Increased numbers of species equivalent to increased success of species.

### B5.1.3 In-text questions
A   19 chromosomes
B   64 chromosomes
C   Twice

### B5.1.3 Spread questions
1   a   23 pairs (or 46) (1 mark)
    b   Diploid
2   Meiosis results in variation in gametes. (1 mark)
    Fusion of gametes produces further variation. (1 mark)
    Genome of offspring produced will be unique. (1 mark)
3   Meiosis leads to variation; mitosis does not / leads to genetically identical cells. (1 mark)
    Meiosis creates gametes / sex cells; mitosis creates body cells. (1 mark)
    Meiosis creates haploid cells; mitosis creates diploid cells. (1 mark)
    Meiosis produces four cells from one parent cell; mitosis produces two cells. (1 mark)

### B5.1.4 In-text questions
A   e.g. brown, blonde, black
B   Brown eyes
C   Dominant – e.g. freckles, ability to roll tongue, pointed chin.
    Recessive – e.g. straight, blonde hair, joined earlobes, upturned nose.

### B5.1.4 Spread questions
1   a   Black (1 mark)
    b   White (1 mark)
    c   Black (1 mark)
2   a   Ff (where F = freckles) (1 mark)
    b   ff (1 mark)
3   Red-eyed flies contain two alleles which code for red eyes / or converse. (1 mark)
    Cross white-eyed fly with red-eyed fly.
    All offspring produced will be heterozygous. (1 mark)
    Allele expressed will be the dominant allele. (1 mark)
    If offspring are white eyed, this is the dominant allele, or converse. (1 mark)

### B5.1.5 In-text questions
A   GG (green), gg (yellow)
B   Because each offspring must contain one dominant and one recessive allele.
C   25%

### B5.1.5 Spread questions
1

|   | H  | H  |
|---|----|----|
| h | Hh | Hh |
| h | Hh | Hh |

(1 mark)

2  a  0%
   b  100%
   c  0%
3  a  Parental genotypes: mother EE (or equivalent), father
      ee (or equivalent). *(1 mark)*
      Gametes: mother  father (e)(e) *(1 mark)*

|   | e  | e  |
|---|----|----|
| E | Ee | Ee |
| E | Ee | Ee |

*(1 mark)*

   b  0 homozygous dominant : 4 heterozygous : 0 homozygous
      recessive. *(1 mark)*

### B5.1.6 In-text questions
A  ¼
B  Male
C  50%

### B5.1.6 Spread questions
1  Females
2  Any three from:
   male gametes carry X and Y chromosomes; female gametes
   only X chromosomes; *(1 mark)*
   during fertilisation the male gamete and female gamete
   combine; *(1 mark)*
   50% of the fertilised eggs will contain the chromosomes XY
   /50% of the fertilised eggs will contain the chromosomes XX;
   *(1 mark)*
   XX codes for a female / XY codes for a male. *(1 mark)*
3  Parental genotypes: round Rr (or equivalent), wrinkled rr (or
   equivalent) *(1 mark)*
   Gametes: round 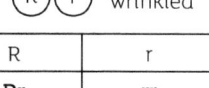 wrinkled (r)(r) *(1 mark)*

|   | R  | r  |
|---|----|----|
| r | Rr | rr |
| r | Rr | rr |

*(1 mark)*

Genotype: 50% Rr : 50% rr *(1 mark)*
Phenotype: 50% round : 50% wrinkled / 50% chance of
producing round-seeded plant. *(1 mark)*

### B5.1.7 In-text questions
A  Sunbathing exposes the body to UV radiation
B  e.g. eye colour, hair colour
C  If the organism lives in a snowy habitat, white fur would offer
   camouflage.

### B5.1.7 Spread questions
1  Cancer, sickle cell anaemia, cystic fibrosis / other named
   genetic disease. *(1 mark)*
2  X-ray would expose radiographer to ionising radiation *(1 mark)*
   which could lead to a harmful mutation. *(1 mark)*
3  Any six from (for one mark each):
   mutation is a change in the sequence of DNA bases;
   this could be an addition, substitution, or deletion to the
   sequence;
   leads to change in the sequence of mRNA bases;
   difference in sequence of amino acids produced;
   protein folds in a different way;
   shape of active site is different;
   active site can no longer bind to the substrate.

### B5.1.8
There are no in-text questions on this spread.

### B5.1.8 Spread questions
1  a  Miescher *(1 mark)*
   b  Mendel *(1 mark)*
   c  Watson and Crick *(1 mark)*
2  To identify and sequence all genes in the human body.
   *(1 mark)*
3  Identification of three named scientists (3).
   Contribution to modern genetics correctly linked (3).
   e.g. Mendel / Miescher / Watson and Crick (3).
   Characteristics determined by hereditary units / identification
   of nucleic acid / determination of DNA structure (3).

## B5.2 Natural selection and evolution
### B5.2.1 In-text questions
A  Unicellular aquatic organisms.
B  E.g. good eyesight (to spot predators), fast runner (to escape
   from predators), camouflaged fur colour (to remain hidden
   from predators).
C  Bacteria reproduce quickly, so any mutation which develops
   antibiotic resistance is quickly passed on to many offspring.

### B5.2.1 Spread questions
1  Organisms which have the most advantageous characteristics are
   the most likely to survive. *(1 mark)*
2  Pale *(1 mark)*
   as most trees are pale coloured / not
   covered in soot / not darker than normal *(1 mark)*
   therefore pale moths are better camouflaged so
   are more likely to pass on their characteristics. *(1 mark)*
3  A mutation could cause resistance to the poison *(1 mark)*
   which would allow these rats to survive for longer *(1 mark)*
   and reproduce (more) *(1 mark)*
   which would pass on their advantageous characteristic to
   their offspring. *(1 mark)*
   Most rats would not be resistant to the poison therefore
   would die if poison was consumed and not pass on their
   characteristics. *(1 mark)*
   Over time, the whole population would derive from rats
   which were resistant to the poison. *(1 mark)*

### B5.2.2 In-text questions
A  The remains of a plant or animal which have mineralised /
   changed to rock over millions of years.
B  It is incomplete.
C  Species which are not adapted to / do not have advantageous
   characteristics for their environment die out.

### B5.2.2 Spread questions
1  Organisms which are now extinct can be viewed *(1 mark)*
   and compared with modern day species to see how the
   species has changed over time. *(1 mark)*
2  Fossils form from the skeletons of organisms / from the
   parts of an organism which do not easily rot away. *(1 mark)*
   Soft-bodied organisms are unlikely to be covered in sediment
   before the decay process takes place. *(1 mark)*
3  Any six from (for one mark each):
   Fossil record;
   which shows the progression of a species from an early
   ancestor to the modern day species.

Extinction;
which shows that only organisms which are adapted to their environment survive.
Rapid changes in a species;
which demonstrate the process of evolution in a very short timescale.
Molecular comparison;
which studies the DNA and proteins of organisms, allowing comparison between species to be made.

## B5.2.3 In-text questions
**A** The fossil record supplies evidence of species which no longer exist / have changed over time
**B** Each island had a different food source. The finches on an island had adaptations to take advantage of a specific food type.

## B5.2.3 Spread questions
1 Lyell, Wallace, Darwin. *(1 mark)*
2 Darwin published a book popularising the topic *(1 mark)*
which meant over time that his name became associated with the theory. *(1 mark)*
3 Any four from (for one mark each):
At the time of publication, most people believed God created all animals and plants.
Darwin's theory was new / opposed this belief.
Darwin was unable to explain how inheritance occurred / Darwin had no knowledge of genes.
Which meant it was hard to convince people that the theory was correct.
It took time to collect further evidence to support the theory.

## B5.2.4 In-text questions
**A** The organism's features are compared with classified species. This enables identification.
**B** Kingdom / phylum
**C** Natural – based on evolutionary links between species; artificial – based on observable characteristics.

**Go further: Binomial nomenclature**
Lion – Genus: *Panthera*, Species: *leo*
Daisy – *Bellis perennis*

## B5.2.4 Spread questions
1 Any two from (for one mark each):
identify species / predict characteristics / find or show evolutionary links / to allow scientists to share research worldwide.
2 **a** Mammoth / *Anancus* / *Primelephas* / *Gomphotherium* / *Paleomastodon* *(1 mark)*
**b** *Gomphotherium* / *Paleomastodon*. *(1 mark)*
3 Any six from (for one mark each):
Early systems based on observable characteristics.
Organisms with similar features were put into the same groups.
This is known as artificial classification.
Credit one example from: (the most commonly used system was based on) seven taxonomic groups / five kingdoms / description of a hierarchical system of classification.
DNA sequencing / study of DNA / similarities in DNA.
Enables scientists to identify genetic / evolutionary links between organisms.
This is known as natural classification.
Enables organisms which do not appear to be similar to be linked with others who share a common ancestor.

# B6.1 Monitoring and maintaining the environment

## B6.1.1 In-text questions
**A** Worm: 5
Spider – ||||  ||
**B** e.g. woodlouse, ladybird
**C** Many will not fall into the trap.
**D** Buttercup – broad leaves, leaf with ragged edge, flowers branch off stem,

## B6.1.1 Spread questions
1 **a** Pooter / tree beating. *(1 mark)*
**b** Kick sampling. *(1 mark)*
**c** Sweep net. *(1 mark)*
2 Broad leaves, leaves have ragged edges, flowers grow from base. *(1 mark)*
3 **a**

| Organism | Frequency |
|---|---|
| Woolly apple aphid | 12 |
| Winter moth caterpillar | 4 |
| Capsid bug | 9 |

**b** 4 caterpillars per tree × 50 trees *(1 mark)*
= 200. *(1 mark)*
**c** It makes the assumption that each tree contains the same number of caterpillars *(1 mark)*
and that all the caterpillars on the sampled tree are collected. *(1 mark)*

## B6.1.2 In-text questions
**A** Animals may move or are hidden.
**B** 1000 dandelions
**C** A transect uses samples taken at pre-determined points.

## B6.1.2 Spread questions
1 Random – position of sample is not pre-determined / collection of organisms is entirely due to chance; non-random – placement of sample is pre-determined.
2 **a** Pooter *(1 mark)*
**b** Estimated population size
$$= \frac{\text{first sample size} \times \text{second sample size}}{\text{number of recaptured marked individuals}}$$
$$= \frac{20 \times 15}{3}$$ *(1 mark)*
= 100 woodlice *(1 mark)*
3 Any six (for one mark each):
Use a random number generator/ other described technique to decide on sample sites.
Sample at least ten different sites on field.
At each site use a quadrat to measure the number and types of plant present.
Set up a pitfall trap and leave overnight to collect crawling invertebrates.
Use tree beating to dislodge invertebrates and collect on sheet.
Use a sweep net to collect any flying insects.
Use a pooter to collect any insects to avoid damaging them / aid identification.
Use an identification key to identity organisms.
Calculate mean average number of organisms at each site sampled (per square metre).
To estimate the total population multiply the mean average by the total field area.

Or estimate population size using capture-recapture (for appropriate organism stated).

## B6.1.3 In-text questions
**A** Trees provide a different habitat to the playing field. Different species are therefore supported in the trees. Losing the trees causes a loss of these species.
**B** Plants are removed. Species which rely on the plants are also lost from an area.
**C** Aquatic plants die. Decomposers multiply, which respire – using oxygen from the lake.

## B6.1.3 Spread questions
1. Any three from:
   Removal of hedgerows; use of pesticides; monoculture; use of herbicides (3).
2. Chemical can (bio)accumulate in target organism. *(1 mark)*
   Other organisms eat many targeted organisms. *(1 mark)*
   Causing high concentrations of (toxic) chemical / leading to death of the organism. *(1 mark)*
3. Any six from:
   Trees are removed.
   Animals which rely on trees for food / shelter will die / move to another area.
   Other organisms which rely on these animals will lose food source.
   So will move elsewhere / die out in an area.
   Plants which would be eaten are allowed to survive.
   Which can outcompete other species, further reducing biodiversity.
   Plant seeds may not be spread by animals.
   Preventing the spread of these plant species.

## B6.1.4 In-text questions
**A** Endangered – few organisms of a species remain; extinct – no organisms of a species remain alive
**B** Restricting access, use of wardens
**C** It may be the removal of / change to the habitat which caused the species to become endangered.

## B6.1.4 Spread questions
1. E.g. may create a tourist attraction / may preserve the natural beauty of the countryside.
2. Any four from (for one mark each):
   Advantages:
     Animals are provided with food / shelter / medical care / protection from predators.
     Which increases organisms' chance of survival.
     Increasing the chance of being able to reproduce.
     So the species' numbers increase.
   Disadvantages:
     Animals are kept in captivity.
     Reduces the gene pool.
     Some organisms may not survive if released back into the wild.
3. Any six from (for one mark each):
   Positive effects:
     Conservation projects;
     Protect / restore habitats;
     So protecting / increasing the numbers of (endangered) species.
     Captive breeding programmes;
     Can help to prevent extinction / increase numbers of endangered species.
     Seed banks;
     Can provide plants in the future if a plant species becomes extinct.
   Negative effects:
     Use of land for building / farming;
     Removes trees, reducing biodiversity.
     Farming;
     Reduces the number of plant species in an area / monoculture;
     Uses pesticides / herbicides which reduces biodiversity;
     Often results in the removal of hedgerows, reducing biodiversity.

## B6.1.5 In-text questions
**A** The birds move freely across countries' borders.
**B** Tourism – visiting an area; ecotourism – visiting an area which results in (some) money being channelled into environmental management schemes to maintain biodiversity.
**C** If biodiversity decreased, people may not visit, so income from tourism would decrease.

## B6.1.5 Spread questions
1. International – CITES; local – stewardship schemes. *(1 mark)*
2. Any four from (for one mark each):
   Advantages:
     Brings money into a region.
     Allows people to view wildlife.
     Ensures income is used to maintain or promote biodiversity.
   Disadvantages:
     May bring more visitors to an area.
     Can lead to erosion e.g. of footpaths.
     Can cause a change in a habitat.
3. Any six from (for one mark each):
   CITES treaty
   IUCN red list
   Rio Conventions
   Stewardship schemes
   Agreements can:
     Make trading in some animal / plant products illegal.
     Highlight species which are at risk of extinction.
     Promote co-operation in conservation programmes.
     Lead to agreements between countries e.g. in reducing $CO_2$ emissions.
     Encourage landowners to conserve or restore natural environments.

## B6.1.6 In-text questions
**A** The required species may not be present in an area / the organisms may be harmed / killed by sampling.
**B** Freshwater shrimp.

### Working scientifically: Air pollution investigation
**a** Independent – distance from town centre; dependent – number of lichen species.
**b** The further you travel from the city centre, the more lichen species present.
**c** As you travel away from the city centre, the air pollution level becomes lower.

## B6.1.6 Spread questions
1. E.g. canary – carbon monoxide; lichen – sulfur dioxide; sludgeworm – sewage. *(1 mark)*

2   Lichens have no root systems (*1 mark*)
    so gain nutrients from the air / rainwater; (*1 mark*)
    if the air is polluted, this is absorbed into the lichen. (*1 mark*)
3   Any four from (for one mark each):
    Upstream of the leak, the mayfly larvae will be found.
    Around the leak site, sludgeworms will be detected.
    As you move downstream, water louse will be detected.
    Then further downstream freshwater shrimp.
    And eventually mayfly larvae again, indicating the water is unpolluted / of a very low pollution level.

## B6.2 Feeding the human race

### B6.2.1 In-text questions
A   Advantage – may increase rate of photosynthesis / increase crop yield; disadvantage – may increase droughts / lead to desertification of some areas.
B   Less energy is wasted in respiration / heating the pigs' bodies, therefore more energy is available for growth.

### B6.2.1 Spread questions
1   One example from:
    Use of greenhouses (*1 mark*)
    to maximise factors required for photosynthesis. (*1 mark*)
    Use of fertilisers (*1 mark*)
    to maximise plant growth. (*1 mark*)
    Use of pesticides / herbicides / fungicides (*1 mark*)
    to prevent pests / competing plants / fungi reducing crop yields. (*1 mark*)
2   a   Intensive, as artificial chemicals used (2).
    b   Organic, as no chemicals used, natural method of weed removal (2).
    c   Organic, as no artificial chemicals used (2). 3. The population eat a more varied diet; (*1 mark*)
    Which is likely to include meat / more diverse foods. (*1 mark*)
    These require greater energy input to produce / transport; (*1 mark*)
    Which reduces the food output compared to the energy input required to produce the foods. (*1 mark*)

### B6.2.2 In-text questions
A   Smaller / younger / immature fish can escape out of the nets. These then grow to an age where they can reproduce, replacing the population.
B   The released predators may eat / compete with other (non-targeted) organisms.
C   Many plants can be grown in a small area / unused mineral solution can be recycled / maximum growth is achieved as plants can be provided with optimum concentration of each mineral.

### Working scientifically: Growing tomatoes
Detailed plan should be produced stating that at least five plants should be grown in a solution containing all three minerals (control). At least five plants should be grown for each of the other three treatments. Each treatment should be solutions containing two of the minerals. Any differences in plant growth from the control treatment can then be attributed to the missing mineral.

### B6.2.2 Spread questions
1   Food production which can be maintained indefinitely. (*1 mark*)
2   Any four (two points, with linked explanations) from:
    Plants can be grown above one another; (*1 mark*)
    which means more food produced in the same land space. (*1 mark*)
    The required minerals for effective growth are supplied to a plant; (*1 mark*)
    meaning no chemical product is wasted / production is an energy efficient process. (*1 mark*)
    Unused minerals can be recycled; (*1 mark*)
    reducing the materials / energy for production of new mineral solutions. (*1 mark*)
    Hydroponic systems exist in controlled environments; (*1 mark*)
    ensuring the rate of photosynthesis can be maximised (e.g. through temperature / light / $CO_2$ level control). (*1 mark*)
3   Any four (two points, with linked explanations) from:
    Fish farming (*1 mark*)
    ensures fish are able to be caught easily / can be fed diet to maximise growth / protects fish from predators. (*1 mark*)
    Fishing quotas have been introduced (*1 mark*)
    to conserve fish stocks / to allow breeding to maintain fish populations. (*1 mark*)
    Fish nets have large holes in the net mesh (*1 mark*)
    to allow smaller / immature fish to escape. (*1 mark*)

### B6.2.3 In-text questions
A   E.g. large volume of milk, fast growing (for meat), low fat content (for meat).
B   Each generation will contain a greater and greater proportion of offspring with the desired characteristics. It will take several generations for most of the flock to be bred with the desired characteristic.
C   Stalks grow to the same height; ears ripen at the same time; seeds remain in the ears of wheat.

### B6.2.3 Spread questions
1   Any two from (for one mark each):
    Reduces the gene pool / variation; may leave a species susceptible to a disease; can cause inherited genetic disorders.
2   a   90th percentile equivalent to 10% of hens. (*1 mark*)
        10% of 80 hens = 8 available for breeding. (*1 mark*)
    b   Percentage gain
        $= \frac{\text{(new yield} - \text{original yield)}}{\text{original yield}} \times 100$ (*1 mark*)
        Percentage gain $= \frac{(200 - 150)}{150} \times 100$ (*1 mark*)
        Percentage gain = 33%. (*1 mark*)
3   Select plants from each species which display the best characteristics (sweetest tomatoes and biggest tomatoes). (*1 mark*)
    Breed / cross-pollinate the plants. (*1 mark*)
    From offspring, select plants with largest tomatoes (*1 mark*)
    and those with the sweetest tomatoes. (*1 mark*)
    Breed / cross pollinate the plants again. (*1 mark*)
    Repeat the process over several generations. (*1 mark*)

# Answers

## B6.2.4 In-text questions
A Occurs in one generation; accurate.
B Crops can be engineered to be pest resistant, so pesticides do not need to be used.
C The gene comes from a different species of organism / it is not naturally occurring in the tomato plant.

## B6.2.4 Spread questions
1 Allows crop to be grown in regions of little rainfall / prevents farmer losing money, as drought would not kill plants. *(1 mark)*
2 The long-term effects are not known *(1 mark)* which may lead to (named example) e.g. genetically modified plants cross-pollinating with wild plants, making the wild plants infertile. *(1 mark)*
3 Any six from (for one mark each):
Benefits – up to three from:
organisms can be modified quickly
process is accurate – individual characteristics can be targeted
can increase crop yields
can make crops pest resistant / lead to reduced use of pesticides
can allow medicinal drugs to be manufactured.
Drawbacks – up to three from:
may lead to long-term negative health effects
many genetically modified crops are infertile
genetically modified crops may cross-pollinate with wild plants – the impacts are unknown
many people do not agree with genetically modifying organisms
some people think that genetically engineering an organism is unethical.

## B6.2.5 In-text questions
A Host – has the required gene for a particular characteristic; donor – receives the required gene.
B Restriction enzymes.
C They do not contain the antibiotic resistance gene, so are killed by the antibiotic.

## B6.2.5 Spread questions
1 Restriction enzymes – to cut the DNA; *(1 mark)* ligase enzymes – to rejoin the cut DNA. *(1 mark)*
2 Insert gene (marker) which codes for fluorescence alongside required gene (into bacterial plasmid). *(1 mark)*
Grow bacteria on agar plate. *(1 mark)*
Place agar plate under UV light. *(1 mark)*
If bacterial colony glows, the gene will have been successfully incorporated. *(1 mark)*
3 Any six from (for one mark each):
Gene which codes for hormone identified.
Restriction enzymes used to cut DNA / remove gene.
Restriction enzymes cut bacteria plasmid.
Identical sticky ends are produced in gene and plasmid.
Growth hormone gene and plasmid DNA are mixed.
Ligase is used to join the gene to the plasmid DNA.
Check to see if desired genes have been incorporated, using markers, e.g. fluorescence or antibiotic resistance.
Bacteria are reproduced many times (in a fermenter).
Bacteria are killed and the hormone extracted.

## B6.2.6 In-text questions
A Golden rice contains beta-carotene which can be used by the body to produce vitamin A. This can preventing blindness due to a vitamin A deficiency.
B Bacteria / plasmid, virus.

## B6.2.6 Spread questions
1 Any three appropriate examples, e.g. selective breeding; genetic modification of crops; production of insulin from genetically engineered bacteria.
2 There is one additional step – the vector is added into the organism to be modified. *(1 mark)*
3 a Land usage for GM crops is increasing in both industrialised and developing countries. *(1 mark)*
More land was used in industrialised countries (than developing countries) for GM crops in all years between 1996 and 2006. *(1 mark)*
b Readings from graph (approx.): Total – 45 million hectares; industrialised – 35 million hectares; developing – 10 million hectares. *(1 mark)*
Industrialised countries used 25 million more hectares / 3.5 times as much land compared to developing countries (accept converse). *(1 mark)*
c Readings from graph (approx.): 2001 – 40 million hectares; 2006 – 60 million hectares. *(1 mark)*
Percentage change = (60 – 40) / 40. *(1 mark)*
Percentage change = 50%. *(1 mark)*

## Chapter 6.3 Monitoring and maintaining health

### B6.3.1 In-text questions
A Health is the absence of disease.
B Pathogen – disease-causing organism; vector – disease-carrying organism.
C Non-communicable (caused by a vitamin deficiency).

### B6.3.1 Spread questions
1 Communicable – can be passed between organisms; non-communicable – cannot be transmitted between organisms. *(1 mark)*
2 Communicable – pneumonia, measles *(1 mark)*
Non-communicable – high blood pressure, haemophilia. *(1 mark)*
3 Disease is communicable *(1 mark)*
so can be passed from tree to tree; *(1 mark)*
Felling and burning infected trees kills the pathogen / prevents the pathogen being passed on. *(1 mark)*

### B6.3.2 In-text questions
A Large numbers of students in close proximity.
B Transferring infected plant material from one area to another, e.g. on the bottom of shoes.
C When the number of new cases stops rising (or starts falling), disease-prevention techniques have worked effectively.

### Using maths: Exponential growth
400 minutes

### B6.3.2 Spread questions
1 Animals – any two from: through insect / animal bites, when foods / drinks are shared, by inhaling pathogens, during sexual intercourse. *(1 mark)*
Plants – any two from: through vectors (such as insects), through direct contact of sap from an infected plant with a healthy one, by the wind. *(1 mark)*

2   a   160, 640
    b   A maximum of four marks can be given for a graph, one for each of the following:
        Axis labels (1 mark)
        Linear axes (1 mark)
        Plots (1 mark)
        Smooth line of best fit (1 mark)
    c   Many pathogens will be produced / replicated in a short period of time (during the incubation period); (1 mark)
        which will release toxins / damage body cells. (1 mark)
3   Some cases may not be reported (1 mark)
    because people are unable to reach a treatment centre / are worried about diagnosis. (1 mark)
    Some cases may be misdiagnosed (1 mark)
    because symptoms may be similar to another disease. (1 mark)
    Other reasonable suggestion (1 mark)
    with supporting explanation. (1 mark)

## B6.3.3 In-text questions
A   The mask prevents microorganisms entering your body through your mouth or nose.
B   Any microorganisms present will be killed.

## B6.3.3 Spread questions
1   Some diseases are spread by touching infected surfaces, and disinfectant chemicals kill the pathogens responsible for the disease. (1 mark)
2   a   More chance of coming into contact with infected people (1 mark)
        who can pass on disease through droplet infection / infecting objects. (1 mark)
    b   Increased risk of exposure to pathogens (1 mark) e.g. through contaminated drinking water. (1 mark)
3   Any six from (for one mark each; three statements, with three explanations):
    Chemical dips / footwashes are installed at the entrance to fields;
    to prevent pathogens being transferred between different areas (on muddy boots).
    Diseased plants are burnt;
    to kill pathogens living on the plant materials.
    Livestock are banned from being transported;
    to prevent the potential of infected livestock transmitting the disease to another area.
    Infected, and potentially infected, livestock are slaughtered;
    to prevent infected animals passing on the disease to healthy animals.

## B6.3.4 In-text questions
A   You may spread the disease (to your other foot / someone else).
B   Herpes is caused by a virus; antibiotics can only treat bacterial infections.

## B6.3.4 Spread questions
1   Untreated water may contain *Campylobacter* (1 mark)
    which is killed by heating / boiling. (1 mark)
2   Condoms provide a barrier between partners (1 mark)
    which prevents the transfer of bodily fluids. (1 mark)
3   Chicken can contain *Campylobacter* / *Salmonella* / *E. coli* (1 mark)
    which is killed when the meat is thoroughly cooked. (1 mark)
    If the meat is raw / undercooked the bacteria may survive (1 mark)
    which can infect the person eating the meat (leading to food poisoning). (1 mark)

## B6.3.5 In-text questions
A   Selective breeding, genetic modification.
B   The bacteria induce the plant to produce excess amounts of growth hormone.

## B6.3.5 Spread questions
1   Tobacco mosaic virus; (1 mark)
    crown gall disease; (1 mark)
    powdery mildew. (1 mark)
2   a   Caused by a fungus (*Erysiphe graminis*) (1 mark)
        which produces spores which are scattered by the wind. (1 mark)
    b   Caused by bacteria (*Agrobacterium tumefaciens*) (1 mark)
        which enter the plant through a cut or wound in the plant. (1 mark)
    c   Caused by a fungus (*Ophiostoma ulmi*) (1 mark)
        which is spread by elm bark beetles. (1 mark)
3   *Agrobacterium tumefaciens* gains entry through a wound. (1 mark)
    The plasmid integrates into the host's genome. (1 mark)
    This causes greater amounts of growth chemicals to be produced. (1 mark)
    This leads to the production of galls (large tumour-like growths). (1 mark)
    The galls can totally encircle the plant's stem or trunk. (1 mark)
    Which cuts off the flow of sap / water / nutrients leading to eventual death. (1 mark)

## B6.3.6 In-text questions
A   Physical
B   To break down pectin / to break cells apart from each other.
C   Antifungal – kills fungi; antibacterial – kills bacteria.

## B6.3.6 Spread questions
1   Any three from:
    Pine resin / citronella, which repel insects which cause disease (1 mark)
    Pyrethrins which kill insects which cause disease (1 mark)
    Antibacterial compounds which kill bacteria (1 mark)
    Antifungal compounds which kill fungi (1 mark)
    Cyanide which is toxic to most living organisms. (1 mark)
2   It provides a barrier (1 mark)
    which stops pathogens entering the leaf (1 mark)
    It repels water (1 mark)
    which prevents fungi from producing spores. (1 mark)
3   Any six (for one mark each, three suggestions, three explanations) from:
    The crop could be sprayed with fungicide;
    which kills the disease-causing fungus.
    Different crops should be grown annually (in a field / area);
    to prevent re-infection of crops the following year.
    Machinery should be cleaned / disinfected after use;
    to prevent the spread of the disease to unaffected areas.
    Crops can be selectively bred for disease resistance;
    to enable future crops to be resistant to the disease.
    Crops can be genetically modified to be disease resistant;
    to enable future crops to be resistant to the disease.

## B6.3.7 In-text questions
A To avoid significant damage to crops/to minimise spread.
B The symptoms of different pathogens may be very similar.
C Each pathogen carries a unique DNA profile which makes diagnosis 100% accurate.

## B6.3.7 Spread questions
1  a  *Erwinia carotovora*; *Plasmodiophora brassicae*. (1 mark)
   b  Causes the cabbage to rot; causes decay of roots. (1 mark)
2  The antigens are present as soon as a pathogen infects a plant/at an early stage of a disease. (1 mark)
   This allows the disease to be identified before significant crop damage occurs. (1 mark)
   The farmer can remove the disease using appropriate techniques to prevent spread. (1 mark)
3  At least two named techniques (no mark), with at least one advantage (one mark each) and one disadvantage (one mark each) for each named technique:
   Observation:
   Advantages – Simple technique / easy to carry out / straightforward diagnosis. (1 mark)
   Disadvantages – Infection must be apparent to diagnose / crop may be damaged / some diseases produce identical symptoms. (1 mark)
   Microscopy (light / electron):
   Advantages – Simple diagnosis of many pathogens (light) / more accurate identification of pathogens (electron). (1 mark)
   Disadvantages – Not all pathogens can be identified (light) / complex/expensive technique (electron) / requires access to laboratory equipment. (1 mark)
   DNA analysis:
   Advantages – Accurate diagnosis if genome previously sequenced / does not require significant infection of plant. (1 mark)
   Disadvantages – May not have genome to compare DNA fingerprint to / complex/expensive technique, requires access to specialised laboratory / techniques / apparatus. (1 mark)
   Antigen detection:
   Advantages – Accurate diagnosis / does not require significant infection of plant / some conditions have simple diagnostic test. (1 mark)
   Disadvantages – Few pathogens have simple diagnostic test / many conditions require access to specialised laboratory / techniques / apparatus. (1 mark)

## B6.3.8 In-text questions
A Platelets change the blood protein fibrinogen into fibrin. This forms a network of fibres in the cut which red blood cells get trapped in.
B Antibodies – bind to an antigen; antitoxins – stop or reduce the effect of the poisonous toxins that some microorganisms make.

## B6.3.8 Spread questions
1  Any three from:
   skin – a barrier; stomach acid – kills ingested pathogens; cilia and mucus – trap inhaled microorganisms; nasal hairs – prevents larger pathogens entering the airways; tears – contain lysozymes which destroy bacteria. (Suggestion and explanation both required in each case for mark.)
2  Phagocytes – engulf the pathogen (1 mark)
   and then digest using enzymes. (1 mark)
   Lymphocytes – produce antibodies (which bind to the antigen) (1 mark)
   allowing phagocytes to destroy the pathogen/ (1 mark)
   produce antitoxins (1 mark)
   which bind to the toxin molecule / reduce or stop the effect of the toxin. (1 mark)
3  The varicella-zoster virus has a specific antigen: lymphocytes produce an antibody to this antigen which enables phagocytes to destroy the virus. (1 mark)
   If reinfection occurs, lymphocytes can produce the antibody more quickly, (1 mark)
   destroying the virus before it causes disease / meaning you now have immunity to the disease. (1 mark)

## B6.3.9 In-text questions
A A drug / cell which can be inserted into the body to destroy a specific cell or pathogen.
B Lymphocyte cells cannot survive outside the body / cell is reproduced indefinitely.
C The use of a monoclonal antibody to confirm the existence of an antigen.

## B6.3.9 Spread questions
1  An antibody produced in the laboratory (1 mark)
   which binds to a specific antigen. (1 mark)
2  The monoclonal antibody will only bind to a specific antigen (1 mark)
   which means the drug is targeted only on the affected cells (1 mark)
   minimising damage to surrounding tissue. (1 mark)
3  Any six from (for one mark each):
   Monoclonal antibodies bind to specific proteins;
   so can be designed to target only one type of (cancer) cell.
   When the antibody binds with the protein, it kills the cell / makes the cell inoperative.
   Monoclonal antibodies can act as markers;
   to highlight the presence of a disease.
   Monoclonal antibodies can carry drugs / radioactive substances to target cells;
   so increasing the effectiveness of the treatment applied.

## B6.3.10 In-text questions
A A dead or weakened pathogen which, when inserted into the body, provides immunity to a disease.
B Any three from: polio, diphtheria, tetanus, whooping cough, Hib meningitis and meningitis C, measles, mumps, and rubella.
C It was 28 times lower in 2000 compared to 1900.

## B6.3.10 Spread questions
1  The vaccine is inserted into your body. Lymphocytes produce antibodies to the antigen. (1 mark)
   If the real pathogen enters your body, the body reacts quickly, destroying the pathogens before they can cause disease. (1 mark)
2  Any two from e.g. better sanitation / better disease diagnosis / better healthcare / better standard of living / warmer houses. (2 marks)
3  a  The vaccination programme has reduced the number of cases of whooping cough in the UK. (1 mark)
      When the vaccination rate is high, the number of cases of whooping cough decreases / converse. (1 mark)

b   Early 1950s – cases averaged around 150 000 (accept 140 000–160 000); early 1990s – cases average around 5000 (accept 3000–6000). *(1 mark)*
There was a decrease of around 30 times (accept 23 times to 53 times) in the number of cases of whooping cough between the early 1950s and the early 1990s. *(1 mark)*

c   Any two sensible suggestions with reasoned argument. Can include one argument for, and one against, e.g.:
Yes, because the population have a right to know; *(1 mark)*
yes, because people need to be able to make an informed decision. *(1 mark)*
No, because newspapers often exaggerate stories to gain a headline; *(1 mark)*
no, because information may be published which does not have a scientific basis. *(1 mark)*

## B6.3.11 In-text questions

A   Antiseptic – can be applied to the skin; disinfectant – applied to non-living surfaces.
B   The antibiotic with the largest zone of inhibition / the bottom antibiotic.

## B6.3.11 Spread questions

1  a  Disinfectant / antiseptic *(1 mark)*
   b  Antiviral *(1 mark)*
   c  Antiseptic *(1 mark)*
   d  Antibiotic *(1 mark)*
2  Radius = 2 cm *(1 mark)*
   Area = $\pi \times 2^2$ *(1 mark)*
   Area = $12.6 \, cm^2$ *(1 mark)*
3  Viruses cannot replicate on their own. *(1 mark)*
   They need to use the host cell's DNA to replicate. *(1 mark)*
   Plus two from:
   Viruses can be prevented from replicating by blocking the virus from entering a host cell / *(1 mark)*
   preventing the virus from releasing genetic material / *(1 mark)*
   preventing the virus from inserting its genetic data into the host cell's DNA. *(1 mark)*

## B6.3.12 In-text questions

A   To sterilise the area before others use it / prevent unwanted contamination of others / others' equipment.
B   A hot loop would kill the microorganisms being transferred.
C   An airtight seal could promote the growth of pathogens.

## B6.3.12 Spread questions

1   Any three from: working area is washed down with alcohol before (and after) working; glassware / growing media is sterilised in an autoclave prior to use; wire loops for transferring bacteria are flamed before use; working should be completed close to a Bunsen burner flame.
2   Microorganisms are subjected to high pressure, high temperature steam for periods of up to 20 minutes *(1 mark)*
this kills the microorganisms, so making the equipment sterile. *(1 mark)*
3  a  Any six from:
      Sterilise all apparatus / growth media before use in an autoclave.
      Wash down working area with alcohol before working.
      Ensure you work close to a Bunsen burner flame.
      Wire loop is used to transfer bacteria from a sample to an agar plate.
      Flame wire loop before the transfer takes place.
      Dip wire loop in the pure sample, and then streak across the agar plate.
      Produce a second series of streaks, crossing over the first set of streaks.
      Produce a third and fourth sets of streaks using the same technique.
      Seal the petri dish (not airtight) and incubate for several days.
   b  Different coloured dots implies different bacterial colonies *(1 mark)*
      meaning the sample was contaminated *(1 mark)*
      because e.g. transfer of bacteria not carried out aseptically / agar contaminated. *(1 mark)*

## B6.3.13 In-text questions

A   Many new drugs are developed from plant compounds.
B   Testing on live cells, bacteria, and tissue cultures.
C   Neither the doctors involved in the test, nor the patients, know who has been given a placebo and who has been given the real drug.

## B6.3.13 Spread questions

1   You expect to feel better when taking a medicine – the placebo effect.
2   Any two from (for one mark each):
    Side effects may take a long time to develop.
    Small samples can lead to anomalies in results which are not replicated across a large number of subjects.
    The people tested may not have been representative of the whole population.
    Different people may respond differently to the drugs than the tested group.
    Different genetic make-up / diets / lifestyles may lead to different results from the tested group.
3   Testing a new drug on animals *(1 mark)*
    plus up to two from (for one mark each):
        The animal has no choice about being involved.
        The research may cause unnecessary suffering for the animals.
        Animal research is required to model the effect on humans / animal testing is more realistic than tissue culture / cell research / bacteria / computer modelling.
    Testing a new drug on humans *(1 mark)*
    plus up to two from (for one mark each):
        The drug may have unpleasant / severe side effects.
        The drug may give false hope of a cure for a disease.
        People know what they are getting involved in.
        Only volunteers are used.
    Performing a double blind test *(1 mark)*
    plus up to two from (for one mark each):
        You may be denying a patient a cure to a disease.
        Withholding a drug may cause some patients to lose their lives, who could have been saved.
        Some people may suffer unnecessarily.
        It's not being 'honest' with the volunteers.

## B6.4 Non-communicable diseases

### B6.4.1 In-text questions

A   Three from: (named) cancer, bronchitis, emphysema, heart disease.
B   Your reaction time increases / you may suffer blurred vision.

# Answers

## B6.4.1 Spread questions
1. (Nicotine in) smoking and ethanol are addictive drugs *(1 mark)*
   heavy users of the drug(s) become dependent on the drug. *(1 mark)*
2. Mucus will build up in the airways of the lungs overnight *(1 mark)*
   causing the smoker to cough to remove the mucus from their lungs. *(1 mark)*
3. a Cancers.
   b Cancers – 40 000 deaths, heart disease – 10 000 deaths; *(1 mark)*
      Cancers 4 times greater. *(1 mark)*
   c Proportion = (quantity / total) * 100; *(1 mark)*
      = (10 000 / 80 000) * 100; *(1 mark)*
      = 12.5%. *(1 mark)*

## B6.4.2 In-text questions
A The blood clot prevents the flow of blood and therefore oxygen to the brain.
B Processed foods contain high levels of salt and / or saturated fats.

## B6.4.2 Spread questions
1. Exercise more, *(1 mark)*
   reduce your intake of salt, *(1 mark)*
   reduce your intake of saturated fats. *(1 mark)*
2. Carbon monoxide in smoke reduces the quantity of oxygen carried by red blood cells / haemoglobin; *(1 mark)*
   heart needs to pump harder *(1 mark)*
   which increases blood pressure *(1 mark)*
   which can lead to blood vessel damage (a form of CVD). *(1 mark)*
3. a The more cigarettes smoked, the greater the risk of lung cancer. *(1 mark)*
      Detail from the graph e.g. smoking small numbers of cigarettes does not lead to significant numbers of lung cancer deaths (in either gender) / both genders are affected in a similar way. *(1 mark)*
      Quoted data trend from the graph e.g. for males, smoking 2000 cigarettes per year caused approximately 10 deaths / year / 100 000 people. Doubling the number of cigarettes smoked caused approximately 120 deaths / year / 100 000 people – around 12 times the number. *(1 mark)*
   b There is no clear correlation *(1 mark)*
      the graph shows that both genders experience approximately similar death rates. *(1 mark)*
      Quoted values from both gender e.g. for 3000 cigarettes smoked per year, males = 40 deaths / year / 100 000 people approx., females = 30 deaths / year / 100 000 people approx. *(1 mark)*

## B6.4.3 In-text questions
A Smoking narrows the arteries (atherosclerosis). This can cause a heart attack if this occurs in the coronary (heart) arteries.
B Statins, beta blockers, nitrates.
C Surgical

## B6.4.3 Spread questions
1. a Stated medical drug *(1 mark)*
      plus explanation of action, *(1 mark)*
      e.g. Statins *(1 mark)*
      which lower cholesterol / prevent cholesterol formation / cause the liver to remove more cholesterol from the blood.
   b Stated surgical procedure *(1 mark)*
      plus explanation of action, *(1 mark)*
      e.g. use of a stent *(1 mark)*
      to widen blood vessels. *(1 mark)*
2. Any **two** examples of dietary change *(1 mark)*
   with associated effect: *(1 mark)*
   Eating less salt;
   lowers blood pressure.
   Eating less saturated fat;
   lowers the level of cholesterol in blood.
   Eating less sugar;
   lowers the risk of developing diabetes.
3. Apply up to four marks for lifestyle / medical / surgical procedures, plus up to two marks for evaluation of choice of surgical / medical / lifestyle procedures:
   Up to two marks for lifestyle procedure, e.g.:
   advice on changing diet *(1 mark)*
   to limit salt / saturated fat / sugar intake to minimise risk of disease recurrence; *(1 mark)*
   support to develop an exercise programme *(1 mark)*
   to lose weight, reducing strain on heart. *(1 mark)*
   Up to two marks for medical procedure, e.g.:
   use of statins *(1 mark)*
   to reduce blood pressure; *(1 mark)*
   use of antiplatelets *(1 mark)*
   to reduce chance of thrombosis of coronary artery; *(1 mark)*
   use of beta blockers *(1 mark)*
   to reduce blood pressure; *(1 mark)*
   use of nitrates *(1 mark)*
   to widen blood vessels. *(1 mark)*
   Up to two marks for surgical procedure, e.g.:
   use of a stent *(1 mark)*
   to widen partially blocked arteries; *(1 mark)*
   heart bypass operation *(1 mark)*
   to replace blood supply to the heart. *(1 mark)*
   Up to two marks for evaluation of effect of different procedures, e.g.:
   surgical operation likely to be required immediately to repair cause of heart attack; *(1 mark)*
   medical drugs may be required to alleviate issues which caused the heart attack; *(1 mark)*
   lifestyle changes will be required in the longer term to significantly reduce risk of recurrence of heart attack. *(1 mark)*

## B6.4.4 In-text questions
A The body's defence system against infection will be depressed / more chance of suffering an infection.
B Divide indefinitely/ additional cells are placed into areas of the body/ might divide to form a clump (tumour)/ other sensible suggestion.

## B6.4.4 Spread questions
1. Creating new brain cells, e.g. for treating Parkinson's; *(1 mark)*
   making new bone or cartilage cells, e.g. for treating arthritis; *(1 mark)*
   making replacement heart valves, e.g. for treating heart disease. *(1 mark)*
2. Foreign tissue would be detected by immune system *(1 mark)*
   which produces antibodies; *(1 mark)*
   immunosuppressant drugs reduce or stop the effect of the immune system (preventing rejection). *(1 mark)*

3   Answer should include at least one argument for the use of embryos, and one against (for one mark each, up to four in total):
    FOR
    Offers ability to treat currently incurable diseases.
    Uses embryos which are unwanted / have been created anyway.
    Allows the potential treatment of conditions using no / fewer drugs than conventional treatments.
    Minimises the risk of rejection compared to organ / tissue transplants.
    AGAINST
    It is not a natural approach.
    Embryos have the right to life.
    Embryos should carry the same human rights as a living person.

### B6.4.5 In-text questions
A   It should have its pathogenic properties removed / be made unable to cause an infection.
B   Gene therapy does not target gametes, so these cells remain unaltered.
C   May cause a person to worry / the disease may never develop / tests are expensive / preventative treatments may be expensive / information could be used by e.g. insurance companies to weight premiums.

### B6.4.5 Spread questions
1   Two appropriate suggestions, e.g. new gene therapy treatments may be developed, *(1 mark)*
    more personalised medicines developed that target particular genes. *(1 mark)*
2   Cells only have a particular lifespan, and so will be replaced by new cells. *(1 mark)*
    These cells may not carry the modified DNA, and so could lead to the disease being re-expressed. *(1 mark)*
3   Any six from (for one mark each):
    The normal version of the insulin gene;
    is removed from the DNA of a donor;
    using restriction enzymes.
    Multiple copies of the normal allele are produced.
    DNA is placed into a modified virus;
    virus inserts the DNA into the target cells.
    DNA is incorporated into recipient's cells;
    targeted cells now produce insulin.

## PAG 1 – Microscopy
### Designing your practical
1   Suitable apparatus:
    - microscope – to view organisms
    - pond water
    - concave slide – to contain water droplet
    - acetate grid – to estimate the size of viewed objects.
2   Suitable method:
    - Add a droplet of pond water to a concave microscope slide.
    - Place a coverslip and acetate grid over the slide.
    - Move the microscope stage to its lowest position.
    - Select the objective lens with the lowest magnification.
    - Place the slide on the stage.
    - Turn the coarse-focus knob slowly until you see the object.
    - Turn the fine-focus knob slowly until the object comes into clear focus.
    - Repeat the steps using a higher magnification objective lens to see the object in greater detail.
3   At least two risks should be identified.

| Hazard | Risk | Control |
|---|---|---|
| microscope | injury from dropping | place in centre of table when not in use |
| glass slide / coverslip | cuts | take care with sharp edges sweep up any breakages immediately |

### Analysing your results
4–6 Answers are dependent on students' results. Suitable drawings should be produced that include:
- scale
- estimated size of structures
- labels of known structures and components.

### Evaluating your practical
7–8 Here are some possible answers.
- Problem – having difficulty focusing on an object. Improvement – locate the object in the centre of the field of view under lowest magnification, then turn the focus knobs very slowly.
- Problem – not being able to see organisms. Improvement – select a different sample of pond water / use staining.
- Problem – difficulty drawing organism. Improvement – draw grid on own paper (at a larger size) and copy square by square.

9   Statement linking student's drawing with other students' equivalents. If drawings contain similar structures, there should be an indication that the method used is reproducible.

### Spread questions
1   Accurately sketched copy of Figure 3, with nucleus and cell wall correctly labelled.
2   × 40
3   Approximately two cells across the width of image Each cell appears approximately 35 mm wide at × 400 magnification.
    Cell size approximately $\frac{35}{400} = 0.09$ mm $= 90$ μm
    Accept answers in range 40 μm to 140 μm
4   To highlight cell components

## PAG 2 – Testing for biological molecules
### Designing your practical
1   Suitable apparatus:
    - reagents – iodine, Benedict's solution, copper sulfate and sodium hydroxide, ethanol and water – to test for biological molecules
    - test tubes – to contain foods / reagents
    - water bath – to safely heat ethanol solution.
2   Suitable method:
    - Place food / food solution in test tube.
    - Add reagent.
    - For glucose (reducing sugars) test, heat in water bath.

# Answers

- (Wait for) colour change:
  - starch (non-reducing sugars) test – iodine from orange to blue-black
  - glucose (reducing sugars) test – Benedict's solution from blue to orange-red
  - protein test – copper sulfate, then sodium hydroxide from pale blue to purple
  - fats (lipids) test – ethanol, then water from clear to cloudy solution

3  At least two risks should be identified.

| Hazard | Risk | Control |
|---|---|---|
| test tube | cuts | care with sharp edges |
|  |  | 1 sweep up any breakages immediately |
| ethanol | highly flammable – burns | do not use in laboratory with naked flames |
|  |  | heat in water bath |

4

| Food tested | Component tested for / colour change detected ||||
|---|---|---|---|---|
|  | Glucose (reducing sugars) | Starch (non-reducing sugars) | Protein | Lipids |
|  |  |  |  |  |
|  |  |  |  |  |
|  |  |  |  |  |
|  |  |  |  |  |

### Analysing your results
5  Answers dependent on students' results.

### Evaluating your practical
6  Answers dependent on students' results.
7  Any appropriate example, such as the food being strongly coloured, making it difficult to judge the potential colour change.
8  Each food test should be completed more than once, by the same person and using the same apparatus. If the same result is gained, the results can be classified as repeatable.
9  If the same results are gained by different groups, the results can be classified as reproducible.

### Spread questions
1  A – starch (non-reducing sugars) test – iodine changes from orange to blue-black
B – glucose (reducing sugars) test – Benedict's solution changes from blue to orange-red
C – Protein test – copper sulfate, then sodium hydroxide changes from pale blue to purple
D – Fat (lipids) test – ethanol, then water changes from a clear to cloudy solution
2  A – starch
B – glucose and fat
C – protein, glucose and fat
**D – glucose**

3  Food A – it contains starch that will provide slow release energy to sustain the player through the match.
4  Food B contains sugar and fat, which may cause a range of health problems (for example, diabetes, obesity, high blood pressure) if consumed in excess / not as part of a healthy balanced diet.

## PAG 3 – Sampling techniques
### Designing your practical
1
- Lay a tape in a straight line, covering a fixed distance (e.g., 4 m) either side of a footpath.
- Select sites along the tape to take samples – for example, every metre.
- Place a quadrat at the first sample site. Note the number of plant species in the quadrat.
- Record any important abiotic factors at the sample site, for example, moisture content, or a description of how compacted the soil is.
- Repeat the procedure for the remaining sampling sites.

2  At least two risks should be identified.

| Hazard | Risk | Control |
|---|---|---|
| plants | irritant | do not touch plants / wear gloves |
|  | 3 sharp thorns – may cause abrasions | 5 check group medical history prior to undertaking work |
|  | 4 allergy risk |  |
| broken glass / sharp objects | cuts | ensure area to be sampled is free of rubbish |

3  Below is a suitable results table (abiotic factors studied will vary).

| Sample site | Number of plant species present | pH | Moisture content of soil | Oxygen content of soil |
|---|---|---|---|---|
|  |  |  |  |  |
|  |  |  |  |  |
|  |  |  |  |  |

### Analysing your results
4  Students should choose suitable scales and axes. They should draw data points as small crosses and a line of best fit.
5–6  Answers dependent on students' results. Students are likely to find that fewer species of plant are present in the region of more compacted soil.

### Evaluating your practical
7  Students should give at least one advantage and one disadvantage. For example, advantage – quicker / should be representative for the whole area. Disadvantage – may not be representative / second sample would check repeatability of the results.
8  Validity implies results were produced using a method that produces (close to) the true result, using a method that leads to repeatable and reproducible results. Students should use comparisons with other groups, and a judgement over whether repeating (or lack of) leads to results that can be defined as valid.

9  Uncertainty is distance in a measurement from the true value. Students should make estimates of uncertainty. If digital sensors were used to measure abiotic factors, uncertainty in these measurements is likely to be negligible. Uncertainty estimates will therefore come from repeat measurements – so the more repeat measurements that are taken at different points along the path, and taking a mean average of the species richness at each sampling point, the lower the uncertainty is likely to be.

**Spread questions**
1  Biotic: number of shrimp
   Abiotic: oxygen concentration and ammonia concentration
2  Correctly plotted line graph from data in table 1.
3  There is a direct correlation between the number of shrimp present and the dissolved ammonia concentration.
   There does not appear to be a correlation between the dissolved oxygen concentration and the number of shrimp. However, there is a weak correlation / general trend that an increase in dissolved oxygen concentration leads to an increase in the number of shrimp.
4  No definitive conclusion can be formed, as two potential independent variables are changing at the same time. However, tentative conclusions can be formed.
   - The greater the dissolved ammonia content, the greater the number of shrimp can be supported.
   - The greater the dissolved oxygen content, the greater the number of shrimp can be supported.
5  To form definitive conclusions, the experiment would need to be repeated in controlled conditions, where only one factor at a time is altered. It is impossible to distinguish between the effect of the dissolved ammonia and oxygen content – both factors are changing. No other biotic or abiotic factors were measured. Therefore another factor may also have affected the results, which is currently unknown.
   The study provides evidence that shrimp may be used as an indicator species, but this is not definitive (see answer to Question 4) – further work would be needed to confirm whether this is the case.

## PAG 4 – Rates of enzyme-controlled reactions
**Designing your practical**
1  Suitable apparatus (for temperature example):
   - boiling tube – to contain solutions
   - water bath – to heat solutions to a constant temperature
   - thermometer / temperature probe – to record temperature
   - starch solution – substance to be digested
   - amylase solution – enzyme
   - iodine – to indicate when starch has been digested
   - stopwatch – to indicate when to take samples
   - dropping tile
   - pipette – to remove starch / amylase mixture.
2  Suitable method (for temperature example):
   - Place a drop of iodine into each dimple in a dropping tile.
   - Place flasks of starch solution and amylase in water baths at 30 °C, 35 °C, 40 °C, 45 °C, 50 °C.
   - Add 3 cm³ starch solution and 3 cm³ amylase to a boiling tube in a water bath at the appropriate temperature.
   - Start stopwatch.
   - Remove small quantity of mixture with a pipette. Add a drop to the first dimple on the spotting tile.
   - Repeat this step every 10 seconds until the iodine no longer changes colour.
   - Count the number of dimples used. Multiply by 10 seconds to measure the time taken for the enzyme to digest the starch solution.
3  At least two risks should be identified.

| Hazard | Risk | Control |
| --- | --- | --- |
| iodine solution | low hazard <1M | 6 refer to CLEAPSS Student Safety Sheet 56 |
| boiling tube | cuts if broken | clear up broken glass immediately with brush and pan<br>ensure unused tubes are stored in a boiling tube rack |

4  Here is an example of a suitable results table.

| Temperature (°C) | Time to fully digest starch (s) | | | Rate of reaction ($s^{-1}$) |
| --- | --- | --- | --- | --- |
| | Result 1 | Result 2 | Mean | |
| 30 | | | | |
| 35 | | | | |
| 40 | | | | |
| 45 | | | | |
| 50 | | | | |

**Analysing your results**
5–7  Answers dependent on students' results. Students should choose suitable scales and axes. They should draw data points as small crosses and a line of best fit. Their conclusions should be appropriate to the results they record.

**Evaluating your practical**
8  Answers dependent on students' results. Students should identify outliers as data points a large distance from the line of best fit, or repeat values that are significantly different from each other.
9  There should be a statement about the likelihood (or not) of measuring the true value of the optimum rate. If the answer implies that the true value has been found:
   - additional results should have been collected around the expected optimum point to confirm the exact position
   - there should be a number of repeats with little variance taken
   - a comparison should be made with other groups to confirm the position of the optimum point.

# Answers

**Spread questions**

1. Two from pH, volume of solution / substrate, concentration of solution / substrate.

2. 

| Temperature (°C) | Time to fully digest protein (s) | | | Rate of reaction (s$^{-1}$) |
| --- | --- | --- | --- | --- |
| | Result 1 | Result 2 | Mean | |
| 25 | 76 | 88 | 82 | 0.012 |
| 30 | 61 | 67 | 64 | 0.016 |
| 35 | 46 | 50 | 48 | 0.021 |
| 40 | 32 | 36 | 34 | 0.029 |
| 45 | 43 | 49 | 46 | 0.022 |
| 50 | 120 | 130 | 125 | 0.008 |

3. Correctly plotted line graph from data in **2**.
4. At low temperatures, increasing the temperature increases the rate of reaction. This occurs because the particles (of solution and substrate) move at a greater speed, and so collide more often and with greater energy. The greatest rate of reaction is around 40 °C. Above 40 °C, the rate of reaction decreases rapidly with temperature. This occurs as the enzymes denature above 40 °C.
5. Take additional results around 40 °C. This will help identify the optimum point with greater accuracy.
6. All of the second set of results takes longer to digest than in the first set of results. This implies there may be a systematic error in the second set of data, for example, the temperature probe may be calibrated incorrectly.

## PAG 5 – Photosynthesis

**Designing your practical**

1. Suitable apparatus (for light intensity example):
   - beaker – to contain solution / plant
   - pond weed – for example, *Cabomba* or *Elodea*
   - desk lamp – to provide varying light intensities
   - ruler – to measure distance from light source to plant
   - glass funnel – to direct oxygen bubbles into inverted test tube
   - marked test tube – to collect oxygen gas.
2. Suitable method (for light intensity example):
   - Place samples of pond weed into dilute sodium hydrogen carbonate solution.
   - Place inverted glass funnel over pond weed.
   - Position light source 50 cm above pond weed / water surface.
   - Fill marked test tube with water, and invert while held underwater. Place over funnel.
   - Switch on light.
   - Measure the time taken for the oxygen level to reach the mark point on the test tube.
   - Repeat for 40 cm, 30 cm, 20 cm, and 10 cm.
   - Repeat the experiment, to gain at least two results for each value of light intensity.

3. At least two risks should be identified.

| Hazard | Risk | Control |
| --- | --- | --- |
| light source | burn – bulb becomes hot | 7 switch off bulb between experiments  8 handle lamp by base |
| glassware | cuts if broken | clear up broken glass immediately with brush and pan  ensure unused tubes are stored in a test tube rack  keep apparatus placed in centre of table |

4. Here is an example of a suitable results table.

| Distance / cm | Relative light intensity | Time for oxygen to reach test tube mark / s | | | Rate of photosynthesis / s$^{-1}$ |
| --- | --- | --- | --- | --- | --- |
| | | Repeat 1 | Repeat 2 | Average | |
| | | | | | |
| | | | | | |
| | | | | | |
| | | | | | |
| | | | | | |

**Analysing your results**

5–7 Answers dependent on student's results. Students should choose suitable scales and axes. They should draw data points as small crosses and a line of best fit. Their conclusions should be appropriate to the results they record.
Expected outcome – initial approximately linear section, followed by decreasing rate of photosynthesis increase, followed by maximum rate of photosynthesis.
Reason – factor initially supplied to enable photosynthesis to occur more rapidly, but rate of increase limited by other (limiting) factors in short supply.

**Evaluating your practical**

8. Outliers may be identified either far from the line of best fit, or from repeats being significantly different to other results for the same value of independent variable. A reasonable reason should be given, for example, at short distances, light supplies increase the temperature as well as light intensity to the pond weed.
9. Students should identify control variables, for example, for light intensity, carbon dioxide concentration, temperature.
10. Oxygen bubbles may be of different sizes to one another, so the volume of oxygen measured may not be accurate.

**Spread questions**

1. The number of bubbles produced per minute is a measure of the rate of photosynthesis.
2. 

| Distance (cm) | Relative light intensity | Number of bubbles produced per minute | | |
| --- | --- | --- | --- | --- |
| | | Repeat 1 | Repeat 2 | Average |
| 4 | 0.25 | 102 | 108 | 105 |
| 8 | 0.13 | 98 | 102 | 100 |
| 12 | 0.08 | 86 | 88 | 87 |
| 16 | 0.06 | 76 | 68 | 72 |
| 20 | 0.05 | 58 | 58 | 58 |

3 Accurately drawn graph of relative light intensity (*x*-axis) versus number of bubbles produced per minute (*y*-axis) from the data in **2**.
4 At low light intensities, supplying additional light energy enables photosynthesis to occur at a greater rate, as there is more energy to drive the photosynthesis reactions. The rate of increase is limited by other (limiting) factors, such as carbon dioxide concentration or temperature, being in short supply.
5 More repeats. This would allow students to judge how repeatable the data produced by the method is / compare results with other groups, to judge reproducibility of data / wider range of light intensities, and to see if the trend continues above or below tested values.

## PAG 6 – Physiology, responses and respiration

### Designing your practical

1 Suitable method:
   - Select study group, for example, students who regularly play for the school netball team versus control group who do not regularly partake in sport.
   - Using a stopwatch to check time, take resting pulse rate over 1 minute.
   - Repeat for two further readings.
   - Ask both groups to complete star jumps for 30 s.
   - Measure recovery time – take pulse rate every minute until the heart rate returns to pre-exercise rate.
   - Ask groups to complete identical exercise for 60 s, 90 s, 120 s, and 150 s.
   - Measure recovery time after each exercise.

2 At least two risks should be identified.

| Hazard | Risk | Control |
|---|---|---|
| exercise | sprains and strains | 9 ensure warm-up and cool-down exercises are completed |
| exercise | asthmatic attack | ensure students do not exercise beyond their comfortable limit<br><br>ensure asthmatics have inhalers to hand |

3 Here is an example of a suitable results table.
Students who play for netball team

| Exercise duration (s) | Student number and recovery time (min) | | | | | | | | Mean recovery rate (min) |
|---|---|---|---|---|---|---|---|---|---|
| | 1 | 2 | 3 | 4 | 5 | 6 | 7 | 8 | |
| 30 | | | | | | | | | |
| 60 | | | | | | | | | |
| 90 | | | | | | | | | |
| 120 | | | | | | | | | |
| 150 | | | | | | | | | |

Students who do not take part in regular exercise

| Exercise duration (s) | Student number and recovery time (min) | | | | | | | | Mean recovery rate (min) |
|---|---|---|---|---|---|---|---|---|---|
| | 1 | 2 | 3 | 4 | 5 | 6 | 7 | 8 | |
| 30 | | | | | | | | | |
| 60 | | | | | | | | | |
| 90 | | | | | | | | | |
| 120 | | | | | | | | | |
| 150 | | | | | | | | | |

### Analysing your results

4–6 Answers dependent on student's results. An appropriate choice of graph would be a bar chart, with comparative bars for each exercise length. Students should choose suitable axes and scales. Their conclusions should be appropriate to their results, for example, students who regularly partake in sport should have a shorter recovery time than those who do not. This is because regular exercise increases the strength of the heart muscle, meaning that it can pump more blood with every beat. This means it does not have to increase as high during exercise to meet the increased oxygen demands required by increased respiration rates. Therefore it is quicker to return to normal.

### Evaluating your practical

7 Individuals within a sample will show variation. Therefore a large sample is required to avoid individuals affecting an overall result and so potentially leading to a false conclusion.
8 Answer will be relevant to student's results. Expected discussion points include:
   - comments on repeatability
   - comments on reproducibility
   - comments on outliers / unexpected results
   - the effect of each of these points weighed up, with a statement about the overall validity of the conclusion.

### Spread questions

1 Correctly plotted line graph for data in Table 1.
2 For all age groups, the more exercise was completed, the higher the maximum heart rate became. All age groups showed an increase in heart rate at a decreasing rate. There was no apparent link between age and resting heart rate.
3 Increase of 175%
4 Any from:
   - sample sizes were small – especially in the over-60 age group
   - no indication of actual ages of the participants – for example, all of the 40–60 group could have been 59, and all the over 60s could have been 61
   - group sizes were not consistent
   - generalised conclusions cannot be made as a group of cyclists is not a typical cross-section of a population
   - the 'exercise' undertaken was not specified, and may not have been the same for all participants – if it was the same, conclusions can only be drawn relating to this exercise
   - only one set of results was taken for each exercise for each group, so it is impossible to say if the data produced is repeatable.

## PAG 7 – Microbiological techniques

**Designing your practical**

1. Suitable apparatus:
   - petri dish – to have a large surface area over which the bacteria are spread
   - molten agar
   - bacteria culture to be studied
   - paper discs – to absorb antimicrobial agent
   - range of antimicrobial agents to be tested
   - tweezers – to move paper discs (without contamination)
   - incubator – to provide a warm environment to speed up bacteria growth
   - Bunsen burner – to work aseptically.

2. Suitable method:
   - Flame an inoculation loop to ensure it is sterile.
   - Transfer a sample of bacteria culture to cooled molten agar in a petri dish.
   - Mix well and allow to set.
   - Divide the petri dish into four quadrants by drawing lines on the bottom of the plate.
   - Dip a sterile paper disc into the first agent to be tested, and place in the first quadrant. (Note which quadrant relates to which antimicrobial agent.)
   - Repeat for the other antibacterial agents to be tested.
   - Seal the plate, but do not form an airtight seal.
   - Invert, and incubate for several days.
   - Without opening the plate, measure the zone of inhibition around each antibacterial agent.

3. At least two risks should be identified.

| Hazard | Risk | Control |
|---|---|---|
| bacteria | contaminating experimenter / others causing illness | 10 choose non-pathogenic form of bacteria; clean benches with antimicrobial agent; autoclave all equipment after use |
| Bunsen burner | burns | keep on visible safety flame when not in use; place in centre of working area; ensure others are aware of burner |

4. Here is an example of a suitable results table.

| Quadrant | Antimicrobial agent | Width of zone of inhibition (mm) | Area of zone of inhibition (mm$^2$) |
|---|---|---|---|
| | | | |
| | | | |
| | | | |

**Analysing your results**

5–6 Answers dependent on student's results.

**Evaluating your practical**

7. Answers dependent on student's results.
8. Reproducible results mean other groups who used different equipment achieved the same pattern in results. Answer dependent on student's own results.
9. Appropriate uncertainty estimate, for example, ±1 mm for width of zone of inhibition. Oxygen bubbles may be of different sizes to one another, so the volume of oxygen measured may not be accurate.
10. Appropriate suggestion to minimise uncertainty, for example, take diameter measurement in different directions and take average of results; ask others to take measurement and compare values.

**Spread questions**

1. To ensure that the bacteria being studied do not contaminate the student or the laboratory, and that no other microorganisms contaminate the sample being studied.

2. 

| pH of paper disc | Width of zone of inhibition (mm) | Area of zone of inhibition (mm2) |
|---|---|---|
| 3 | 18 | 254 |
| 4 | 12 | 113 |
| 5 | 4 | 13 |
| 6 | 1 | 1 |
| 7 | 0 | 0 |

3. The more acidic the solution, the larger the zone of inhibition (the more the bacteria are prevented from growing). No alkaline solutions have been tested. The experiment only tested acidic and neutral solutions.

   Any suitable suggestion stated and explained. For example:
   - test pH 2 to see if this causes an even greater zone of inhibition
   - repeat with another species of bacteria to see if the conclusion can be generalised for other species
   - repeat whole test to ensure method is reliable.

## PAG 8 – Transport in and out of cells

**Designing your practical**

1. Suitable apparatus:
   - corer – to cut potato samples to identical diameters
   - ruler – to measure length of samples
   - boiling tube – to contain solutions
   - stopwatch – to measure time
   - top pan balance – to measure mass of potato samples
   - sugar solutions of different concentration.

2. Suitable method:
   - Cut potato samples.
   - Dry on paper towel.
   - Measure mass using top pan balance.
   - Place a potato sample in a boiling tube containing distilled water.
   - Leave for 15 minutes.
   - Dry potato on paper towel.
   - Remeasure mass of potato sample.
   - Repeat above procedure for solutions of varying sugar concentration.
   - Collect at least results for each concentration of sugar solution.

3   At least two risks should be identified.

| Hazard | Risk | Control |
|---|---|---|
| top pan balance | heavy if dropped – potential broken bones | 1 place balance away from edge of table<br>2 ensure power cord is not dangling over the table side |
| boiling tube | cuts if broken | clear up broken glass immediately with brush and pan<br>ensure unused tubes are stored in a boiling tube rack |

4   Here is an example of a suitable results table.

| Solution concentration / mol/dm³ | Mass / g | | | | | | Average mass change / g |
|---|---|---|---|---|---|---|---|
| | Before 1 | After 1 | Change 1 | Before 2 | After 2 | Change 2 | |
| 0.0 | | | | | | | |
| 0.2 | | | | | | | |
| 0.4 | | | | | | | |
| 0.6 | | | | | | | |
| 0.8 | | | | | | | |

## Analysing your results

5–6 Answers dependent on student's results. Students should choose suitable axes and scales. They should draw data points as small crosses and a line of best fit.

## Evaluating your practical

7   Answers dependent on student's results. Students should identify outliers as data points a large distance from the line of best fit / repeat values that are significantly different from each other.

8   a   Include the following points:
   - accurate results = close to true value
   - use of top pan balance to ensure measurements of mass were precise
   - use of corer to ensure potato samples had consistent cross-sectional area
   - calculation of percentage change in mass to allow for small differences in starting mass of potato
   - removal of outliers from calculations of mean average.

   b   Any from:
   - Take additional readings just above and just below the estimated position of zero mass change to isolate the exact concentration of sugar solution that produced no change in mass.
   - Take additional repeat readings of results to reduce effect of smaller outliers.
   - Repeat experiment using different solution, for example, salt solution, to see if the result is repeated.
   - Compare results with those of other groups.
   - Allow surface of potato chip to dry prior to taking mass – patting on paper towel will not remove all moisture, which may lead to incorrect measurements of mass change.

## Spread questions

1   Any two from: temperature of solution, cross-sectional area of potato chip, length of potato chip, time chip left in solution.

2

| Sugar concentration (mol/dm³) | Mass before (g) | Mass after (g) | Change in mass (g) | Percentage change in mass (%) |
|---|---|---|---|---|
| 0.0 | 5.0 | 5.6 | 0.6 | 12% |
| 0.2 | 5.0 | 5.4 | 0.4 | 8% |
| 0.4 | 5.2 | 5.4 | 0.2 | 4% |
| 1.0 | 5.0 | 4.6 | −0.4 | −8% |
| 2.0 | 5.0 | 4.4 | −1.0 | −19% |

3   Correctly plotted graph from data in 2.
4   0.6 mol/dm³
5   If the water potential in the potato was higher than the solution, water moved out of the potato by osmosis, so the mass of the potato decreased.
   If the water potential in the potato was lower than the solution, water moved into the potato by osmosis, so the mass of the potato increased.
   Where the water potential of the potato and the solution were equal, no osmosis occurred so the mass did not change.
6   The starting mass of the potato chips was slightly different. Calculating percentage change allowed a fair comparison to be made between samples.

Great Clarendon Street, Oxford, OX2 6DP, United Kingdom

Oxford University Press is a department of the University of Oxford.
It furthers the University's objective of excellence in research,
scholarship, and education by publishing worldwide. Oxford is a
registered trade mark of Oxford University Press in the UK and in
certain other countries

© Oxford University Press

The moral rights of the authors have been asserted

First published in 2016

All rights reserved. No part of this publication may be reproduced,
stored in a retrieval system, or transmitted, in any form or by any
means, without the prior permission in writing of Oxford University
Press, or as expressly permitted by law, by licence or under terms agreed
with the appropriate reprographics rights organization. Enquiries
concerning reproduction outside the scope of the above should be sent
to the Rights Department, Oxford University Press,
at the address above.

You must not circulate this work in any other form and you must
impose this same condition on any acquirer

British Library Cataloguing in Publication Data
Data available

978 0 19 835987 6

10 9 8 7 6 5 4 3 2 1

Paper used in the production of this book is a natural, recyclable
product made from wood grown in sustainable forests.
The manufacturing process conforms to the environmental regulations
of the country of origin.

Printed and bound by CPI Group (UK) Ltd, Croydon, CR0 4YY

### Acknowledgements

**COVER**: Rich Reid / National Geographic / Offset

The authors and series editor would like to thank Sophie Ladden and
Margaret McGuire at OUP for their patience, encouragement, and
attention to all the small - but important - details.

The authors would like to thank all the editorial staff at OUP, for their
support throughout this project. We would particularly like to thank
Claire Gordon for her clear guidance at the start of the project, and
Philippa Gardom Hulme, for her positive encouragement with all of
our ideas.

Philippa Gardom Hulme would like to thank Barney, Catherine, and
Sarah for their never-ending support and patience, and for keeping
quietly out of the way in the early mornings. Thanks, too, to Claire
Gordon for her wise counsel over tea and scones, and for getting us all
going in the first place!